Dr. Eddie Anderson,
Hall of Fame College Football Coach

Dr. Eddie Anderson, Hall of Fame College Football Coach

A Biography

KEVIN CARROLL

McFarland & Company, Inc., Publishers
Jefferson, North Carolina, and London

LIBRARY OF CONGRESS CATALOGUING-IN-PUBLICATION DATA

Carroll, Kevin, 1950–
    Dr. Eddie Anderson, Hall of Fame college football coach : a biography /
Kevin Carroll.
    p.   cm.
    Includes bibliographical references and index.

    ISBN-13: 978-0-7864-3007-9
    (softcover : 50# alkaline paper) ∞

    1. Anderson, Eddie (Edward Nicholas), 1900–1974.
2. Football coaches — United States — Biography.
I. Title. II. Title: Doctor Eddie Anderson.
GV939.A62C37   2007
796.332092 — dc22   2006038053
[B]

British Library cataloguing data are available

On the cover: Holy Cross quarterback Pat McCarthy and Dr. Eddie
Anderson during a game at Fitton Field in the early sixties *(Courtesy of
Mel Massucco)*

Manufactured in the United States of America

McFarland & Company, Inc., Publishers
  Box 611, Jefferson, North Carolina 28640
  www.mcfarlandpub.com

To Herbert "Buster" Carroll

Acknowledgments

The author is especially indebted to members of the Anderson family —
Nick, Jerry, Jim and Judy — who so generously gave their time for lengthy
interviews and answered numerous phone calls and e-mails about their father.
They also allowed me access to family photos and scrapbooks that proved to
be invaluable. Heartfelt thanks to the late Mel Massucco and the former Holy
Cross and Iowa football players, trainers, managers and coaches, who interrupted their busy schedules and often invited me into their homes to talk
about their old coach. Each and every one was a class act.

A big salute goes to the gracious and helpful archival staff at Holy Cross
College in Worcester, Massachusetts: Mark Savolis, Head Archivist; Lois
Hamill, Assistant Head Archivist; and Archival Assistant Jo-Anne Carr. Their
unlimited patience and alacrity during my multiple visits to Dinand Library
even outweighed the reams of information they made available to me. Lois
Hamill hunted up numerous archival photos to enhance this project, while
Jo-Anne Carr photocopied hundreds of newspaper articles. Just as eager to
help were David McCartney and the wonderful archival staff of the Depart-
ment of Special Collections at the University of Iowa. I'm also indebted to
Renee Bartley and Kathryn DeGraff at the DePaul University Archives in
Chicago. Archivist Michael D. Gibson of Loras College was most accommo-
dating during my visit to Dubuque and in subsequent correspondence.
Charles Lamb and Elizabeth Hogan at the University of Notre Dame Archives
also provided valuable assistance. Thanks to the library staff at Albuquerque
Academy and in particular Nancy Madigan, Barbara Trussell, Barbara Spivey
and Mary Beth Jordan for all their help in so many ways.

I will be eternally grateful to Sally Prince Davis, whose meticulous edit-
ing of the manuscript and overall input were indispensable. Thanks to my

good friend and sports buff Mike Nadler, for proofreading segments of the manuscript, and to Mike Fanning for his research help during his undergraduate days at Notre Dame. A tip of the hat goes to my Albuquerque Academy colleague and computer whiz, Dave Schifani, for his technical assistance. My daughters, McKinnon and Letitia, also provided aid and moral support to their computer-illiterate father.

Finally, I'd like to thank my loving wife, Linda, who encouraged me to undertake this project and was my biggest booster every step of the way.

TABLE OF CONTENTS

PREFACE

I first learned of Eddie Anderson as a young boy from my father. It was either in the late fifties or early sixties. Dad was watching a football game on our black and white Sylvania television set when I plopped onto the living-room couch of our small apartment in College Point. Located in the New York City borough of Queens, College Point was predominantly an Irish-German neighborhood in those days.

After a minute the camera panned to a sideline shot of a well-dressed older man in a suit. This was before handheld, roaming cameras provided television audiences with sideline close-ups. While the camera was too far away to clearly see the man's face, his stylish fedora and dark horn-rimmed glasses were quite distinctive. "That's Eddie Anderson," my father informed me. "Not only is he the Holy Cross coach, but he's also a medical doctor. Years ago he was an All-American football player at Notre Dame for the great Knute Rockne."

My first reaction to Dad's words was to wonder how a doctor could be a coach and, conversely, how a coach could be a doctor. What doctor had time to coach? What coach knew enough to be a doctor? Could my father have been misinformed or was he pulling my leg? At that age I was ignorant of the term "subway alumni," a moniker applied to thousands of working class Americans who never attended college, but nevertheless adopted Notre Dame as their *alma mater*. When it came to Notre Dame football, Dad was not only a subway alumnus, but a *magna cum laude* graduate.

To my father, Herbert "Buster" Carroll, Notre Dame football was sacrosanct. He even kept his own Holy Scripture of the school's gridiron legacy. The sacred text was a thick, black, loose-leafed binder, the contents of which included the score of every Notre Dame game between 1935 and 1941. Each

1

season's game scores were written in ink on lined loose-leaf paper in "Buster's" own hand, followed by pages of faded newspaper articles describing the epic contests. Like a calligrapher's stylized letter, a colored action photo occasionally stood out amongst the continuous pages of black and white pictures and newspaper print. The annual missal ended only when its scribe answered his country's call by joining the Marine Corps in January of 1942.

As a youngster it seemed unfathomable to me that anyone could be both a doctor and a football coach. If Dad's words weren't proof enough, however, his loose-leafed Holy Writ provided conclusive testimony. The scripture's Iowa verses detailed how Dr. Eddie Anderson led his undermanned Hawkeyes to stunning upsets over previously undefeated Notre Dame squads in 1939 and 1940. This initially struck me as sacrilegious, a Notre Dame graduate coaching another school to victory over the Irish. However, Dad assured me that as a former All-American end under Knute Rockne and a medical doctor, Anderson had been granted dispensation.

In 1962, I began to routinely follow the fortunes of Holy Cross football. I was still awed by Dr. Anderson's reputation when I matriculated at the college in 1968. By that time the legendary coach had been retired from the game for several years and most of the current players and coaching staff had never met Anderson. I first heard Anderson's name mentioned on campus when I hobbled into the training room one October afternoon before practice to get my ankle taped. As a substitute halfback on the freshman team I had sprained it a week earlier. Despite the injury I continued to practice. In those days freshman squads served mainly as cannon fodder for the varsity. We did however, play an abbreviated schedule and were slated to open against Dartmouth the next day. After six weeks of practice, I wasn't about to let a sore ankle rob me of my slim chance of seeing some game action. Boosting myself onto the taping table, I came under the scrutinizing gaze of Jack "Skitchy" Scott.

Scott, the team's roly-poly athletic trainer, was overworked, underpaid and universally loved. Visibly annoyed, the perspiring, red-faced Scott glared at me and announced, "You know, when Dr. Anderson was here, if a player needed taping the day before a game he didn't play the next day!" Stung by the reprimand, I began to slide down from the table. Scott's bark was worse than his bite however, and he had me sit still and then proceeded to ply his craft. As I watched Jack's pudgy hands adroitly tape my ankle in what was called a "basket wrap," it dawned on me that Anderson was right. Pre-game practices were always light; no sprinting, live contact or sled work. If a guy couldn't endure what amounted to a limbering-up session without being taped, he probably shouldn't be playing in a football game the next day. It was a policy I would implement with my own teams as a high school coach years later.

During later taping sessions I would occasionally grill Scott about Dr. Anderson. Because there was usually a line of players anxiously waiting to be taped, the hurried trainer only provided snippets of information. Yet, he always spoke of Anderson in glowing terms which made me want to learn more about the man.

I only saw Dr. Anderson in person once, on April 25, 1970. Bob Curran, the school's baseball coach, "volunteered" another teammate and me to check coats at the school's annual Athletic Hall of Fame Dinner. Dr. Anderson was one of four honorees being inducted. Our station was located in the basement of cavernous Kimball Hall where the event was being held. After the coat-check rush subsided, I snuck upstairs for a peek. Sitting at the dais in a dark business suit, the 69-year-old Anderson was viewing the proceedings with a critical eye and a no-nonsense, almost intimidating demeanor. While I was researching this book, many former Crusaders recalled that when it came to reprimanding a player, Anderson wasn't a "yell at you" coach, but rather a "look at you" coach, and that the patented Anderson "look" often sent future Marine Corps officers scurrying for cover. Thinking back to Anderson's visage on that April night, I understood what they meant.

Through the years I learned about Dr. Anderson's career in bits and pieces. How he became both a football coach and a medical doctor was still intriguing to me. His life would make a fascinating topic for a book. Since there was no such book, I decided to write one.

Anderson was a man of indefatigable spirit, an All-American football player who learned his trade from the most well-known and romanticized coach in the history of the game. With a quiet confidence and a fierce determination to succeed, Anderson plunged headlong into the Roaring Twenties by coaching college teams while simultaneously attending medical school in Chicago. In his "spare time" on Sunday afternoons he played for the NFL's Chicago Cardinals. As a doctor he established himself as an ear, nose and throat man and later as a urologist, while leading both Holy Cross and Iowa to memorable football seasons. A devout family man, he practiced moral ethics daily and instilled them into his players over a coaching career that spanned 43 years. As college football increased in popularity through the decades, so did Anderson's influence on the young men who played for him.

Retracing Anderson's life was a wondrous adventure. I hope that, readers will enjoy the journey as much as I did.

INTRODUCTION

As dusk descended upon Boston College's Alumni Field on November 28, 1964, the scoreboard's numbers glowed steadily brighter, heralding not only the game's climactic finish, but also the end of one man's storied coaching career.

Swaying pensively on the visitors' sideline was Dr. Eddie Anderson. For 39 seasons at four different schools, Anderson had spent autumn Saturday afternoons roaming the sidelines of college and university gridirons across America. Always impeccably attired in suit and tie on game days, his wing tip shoes buffed to a glossy shine, the bespectacled coach scrutinized his team's performance from under the brim of a stylish fedora. Cold and cloudy days like this one often found Anderson wearing a ¾-length overcoat and brandishing a rolled-up game program in his gloved hands.

Reacting to events on the field, Anderson sporadically pressed an open end of the program to his lips and used it like a megaphone to growl warnings or bellow words of encouragement to his players. Despite these Rudy Vallee–like efforts, cheering fans and blaring band music often rendered the coach's commands either indiscernible or inaudible. Yelling through an improvised megaphone was as demonstrative a behavior as Anderson's conservative midwestern upbringing would allow. Throughout his career, dignity, composure and a penetrating focus were hallmarks of the "good doctor's" sideline decorum.

Perhaps it was fitting that Anderson's coaching swan song would pit his Holy Cross squad against Boston College. For many fans in New England the traditional season finale between these Jesuit institutions was the biggest football game of the year. It was the Catholic schools' equivalent of the Army-Navy game. Held annually on the Saturday after Thanksgiving, the contests were always bitterly fought with the outcome usually undetermined until the game's waning moments.

The rivalry had been great because the competitors were so much alike. For the most part, they hailed from working class families, the sons and grandsons of Irish, Italian, French and Polish immigrants, who often lived on one of the floors of the three-decker houses that lined the streets of mill towns throughout New England. They were tough kids and skilled athletes who yearned for the opportunities a college education could provide.

Winning was paramount for each school, with the spoils of victory savored by students, alumni and faculty alike. A win gave the victorious student body a year's bragging rights over its lesser Jesuit rival 40 miles down the road. Alumni often bragged louder and longer than the students because they viewed their alma mater's victory as another validation of their hard-earned diplomas. It infused their steps with new bounce and swagger as they returned to work on Monday morning.

While the Jesuit rivalry received extensive news coverage throughout New England, it rarely captured center stage of the national sports spotlight. However, 1964 was different. During the Thanksgiving week, sports journalists and camera crews flocked to the central Massachusetts city of Worcester to cover football practices at Holy Cross. The purpose of the media pilgrimage was to pay homage to Dr. Eddie Anderson, who was stepping down as the "Dean of America's College Football Coaches."

Anderson had ascended to the deanship in 1957 when Columbia's venerable Lou Little retired. It was a well-deserved honor. As a player Anderson had mastered the game as an All-American end under Notre Dame's legendary Knute Rockne. Armed with a firm command of the so-called Notre Dame system of football, Anderson entered the collegiate coaching ranks in 1922 and served as a head coach for all but four of the next 43 years. (Anderson's brief respites from coaching occurred in 1932 when he left DePaul University to finish his medical internship and again between 1943 and 1945 while serving as an officer in the U.S. Army Medical Corps.)

In 1929 he married Mary Broderick in Chicago and together they raised four children. As an ear, nose, and throat man, and later a urologist, Anderson practiced medicine over the years at the Massachusetts Eye and Ear Hospital, the Iowa University Medical Center and the Rutland Veterans Hospital while guiding his teams to over 200 victories. More importantly, his coaching techniques and methods left an indelible impression on hundreds of young men who had played for him. Men who, years later, would credit the major impact Dr. Anderson's tutelage had had on their own successful careers as doctors, lawyers, military officers, educators and coaches, as well as prominent business men and civic leaders.

By 1964 a new wave of coaches was sweeping across the scene of college football — young men with high energy levels well suited for the frantic pace of big time college recruiting; coaches with colorful personalities who would soon jettison the traditional coaching garb of ties and jackets in favor of open-collar shirts; young men who would capitalize on the National Collegiate Athletic Association's (NCAA) permanent adoption of two-platoon football and the impending racial integration of college athletics that would dramatically increase the number of gifted athletes on college campuses.

Eddie Anderson was the last of an era of gentlemen coaches who had cut their teeth on football during the Rockne era, a coaching genre that included Columbia's Lou Little, Colgate's Andy Kerr, Michigan's Fritz Crisler, Tuss McLaughry at both Brown and Dartmouth, Indiana's Bo McMillin and Notre Dame's Elmer Layden. On the eve of his retirement from college football Dr. Anderson was the game's elder statesman. While he was revered by players, fellow-coaches, fans and members of the press, some viewed Anderson as reserved, austere and even aloof. These perceptions might have been accurate, but Anderson was a complex man who could not be readily pigeonholed or typecast to any prescribed mold.

His skill at wringing the most out of limited talent and his ability to get his teams "up" for big games came to be irrefutable trademarks of Anderson's prolific coaching success. Only the year before, in 1963 at Worcester, Anderson's Crusaders had clawed out a 9 to 0 upset victory over heavily favored Boston College. Now, a year later, sportswriters, coaching colleagues and sentimental fans were hoping that the "good doctor" could conjure up one more upset in his coaching farewell.

By 1964 Boston College had a significantly larger student body than its Worcester rival. In recent years the Chestnut Hill school had increased its allotted number of football scholarships and scheduled more intersectional games in hopes of seeing the Eagle football program soar to the big time. Cognizant of the widening talent gap between Boston College and the "Cross," Anderson shared his concerns with his son, Jim, before a game against the Eagles in the early sixties.

"I sure hope that we can get these guys this year, because I don't know if we'll be able to get them in the future," predicted Anderson. "They just have so much depth. They have eleven guys that can play offense, another eleven to play defense, and still another eleven who excel on kicking teams. Heck, they even have eleven guys that go to class."[1]

Despite having fewer scholarship athletes and regularly having to line up against bigger and stronger Boston College squads, Anderson's teams remained competitive. In fact, during Anderson's previous seasons at Holy Cross, the Crusaders had prevailed in 11 of the 20 contests.

Introduction

In 1964 Boston College would again be a 13-point favorite over Holy Cross. The Eagles had defeated both Syracuse and Villanova, two teams that had easily handled the Crusaders earlier in the season. Sportswriters, friends and coaching colleagues held faint hope that Anderson could "doctor up" one final upset. Some nostalgically wished that Anderson had retired after the 1963 season, thus assuring his exiting a winner. But in 39 years of coaching Anderson was never one to look back. He wouldn't start now.

Holy Cross entered the game with a record of 5 wins and 4 losses, while Jim Miller's Boston College squad, having played a more formidable schedule, had won 5 and lost 3. The '64 game was another classic Holy Cross–Boston College thriller, with both teams going at it hammer and tongs from the opening kickoff. Early gang tackles and punishing blocks yielded only more of the same as the afternoon wore on. It was a crisp, fast-moving game with few penalties and the fans loudly cheering any offensive play that netted more than a few yards. At the end of the third quarter Holy Cross held an 8 to 3 lead. With 12 minutes remaining, however, Boston College seized the lead with a touchdown and field goal, and everything changed. .

A coaching colleague once described Anderson as "coaching by the end of his nose."[2] The expression meant that Anderson would deviate from a well-devised game plan if he sensed the winds of the football fates changing. Like a wily grizzly sticking its snout to the wind to determine whether to continue the hunt upstream or downstream, Anderson would follow his coaching nose during a game's critical moments. The scent now told him to send in the field goal team.

It was a bold decision in the face of Holy Cross' questionable place-kicking game. The Crusaders had not successfully attempted a field goal since 1960 when a kid from Nebraska named Bill Joern booted one that more resembled a sliced 9-iron shot than it did a field goal. Nevertheless, Joern's kick possessed enough distance and "body English" to sail inside the uprights, giving Holy Cross a last second 9 to 8 victory over Dartmouth at Hanover.

The Crusaders had lacked a reliable place-kicker for years, which forced Holy Cross to attempt two-point conversions after touchdowns scored during the early sixties. In recent weeks, however, perhaps anticipating such a predicament, Anderson had made his team resume practicing field goals. He tried numerous kickers and had decided upon one whose success rate was improving daily.

As the purple-and-silver clad Crusaders aligned for what could be the game-winning 14-yard field goal, 26,909 spectators sat taut with anticipation throughout Alumni Field. Dr. Anderson merely set his jaw and cocked his head slightly to the right.

The play never had a chance. The center's snap sailed high and behind the holder Charlie Hinckle. Only by reaching his outstretched arms behind him was Hinckle able to get a hand on the ball that sent it flying about 12 feet into the air. Like a basketball player leaping for a rebound, kicker Ray Weaver grabbed it in mid-air before being swarmed under by a wave of maroon-and-gold jerseys.

On the Holy Cross sideline several players cringed, covering their eyes in agony and shaking their heads in disbelief. Among the coaches, however, no profanities were uttered or clipboards thrown. No verbal tongue-lashings were administered. They stoically eyed the clock while secretly praying for another Boston College turnover.

No miracles were on top that day, and Dr. Anderson's coaching career ended with a 10 to 8 defeat.

The vibrant clatter of metal-tipped cleats on the concrete floor contrasted sharply with the locker room's somber mood as dejected, teary-eyed players lumbered and limped in single file to take a seat on one of the long wooden benches around the room. Now with heads bowed, bloodied and emotionally drained, players sat in anguish over the gut-wrenching loss.

Dispersed among the line of players were numerous sportswriters who, upon entering the room, quickly scattered to perch at various openings along the walls. With pencils and notebooks at the ready, they waited self-consciously, intruders in the players' sanctuary. They would remain interlopers until Doctor Anderson arrived. Then, by scribbling notes while the coach addressed the team, their presence would be validated. They didn't have to wait long.

After entering the room Anderson led his team in a short prayer. Poking his glasses higher upon his nose, the coach rose to speak.[3]

There were no tears or melodramatics. Anderson's last words to his team were dignified and direct, just the style in which he had coached through the years. He told them they had played like men. He expressed his pride in the team. He then turned to meet the press. As always, he fielded all questions patiently, giving candid and concise answers.

"I would have [liked] to have won it," confessed Anderson, "especially for the boys. And it would have been nice for me too."

Occasionally, Anderson broke away from the reporters' questioning to congratulate a passing player on a game well played. Players intermittently approached to extend their personal best wishes.

"Coach," said junior Bob Noble, "I just wanted to let you know what an honor and privilege it was to have played for you."

"No," replied Anderson while shaking the defensive end's hand, "I want you to know what an honor it was for me to have coached fine young men like you."[4]

Almost an hour passed before the last of the reporters scurried off to meet their deadlines and the throng of alumni and players finished paying their respects. It was dark when the coach departed the locker room. Only a few players and fans lingered in the parking lot as Anderson and his youngest son, Jim, headed to the car for the drive back to Worcester. Sliding into the passenger seat and closing the door, out of earshot of everyone except his son, Anderson slammed his right fist into the open palm of his left hand, shook his head and growled, "Boy, I wish I had one more shot at those guys!"[5]

To Jim Anderson his father's words were an epiphany. He realized that all of the fanfare, honors and publicity of the previous week — the countless television and newspaper interviews, the crew from *Newsweek* covering his team's practices, the career awards had meant nothing to his father. What did matter to the good doctor, however, was the thrill of football's competition and how the young men he coached played the game.

"It was then," recalls Jim Anderson, "that I realized why my father had been so good at the game."[6]

1

THE EARLY YEARS

Edward Nicholas Anderson was born on November 13, 1900, in Oskaloosa, Iowa. His father, Edward Martinius Anderson, was a native of Horten, Norway, who at age 14 signed on with a sailing ship and spent the next five years literally sailing the seven seas. Ports of call took the young Argonaut throughout the Mediterranean and to the distant lands of China and Australia. Deciding to follow one of his brothers to America in 1887, the 19-year-old sailor joined the crew of a schooner sailing from Rotterdam, Holland, to the United States.[1]

Arriving on the eastern seaboard, the adventurous Anderson jumped ship and made his way west to Duluth, Minnesota, where he worked the big log drives in St. Louis Bay. Like many Scandinavian immigrants at that time, Anderson changed the spelling of his name from Andersen with an *e* to Anderson with an *o*.[2]

Procuring employment with the railroad, the ex-sailor eventually met and fell in love with an Irish-American beauty named Nellie Dinon. In early 1900 they were married in St. Paul before moving to Oskaloosa where Eddie was born. When Eddie was 13, the family moved to Mason City, Iowa, where Mr. Anderson worked for many years as an engineer for the Minneapolis & St. Louis Railroad.

Residing in a comfortable house at 718 North Pennsylvania, young Eddie often entertained himself for hours at a time by throwing a baseball against the barn wall and catching it on the rebound. Schoolwork came easy to Eddie, especially mathematics, in which he excelled. Breezing through his daily homework assignments allowed him ample time for afternoon athletic contests and games in the neighborhood.

Although an athletic child, Eddie didn't play football until his junior year in high school — and that almost didn't happen. When the youngster announced his plans to play, his father was less than thrilled. The old gent simply couldn't see the boy deriving any benefits from participating in this strange new game. In hopes of enticing his son to do something more productive with his time, Mr. Anderson offered to buy Eddie a bike so he could obtain an after-school job.[3] The teenager agreed.

This change of plans, however, prompted the Mason City coach, C.A. West, to pay a visit to the Anderson home. Pleading that Eddie's playing was vital if Mason City was to field a winning team, West argued a compelling case that won over both father and son. Eddie agreed to play and Coach West's words proved to be prophetic.

In Eddie's senior season Mason City went undefeated and won the state championship. Steam-rolling to nine shutout victories in ten games, Mason City scored 536 points while only yielding 7.

A stellar performer at right end, Anderson's play was instrumental in his team's narrow 3 to 0 win over North Des Moines. In the sports vernacular of the day a local newspaper reported, "Steffan and Anderson played a whale of a game at ends and worked under punts and covered forward passes attempted by the Des Moines team, so that the opponents were hopeless most of the time.

"It was Anderson who made Funk's kick (a 25-yard dropkick field goal) possible, for he took a pass from a Des Moines man in the final quarter and carried it to the 20-yard line, where Funk had no trouble making the count."[4]

The 1917 Mason City squad was loaded with talent. Anderson's teammates included center John McConnell and halfback Lester Belding. Both went on to play at the University of Iowa and fullback Red Weston later played at Wisconsin. Belding and Weston would both earn All-American honors in 1920.

So proud of its team were local residents that school officials agreed to host a post-season exhibition game against Chicago's city champions. Attired in shiny and well-fitting uniforms, the brawny visitors from the Windy City openly guffawed when their shoddily clad hosts took the field. During the coin toss Anderson overheard one of the Chicago team captains scoff, "Let's get this game over with and get back to *Chi*!"[5] When the final gun sounded, the Mason City yokels had pummeled their big city opponents by 50 points.

Anderson's athletic prowess extended well beyond the gridiron. Winter's falling snow found the railroader's son playing guard on the school's basketball team, and when April's winds blew, he would don a catcher's mask and chest protector for the baseball team. Throughout the spring Anderson occasionally shed the "tools of ignorance" to compete in track and field. At the Cerro Gordo County Schools' track meet on May 17, 1917, Anderson demonstrated his athletic versatility by finishing second in four events: the high hurdles, shot put, and both the broad and high jumps.[6]

With his high school graduation looming in the spring of 1918, Anderson set his sights beyond the multi-globe streetlights that bordered Mason City's major thoroughfares. He had no desire to follow in his father's footsteps as a railroader. He wanted to attend college.

Having maintained good grades throughout his school years, Anderson dreamed of one day becoming a doctor. During summer vacations he often accompanied his mother on trips to St. Paul, Minnesota, where they visited relatives. Aside from enjoying the area's many lakes and tree-shaded lanes that provided an escape from Iowa's sweltering heat, it was there that Anderson got his first glimpse of a major university — the University of Minnesota. Encouraged by aunts and uncles, he fostered hopes of matriculating there and, perhaps, eventually gaining entrance into its prestigious medical school.

Certainly he must have entertained these thoughts as he sat in cap and gown with the 1918 graduating class of Mason City High School. Family, faculty and friends all believed that the serious-minded teenager would one day make his mark on the world. Among the evening's throng of well-wishers, Anderson shook hands and shared congratulations with another schoolmate destined for bigger things, Meredith Willson.

Willson had grown up at 314 South Pennsylvania, 10 blocks south of the Anderson house. Several weeks after his own graduation in 1919, the aspiring musician and composer packed his slightly bent flute into a battered suitcase and boarded a train to New York. By 1921 he would be playing in John Phillip Sousa's famous band before joining the New York Philharmonic Orchestra. He eventually composed numerous hit songs but his most famous work was the 1957 musical, *The Music Man*. It is widely accepted that the musical's mythical setting of River City, Iowa, is actually a depiction of Willson's hometown of Mason City.

Anderson was also delighted to bump into an old friend and Mason City alumnus, Carmen Lombardo. Having graduated the previous year, Lombardo spent most of their conversation raving about a small Catholic university he was attending in northern Indiana called Notre Dame.[7]

2

UNDER THE
GOLDEN DOME

Why Eddie Anderson decided to matriculate at Notre Dame is not known. In the fall of 1918 it had neither the academic nor athletic reputation that it enjoys today. It did have, however, a dynamic rookie football coach named Knute Rockne.

Arguably, Rockne would do more to promote the game of football than any other individual in the history of the sport. While not inventing the forward pass, he and Notre Dame teammate, Charles "Gus" Dorais, pioneered its exciting and devastating offensive capabilities on November 1, 1913. With Rockne doing most of the catching, Dorais completed 14 of 17 heaves for 243 yards in a stunning 35 to 13 upset of Army at West Point. The duo's dazzling performance would revolutionize the game and garner Notre Dame its first national headlines. During his 13-year tenure as Notre Dame's head coach, Rockne compiled an incredible record of 105 wins, 12 losses and 5 ties while making the University of Notre Dame synonymous with college football. He became an evangelist for the game's virtues and would bequeath to later generations of coaches an unrivaled legacy for visceral locker room pep talks.

In later years Anderson relished recounting his first meeting with the fabled coach. Upon eyeballing the 17-year-old freshman, the balding Rockne asked, "How big are you, son?"

"Five-ten and 149 pounds, sir," Anderson replied.

"What position do you play?"

"End, sir."

"Hmm, I've got 16 right ends and 14 left ends," the coach growled.

"I guess I'm a left end, then," said Anderson.

14

Rockne laughed and tossed Anderson a pair of tattered football pants way too large for him.

"These are lucky pants, son," instructed Rockne. "Don't lose them. Take them to a tailor and have them sewed up."

"Only a skinny kid like me could have worn those pants after all the tears in them had been mended." Anderson recalled. "Rock again told me they were lucky pants, but I also knew that they were the only pair left at Notre Dame."[1]

This quaint tale may have been apocryphal, for according to Anderson's younger brother, Bill, Rockne had visited Mason City several times during the summer of 1918 in hopes of persuading the star end to attend Notre Dame.[2] In those nascent years of intercollegiate football the athletic recruiting process was haphazard at best, and although limited financial aid was available, few colleges offered football scholarships that covered the total cost of room, board, tuition, and books. Anderson initially received no financial aid for attending Notre Dame.

An inducement for Anderson enrolling at the South Bend campus may have been the school's Student Army Training Corps (SATC) program. With the country immerged in World War I, the United States' armed services had an insatiable demand for recruits. In an attempt to satisfy this need, Secretary of War Newton D. Baker announced the creation of the SATC program to all college and university presidents on May 18, 1918. Institutions of higher learning with enrollments of 100 or more were eligible. In his book, *Thy Honored Name,* Father Anthony Kuzniewski, S.J. explains the program. "Its purpose was to enroll all able-bodied male students above the high school level as army privates in what one historian called, 'a vast network of pre-induction centers where young men could be temporarily held prior to call-up for active military duty.' Student corpsmen were issued uniforms, subjected to military discipline and given about a dozen hours a week in military drill and related courses."[3]

Cutting a dashing figure, Private Eddie Anderson posed proudly in his uniform for pictures that he sent home to his parents. He was also grateful for the monthly stipend he received from the government for participating in the SATC program, money he sorely needed. (Some student corpsmen received up to $30 a month.)

Because the war precipitated a manpower shortage on many college campuses, freshmen were allowed to compete on varsity teams in 1918. If Anderson, as legend proclaims, did indeed begin his Notre Dame football career as a 15th string end, he rose quickly through the ranks. The Iowa native's blocking, tackling and overall toughness soon caught the coach's eye. So impressed was Rockne with Anderson's pass-catching skills and football savvy, that Anderson found himself traveling with the team to Cleveland for its season opener against Case Tech.

Rockne's squads were so talent-laden that he sometimes started his so-called "shock troops" or second team against an opponent. The shock troops would hammer the adversaries well into the game's opening quarter before their cagey coach would send in the first team. The Notre Dame regulars, who had eagerly been awaiting Rockne's call to action, then made quick work of their battered and winded opponents. Against Case Tech, veterans George Gipp and Captain Pete Bahan joined young Anderson in watching the game's opening minutes from the bench.

Near the end of the first quarter Rockne turned to his freshman end and asked, "How are you feeling, Eddie?"

"Fine, coach," replied Anderson.

"Good. Get in there at right end," barked Rockne.

"Yes, sir!" eagerly snapped Anderson as he sprinted into the fray.[4]

Eddie Anderson was the first player Knute Rockne ever substituted into a game. Once in the lineup, however, Anderson seldom left it. During his remaining four years at Notre Dame, he started all but one game at right end.

The players had over a month to savor their 26 to 6 victory over Case Tech. A deadly outbreak of Spanish influenza forced Notre Dame to cancel its game with Washington & Jefferson and to postpone its remaining October games until November.

In John Barry's *The Great Influenza*, the author suggests that this strain of flu may have originated in February of 1918 in Haskell County in southwestern Kansas. It then traveled east to the nearby Army base at Fort Riley where early on the morning of March 11 a soldier reported to sick bay. By noon over 100 soldiers had reported to sick bay with the flu. By the week's end, over 500 of the camp's soldiers were hospitalized with the ailment.

Soldiers carried the flu with them from one military base to another as they rode jam-packed troop trains to eastern seaports to embark for Europe. In a single day in September, 1,543 soldiers at Massachusetts' Camp Devens reported ill with influenza.

In October, the epidemic swept down the eastern seaboard claiming 11,000 lives in Philadelphia. To combat the lethal flu, Kentucky's Board of Health prohibited public meetings of any kind. The state of Pennsylvania shut down all places of public amusements. Across the nation towns were quarantined and laws were passed requiring people to wear masks in public. Schools and theaters were closed and colleges cancelled or postponed football games.

The Spanish influenza epidemic of 1918 would eventually claim over 675,000 American lives — more than all the wars of the 20th century combined — before disappearing as mysteriously as it began.[5] In October alone over 195,000 Americans succumbed to the dreaded disease, resulting in a nationwide casket shortage.

Rockne's squad returned from its five-week hiatus on November 2 by pummeling Wabash College 67 to 7, a contest arranged with the tiny Indiana school the day before the actual game. At South Bend the following week Notre Dame tied Great Lakes Naval Training Station. Great Lakes featured star halfback Paddy Driscoll, a future teammate of Anderson's with the Chicago Cardinals, and George Halas. Halas, of course, later co-founded the National Football League and the Chicago Bears.

After losing to Michigan State and defeating Purdue, Notre Dame ended its aborted season by traveling to Nebraska for a Thanksgiving Day game. Played in a sea of mud, the futile struggle ended in a scoreless tie. The final curtain descended on the 1918 season with Notre Dame posting a record of 3 wins, 1 loss and 2 ties.

Anderson's first season at Notre Dame was almost his last. Although bruised and sore, the freshman end was in good spirits when he departed the team train in Iowa to spend the Thanksgiving weekend with his parents in Mason City. Upon his arrival, however, Eddie discovered that his mother was ailing. Nellie Anderson had developed a heart condition that was also putting a strain on the family's finances. During a late night conversation with his dad Eddie learned that there was no money for him to continue college.[6] With the armistice of November 11 ending the war, Notre Dame would be disbanding its SATC program in December. With it would go the monthly stipend Eddie received as a student corpsman.

Showing a calm resolve to make the most of a bad situation, a personality trait that would remain with him throughout his life, Anderson procured a job at the local cement factory the next day. In a telegram explaining his predicament, he informed Rockne that he would not be returning to Notre Dame.

No sooner had the gray cement dust settled on Anderson's work boots than Rockne wired back:

"Everything paid for! Don't worry. Get back."

— Rock[7]

Years later in conversations with his sons, Anderson occasionally reflected on how different his life might have been had Rockne not sent that telegram.

Prospects for Notre Dame football seemed bright in 1919. With the war over, stars like "Slip" Madigan and Joe Brandy were returning from military service. Joining them were newcomers "Buck" Shaw and George Trafton, whom Rockne had discovered playing on service teams. The soon-to-be-legendary George Gipp, who led the team in scoring, passing and rushing in 1918, and leading receiver Bernie Kirk spearheaded a returning cast that included Anderson, team captain Pete Bahan, halfback Johnny Mohardt and guard Heartley "Hunk" Anderson.

Despite its advance billing, Notre Dame struggled in a close 14 to 0 win over Kalamazoo in the season's home opener. Rockne was not in attendance, however, opting instead to scout Nebraska while leaving his old teammate and new assistant, Gus Dorais, to handle the coaching chores. Throughout his career Rockne occasionally delegated an assistant to coach the team against a lightweight opponent while he traveled elsewhere to scout a more formidable upcoming foe. This strategy would drastically backfire in 1926, when undefeated Notre Dame was playing in Pittsburgh while Rockne was spending the weekend in Chicago attending a Western Conference meeting of athletic directors and scouting future opponent Navy. Upon learning of Rockne's absence, opposing coach Wally Steffen informed his squad that Rockne thought so little of Carnegie Tech's chances that he deemed it unnecessary to be there. Enraged by this slight, Carnegie Tech roared to a 19 to 0 upset victory. The loss cost Notre Dame the national championship and left Rockne with egg on his face.[8]

With Rockne back on the sidelines the following week, Notre Dame trounced Mount Union 60 to 7 before boarding a train to play at Nebraska for the fifth consecutive year. Due to the small seating capacity at Cartier Field, Notre Dame was compelled to play most of its games on the road in those early days. Since Nebraska split the gate 50/50, playing before 10,000 avid fans at Lincoln always resulted in a lucrative payday for the Indiana school. Furthermore, much of the anti–Catholic sentiment directed at the South Bend visitors during their early meetings had dissipated as the gate receipts increased. This was clearly demonstrated on the eve of the 1919 game when over 1,000 Nebraska students and fans, following behind a 70-piece band, marched on Notre Dame's hotel chanting, "We want Rockne! We want Rockne!"

It was only when Rockne and many of his players, Eddie Anderson among them, assembled on the hotel's 9th Street balcony that the crowd finally quieted. "It is always a pleasure for us to visit Lincoln," Rockne addressed his admirers, "because we are sure of a good game."[9]

The next day Rockne witnessed a better contest than he may have liked as a physically punishing Nebraska team knocked several of Notre Dame's starting players out of the game. With George Gipp masterfully burning time off much of the fourth-quarter clock, Notre Dame escaped with a 14 to 9 win and a net payday of over $3,500.

After successive wins over Western Michigan and Indiana, Rockne and a traveling squad of 25 players boarded a train east to resume what was fast becoming one of the fiercest football rivalries in the country — the Army-Notre Dame game. Due to traveling restrictions imposed by the war, the two schools had not met in 1918.

Stepping off the noon train at West Point on Friday, November 7, Anderson learned that Cadet Earl "Red" Blaik, the Army end he was scheduled to line up against the next day, was ill and unlikely to play. Anderson and Blaik would meet on the gridiron 17 years later, matching wits as coaching rivals in 1936. That was before Blaik returned to West Point to lead his alma mater to the zenith of the college football world during the 1940s.

However, on November 8, 1919, the cadets were unaffected by Blaik's absence as they jumped to an early 9 to 0 lead over the visitors. With only seconds remaining in the half, Notre Dame had the ball at the Army 1-yard line. As Knute Rockne remembered it, "Gipp had had a flash of the head linesman lifting his horn to blow the end of the half. While both teams looked on in surprise Gipp grabbed the ball from Larson (the center) and dove over the goal line for a touchdown. The horn sounded the instant Gipp took the ball, but the half wasn't over until the ball was dead, and the ball wasn't dead until the touchdown was made. I've never seen a quicker piece of thinking on the part of a player."[10]

Gipp's impromptu plunge narrowed the score to 9 to 6.

Early in the second half Notre Dame had the ball at mid-field when Eddie Anderson raced behind the West Point secondary and was waiting with open arms for Gipp's beautifully thrown pass. Tackled at the Army 10-yard line, Anderson's catch set up Walter Miller's touchdown run two plays later to give Notre Dame a 12 to 9 win.

After successive wins over Michigan State and Purdue, an undefeated season was on the line when Notre Dame traveled to Sioux City, Iowa, for the season finale against Morningside College. Playing on a snowy Thanksgiving Day before 10,000 fans, Notre Dame running backs Fritz Slackford and Gipp would mush at will through both the heavy snow and the Morningside defenders to give Notre Dame a 14 to 6 win and Rockne his first undefeated season.

After the exultation and festivities subsided hours later, Anderson bid his teammates adieu at the Sioux City railroad station and boarded a northbound train for Mason City to spend the holiday weekend with his parents. The passenger car in which he rode rocked gently as the locomotive barreled into the night. Gazing out the window into darkness and alone with his thoughts, Anderson must have taken solace in his own good fortune. Just a year earlier circumstances nearly coerced him into leaving school. However, fate and Knute Rockne intervened by granting him financial aid to continue with his education. He had good grades and being a starter on one of the finest college football teams in America had allowed him to travel the country from Nebraska to New York. It was a far cry from working at Mason City's cement plant.

Like most students who venture off to college, Anderson's most reward-ing experiences may have been the people he met and the friends he made. Affable and out-going, he had already achieved a degree of popularity on campus, while his tenacity and athletic talent on the gridiron earned him the cherished respect of teammates and coaches.

One of Anderson's closest friends at Notre Dame was teammate Heart-ley "Hunk" Anderson. Eddie and Hunk shared more in common than just a last name. Hunk was two years older, but both were of Norwegian descent. The sons of railroaders — Eddie's father, an engineer and Hunk's, a yard mas-ter in the northern Michigan town of Calumet — both had earned starting positions on Rockne's 1918 varsity squad as freshmen. That fall both served in the SATC on campus. Both were excellent students, Eddie in pre-med and Hunk in civil engineering. Both played on the basketball and baseball teams at Notre Dame. Yet, neither earned a letterman's monogram in the latter sport. As mid-year seniors, both would be involved in regrettable incidents that resulted in the university banning each from further participation in var-sity athletics.

Throughout his life Eddie would call Hunk Anderson the "toughest man I ever met."[11] That's a colossal tribute when one considers the myriad of coura-geous and talented men Anderson played with and coached during his 45-year association with the game of football. An early inkling of Hunk Anderson's exceptional toughness occurred in their freshman year when the kid from Calumet entered Eddie's dormitory room one evening and asked, "Do you know a guy from Davenport (Iowa) named Freeberg?"

"No, but I've heard of him. Why?" Eddie inquired.

Hunk then explained that Lt. Kirkohr of the Army's SATC program on campus had asked Hunk to represent the unit in a series of scheduled box-ing matches. Seeing that Kirkohr was desperate, Hunk agreed to fight as a heavyweight even though he weighed only 168 pounds.

Well aware of Freeberg's reputation as a fighter, Eddie warned, "You bet-ter not fight this guy, Hunk. Hell, he's good. He'll probably kill you."

"Bull," replied Hunk confidently. "I'm not afraid of anyone I can see or touch."[12]

Worried about his friend, Eddie was at ringside for the event several nights later when the larger Freeberg staggered Hunk with a couple of rights in the first round. But in the second round Hunk unleashed a devastating left hook over his opponent's right cross that sent Freeberg sprawling to the can-vas. Freeberg didn't get up until after he was counted out.

In December of 1919, in what seemed like déjà vu, Eddie again witnessed Hunk's ferocity in the ring. This time, however, the local Elks Club wanted to give hundreds of veterans returning from the war a "beer bust" and a night of recreation. The Elks prevailed upon Knute Rockne to supply the entertainment by promoting some boxing matches. Feeling obligated to their coach, several players, including Hunk Anderson, complied when asked to participate.

This time Hunk was matched against a teammate named George Trafton. Trafton, who had a 45-pound advantage as well as four inches in height and reach, gloated in anticipation upon informing Hunk that he would be his opponent that evening. As a member of the Chicago Bears in the 1920s, Trafton's rugged style of play earned him not only a reputation as the team's hatchet-man, but also an eventual place in the Pro Football Hall of Fame.

With George Gipp in Hunk's corner, an amazed Eddie Anderson watched the second round from ringside as Hunk rocked Trafton with a vicious left that sent him through the ropes in an unconscious heap. Scrambling frantically into the ring after the fight, Knute Rockne, the evening's promoter, excitedly announced, "No more fighting for Hunk. He'll kill anyone we put against him. He doesn't give a damn if they weigh 200 or 400 pounds ... he'll wreck 'em good."[13] With Rockne's declaration, Hunk was prohibited from advancing to the finals.

Years later, NFL-great Paddy Driscoll would claim, "Hunk Anderson would have been in his element in the Roman Colosseum — and God help the lions!"[14]

Hunk Anderson's street savvy almost matched his physical toughness. At the close of one school year Eddie and Hunk decided to "ride the rails" home together. Unable to hop a freight train, they resorted to hitchhiking. After a day-and-a-half on the road the two found themselves hungry and broke and still a long way from home. On the outskirts of a small midwestern town the weary travelers came across a carnival.

"Come on, Eddie," Hunk advised. "I think I know where we can get some money."

Each carried a suitcase and had a jacket slung over the opposite shoulder as they meandered through the carnival grounds taking in the sights and sounds. The aromatic smells emanating from the inviting booths of various food vendors only exacerbated their hunger. Unresponsive to Eddie's occasional inquiries, Hunk pensively scanned the rides and games of chance until the pair came upon a small crowd watching the antics of a monkey chained to an organ grinder. Flashing its teeth and tipping its hat to the delighted crowd, the monkey pirouetted and did an occasional back flip to the organ grinder's blaring music before holding out a tin cup to collect coins from appreciative spectators. The clinking of a few coins into the cup sent the monkey scurrying back to the organ grinder, who graciously pocketed the change.

After watching these proceedings for a few minutes, Hunk inconspicuously made his way to the front of the crowd. The garrulous organ grinder, greeting and chatting with passers-by, was not always watching the monkey at the end of the 15-foot chain. Whenever Hunk spied the organ grinder looking elsewhere, he would sneak a kick at the monkey. After several such stealthy jabs, the monkey became visibly upset and launched into a scolding chatter. A final kick resulted in the irate monkey lashing out at Hunk's pant leg and ripping a two-inch gash in the material.

Feigning indignation, Hunk threatened to call the police unless he was reimbursed for the pants ruined by the monkey's vicious attack. Ignorant of Hunk's provocation of the animal, the startled organ grinder offered $2 to resolve the matter. Thus, the Anderson boys had meal money that night.

Shaking his head incredulously years later, Eddie Anderson related, "You have to realize, a guy just doesn't pick an organ grinder as a target out of a whole group of carnival workers. But Hunk knew what he was doing, because we got the money."[15]

As a sophomore Eddie Anderson earned a starting position on the varsity basketball squad during the 1919–20 season. With Joe Brandy at the other guard, and Harry Mehre and Roger Kiley at the forwards, the starting line up was comprised of four varsity football players. Gus Dorais, who also assisted Rockne in football, coached the team to a season record of 5 wins and 13 losses.

In an era before fast-break offenses and slam-dunks, basketball was a slow-paced game of methodical passing and two-handed set shots. It was an anomaly when a team scored 40 points. Despite an anemic scoring average of only 0.6 points per game, the sophomore's overall play was solid. Anderson's performance in a 44 to 17 win over Kalamazoo on January 14, 1920, prompted a young sportswriter named Archie Ward (later to become nationally known as "Arch" Ward) to write, "Eddie Anderson gives promise of developing into one of the greatest guards that ever wore the Gold and Blue..."[16]

Anderson's most productive basketball season was his junior year under new coach, Walter Halas, the brother of longtime Chicago Bear coach, George Halas. The season's highlight occurred before 3,000 exuberant fans at Creighton University on February 17, 1921. In the words of local sportswriter Carroll R. Mullen, "Creighton defeated Notre Dame 24 to 20 in one of the hardest fought and most eventful games ever played on an Omaha court." What made this contest so unique initially had nothing to do with the game itself. Like many gymnasiums of that era, Creighton's basketball court was surrounded by an elevated running track that served as a viewing platform for spectators during games. In the closing minutes of the first half the ceiling under the running track on the south end of the court began to give way.

The game came to an immediate halt when hundreds of frenzied spectators raced onto the court to escape the falling debris. Fortunately, the fans on the elevated section of the track calmly evacuated the crumbling area. The section sagged but didn't collapse, and no one was injured.

After a cursory inspection, local officials roped off both of the affected upper and lower sections. Believing that the show must go on, they then allowed the game to resume.

The intense play of the second half and the game's close score only heightened the crowd's frenzy. The fans' rabid cheering often made it impossible for players to hear the referee's whistle. Near the end of the game a particularly hard foul led to a scuffle between the team's respective captains, Creighton's Charlie Kearney and Notre Dame's Harry Mehre, which triggered a rush of angry fans onto the floor to exchange blows with the visiting players. Halas' lads closed ranks and held the attackers at bay until police managed to clear the court. (Fortunately for the Creighton zealots, Hunk Anderson had jettisoned basketball that season in favor of playing club hockey or several probably would have been cold-cocked.)

Emerging brightly from the chaos of fallen debris and flying fists was the play of the guard from Mason City, for the next day Carroll Mullen wrote, " ... the individual work of Eddie Anderson was in evidence all evening."[17] Despite the yeoman efforts of Anderson and his teammates, Notre Dame could only muster a record of 9 wins and 14 losses for the 1920–21 season.

3

GEORGE GIPP

With the undefeated 1919 season under his belt and a talent-laden team returning, Rockne confidently set about beefing up his team's schedule for 1920. Hoping that Notre Dame would eventually gain entrance into the Western Conference (the forerunner of the Big Ten), Rockne continually sought to schedule its member schools. In this pursuit Rockne managed to add Northwestern to the 1920 slate that already included Indiana and Purdue. Somehow, the slick-talking Rockne persuaded Purdue to visit South Bend for the first time. Then, in a two-pronged maneuver to make financial hay, Rockne convinced the Notre Dame fathers to expand the seating capacity at Cartier Field while announcing that the November 6 contest with Purdue would be the school's inaugural homecoming game.

Like a bulldog eye-balling a pork chop, Rockne was salivating to start the 1920 season. Notre Dame was loaded with talented players. As reserve quarterback Chet Grant reflected years later, "We had two distinct teams with which to wage our campaign, and for the first time in Notre Dame history — probably in collegiate football history — two elevens operated almost entirely as separate units."[1] Rockne's prognosis changed dramatically, however, when on March 8, 1920, Notre Dame expelled star halfback George Gipp.

A native of Laurium, Michigan, Gipp came to Notre Dame on a baseball scholarship in the fall of 1916 as a 21-year-old freshman. The scholarship itself was really a job in the university's dining hall to pay his way. There are several stories of how Gipp came to play football at Notre Dame. The first claims that Rockne invited him to try out after spying Gipp in street clothes dropkicking a football behind Brownson Hall. Another maintains that while practicing baseball one fall day, a football sailed over the outfield fence and rolled dead at Gipp's feet. Gipp supposedly punted it back over the fence

24

where it landed squarely on Rockne's balding dome. Seeking the cause of his sudden headache, Rockne poked his head over the fence and yelled, "Who kicked that football?"[2] Realizing that Gipp had punted the ball over 60 yards in the air, the coach offered him a tryout.

Gipp quickly distinguished himself during a freshman game against Western Michigan. Late in the fourth quarter with the score tied at 7, Notre Dame had the ball at mid-field with a fourth down and four yards to go for a first down. Gipp dropped back into what everyone thought was a punt formation. Instead of punting, however, Gipp boomed a 62-yard dropkick field goal to give Notre Dame a 10 to 7 victory.

A spirited and gifted competitor on game days, Gipp was a prima donna during the week. He seldom practiced until mid-week, skipping practice on Mondays and Tuesdays. When he did show, Rockne occasionally banished him to work out with the scrubs, which he did half-heartedly. But on game days, Gipp again would be in the starting line up.

In *Rockne of Notre Dame*, Ray Robinson writes, "Gipp continued to receive special treatment from Rockne. A lesser player would have had a tongue-lashing administered to him by the coach and probably would have been thrown off the team. Instead, Rockne pampered his star pupil..."[3]

Gipp missed the first two games of the 1917 season because he failed to show up for school until mid–October. Nevertheless, Gipp's passing, running and punting saved the day for Notre Dame in its 7 to 2 win over Army. Unfortunately, Gipp's season ended prematurely the following week at Sioux City, Iowa, when two Morningside tacklers broke his leg by knocking him into a metal post along the sidelines. Gipp left school for the spring semester to recuperate but returned to star for the team in both 1918 and 1919. Because of the war and Notre Dame's aborted schedule in 1918, Gipp had been granted a fifth year of football eligibility for 1920.

Off the field, Gipp refused to let his studies interfere with his late night pool hustling and card playing. He seldom attended classes, preferring to ply his craft at Hullie and Mike's pool hall on Michigan Avenue. Even the *South Bend Tribune* heralded his pool-playing exploits. His substantial winnings at billiards and poker allowed Gipp to quit his dining hall job after only one semester. He later moved off campus and spent most of his South Bend years living at the lush Oliver Hotel.

Although prohibition was in full swing by 1920, Gipp always had access to hard liquor and often drank heavily after games. On paydays in nearby Elkhart, Gipp often visited the town to fleece its poker-playing citizenry of their hard-earned wages. He usually departed these high-stake games with his pockets bulging with cash winnings.

After one such game broke up at about 3 a.m., Gipp and his cronies realized that there was no public transportation available to take them back to South Bend. The only vehicle on the downtown streets of Elkhart was a horse-drawn milk wagon. As Hunk Anderson explained in his autobiography, "The milkman was delivering milk at the back door of a closed restaurant when Gipp yelled, 'Hurry up, let's get into that milk wagon.' Gipp took the reins and managed to navigate his way back to South Bend and the Oliver Hotel. He then turned the horse and wagon around, pointed them toward Elkhart, and with a yell and a slap on the horse's behind, the horse took off in a gallop."[4] It was never determined if the milk wagon ever reached Elkhart.

By March of 1920 the Notre Dame fathers had had enough of Mr. Gipp. Publicly citing "excessive class absences" as the reason for their decision, but privately fed up with his incessant disobedience of university rules, the "powers that be" expelled him.

The news stunned coach and teammates alike. Gipp, however, took the news with his characteristic indifference. Rockne's bewilderment quickly turned to panic when he learned that schools such as Michigan, Detroit and even West Point were feverishly recruiting the exiled Gipp.[5] Dreading the loss of his triple-threat halfback, the pudgy-nosed coach began petitioning university officials for Gipp's readmission. Rockne also pleaded his case to sympathetic downtown businessmen, who over the next few weeks continuously petitioned Notre Dame President Father Burns to reconsider Gipp's expulsion. With his patience at an end and afraid of alienating many of the school's financial boosters, Father Burns finally agreed to reinstate Gipp on April 29, 1920.

As Murray Sperber writes in *Shake Down the Thunder*, "When President Burns acted in April 1920, no doubt he hoped and even assumed that the incident would soon be forgotten. He had no way of knowing that within nine months George Gipp would become Notre Dame's first consensus All-American, would die, and then, twenty years later, would be sanctified in a Hollywood film."

Although tired and out-of-shape from his nocturnal carousing, George Gipp reported punctually for the opening day of practice in 1920. Voted captain-elect by teammates the previous November, his six-week expulsion resulted in the forfeiture of that honor to senior tackle Frank Coughlin.

Kicking off the season with consecutive home shutouts over Kalamazoo (39 to 0) and Western Michigan (42 to 0), Notre Dame then traveled to Lincoln for the sixth consecutive year to meet Nebraska. Although the relationship between the two schools had improved in recent years, many of Nebraska's 9,000 homecoming fans now showered the visitors with vitriolic anti–Catholic taunts all afternoon.

The bigotry was indicative of a nativism sweeping across much of America in the early twenties. Disillusioned with the country's recent involvement in the Great War and violence spurred by immigrant anarchists on the radical fringes of the national labor movement, many Americans longed to return to the halcyon pre-war days. An alarming offshoot of this movement was the re-emergence of the Ku Klux Klan. Like its Reconstruction predecessor, the new Klan began as an instrument of black oppression in the South but soon sprouted in middle-size cities and small towns throughout the Midwest, with an especially active contingent in Notre Dame's home state of Indiana.[6] As self-professed guardians of public and private morals, the Klan espoused anti–Semitism, anti–Catholicism and xenophobia. Its brief revival would culminate in 1923 with a nationwide membership of nearly five million before internal squabbling and emerging national resistance reduced it to 9,000 members by 1930.

Trailing Nebraska 7 to 2, Eddie Anderson jump-started Notre Dame's sputtering offense by hauling in three passes for a total of 59 yards during the visitor's first touchdown drive. With Rockne's lads nursing a two-point lead in the fourth quarter and Nebraska marching deep into Notre Dame territory, the opportunistic Anderson recovered a key fumble that stymied Nebraska's scoring threat. Notre Dame then scored again for a 16 to 7 win.

At home the following Saturday Notre Dame beat Valparaiso 28 to 3. It would be their only meeting on the gridiron and one that Rockne really wanted. Hoping to fill Notre Dame's schedule with big-name opponents, Rockne had approached Harvard for a game in 1920. The Cambridge school's curt and icy reply that "such a meeting was inadvisable" left Rockne chagrined.[7] When Harvard later agreed to play Valparaiso that season, a tiny Indiana school only 80 miles from South Bend, Rockne hastily added Valparaiso to Notre Dame's 1920 schedule so he could beat them by a larger margin than Harvard would. (Rockne succeeded; Harvard only beat Valparaiso 21 to 0).

The weather weighed heavily on Rockne's mind as Notre Dame's train arrived in a driving rain at West Point on Friday, October 29. "Rock" need not have worried, for Saturday's sunshine and brisk breeze dried the field by kick-off. Rockne relished playing Army at West Point, for although the military academy did not yet charge admission, it nevertheless paid visiting teams a substantial fee. With key New York City sportswriters in attendance, the game always received the expansive publicity that Rockne so coveted.

The Army-Notre Dame game had rocketed in stature in only six short years. Its dramatic surge in popularity was attributable to the interest the game sparked among the Catholic working class in New York City. Never having attended college themselves, many now professed loyalty to the small midwestern Catholic school that annually pitched battle with mighty Army. During the rivalry's early years they traveled by train 50 miles north to cheer their "adopted" school on to victory. The contest was later switched to New York City where for many years local blue-collar Notre Dame fans rode the city's subways to the games. Thus, the origin of Notre Dame's so-called "subway alumni."

Both teams entered the 1920 game undefeated and would play before a capacity crowd of 10,000 at Cullum Hall Field. In a prelude to his afternoon's performance, George Gipp engaged in a dropkicking duel with Army's Russell "Red" Reeder during the pre-game warm up. When Reeder dropped out at the 40-yard line, Gipp walked to the 50-yard line and called for four footballs. He then kicked two over one crossbar before turning and nonchalantly kicking the remaining two over the other bar.[8]

If *New York Times* sportswriter Arthur Robinson's account was accurate, the game's early action resembled a back alley brawl. "The play became rough. Blood poured from the noses of several players, but the roughness subsided suddenly when Notre Dame was penalized half the distance to its goal for assault and battery."[9]

Undaunted by Gipp's kicking display and a few bloody noses, Army jumped to an early 7 to 0 lead. Early in the second quarter Gipp unleashed a 50-yard touchdown pass to left end Roger Kiley and dropkicked his second extra point to give Notre Dame a 14 to 7 lead. But behind the talented running of Walter French, a transfer student and former All-American from Rutgers, Army continued to give Notre Dame fits. The speedy French returned Gipp's punt 60 yards for a touchdown to tie the game at 14. When the multi-talented French later booted a 20-yard field goal Army took a 17 to 14 halftime lead.

During the first half, Archie Ward, a student-reporter covering the game for the *South Bend Tribune*, heard several Notre Dame fans repeatedly cheering, "Let's go Irish!" The chant obviously referred to the abundance of Irish names on the Notre Dame roster. In his account of the game young Ward substituted the nickname "Irish" for terms previously used to describe Notre Dame such as "Hoosiers," "Catholics" or "Benders." The press wire services picked up the new moniker and the sports world soon came to acknowledge Notre Dame as the Irish.

Recognizing the game's importance for both his own career and the school's athletic reputation, Rockne was not about to lose it. The irate coach lashed into his team at halftime. According to teammate Chet Grant, Rockne's wrath initially descended on the end from Mason City.

"'Eddie, where the hell were you on French's runs?'

"Eddie Anderson begins to explain, 'It wasn't my fault, Rock."

Rock then blew up. "I had never seen him in such a rage. I thought he was going to sock Eddie."

"'Shut up, Anderson!' he shouted. 'Don't talk back to me. You go back in there and play football.'"[10]

There are no other accounts of Rockne ever berating Anderson. Rarely, if ever, did Anderson allow a ball carrier to run around his end. Usually the first defender down on punt coverage, Anderson dropped many a punt returner like he had been shot with a deer rifle. Walter French, however, had obviously eluded Anderson on his 60-yard punt return for a touchdown. It would be the last such touchdown on Anderson's watch.

Rockne continued his tirade upon spying Gipp leaning against a wall, calmly smoking a cigarette. "What about you, Gipp? I don't suppose you have any interest in this game?"

To which Gipp indignantly replied, "Look, Rock, I've got $400 of my own money bet on this game, and I'm not about to blow it."[11]

In fact, Gipp and his teammates had a total of $2,100 bet with West Pointers on the game's outcome. Such student betting had been common practice between the two schools since the series' inception in 1913.[12]

In the second half Gipp protected his investment by playing superbly on both sides of the ball. After a scoreless third period, Gipp's runs and accurate passing led to John Mohardt's second touchdown run. Gipp then drop-kicked the extra point giving Notre Dame a 21 to 17 lead. Later Gipp again demonstrated great speed and agility by returning a punt 50 yards down the middle of the field to set up his team's last touchdown.

Playing the greatest game of his career in Notre Dame's 27 to 17 win over Army, Gipp personally accounted for 332 yards in rushing, passing and kick returns. The 6-foot, 185-pound halfback also kicked three extra points and threw a touchdown pass. Eastern newspapermen viewed Gipp's performance as a godsend and zealously set about the task of transferring his heroic deeds to paper. While pounding their typewriter keys to meet their respective deadlines, sportswriters began the process of chiseling the name of George Gipp forever into the Golden Age of American sports.

Sportswriters now heaped lofty accolades on the Notre Dame halfback such as the one that appeared in the next day's *New York Times*. "A little Hoosier football player named George Gipp galloped through Army on the Plains here this afternoon giving a performance which was more like an antelope than a human being."

Esteemed sportswriter Ring Lardner wrote that for Notre Dame to insure future success all it needed was to "...have the team line up, pass the ball to Gipp and let him use his own judgement."

Notre Dame returned home on November 6, 1920, to play Purdue in its first-ever homecoming game. In an early testimonial to the "build it and they will come" mentality, a record crowd of 12,000 packed their fannies into recently expanded Cartier Field to welcome back former gridiron heroes such as Louis "Red" Salmon (Class of '04) and Ray Eichenlaub (Class of '15).

Rockne's decision to start the second team caused Eddie Anderson to miss his first starting assignment since the opening game of his freshman year against Case Tech. From his unaccustomed seat on the bench, Anderson watched as the second-stringers took a 7 to 0 lead. Only when Purdue marched to Notre Dame's 10-yard line early in the second quarter did Rockne insert the first team. Replacing Dave Hayes at right end, Anderson and company kept Purdue from scoring.

Once in the line-up, George Gipp lived up to his press clippings by running 92 and 80 yards for touchdowns. Gipp's long-scoring runs were sandwiched around Anderson scooping up teammate Norm Barry's fumble and advancing it 20 yards for a touchdown. By the fourth quarter, Rockne's starters were back on the bench watching the third team mop up in Notre Dame's 28 to 0 win.

The Irish had a tougher time of it the following week before 14,000 fans at Indianapolis. Pounded early and often by Hoosier tacklers, a battered Gipp left the game with what was diagnosed as a separated shoulder and possible broken collarbone. Indiana took a 10 to 0 halftime lead into the locker room.

For most of the season Notre Dame's Norm Barry and Johnny Mohardt had competed ferociously for the team's starting right half back spot. Mohardt prevailed, but the struggle resulted in hard feelings between the two. When Rockne announced that Barry would start the second half at left half back for Gipp, the two temporarily shelved their differences and worked in earnest as teammates. Blocking for one another, Barry and Mohardt took turns ripping off chunks of yardage until the quarter ended with the ball at Indiana's 5-yard line. It was at that point that Rockne decided to re-enter Gipp for Barry, a move that caused Barry to explode in anger.

Ray Robinson writes, "As Gipp ran onto the field, taped from shoulder to wrist like a mummy, the incensed Barry tossed his helmet in the direction of Rockne. Fortunately, Rockne ducked. Barry didn't stay around to watch Gipp plunge over for a touchdown, then add the extra point to make the score 10 to 7, still in favor of Indiana. By that time Barry had hailed a cab outside the stadium and was headed for a local hotel."[13]

Late in the game Notre Dame moved the ball to the Hoosiers' 15-yard line. With Indiana anticipating Gipp attempting a game-tying field goal on fourth down, Gipp surprised the home team by passing to Eddie Anderson at the 1-yard line. However, Gipp's deception didn't end there. After three running plays gained only inches, Notre Dame lined up for fourth and goal with less than a minute remaining. Quarterback Joe Brandy called for a "sneak" play, whereupon Gipp, from his left halfback position, turned his face away from the crouching Indiana line and cried out in a loud voice, "Wait a minute, Joe! My headgear is caught and I can't get my breath. Wait till I pull it off!"

As Gipp proceeded to remove his headgear, the Indiana players relaxed and raised their eyes to watch him. Brandy, standing a yard from the center, simulated a yawning man stretching out his arms. As Gipp finished the last word of the sentence, the center snapped the ball to Brandy and the whole Irish line, from end to end, charged, shoulder to shoulder, against the Indiana players. Brandy then plunged into the end zone for the winning touchdown.[14]

On the jubilant trip back to South Bend, Gipp departed the team train in Chicago to help his friend and former Notre Dame teammate, Grover Malone, coach a high school football team for a few days.[15] Somehow the coaching sojourn turned into a three-day drinking binge. When he boarded the train to return to South Bend, Gipp had developed a nasty cough. By kick-off the following Saturday the cough was worse, and he was suffering from a fever and sore throat as well. Rockne had no plans of playing his weakened halfback against Northwestern.

Almost 1,100 Notre Dame students, about two-thirds of the student body, rode the South Shore electric train to Evanston to cheer on the Irish. Making the trip from Iowa, Eddie's father and brother, Bill, were also in attendance. It would be one of the finest games Eddie Anderson ever played and George Gipp's gridiron swan song.

Joining the ailing Gipp on the bench was his good friend Hunk Anderson, who was sidelined with a shoulder injury. Together they watched as Notre Dame drew first blood when Johnny Mohardt tossed a two-yard touchdown pass to Eddie Anderson. The end from Mason City would later make another two-yard scoring catch on a pass from Joe Brandy to give the Irish a 21 to 7 lead.

In the middle of the third quarter Notre Dame fans began yelling, "We want Gipp!" Northwestern supporters joined in so that by the end of the quarter the chanting had reached a crescendo. Usually indifferent to the cheering throngs, the crowd of 20,000 must have struck an emotional cord with Gipp, for he left his seat on the bench and gradually inched closer to Rockne who was standing near the sideline. Early in the fourth quarter Rockne looked over his shoulder and spied Gipp, bundled in blankets, standing near his elbow. He asked Gipp if he felt like playing, to which Gipp replied nonchalantly, "Sure, let's go."[16]

When Notre Dame regained possession compliments of an Eddie Anderson interception, Rockne sent Gipp into the game for Mohardt. To the fans' delight, Gipp, despite his heavily bandaged shoulder, dropped back on the first play and side-armed a 35-yard touchdown pass to the glue-fingered Anderson. It was Anderson's third touchdown reception of the day, and it would stand alone as a Notre Dame single-game record until Bill Barrett equaled Anderson's feat against North Carolina in 1949.

On Notre Dame's next possession Gipp showed that he held no grudge against Norm Barry for his angry outburst of the previous week by tossing him a 54-yard touchdown pass to give Notre Dame a 33 to 7 win.

It was an admirable performance for a healthy athlete, but considering Gipp's deteriorating condition, it was truly amazing. It would be Gipp's last hurrah, for his condition worsened during the week.

Gipp rallied briefly to attend a team banquet at the Oliver Hotel two days before the season's finale. A sudden relapse, however, forced him to leave halfway through the ceremonies.

As his teammates were blanketing Michigan State 25 to 0 on Thanksgiving Day to complete an undefeated season, Gipp lay gravely ill at St. Joseph's Hospital in South Bend. He was diagnosed with pneumonia and strep throat. This was before the days of antibiotics, and the streptococcus infection quickly spread through his body. Gipp slipped into critical condition.

Notre Dame's students began a vigil while waiting for medical updates on Gipp's condition. The university's Father Patrick Haggerty became a constant companion at the patient's bedside during Gipp's last days.

The last hours of Gipp's life have given birth to two controversial Notre Dame legends. The first maintains that Gipp, a lifelong but non-practicing Protestant, converted to Catholicism on his deathbed. Mrs. Matthew Gipp, a devout Protestant who was at her son's side during his last weeks, emphatically denied this claim. However, Hunk Anderson wrote in his autobiography, "It was on his death bed that George indicated a desire for conversion and before eternity claimed him, he was baptized into the Catholic faith and given the last rites of the church."[17]

Because it was Hunk Anderson who gave his blood to Gipp in a transfusion process that required him to lie alongside the dying friend who had actually recruited him to Notre Dame, Anderson's words carry considerable weight.[18]

The second and more famous legend deals with the alleged request Gipp made to Rockne shortly before he died. Rockne supposedly leaned over the dying hero and said, "It must be tough to go."

Barely able to whisper, Gipp supposedly replied, "What's so tough about it? I've got to go, Rock. It's all right. I'm not afraid. Sometimes when things are going wrong, when the breaks are beating the boys, tell them to go out

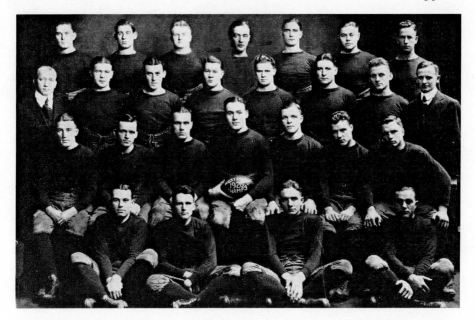

The undefeated 1920 Notre Dame lettermen. Eddie Anderson is seated on the far right, second row. His good friend "Hunk" Anderson is seated third from the right, second row. Because the terminally-ill George Gipp was hospitalized when this late season photo was taken, the resourceful Knute Rockne (standing on the far left, third row) positioned a stand-in in the middle of the back row and later had a photo of Gipp's face superimposed on the stand-in. (Notre Dame Archive)

and win one for the Gipper. I don't know where I'll be then, Rock, but I'll know about it and I'll be happy."

Millions would later accept this account as gospel after watching the actor Ronald Reagan, portraying Gipp, deliver these words to Pat O'Brien, portraying Rockne, in the 1940 Hollywood movie *Knute Rockne: All-American*. The movie immortalized the legend of George Gipp.

If such an incident ever occurred, skeptics ask, why did the charismatic Rockne never mention the event publicly or privately for eight years? Many of his former players say that Rockne was not above fabricating an emotional story to inspire his teams to a higher level of play. For example, in the 1922 Georgia Tech game, a teary-eyed Rockne read a telegram supposedly from his deathly ill son hospitalized in South Bend, whose only wish was to see his dad's team beat Georgia Tech. Playing like men possessed, the emotionally choked Irish players upset a physically superior Tech team 13 to 3 in a grueling contest. Upon detraining in South Bend the limping and bruised team members were stunned to see little Billy Rockne, the picture of health, running wildly up and down the railroad platform yelling, "Yay, my daddy's team won! My daddy's team won!"[19]

Others deny the legend's authenticity because no one, not teammates or family members or Gipp himself, referred to Gipp as the "Gipper."

Throughout his life, Eddie Anderson, who knew both men well, refused to believe that Gipp ever uttered such words. He too chalked up the episode to one of Rockne's master motivational ploys.[20]

Gipp died in the early morning hours of December 14, 1920, at the age of 25. Over 1,500 Notre Dame students and townspeople attended the funeral in a blinding snowstorm and later escorted the coffin to the train to send Gipp's body back to northern Michigan. The pallbearers included Notre Dame teammates Hunk Anderson, Ojay Larson, Joe Brandy and Norm Barry. The coffin was transported by sled the last six miles to the cemetery in Laurium.

Francis Wallace in his book, *The Notre Dame Story,* may have described it most poignantly when he wrote, "And the snows of Christmas powdered the grave of Thanksgiving's hero."

4

CAPTAIN EDDIE ANDERSON

On January 12, 1921, the Notre Dame football team held its annual post-season banquet. The usually festive occasion began on a somber note with a toast to the late George Gipp followed by a moment of silence. Miniature gold footballs with the inscription "Western Champions" were then distributed to the squad's 23 monogram letter winners. Turning to new business, the squad overwhelmingly elected Eddie Anderson as team captain for the upcoming season.[1]

Both proud and humbled by the honor, Anderson was a worthy recipient. A gritty defensive player with a nose for the ball, in his three seasons at Notre Dame he had never missed a game due to injury and had started every game but two. Teammates joked that if Eddie tackled you in the open field and you didn't go down, you'd better look behind you to see what was holding you up. Anderson also led the 1920 team with 17 receptions for 293 yards and 3 touchdowns. At 5'10" tall and weighing 166 pounds, the speedy end also possessed tremendous hand and wrist strength, strength developed from constantly squeezing a rubber ball and repeated sets of finger-tip pushups. His vise-like grip facilitated plucking passes out of the air and shedding blockers.

The next day congratulatory telegrams from T.J. Shaughnessey, president of the Chicago Alumni Association, and Bob O'Connor, secretary of the Indianapolis Alumni Association, alerted Anderson to the fact that there was a regional, if not yet national, network of alumni and boosters that took Notre Dame's gridiron fortunes very seriously. Anderson was not about to let them down.[2]

In the fall of 1921, Notre Dame adhered to Western Conference rules that prohibited coaches from conducting or supervising practices before September 15. So determined was Anderson, however, to extend Notre Dame's winning streak through the 1921 season (Notre Dame had been undefeated in both 1919 and 1920), that he called for "voluntary" team practices to begin in South Bend shortly after Labor Day and run until the official practice starting date. Although Anderson and Buck Shaw were the only returning starters in attendance, over 30 aspirants participated in the daily workouts.

In assessing these informal practices, the *South Bend News Times* reported on September 7, 1921: "The most notable feature was the outstanding good condition of Eddie Anderson. The husky leader has devoted the greater part of the summer vacation to conditioning himself and looks to be in mid-season form right now."

One reason for Anderson's being in such great shape may have been attributable to the job he held that summer. Returning to Mason City in June, Anderson acquired work firing the furnace in the local cement factory. He stoked the furnace 12 hours a day, seven days a week, forging his own physical toughness and determination in the process. Eddie finally got a day off when the plant changed shifts a month later, but when they changed back Anderson had to work 24 hours straight. Years later, when Anderson occasionally related the experience to his son, Jerry, he always summarized his remarks by enthusiastically proclaiming, "It was the best summer job in Mason City!"

Over a quarter century after his father's death Dr. Jerry Anderson recalls, "It never sounded too great to me!"[3]

Notre Dame hosted Kalamazoo in the season opener on September 24. The Irish starters included Eddie Anderson (right end), Lawrence "Buck" Shaw (right tackle), Hunk Anderson (right guard), Harry Mehre (center), Ed Degree (left guard), Arthur "Hec" Garvey (left tackle), Roger Kiley (left end), Dan Coughlin (left half back), Chet Wynne (fullback), Johnny Mohardt (right half back) and Frank Thomas (quarterback).[4]

The above line-up read like a future "Who's Who" list of nationally celebrated football coaches. Seven of the starting eleven went on to coach in the collegiate ranks. Right tackle Lawrence "Buck" Shaw later held head coaching jobs at North Carolina State, Nevada and Santa Clara. When the war forced Santa Clara to drop football in 1942, Shaw moved on to the professional ranks. In 1946 he became the first head coach of the San Francisco 49ers where he remained until 1955. The next year Shaw became the first coach of the U.S. Air Force Academy. In 1958 he returned to the pros as head coach of the Philadelphia Eagles. His team upset Vince Lombardi's Green Bay Packers 17 to 13 for the NFL Championship in 1960. Shaw then retired.

The right guard, Hunk Anderson, would be head coach at the University of St. Louis in 1927 and 1928 before re-joining Rockne's staff at Notre Dame. When Rockne was killed in a plane crash in early 1931, Anderson took over as head coach. Anderson managed a three-year record of 16 wins, 9 losses and 2 ties before being fired. He then served as head coach at North Carolina State and as an assistant for the Detroit Lions before finishing his coaching career as an assistant with the Chicago Bears from 1940 until his retirement in 1951.

Center Harry Mehre would serve as the head coach at the University of Georgia from 1928 until 1937, compiling a record of 59 wins, 34 losses and 6 ties. In 1938, he resigned to assume the head duties at the University of Mississippi, where his teams won 31 games, lost 8 and tied 1.

A grinning Eddie Anderson posed in his letterman's sweater. Anderson was the first player Knute Rockne ever substituted into a game. Anderson captained the 1921 squad and during his four varsity seasons the Irish compiled a record 31 wins, 2 losses and 2 ties. (Notre Dame Archives)

Left end Roger Kiley coached at Chicago's Loyola University in the 1920s, where he locked coaching horns with his ex-teammate, Eddie Anderson, who was then at DePaul. Kiley left coaching to concentrate on a law career, eventually becoming an appellate court judge in Illinois.

Fullback Chet Wynne later held head coaching positions at Creighton, Auburn and the University of Kentucky. His 1932 Auburn team, starring All-American halfback Jimmy Hitchcock, was undefeated.

Quarterback Frank Thomas enjoyed a successful reign at the University of Chattanooga before taking the head job at the University of Alabama. During his 15-year tenure at Tuscaloosa, Thomas coached four undefeated teams and compiled an enviable record of 114 wins, 24 losses and 7 ties. Due to poor health, he stepped down from coaching in 1947 to concentrate on his duties as athletic director until his retirement in 1952.

It should be noted that several of Anderson's earlier Notre Dame teammates also enjoyed storied coaching careers. Curley Lambeau, for example, Anderson's teammate in 1918, later became the long-time head coach of the Green Bay Packers. Edward "Slip" Madigan, from Notre Dame's 1919 team, had a lengthy and successful coaching career at St. Mary's in California. Maurice "Clipper" Smith, Anderson's teammate from 1918 until 1920, also headed the football programs at both Santa Clara and Villanova.

With all deference to Yale University and Walter Camp, the combined coaching accomplishments of all these "Golden Domers" make a compelling case for Notre Dame being labeled the first "cradle of America's football coaches," especially when one considers that Anderson and Lambeau each chalked up more than 200 career coaching victories.

Notre Dame steam-rolled over Kalamazoo 56 to 0 before 8,000 elated fans in the season opener at Cartier Field. The same number of spectators returned the following week when DePauw University's "Little Giants" came to town with a team that Rockne heralded as being worthy of its nickname. Despite Rockne's repeated warnings of DePauw's potency, Notre Dame quickly turned the game into a rout by exploding for 34 first-quarter points. The Irish second and third teams played the entire second and fourth quarters respectively. Captain Anderson played only long enough in the third quarter to make a spectacular leaping catch of a John Mohardt pass for a 35-yard gain.

With its 57 to 10 win over feisty DePauw, it was a confident Notre Dame squad that boarded the train the following week for Iowa City. During such road trips Eddie enjoyed visiting with Hunk Anderson. As the train rumbled across the Midwest, Hunk often regaled Eddie with vivid accounts of his youth in northern Michigan. The tales usually highlighted the physical toughness or Herculean escapades of one of Hunk's neighborhood pals or relatives.

Intrigued by the rugged characters Hunk described, Eddie would inevitably ask after each tale, "Hunk, he sounds like a tough guy. Do you think you could take him?"

Like clockwork, Hunk would merely shrug and reply unequivocally, "Oh, sure."[5]

Howard Jones coached a University of Iowa team that was spearheaded by fullback Gordon Locke, quarterback Aubrey Devine and All-American tackle Duke Slater. Slater, one of the few African-Americans playing college ball during that era, refused to wear a helmet in games.

Trailing 10 to 0, Notre Dame opened the second quarter with Eddie Anderson snagging a pass from Johnny Mohardt and rambling to the home team's 5-yard line. On fourth down Iowa's Aubrey Devine intercepted Mohardt's pass in the end zone and returned it to the Hawkeye 40-yard line. After forcing Iowa to punt, the Irish drove to mid-field where Mohardt connected on a 50-yard touchdown pass to Roger Kiley. The half ended with the Irish trailing 10 to 7.

At halftime Rockne chided his team, "You guys should be penalized for abusing the ball."[6]

Late in the third quarter Eddie Anderson caught another Mohardt pass to put the ball on Iowa's 14-yard line. On the next play, however, Iowa end Lester Belding, Anderson's old Mason City High School teammate, intercepted to end the threat. A second Belding interception squelched another Irish drive moments later.

With its offense stymied, Iowa again punted, but Roger Kiley blocked the kick and advanced it to Iowa's 25-yard line. Mohardt then drilled a pass to Anderson at the Iowa 8-yard line with only minutes remaining.

Years later while coaching at DePaul, Anderson reflected on that afternoon in one of a series of articles composed by Chicago sportswriter Edgar Munzel titled "The Greatest Game I Ever Saw."

"Notre Dame fired passes all over the field in a desperate attempt to score, but it always seemed that Aubrey Devine was there to knock them down. He had an uncanny sense of being at the right spot.

"Finally, Mohardt got one past Devine to me on the Iowa 7-yard line. Our chances for a score seemed bright, though there were only a few minutes left. But for some reason we drew a 15-yard penalty at this point. Then on [our fourth down] pass the ubiquitous Aubrey (Devine) bobbed up to grab it and secured Iowa's triumph as well."

The 10 to 7 loss ended Notre Dame's 20-game winning streak. Making it especially painful was the fact that Notre Dame gained twice as much yardage as Iowa, while accumulating 22 first downs to Iowa's 11.

Anderson elaborated, "One of our troubles, of course, was overconfidence. Being captain of the team, I tried to talk some of the fellows into the fact that I thought it would be a tough game, but I was really just as 'fat-headed' as the rest of them. I was equally smug in the belief that on the whole we had little to fear."[7]

After the game a surprisingly compassionate Rockne tried to console a

An unidentified Hawkeye carries the ball in Iowa's 10 to 7 upset of Notre Dame in 1921. Eddie Anderson is clearly identifiable on the far right. The helmet-less African American player on the ground is Iowa's All-American tackle Fred "Duke" Slater. Slater, who refused to wear a helmet, later achieved a distinguished career as a municipal court judge in Chicago. (University Archives, Dept. of Special Collections , University of Iowa Libraries)

dressing room full of teary-eyed players. He credited Iowa with being a good team that had extended an excellent effort. (Iowa would go undefeated in both 1921 and 1922.) "Remember, there are no alibis," counseled Rockne. "This defeat will do us some good and may teach something to our followers, who think we can't be beaten."[8]

In an interesting side note to the game, Ray Robinson writes in *Rockne of Notre Dame*, "Notre Dame's colors were blue and gold, and it wore jerseys that were dark blue. Iowa's jerseys were black. In the gloom and darkness of the final period... Notre Dame resorted to forward passes. It was then that Iowa came up with its crucial interception. There were some in the Notre Dame camp who blamed the similarity of jerseys for the loss, for they felt Mohardt had mistakenly thrown into the arms of a Hawkeye defender. Whatever Rockne may have thought about this theory — and he publicly never endorsed it — all his future teams were decked out in *green* jerseys."[9]

Hours later a sense of gloom permeated the lobby of the Iowa City train station as Notre Dame players tried to cope with the team's first loss in over two years. Many sprawled on benches, seeking succor in sleep. Others lost themselves in newspapers or textbooks. The gloom suddenly turned to curious excitement when a player dashed into the lobby and cried, "Rock, you better come quickly!"

Emerging from the lobby, Rockne saw police cars across the street and several cops filing into a beer joint. Twenty minutes earlier Hunk Anderson had leisurely exited the railroad depot. With the train to Chicago not due for another hour, Anderson hoped to kill some time and get his mind off the Iowa loss with a beer. Across the street a rundown tavern sported a paint-blistered sign that read "Depot Lunch." It wasn't much, but it would do.

Sipping his beer, Hunk realized from the bar room banter that many of the noisy tavern's revelers had attended that afternoon's game. Assessing the situation, Hunk intended to quickly finish his beer and leave. Unfortunately, a well-lubricated Iowa fan recognized him and eagerly announced to the house of Hawkeye rooters that a Notre Dame football player was amongst them.

It took a moment for the coach's vision to adjust to the darkness inside the tavern. When his eyes did focus, Rockne first noticed several groggy and shaken men being helped to bar stools. Glancing away from the bar he saw several bodies crumpled on the floor between over-turned tables and chairs. Negotiating his way through the debris and carnage, the coach hustled to the back of the bar where several police officers were questioning a slightly disheveled Hunk Anderson. As Rockne approached, the interrogators left Anderson momentarily to ascertain the body count around the room. Ushering Anderson into a corner and out of earshot of police and customers, Rockne anxiously asked, "Hunk, what happened?"

"Well, Rock," Hunk calmly explained while rubbing his swollen right hand, "when these folks started heckling me for being Irish it didn't bother me because I'm not Irish. Then they started mocking me for being an Irish Catholic. That didn't bother me either because I'm not Catholic. But when they started calling me an Irish Catholic [*@&!], well, that's when I decided to clean out the joint."[10]

Although no one had been killed, several of the bar's patrons would be taking their food through a straw for several weeks. Spewing assurances that Anderson and his team would be leaving Iowa City within the hour and had no plans to return, Rockne persuaded the police to let Hunk go without pressing charges.

In the decades that followed, Iowa fans would delight in recalling the 1921 upset of Notre Dame. In the same breath, Iowa City's old-timers would inevitably pay equal reverence to the post-game fight in which Hunk Anderson cleaned out the Depot Lunch.

Any compassion Rockne displayed in his Iowa post-game talk had evaporated by Monday. Instead, he cracked the whip mercilessly at practice. Subjected to a week of punishing drills laced with Rockne's stinging sarcasm, the Irish eagerly sought redemption at Purdue. As 7,500 Boilermaker fans watched in abject disbelief, Hunk Anderson played like a man possessed, blocking two first-half punts within three minutes and returning both for touchdowns as Notre Dame stampeded to a 33 to 0 win.

After six consecutive seasons of playing at hostile Lincoln, the University of Nebraska finally agreed to visit South Bend on October 22, 1921. The sun's brilliant rays piercing through the golden-leafed trees of northern Indiana provided a beautiful setting for Notre Dame's homecoming game. In contrast to the afternoon's majestic setting, the contest itself resembled a grim slugfest between two plodding heavyweights standing toe to toe. Despite a slight size advantage, the visitors couldn't crack Notre Dame's determined defense.

Eddie Anderson twice recovered Cornhusker fumbles to thwart Nebraska drives. On offense, Anderson and Buck Shaw's combined blocking provided an off-tackle play that consistently gained yardage throughout the day. Johnny Mohardt would score the game's lone touchdown on such a play to give the Irish a 7 to 0 win.

Eddie Anderson described Hunk Anderson as "the toughest man I ever met." This photo of Hunk Anderson is believed to have been taken in 1930, while Hunk was serving as an assistant coach under Rockne. When Rockne was killed in a plane crash in 1931, Hunk succeeded him as Irish head coach. (Notre Dame Archives)

A motivated Notre Dame squad was bent on pummeling Indiana the next week. Several Irish players were convinced that the severe physical pounding George Gipp had incurred the previous year at Indianapolis was the result of late hits and dirty play. Some even speculated that the beating weakened Gipp's resistance and left the star player susceptible to the strep throat that eventually killed him. Rockne, however, held no such enmity and started the second-team backfield against the Hoosiers. After inserting the starters in the second half, the Irish easily pulled away for a 28 to 7 win.

With a record of 5 wins and 1 loss, Notre Dame embarked on an ambitious slice of their schedule that had them playing three games in eight days. With hopes of both showcasing his team before the eastern press and earning another big payday, Rockne had scheduled to play Rutgers in New York City's Polo Grounds on November 8, just three days after their game at West Point. The Irish would then return home on Saturday, November 12, to meet the Haskell Institute Indians.

As previously mentioned, the Army-Notre Dame game was rapidly blossoming into one of the nation's premiere sporting events. Army officials erected extra bleachers to accommodate the anticipated crowd. Over 20,000 fans, the largest crowd ever to see an Army game, jammed into the wooden stands.

The opening kick-off was delayed when fans, jostling for seats, impeded the Superintendent of West Point General Douglas MacArthur's access to his customary box seat. Clearly irritated by such unruly behavior, MacArthur, America's most highly decorated officer in World War I, summoned additional military police to the site to clear a path to the superintendent's box.

A major reason for Notre Dame's gridiron success was Rockne's implementation of the so-called Notre Dame or Rockne Shift. Rockne didn't invent the shift. He had learned it from his coaching predecessor at Notre Dame, Jess Harper. Harper in turn had picked it up during his days at the University of Chicago. While numerous schools across the country employed the shift, none had mastered it as proficiently as Rockne's Irish.

The shift entailed the entire Irish backfield changing its alignment as the quarterback called the signals. The ball was often snapped before the backs came to a complete stop. Critics of the shift railed that it gave offensive backs an unfair forward momentum at the start of the play and denied the defense a fair chance to adjust to the new formation.

As General MacArthur's gendarmes were restoring order in the stands, another confrontation was occurring at mid-field where Army coach Charles Daly was voicing the above objections to both the game officials and Rockne. At one point, there was a threat of canceling the game if Notre Dame's backs did not come to a dead stop before hiking the ball. With rulebook in hand, Rockne diplomatically argued that Daly's interpretation of a dead stop did not comply with the written rules. The officiating crew agreed with Rockne.

The first half went well for the Irish with Johnny Mohardt tossing two scoring passes and Eddie Anderson thwarting Army's lone scoring threat by blocking their early field goal attempt.

When the teams returned for the second half, Army coach Charles Daly resumed vehemently challenging the legality of Notre Dame's shift with the officials. Overhearing Daley's urgent pleas and possibly sensing that he wouldn't need it, Rockne, wanting to keep good relations with West Point, informed referee Ed Thorp that his team would not employ the shift for the rest of the game. The coach was true to his word.[11]

Early in the second half, the ball-hawking Anderson recovered a muffed Army punt return which set up a 15-yard scoring pass from Mohardt to Kiley. Mohardt later scored on a 20-yard run, and Rockne emptied the bench in the fourth quarter as Notre Dame rolled to an impressive 28 to 0 win.

After the game the Irish traveled to Deal, New Jersey, to spend the remainder of their eastern sojourn as guests at the country estate of Mr. Joseph M. Byrne. A prominent Notre Dame alumnus, Byrne became a hero in the annals of the school by reportedly crawling into the university's Dome during the campus fire of 1879 to save the statue of the Blessed Virgin, which then adorned the top of the main building. An active and generous alumnus, Byrne became extremely influential in getting many outstanding athletes to enroll at Notre Dame.

Selected to serve as ambassadors for the university in the spring of 1921, Eddie Anderson and Johnny Mohardt traveled to New York's Grand Central Station to meet and accompany Byrne and his son and fellow alumnus, Joe, Jr., back to South Bend for commencement exercises. The university band and numerous monogram winners were on hand to greet and thank the wealthy benefactors for all they had done for the school.

In return, Byrne was now rolling out the red carpet for Anderson and his victorious teammates. Byrne helped the team relax for the upcoming Rutgers game by hosting several dinner parties and arranging for Broadway show tickets, including a performance by the incomparable Ziegfeld Follies at the Globe Theater.[12]

The Rutgers game was played on Election Day, Tuesday, November 8, at New York's Polo Grounds. The cover of the 15-cent game program pictured each team's captain. Duffy, the Rutgers quarterback, appeared grim and concerned, with his hair neatly combed straight back. In contrast, a smiling Eddie Anderson seemed confident and relaxed, with a healthy clump of hair masking part of his forehead. The photos foretold the game's outcome.

Rutgers' coach Foster Sanford and his starting eleven had scouted Notre Dame at West Point the previous Saturday. Like Army coach Charles Daly, Sanford also protested to officials about the legality of the Notre Dame shift during their pre-game talk.[13] Although the Irish were penalized a total of 75 yards for their backs not coming to a complete stop after shifting, in the end it didn't matter, as Notre Dame simply had too much speed and depth for the larger but slower New Jersey team.

Before a disappointing crowd of 12,000, Notre Dame's Paul Castner ran 50 yards for a touchdown on the game's first play from scrimmage. Taking a 27 to 0 lead into the locker room at halftime, Notre Dame resumed the onslaught in the third quarter. Mohardt hit Eddie Anderson on an 8-yard scoring pass before Castner and Gus Desch (the world's champion in the 440-yard low hurdles and a Joe Byrne recruit) added scoring runs of 5 and 20 yards respectively in the 48 to 0 win.

Although the Rutgers game was not the financial boon Rockne had hoped, his team's brilliant performance in the Polo Grounds garnered extensive and glowing newspaper coverage along the eastern seaboard. Having thoroughly enjoyed the social and cultural aspects of their eastern sojourn, the Irish players bid Broadway a fond farewell as they boarded the train for the return trip to South Bend.

Notre Dame hosted Haskell the following week before a slim crowd at Cartier Field. Regarding Haskell as a lightweight opponent, Rockne turned the game-day coaching over to assistant coach Walter Halas, opting instead to spend the afternoon in Milwaukee scouting their next opponent, Marquette. Rockne's assessment of Haskell was verified by Notre Dame's easy 42 to 7 victory.

It was cold and snowy the following week when Rockne returned to Milwaukee on November 19 with his team in tow. Coach John Ryan's Marquette squad was game, but Notre Dame jumped to an early 14 to 0. The afternoon heated up briefly in the second quarter when Hunk Anderson was ejected for slugging one of two Marquette players that had piled on teammate Chet Grant who was clearly out of bounds at the time.

In the second half, Mohardt connected with Eddie Anderson, who was barely visible downfield through heavily falling snow, on a 50-yard scoring pass to give Notre Dame a 21 to 7 victory.

Bundled and shivering in a blanket on the Marquette sideline for most of the game was a reserve halfback named Pat O'Brien. The sub made the most of his brief fourth-quarter appearance by ripping off a 30-yard run against the Irish second team. O'Brien eventually became a popular Hollywood actor and, nearly two decades later, starred in the movie titled *Knute Rockne: All-American*.

Captain Eddie Anderson closed out his collegiate football career the following Thursday, when he and his teammates steam-rolled to a 48 to 0 win over Michigan State before a record 15,000 fans at Cartier Field. During his four years at Notre Dame, Anderson never missed a game due to injury, and the teams on which he played lost only two games. The 1921 squad Anderson captained finished with a record of 10 wins and 1 loss. While playing brilliantly on defense, he once again led the team in receptions with 26 catches for 394 yards and two touchdowns. His football exploits merited him numerous honors.

On December 11, 1921, renowned *Chicago Tribune* sportswriter, football official and former All-American quarterback at the University of Chicago, Walter Eckersall, named Anderson to the *Tribune's* All-American First Team. Eckersall would write years later, "I have been identified with football as a player and official for over a quarter of a century, and I can truthfully state that I have never seen a better end than Eddie Anderson, the present coach at DePaul.

"I have officiated at many games in which Anderson was on the end of the Notre Dame line. On several occasions I could not help but admire the way he turned ball carriers to the inside, how he snared forward passes or broke up the forward pass attack of an opponent by beating the receiver to the ball ... Eddie was a deadly tackler ... To my mind he is one of the greatest ends who ever played the game."[14]

Football News magazine also selected Eddie as First-Team All-American, while Walter Camp and the International News Service selected him as Second-Team All-American.

Things were also going well for Anderson off the gridiron. He had high academic grades and was active in campus life, serving both on the university's Student Activities Committee and as warden of the university's branch of the Knights of Columbus. The handsome All-American also enhanced his celebrity status by modeling men's clothing for Stephenson Mills in South Bend. In one newspaper ad a smiling, debonair Anderson posed in a garment known as the Rockne Training Shirt (RTS) while the caption below claimed, "The fabric of this garment was recognized at once by Coach Knute Rockne as ideal for football and track men — for athletes in any sport." The ad closed with the comforting guarantee that, "When used as a shirt the RTS can be dried out and does not become repulsive after a few wearings as do fleece-lined shirts."[15]

Things were good, but things were about to change.

5

THE CARLINVILLE EIGHT

The Roaring Twenties catapulted the United States into the modern age. Thanks to Henry Ford's efficient use of the assembly line, his Rouge River plant near Detroit rolled out a spanking new Model T every 10 seconds. Americans fell headlong in love with the automobile, a torrid affair that still burns white-hot today. By the end of the decade Americans would own over 30 million cars. Radios became commonplace in living rooms nationwide where families gathered nightly to hear broadcasts of programs advertising everything from baking soda to electric fans. Buying on the installment plan became a way of life for Americans, while Hollywood emerged as the vortex of a burgeoning movie-making industry. Aviational advances during the Great War led to the advent of commercial air travel a mere 25 years after the Wright Brothers' first flight.

The 1920s have also been hailed as the Golden Age of sports. Syndicated columnists, such as Grantland Rice and Ring Lardner, made national icons of Babe Ruth and Walter Johnson in baseball, Jack Dempsey and Gene Tunney in boxing, Bill Tilden in tennis and Gertrude Ederle in swimming. The sports scribes' beatific accounts of the exploits of college football's Red Grange and the Four Horsemen of Notre Dame also secured their berths in the decade's pantheon of athletic icons.

The college gridiron was the chariot that carried football to soaring heights of popularity in the 1920s. Teenagers and young men saw the game as heroic, with the donning of helmet and shoulder pads as a true test of one's manhood. Dramatic newspaper accounts of Saturday afternoon clashes between the University of Chicago and Northwestern or Harvard and Yale stoked the desire within tens of thousands of virile young men to play the sport in high school and beyond. However, many football aspirants had neither the financial

47

resources nor aptitude to attend college. For these young men, semi-pro teams afforded a salve for their football itch.

By 1920, hundreds of semi-pro teams had sprouted throughout the Midwest. Playing their games at public parks, county fair grounds or even vacant lots, teams were often shabbily equipped and poorly coached. Tickets were sometimes sold, but passing the hat among the spectators was the common method of garnering gate receipts. Well-organized squads practiced once or twice a week, but many never practiced at all. Schedules were haphazard with clubs frequently folding operations in mid-season. Yet, some semi-pro teams actually flourished.

Many small towns were proud of their teams. As the only game in town, the local citizens turned out en masse to cheer their hometown heroes. In a show of community spirit, local businesses sometimes sponsored the teams. With sponsors defraying some, if not all, of a team's expenses, a good afternoon's take from passing the hat often allowed the players to be paid a few bucks.

Intense rivalries developed between neighboring hamlets and towns that sometimes resulted in heavy betting. One such rivalry emerged between the central Illinois towns of Taylorville and Carlinville. Founded in 1839, Taylorville is the county seat of Christian County. Carlinville, located about 80 miles to the southwest, was established as the county seat of Macoupin County in 1825. When Standard Oil of Indiana opened two new coal mines in the area in 1917, Carlinville experienced an economic boon that sent the town's population skyrocketing from 4,000 to 6,000 almost overnight. Organizing its first semi-pro football team in 1920, Carlinville filled its ranks with many of the area's hard-nosed miners.

The Taylorville Independents were organized in 1914 and coached by Grover Cleveland Hoover. Well-versed in the game and a stickler for physical conditioning, the burly Hoover conducted organized practices nightly during the season. Under Hoover's guidance, Taylorville dominated "downstate" semi-pro football for the next six years. Upon his retirement from coaching after the 1919 season, Taylorville had compiled an incredible record of 45 wins and 2 losses.

In 1920, the upstart Carlinville team, coached by Lionel Moise, capped its undefeated inaugural season with a 10 to 7 home victory over Taylorville. The Independents vowed to settle the score if Carlinville visited Taylorville the following year. Having played the 1920 season without the benefit of a coach, Taylorville slipped to a record of 5 wins and 3 losses. Dissatisfied with the season, the players coaxed Hoover out of retirement to again coach the team.

Demonstrating that they still had the winning touch, Hoover's Taylorville club won its first three games in 1921. Then it was announced that a Carlinville rematch would take place at Taylorville on November 27.

As the match-up approached, there was speculation that zealous Carlinville fans had wagered over $30,000 on the game's outcome. With so much at stake, and in view of the fact that Taylorville was undefeated in six games, Carlinville officials hedged their bets by bringing in talented "ringers." Frank Seyfrit, a Carlinville resident and reserve end on the Notre Dame football squad, had often played for Carlinville on Sundays. Occasionally, he brought along an Irish teammate to play as well. Team officials now persuaded Seyfrit to recruit more Irish players for the Taylorville contest. Acting as the "roper," Seyfrit convinced Eddie Anderson and six other Irish teammates to play.[1]

Although newspaper accounts from the era reported that the "Carlinville Eight" denied receiving any money, rumors abounded that the Notre Dame players each received $200 plus expenses to play against Taylorville. Supposedly, the money was delivered to South Bend in advance. Surely, the players must have been paid. It's inconceivable that all eight would have given up their Thanksgiving weekend to play in a semi-pro game on a lark. After playing a grueling 11-game schedule against the likes of Iowa, Nebraska and West Point, and with the prospect of enjoying their first free weekend in nearly three months, what possible appeal could the Carlinville game have held for any of them unless they were being well compensated?

When word leaked that most of the Notre Dame squad would be in the line-up against Taylorville, Carlinville fans, thinking they had a sure winner, bet even larger sums. By kick-off, Carlinville fans were claimed to have wagered a total of $50,000 on the game's outcome.

It was only when Coach Hoover received an anonymous letter warning that Carlinville was loading up with ringers that Taylorville suspected something might be afoot. Hoover sent a man named Carroll Hill to Carlinville with instructions to eavesdrop in restaurants and saloons to verify the rumors. Hill reported back that the rumors were indeed true.[2]

Deciding to fight fire with fire, Hoover apprised a Taylorville player, Dick Simpson, of the Carlinville caper. Simpson telephoned his brother, Roy "Dope" Simpson, who was a reserve end on the University of Illinois squad on Saturdays and a starter for Taylorville on Sundays. "Dope," in turn, "roped" eight of his Illini teammates into the Taylorville camp. Each of the nine players would receive $100, a suit of clothes, a pair of shoes and a hat for doing battle against Carlinville.[3]

The Carlinville Eight were still a little bruised from their Thanksgiving Day win over Michigan State two days earlier when they arrived by train in Springfield. There they spent a restful night at a local hotel under the watchful eye of Carlinville coach Lionel Moise. Wearing their game uniforms the next morning, Anderson and company traveled by car to nearby Taylorville.

In anticipation of the much-ballyhooed rematch, the entire town had taken on a carnival atmosphere. Vendors hawked food from dozens of colorfully decorated wagons that surrounded the stands, and calliope music filled the air. The Baltimore & Ohio Railroad ran a special 15-car train from Carlinville that disgorged hundreds of excited fans, who expected to soon be counting their winnings.

Over 4,000 fans mobbed into Hoover Field with 1,800 customers paying a whopping $3 per grandstand seat while others paid $5 to park a car packed with fans around the field's perimeter. The day was sunny and crisp and ideal for football as the visiting team trotted onto the field to warm up. Seeing so many strange faces among the squad, Carlinville fans initially refused to applaud because they mistakenly thought it was Taylorville running onto the field. Adding to the confusion was the fact that both squads wore unnumbered blue jerseys, with Taylorville's a slightly lighter shade.

Attempting to protect their identities, several of the Carlinville Eight wore tape across the bridge of their noses or partially smeared their faces with shoe polish. A few resorted to wearing phony moustaches, which were quickly knocked askew once the game started. Whether he forgot his jersey or because playing incognito was unimportant to him, Notre Dame fullback Chet Wynne played in a white sweatshirt that made him stand out like a seagull dropping on a navy peacoat.

Taking a calculated risk, Taylorville's Coach Hoover decided not to start the Illinois ringers. Instead, he kept them hidden in cars around the field from which they could watch the game while warmly bundled in blankets.

Shortly before the game, Eddie Anderson learned that he would not be starting at his customary right end position. Whether it was because the regular Carlinville quarterback was injured or because the ringer hired to play that position didn't show, it was decided that Eddie should quarterback the team against Taylorville. Anderson had never played quarterback in his life. While he may not have appreciated the gesture at the time, the decision undoubtedly reflected his Irish teammates' high regard for Eddie's leadership and athleticism.

With Anderson calling the plays, Carlinville immediately drove to the Taylorville 15-yard line on the game's opening drive. A penalty set the visitors back, and after a short gain and an incomplete pass, Taylorville's Vern Mullen blocked Chet Wynne's punt and recovered the ball at mid-field. Failing to gain a yard in three tries, Taylorville's Don Murray punted into the visitor's end zone.

Wearing a perpetual grin throughout the afternoon that was almost as prominent as his white sweatshirt, Chet Wynne was obviously enjoying himself, especially when churning out significant chunks of yardage on runs that soon had Carlinville again across mid-field. The drive was thwarted, however, when Don Murray picked off Anderson's pass and returned it 20 yards. Unable to gain a first down, the home team punted again.

Carlinville picked up a couple of first downs before Wynne was forced to punt from mid-field. Lightning struck twice when Taylorville's Vern Mullen blocked yet another punt. With Wynne and several of the Independents in hot pursuit, the pigskin bounced to the Carlinville 1-yard line where Andy Newman recovered it for the home team.

Taylorville ran three consecutive dive-plays with three different backs carrying the ball, but failed to gain an inch. With fourth-and-goal from the 1-yard line, Taylorville quarterback, Charlie Dressen, who would one day manage major league baseball's Brooklyn Dodgers, took the snap from center, faked to one halfback, then to the other, before running wide around right end to score standing up. Although the Notre Dame boys pushed Taylorville up and down the field for the rest of the half, the home team led 7 to 0 at halftime.

Realizing that his Taylorville regulars had probably accomplished all that they could, Coach Hoover played his trump card by starting his Illini ringers in the second half. The Carlinville team, resting on the eastside of the field during halftime, sensed something was up when a fresh Taylorville squad began running plays to warm up. Running plays was customarily reserved for pre-game warm ups only.

Roger Kiley, another Notre Dame accomplice in the Carlinville caper, approached Anderson shortly before the second half kick-off. Born and raised in Chicago, Kiley had never before set foot in Taylorville. "Eddie," Kiley informed Anderson, "one of those Taylorville guys looks real familiar."[4]

Kiley indeed recognized Jack Crangle, an All-Western Conference end for Illinois. Moments after the kickoff, the Carlinville Eight realized that this fresh Taylorville squad was as skilled and as well conditioned as any college team.

While neither team scored a second half touchdown, the Illini ringers controlled the action. On three occasions they drove deep into Carlinville territory. Joey Sternaman, the starting quarterback for Illinois who had replaced Charlie Dressen at the half, capped each drive with a dropkick field goal to give Taylorville a 16 to 0 win.

The Carlinville rooters were crestfallen after the loss. Those who had bet heavily on the game meandered about the streets in a daze. One Carlinville merchant realizing that he had lost his fruit and vegetable store on the game's outcome openly wept.

It was a different story for those who had wagered on Taylorville. Immediately after the game, one fan embraced Coach Hoover while sobbing, "You wonderful man. You saved my home for me." He had mortgaged his home and business for $2,000 to bet on Taylorville.[5]

Relishing their victory, a spontaneous parade of ecstatic Taylorville fans marched down Walnut Street. A donkey wearing a sign labeled "Carlinville" led the marchers. With the band playing "Under the Double Eagle," the revelers reached East Main and headed west past Milligan's Smokehouse. Many celebrants briefly left the parade to enter the Smokehouse and collect their winnings that were being held by the stakeholder, Charlie Milligan. The parade finally ended at the Antlers Hotel on Market Street, but the drinking and celebrating went on well into the night.

In his 1967 copyrighted manuscript, *Touchdown Taylorville!*, Scott Hoover, the son of Taylorville coach Grover Cleveland Hoover and an 11-year-old spectator on that day, described the following post-game scene. "The Notre Dame boys showered and dressed and stood out in the street watching the small town celebrate... One of them approached an Illinois boy and said, 'We know who you are and I guess you know us. We won't say anything and hope you won't.'

"The Illini assured him that they didn't want any trouble and that 'mum was the word.'"

That was the extent of the pleasantries exchanged between the players from the two schools.

More chagrined than bruised, Eddie Anderson dozed fitfully on the evening train to Chicago as he tried to forget the Taylorville escapade. Nearly two weeks later, however, a bombshell hit the South Bend campus that again dredged up the specter of the Taylorville game. University officials announced that football players Hunk Anderson, Arthur "Hec" Garvey and O.J. Larson were barred from future participation in intercollegiate athletics for having played in a professional football game for the Green Bay Packers on November 27.[6]

The news must have sent chills down the spines of Eddie Anderson and other members of the Carlinville Eight. Couldn't the "good fathers" just as easily learn of the Carlinville-Taylorville clash that had also been played on the same day?

To exacerbate matters, the Notre Dame faculty in control of athletics announced that negotiations for a possible post-season game against Centre College were off. The San Diego Chamber of Commerce had offered to host a contest between the two schools on December 26.[7] The tiny college from Danville, Kentucky, had earned the reputation as a giant killer by upsetting powerful Harvard 6 to 0 en route to an undefeated season. Many sportswriters hailed Centre's Alvin "Bo" McMillin as the most exciting football player in America. Missing out on the national exposure that the Notre Dame-Centre game would surely have generated was extremely disappointing for Knute Rockne, who also served as the university's athletic director.

In reality, however, Notre Dame's administration and faculty had previously viewed post-season games with disdain, regarding them as an over-emphasis that smacked of professionalism. University officials may have nixed the Centre game even in the absence of the Green Bay scandal. But there's no question that the scandal considerably weakened Rockne's negotiating hand. (As it turned out, Centre's "Praying Colonels" agreed to meet the University of Arizona in San Diego on December 26, where they blanketed the Wildcats 38 to 0.)

Notre Dame authorities then summarily dismissed a "feeler" from local promoters in Butte, Montana, seeking to arrange a post-season contest between the Irish and Gonzaga University of Spokane, Washington.[8]

School officials were unaware of the Taylorville episode when Notre Dame closed for the Christmas vacation. With the secret still safe when classes resumed in January, the Carlinville Eight breathed easier in the hopes that the "Ghost of Thanksgiving Past" was buried forever. Unbeknownst to them, however, external forces were at work.

In her 1989 article for the *Taylorville Breeze-Courier*, "The Game That Never Was," Johanna Tinnea describes how the scandal began to unravel. "Shortly after the New Year the University of Wisconsin protested that Laurie Walquist, a star basketball player for Illinois, was ineligible to play because he had participated in a semi-pro game in November. Walquist denied the charges but Wisconsin had proof."

Back in South Bend, the Notre Dame basketball squad lost its first six games of the New Year. Although Eddie Anderson was no longer in the starting line-up, he saw plenty of action coming off the bench. On the evening of January 25, 1922, Anderson would make his last hardwood appearance for the Irish in a 44 to 18 win over Armour Institute.

Two days later, on January 27, the Taylorville incident exploded onto the national scene when University of Illinois officials declared nine star athletes ineligible for further intercollegiate competition because they had played in a semi-pro football game on November 27, 1921, at Taylorville, Illinois.[9]

Sitting on the bed of his dormitory room, Anderson read aloud the names of the banned Illini players from a local evening paper. The nine were Laurie Walquist, Jack Crangle, Joey Sternaman, R.T. Green, "Dutch" Kaiser, Roy "Dope" Simpson, John Teuscher, D.A. Milligan and H. Gamage. Lowering the paper, Anderson looked forlornly at Roger Kiley. Also in the room sat a disconsolate Harry Mehre. All three were members of the Carlinville Eight and presently teammates on the Irish basketball squad.

The other shoe dropped on Sunday, January 29, 1922, when Irish half-backs Gus Desch and Johnny Mohardt were asked to appear at an informal meeting of the university's athletic committee, where they vehemently denied any role in the Taylorville contest. Presented with compelling evidence that the pair was actually on the South Bend campus on the day in question, the committee decided that Desch and Mohardt were merely innocent victims of mistaken identity.[10] (While the evidence cleared Mohardt of involvement in the Carlinville affair, he was not totally innocent of the charges. He later admitted to playing pro football for George Halas' Chicago Staleys against Green Bay and Hunk Anderson, Jay Larson and Hec Garvey on the day in question.) Word was then sent to eight other Notre Dame students to appear the next morning before a formal meeting of the athletic committee chaired by Father William Carey, C.S.C.

On January 30, with overwhelming evidence stacked against them, the eight sullen athletes confessed to school officials that they had played for the semi-pro Carlinville team on November 27. The Associated Press claimed, "They insisted that they received no pay and agreed to play simply as a Thanksgiving holiday lark, and without knowledge that the affair was the out-growth of a town rivalry, which became so acute that about $100,000 was said to have been bet on the game." The Carlinville Eight also denied any prior knowledge of any Illinois athletes playing for Taylorville.

Rendering a swift decision, the athletic committee banned all eight from further intercollegiate competition. "We will stand for no taint or hint of pro-fessionalism here," declared Notre Dame's Father Carey, "not even if it wrecks our teams forever."

While the university teams were not wrecked, the committee's decision took a heavy and immediate toll. Anderson, Harry Mehre and Roger Kiley were dismissed from the basketball team on which Kiley served as captain. Anderson and Kiley were also banned from baseball and Mehre from track. Other members of the Carlinville Eight included Chet Wynne, who also cap-tained the track team, and tackle Lawrence "Buck" Shaw. Shaw had been a champion shot-putter. Robert Phelan of Fort Madison, Iowa, Earl Walsh of Adrian, Iowa, and Frank Seyfrit of Carlinville were all banned from future participation in football.

Immediately upon learning his fate, a contrite Eddie Anderson made a beeline for Rockne's office. The first of the Carlinville Eight to reach his coach, the All-American end confessed, "Rock, I've come to tell you that it's true that I played in that Taylorville game."[11]

For several seconds the stunned Rockne sat staring at his former team captain, unable to utter a reply.

The Carlinville-Taylorville episode was the biggest scandal in the history of college sports up to that time. In all, 17 college athletes were banned from future intercollegiate participation. The incident also served as a catalyst in forming a united front of college coaches, headed by Chicago's Amos Alonzo Stagg, condemning the professional menace encroaching upon college football.

In later years, Eddie Anderson seldom spoke of his Carlinville experience with his family, but when he did, it was always with the same pained expression. "Dad regretted that incident for the rest of his life," recalls his son, Dr. Jerry Anderson, "not because he got caught or because he was punished. But because of the embarrassment it caused the university."[12]

6

COLUMBIA (LORAS) COLLEGE

Banned from competing in both basketball and baseball during his last semester under the Golden Dome, Anderson now found himself with an inordinate amount of free time. Academic pursuits alone weren't enough for Eddie. Seeking to keep physically active, he entered a campus bodybuilding competition sponsored by BHB Lange, C.S.C., the university's director of physical culture.

Vastly different from today's strength and conditioning techniques, bodybuilding was then limited to hoisting light dumbbells, assorted medicine ball exercises, push-ups, pull-ups and calisthenics. Several weeks of intensive training resulted in Anderson earning a medal for his fourth place finish in the competition. Attired in tights and seated with arms and legs crossed, Anderson and the other medal winners posed grimly with Father Lange for a photo in the school paper.[1]

The bodybuilding success of the 5'10", 172-pound Anderson only enhanced his reputation within the Notre Dame student body. Despite his role in the Carlinville Eight scandal, his classmates still held Anderson in high esteem. Because the incident had occurred after Notre Dame's gridiron season when Anderson's football eligibility had expired, many viewed the Carlinville episode as innocuous and Anderson's punishment as unjustly harsh.

Although initially angered and hurt by the scandal, Rockne couldn't stay mad at his former team captain for long. Weeks after the scandal broke and particulars of the Carlinville game had surfaced, Rockne sat Eddie down and asked how he had let the Taylorville quarterback, Charlie Dressen, slip around his end for the game's only touchdown.

"I wasn't playing end," Anderson explained. "Frank Thomas (a Notre Dame quarterback who later coached at Alabama) was supposed to play quarterback, but 'Sleepy' overslept and I had to take his place. Dressen would never have gotten around me because you taught me better than that."[2]

Exhaling a plume of cigar smoke skyward, Rockne's eyes twinkled as he broke into a broad grin that revealed a mentor's pride in his prize pupil.

Shortly thereafter a newspaper reporter asked the pug-nosed coach, "Rock, what do you think of the boys who played for Carlinville?"

"I'm glad they won't be back next year," Rockne replied gruffly.

"Why?" bit the reporter, readying his pad and pencil for what he anticipated would be a juicy scoop.

"Because," Rockne said, "those guys all know a heck of a lot more football than I do."[3]

Privately Rockne must have empathized with those banished by the Carlinville and Green Bay scandals. Why? Because in 1914 Rockne himself was paid for coaching a South Bend semi-pro team at night while working afternoons as an unpaid assistant under Notre Dame's Jess Harper. Rockne had also played professionally for several teams, supposedly for one as late as 1919.[4] How could he now condemn his players for what he had done only a few years earlier? Nevertheless, after the scandals of 1921, Rockne grew steadily critical of pro football and increasingly steered his lads into fields of coaching and teaching, law or medicine.

One afternoon in the spring of 1922, Rockne summoned the Mason City lad to his office and offered Eddie a coaching position on his staff for the upcoming season. Flattered, Anderson admitted that he had often contemplated coaching as a means of earning enough money to one day attend medical school.

Rockne regretfully explained that Notre Dame had not yet sanctioned a paid assistant's position, but the job would provide Eddie with valuable coaching experience. Whether feeling compelled to begin making money immediately or wanting to be out from under the great coach's shadow or both, Anderson declined Rockne's offer.

Rockne, who had once applied to medical school at St. Louis University, was nevertheless excited about Anderson's future plans to become a doctor and encouraged Eddie to pursue his dream. He also promised to use his influence to help him procure a coaching job, one that within a few years might pay enough for Anderson to afford medical school.[5]

Acting upon Rockne's recommendation, tiny Columbia College in Dubuque, Iowa, interviewed Anderson for its head football position. Impressed with the All-American end's maturity and football knowledge, Columbia offered Anderson an annual salary of $2,700 to coach the school's football, basketball and track teams. When a small Nebraska college simultaneously expressed interest in procuring Eddie as its football coach, Anderson proved to be a tough negotiator. Using the Nebraska offer as leverage, Anderson bargained with Columbia's financial officers for over a month before finally accepting the position at a yearly salary of $3,000.[6]

As fate would have it, this was the second time Knute Rockne had a role in determining the football coach at the Dubuque school. Eight years earlier in the spring of 1914, then Notre Dame Coach Jess Harper summoned the famous Irish passing duo of Gus Dorais and Rockne to his office. They found the professorial Harper perched behind a cluttered desk. In his hands was a letter from St. Joseph College officials (soon to be renamed Columbia College) asking Harper to recommend someone to serve as the school's next football coach.

"Either of you would make a fine coach," Harper advised. "However, it's only a one-man job. Which one of you would like to have it?"

Both Dorais and Rockne expressed interest in the position. Unwilling to recommend one above the other, Harper suggested that the matter be decided by a coin toss. Both agreed. Dorais won the flip and served as Columbia's coach from 1914 through 1917.[7] Rockne remained at Notre Dame, serving as an unpaid football assistant until succeeding Harper in 1918. It's amusing to speculate how Notre Dame's football fortunes might have been altered had Rockne won the toss.

On July 22, 1922, the athletic authorities of Columbia College announced the hiring of Eddie Anderson as football coach. "He will succeed Ira N. Davenport whose increasing business responsibilities make it impossible [for him] to continue coaching."[8]

At the time of Anderson's hiring, the college had endured five name changes during its 82-year existence. Originally established as the St. Raphael Seminary to train young men for the priesthood, the Catholic institution came to function under a series of names including Mount St. Bernard, Dubuque College, St. Joseph College and Columbia College. (During its centennial in 1939, the school adopted its present-day name of Loras College, after the Most Reverend Mathias Loras, the first bishop of Dubuque and founder of the college. That same year the college amended its charter forbidding the school to ever again change its name.)

When Anderson arrived at the serene hilltop setting on September 6, 1922, there were over 500 students on campus, approximately 300 of whom were enrolled at the college and the remainder at Columbia Academy, a four-year feeder high school. Both were all male institutions. Besides coaching three sports at the college, Anderson's duties included teaching physics at Columbia Academy. Before departing the Dubuque campus in 1925, Eddie would also teach English and history.

Anderson immediately set to work building Columbia's football team. Inheriting eight starters from the 1921 squad that posted a record of 7 wins against 1 loss provided Eddie with an experienced nucleus. With only three weeks until Columbia's season opener, Anderson's decision to implement the Notre Dame "system" posed a formidable challenge. The system with its infamous shift depended on precise timing that could only result from endless repetition under watchful eyes. Eddie could use some coaching help.

Although business demands forced his resignation as Columbia's football coach after the 1921 season, local entrepreneur Ira Davenport now offered Anderson his part-time assistance. Anderson readily accepted. Anderson then persuaded Max Kadesky, a Dubuque resident and All-American caliber end who had played opposite Eddie in 1921, to spend a few days working with the squad before departing for his senior season at Iowa.[9]

Additional coaching help came from Eddie's former Notre Dame teammate, Johnny Mohardt. After a five-game stint earlier that summer with the Detroit Tigers, Mohardt was now playing center field for a semi-pro team in Shullsberg, Iowa. After Shullsberg visited Dubuque for a weekend series in early September, Mohardt remained behind to help Eddie coach. He stayed for nearly two weeks.[10]

Calisthenics and exhaustive running predominated the early days of practice. Wedged between grueling conditioning sessions were tutoring periods where Kadesky mentored the receivers, Mohardt, the backs and Anderson, the linemen.[11] When scrimmaging later in the week, Anderson and Mohardt donned helmets and played offensive halfback and quarterback respectively. With Anderson toting the ball through and around defenders for large chunks of yardage and Mohardt zipping passes to wide-open receivers, Eddie realized that the athletic talent at the West Fourteenth Street campus was a far cry from what he'd been accustomed to at Notre Dame.

Scrimmaging with the team may have been Anderson's way of determining his players' physical toughness or a method of earning their respect. It's more likely, however, that Eddie just couldn't resist playing the game he loved. As future events soon proved, Anderson was a long way from hanging up his cleats as an active player.

Drills began on September 11 and dozens of curious townspeople visited the practice field daily to observe the rookie coach at work. The scene often resembled a three-ring circus with two separate groups of players engaged in assorted conditioning drills while Anderson worked a third group at the tackling dummy. By the week of the 1922 season opener Anderson was virtually coaching the team by himself. Kadesky and Mohardt had departed and Ira Davenport's business demands only allowed him to attend practice sporadically.

Privately Anderson was pleased with his young squad's progress. The defense especially was showing marked improvement evidenced by the fact that the coach was making fewer long runs during scrimmages and garnering more bumps and bruises. When carrying the ball resulted in Anderson taking an occasional physical shellacking, he would just grin and bear it, earning the additional admiration of players who already marveled at their coach's athletic prowess.[12] For the most part, however, Anderson delivered more physical punishment than he received.

Over coffee and the morning paper on Tuesday, September 26, Eddie was amused to learn that his good friend and former teammate Hunk Anderson had signed to play pro football with the Chicago Bears.[13] Originating as the Decatur Staleys in 1920, the team moved to the Windy City the next year under new owner and player-coach, George Halas. Hoping to ride the coattails of the city's most popular major league baseball team, the Cubs, Halas renamed his Chicago club the Bears in January of 1922.

At breakfast two days later, Anderson was startled to read that Johnny Mohardt had agreed to play with pro football's Chicago Cardinals.[14] Tucking the folded newspaper under his arm, Eddie bolted off to teach a class with no inkling whatsoever that he would be hearing from Mohardt again soon.

On the afternoon of Friday, September 29, an estimated 600 students, faculty and townspeople streamed down the hillside that abutted the team's practice field. Many were shouting and waving pennants while others rang cowbells or blew assorted horns. As the cheering throng pooled on the sidelines chanting encouragement, Anderson realized that to continue practice was pointless. Assembling his squad around him, the new coach led his lads to the sideline to meet their fans. Some players were embarrassed by the proceedings, but most were grateful and happy at the show of support. Even Anderson, who had experienced many a spirited pep rally at Notre Dame, was genuinely humbled by the turnout.

After thanking the crowd for its support and promising that the team would do its best in its season opener the next day, Anderson waded into the crowd to shake hands. The players quickly followed suit. The well-wishing and backslapping continued for 20 minutes before the partisans dispersed and the last of the players straggled to the gym to shower and change.

The Dubuque Athletic Field was the site of Eddie Anderson's coaching debut on September 30, 1922. That year Columbia officials, hoping to increase the team's gate receipts, opted to play its home games at the centrally located municipal park rather than on campus.[15] Serving as Columbia's home field until 1926, the park's playing surface was less than ideal.

In his autobiography, *It Was a Different Game,* Elmer Layden, one of Notre Dame's Four Horsemen and Rose Bowl hero who would succeed Anderson as coach at Columbia in 1925, described the field as he found it: "Home football games were played in a baseball park that was as devoid of grass as the Sahara Desert. When the weather was dry, the field was like concrete. When it rained, the field became a mud hole."[16]

Columbia's opponent for the three o'clock kick-off was the Wisconsin School of Mines. The visitor's 24-man roster comprised nearly one-third of the tiny Platteville school's student body. Playing before a fair-sized crowd under threatening skies, Columbia's stingy defense kept the Miners from earning even one first down en route to a 14 to 0 win. Little did Anderson realize that it would be the first of over 200 wins that would span his 39-year coaching career.

Anderson's shot at a second win would have to wait a couple of weeks as Columbia's next scheduled opponent, the University of Des Moines, cancelled their October 7 meeting. In those years small colleges frequently reneged on contractual agreements due to either a lack of funds or healthy players.

After defeating Wisconsin State Normal (today's University of Wisconsin at LaCrosse) 21 to 0 on Friday, October 13, a resounding cheer rocked the dining car with Anderson's announcement that the team would not practice until Monday. Eddie had originally scheduled a light workout for the squad on Saturday morning, but Chet Wynne's last telegram altered those plans.

As Anderson was blowing his first coaching whistle at Columbia that September, Chet Wynne was breaking into coaching in New York. Wynne wrote his former Notre Dame teammate a congratulatory letter and included the news of his own plunge into coaching. The letter generated a correspondence in which both men compared coaching notes, swapped stories and sometimes commiserated over the lack of talented players at their respective schools. Wynne also wrote that to supplement his meager coaching salary he had signed on to play football with a local pro team, the Rochester Jeffersons. In his reply, Anderson offered that moonlighting in pro football sounded like a "good deal."[17]

Rochester's early schedule included an 18-day, four-game road swing through the Midwest. In these budding years of pro football, however, the game was still a part-time job for its participants, and several Rochester players refused to leave their regular weekday jobs for the team's shakedown cruise. Realizing his club's acute manpower shortage, Wynne offered Eddie's name to Rochester player-coach Joe Alexander as a last-minute recruit.[18] With Alexander's endorsement, Wynne wired Anderson an invitation to join the team in Chicago for its game against the Bears at Cub Field (today's Wrigley Field) on Sunday, October 15.

Anderson viewed it as a one-time chance to pick up between $60 and $70 while seeing Chicago's sights. Besides, he'd love to see the look on the faces of former Irish teammates Hunk Anderson, Hec Garvey and Ojay Larson when he lined up against them. All three were now playing with the Bears.

Meeting with Wynne and Joe Alexander on the eve of the game, Anderson was pleasantly surprised to learn that due to injuries sustained by several players in Rochester's 13 to 13 tie with Akron two days earlier, he'd be starting at right end.

Over 7,000 fans turned out on a glorious autumn afternoon to watch the Bears defeat the visitors on Pete Stinchcomb's fourth-quarter touchdown. Despite the 7 to 0 loss Anderson had thoroughly enjoyed himself and readily agreed when Alexander asked him to play with the Jeffersons again the following Sunday at Rock Island.

Rock Island's Douglas Field was a quagmire, but neither the sloppy turf nor Anderson could slow the Independents' punishing ground game. Player-coach Jimmy Conzelman and Buck Gavin each ran for two touchdowns as Rock Island hammered Rochester 26 to 0.

With Columbia College idle the following weekend, Anderson traveled to Racine, Wisconsin, to play in the final game of Rochester's western road swing on October 29. After a scoreless first half, Racine captain Hank Gillo booted three field goals to give Racine a 9 to 0 victory.

On the evening train home Anderson reflected on the fun he'd had playing over the last three weeks. He was grateful to emerge from the experience healthy while pocketing nearly $200 in the bargain. In his mind, the lark was over and he could now concentrate on coaching and teaching at Columbia.

On October 21, 1922, the day before he played against Rock Island, Anderson had accompanied 20 Columbia players to Decorah, Iowa, to meet a strong Luther College team. Late in the half Anderson inserted 126-pound Albert Entringer at quarterback for the Purple and Gold. Possessing slick ball-handling skills and a strong passing arm, the fleet-footed freshman made an impressive showing by returning two punts for 40 yards each and scampering 30 yards on a run from scrimmage in Columbia's 12 to 0 win.

Throughout his career, one of Eddie Anderson's great coaching strengths was his willingness to give the little man a chance. Few college coaches of that, or any, era would have risked a 126-pounder in the line-up let alone at the crucial quarterback position. But Anderson was no ordinary coach. Weeks earlier, thinking that he was too small to see any playing time, the forlorn Entringer had stopped attending practice. When Anderson later bumped into the AWOL Entringer on campus he convinced him to give football another chance.[19] Recognizing Entringer's ability, the coach knew it was only a matter of time before the bantam-sized freshman would crack the line-up. Not only did Entringer earn a starting position, he would captain the squad in his senior year and eventually be elected to the college's Athletic Hall of Fame.

Tallying its fourth consecutive shutout in a 29 to 0 win over Campion College on November 4 in Prairie du Chien, Wisconsin, the Columbia team's mood was festive. Few players noticed that their coach didn't accompany the squad from the Dubuque train station back to campus. Instead, Anderson quietly slipped away to catch the evening train to Chicago. Just days earlier the National Football League's Chicago Cardinals contacted Eddie about playing for them on Sundays. Whether it was Cardinal owner Chris O'Brien or halfback Johnny Mohardt who initially sent the telegram remains uncertain. It is a certainty, however, that Mohardt turned the Cardinals on to his former Notre Dame teammate.

In those days pro teams were comprised of 16-man rosters. It wasn't unusual for a team's starting 11 players to play the entire game. Substitutions were rarely made; usually when a starter broke a leg or was rendered unconscious. Early pro football exhibited such barbarity that Sunday afternoons became living testimonies to Darwin's theory of survival of the fittest. Anderson had already had a taste of it playing with Rochester.

Eddie Anderson didn't need to play pro football. He was making a fine living as a teacher and rapidly gaining notoriety as a coach. Yet the prospect of earning almost $100 a game to add to his medical school kitty was too attractive for Anderson to refuse. Scrimmaging with his Columbia squad and his brief fling with Rochester had kept him in football-playing shape. Several trains that provided daily service between Dubuque and Chicago made it logistically feasible. Only 21, Anderson had not yet reached his athletic prime. He was still a gridiron warrior. When the Cardinals wired him the price of a round-trip train ticket and expense money, Anderson was off to the pro football wars.

It was raining on Sunday, November 5, 1922, when Eddie Anderson arrived at Chicago's Comiskey Park. Entering the Cardinal locker room he was greeted warmly by his old friend Johnny Mohardt. After being introduced to team owner Chris O'Brien, player-coach Paddy Driscoll and his new teammates, Anderson was issued a uniform and informed that he would start at right end for the Cardinals that afternoon. Driscoll preferred to let a new man get a practice or two under his belt before inserting him in the line-up. However, Mohardt's insistence that "Eddie could handle it," convinced Driscoll to throw the rookie into the breach immediately.

Paddy Driscoll, a great triple-threat halfback and arguably the NFL's first superstar, had led the Cardinals to four straight wins prior to Anderson's join-ing the club. A crowd of 6,000 endured a steady downpour to see the Cards eke out a 9 to 7 victory over the Buffalo All-Americans. Anderson didn't dis-appoint his new teammates. Playing well especially on defense, Anderson was urged by both O'Brien and Driscoll to return the following week.

That evening when the conductor asked for his ticket, Anderson pulled an envelope from his suit coat pocket. Opening it, he spied his ticket among the wad of bills O'Brien had paid him from that afternoon's gate receipts. When the conductor returned his punched ticket, Anderson placed it in the envelope, which he promptly stuffed back in his suit coat pocket. Tired and bruised but nearly $100 richer, he folded his arms across his chest and settled in for the tedious 175-mile train trip back to Dubuque. It was a wearisome trip he would grow accustomed to making over the next three years.

On Saturday, November 11, Columbia hosted St. Viator, a Catholic col-lege from Bourbonnais, Illinois. Named after a sanctified third century lec-tor in Lyons, France, St. Viator became a college in 1868. While the two schools had nearly equal enrollments in 1922, Viator's football reputation far exceeded that of Columbia's. That very week noted *Chicago Tribune* sports-writer Walter Eckersall hailed St. Viator as one of the Midwest's strongest small college teams. Despite Columbia being undefeated and un-scored upon in four games, the *Chicago Herald and Examiner* predicted an easy Viator win, a prediction that Anderson emphatically pointed out to his players.

After viewing that morning's Armistice Day parade, nearly 2,800 patri-otic fans poured through the turnstiles of the Dubuque Athletic Field to cheer on Columbia. Anderson's lads didn't disappoint the hometown faithful. Bill Blake's second quarter touchdown pass to John Fisher and Albert Entringer's late-game scoring plunge gave Columbia a 13 to 0 win.

Within hours after the game Eddie Anderson was on a train speeding to Chicago. It was nearly midnight when the stylishly dressed Anderson checked into a South Side hotel near Comiskey Park. At the front desk he purchased a copy of the *Chicago Tribune*. Turning to the sports section, he was pleas-antly surprised to see his photo accompanying an article heralding the Car-dinals' game on Sunday.[20]

The next day, on a muddy field before only 2,500 fans, Anderson's excep-tional defensive play helped the Cardinals shut out Akron 7 to 0. The game's only touchdown came on a long pass from A. McMahon to Paddy Driscoll. A. McMahon was actually an alias for one Arnie Horween. Both Arnie and his brother, Ralph, were Harvard graduates and Cardinal teammates. In an era when many viewed pro football as a shady enterprise unworthy of any college graduate, the Horween brothers played their entire pro careers under the name McMahon to keep the fact a secret from their mother.[21]

It was after midnight when a sleepy and sore Anderson climbed the dormitory steps to his room on campus. Emptying his pockets onto the desk, the weary traveler recounted the money in the Cardinals' pay envelope. On the eve of his twenty-second birthday Anderson was coaching an undefeated college team on Saturdays, while starring for an undefeated professional team on Sundays. Anderson loved it. Furthermore, it was a means to an end. If he could sustain the unflagging pace, attending medical school would be a reality in a year or two.

In the early twenties college homecomings were still a novelty. Columbia originally had not designated a game for homecoming in 1922. In the wake of its team's successful start, however, school officials hastily ordered posters to be printed and flyers mailed to alumni announcing the season's finale on Saturday, November 25, as the homecoming game.[22] Chicago's DePaul University would be the opponent.

Although confident of victory, Eddie was especially concerned about the DePaul game. His Chicago Cardinals were playing in Canton, Ohio, on Sunday, November 26. The Canton Bulldogs had defeated the Cards a week earlier and the rematch might well determine the league's champion. To make the kick-off in Canton, Anderson would have to leave the DePaul game early to make the train connection in Chicago. Realizing the Cardinals would be hard pressed to find a suitable late replacement for him and not wanting to jeopardize his future with the team, Anderson felt compelled to play. Uncertain as to how college officials would react to his decision, Eddie knocked warily on the door of the school's athletic director, N.A. Steffen.

After hearing Anderson's predicament, the Reverend Steffen acceded to his coach's extraordinary request. Under the circumstances, Steffen's decision was most magnanimous. School officials had scheduled a post-game dinner at St. Francis Hall that would be immediately followed by a homecoming program at the Columbia Auditorium. With college president Reverend Edward Howard and other local dignitaries scheduled to speak, Anderson's absence may have been deemed as inappropriate.[23] His absence would certainly disappoint alumni and fans wanting to meet the school's new winning coach.

Hoping to allay their coach's anxiety over his early departure, Anderson's boys quickly seized control of the DePaul game. Behind several long scoring runs by Tom Wiley, Columbia took a 32 to 0 halftime lead into the locker room. Pleased and proud of his lads, Anderson quickly issued his team instructions before grabbing his valise and exiting the ballpark for the Illinois Central train station located several blocks away.

As fate would have it, the train tracks ran by the Dubuque Athletic Field. The field had no scoreboard, but as the train trundled past in the fading afternoon light Anderson observed DePaul lining up to kick off. He then realized that his Columbia team had finally been scored upon.[24]

Anderson learned in the paper at breakfast the next morning that DePaul had blocked an early third quarter punt and recovered it on Columbia's 3-yard line. DePaul scored two plays later to end Columbia's shutout streak. It would be DePaul's only points as Columbia stormed to a 50 to 6 win.

As a rookie coach, Anderson had led Columbia to a perfect 7 and 0 season. His 1922 squad surpassed even Gus Dorais' 1916 team, which won 6 games and tied 1 during its seven-game schedule. Nevertheless, Anderson undoubtedly regretted missing the second half of the DePaul game, not that he might have kept his team's string of shutouts intact but because he could have "pulled in his team's reins" and prevented running up the score. Throughout his coaching career, whenever Anderson's teams had a commanding lead, he cleared the bench and ran out the clock. He didn't run up the score on an opponent. He had cleared his bench in lopsided games earlier that season against Campion and Mount Morris and had he been on the sidelines in the second half, he undoubtedly would have done the same against DePaul. Instead, angered that DePaul's touchdown had ended their shutout streak, the West 14th Street boys poured it on the undermanned Blue Demons. Columbia's last two touchdowns came on fourth quarter passes of 50 and 60 yards from John Fisher to Tom Wiley. To make matters worse, DePaul coach Frank Haggerty saw one of his injured players helped off the field after nearly every play.

Whatever sympathy Anderson may have felt for Haggerty and DePaul vanished that afternoon when Canton kicked off to Anderson's Cardinals. The Cards led 3 to 0 entering the fourth quarter when Bulldog player-coach and future NFL Hall of Famer Guy Chamberlin took charge. First, he blocked Driscoll's punt, which Bird Carroll recovered on Chicago's 3-yard line. Three plays later the Bulldogs' "Wooky" Roberts scored the game's first touchdown. Chamberlin then thwarted the Cardinals' comeback hopes by intercepting two passes and returning them 50 and 15 yards respectively for touchdowns. Chamberlin's heroics gave the Bulldogs a 20 to 3 win. Now saddled with two losses to Canton in as many weeks, the Cardinals' title hopes seemed bleak.

Returning to Dubuque on Monday, Anderson learned that Columbia officials were seeking a post-season game. Invitations were extended to both Lombard College in Galesburg, Illinois, which hadn't been defeated in two years, and to Lawrence College in Wisconsin, but both declined.

In the meantime, letters of congratulations poured in from throughout the Midwest including one from Chicago White Sox owner Charles Comiskey. Two referees who had worked several of Columbia's games during the season, former All-American Iowa quarterback Aubrey Devine and ex–Kansas State player M.H. Sims, also sent letters.

Devine wrote, "Tell Eddie Anderson for me that I think he has an excellently coached team, one which knows and executes football as well or better than some of the so-called larger schools."[25]

Sims added, "It has never been my experience to officiate behind a cleaner playing team than represented by your college this season. Because of this very high degree of sportsmanship I desire that you express my heartiest congratulations to the team..."[26]

While Anderson's football coaching may have ended for the year, he still had several games to play with the Cardinals. On Thanksgiving Day, November 30, just three days after returning from Canton, Anderson was back in Chicago playing in the inaugural game of the Cardinals-Bears' rivalry. (After playing the 1921 season as the Chicago Staleys, the club changed its name to the Bears in 1922.)

This first encounter was one of the most fiercely contested in the teams' long and bitter rivalry. With the home team Cardinals leading 3 to 0 in the third quarter, events turned ugly when Cards' star halfback Paddy Driscoll was viciously tackled. In *The Football Chronicle*, co-authors Dan Daly and Bob O'Donnell describe the action. "On an end run, Driscoll was lifted off his feet by end-co-owner George Halas and defensive back Joey Sternaman and heaved five yards back. When he got up, he threw a punch at Sternaman...

"A free-for-all followed. Players rushed in from the sideline and at least 100 fans and several policemen came out of the Comiskey Park stands."[27]

Order was finally restored but not before one of Chicago's finest put his .38 caliber service revolver to the head of a disheveled George Halas. Halas, Sternaman and Driscoll were all ejected. When play resumed the Cardinals' B. McMahon [the alias of Ralph Horween] added a 34-yard field goal to give the home team a 6 to 0 win.

In those nascent years of pro football, teams had to play when stadiums were available and travel most affordable. As a result, teams sometimes played games only days apart. Such was the case in 1922 when the Cards played the Bears on November 30 and then entertained the Dayton Triangles on December 3. Because Eddie was banged up from the Bears game, he saw only limited action in the Cards' 7 to 3 loss to Dayton.

Realizing the potential for a lucrative gate, the Bears' George Halas convinced the Cardinals' Chris O'Brien that their teams should play a rematch on December 10. Halas agreed to play at Comiskey Park for a percentage of the gate. Although it was professional football, at times there wasn't much professional about it. Both teams entered the stadium attired in red jerseys. The mix-up delayed the kick-off until someone scrounged up white scrimmage vests for the visiting Bears to wear.[28]

The game was played in chilly winds before a crowd of 12,000—the largest crowd ever to see a pro game in Chicago up to that time. Eddie Anderson's defensive play was instrumental in the Cardinals 9 to 0 win. As the *Chicago Tribune* reported on December 11, "It seemed as if Anderson was always there to take advantage of a break. Once, when the Bears tried a lateral pass after catching a kick-off, Anderson intercepted the ball on the visitor's 5-yard line. That put Paddy Driscoll in a position to score a 12-yard field goal from a difficult angle a few moments later.

"Again, when Sternaman fumbled a punt along the sideline, it was Anderson who dropped on the ball. He was there ready to nail the receiver of punts at all times."

Three Paddy Driscoll field goals provided the game's only scoring. The win gave the Cardinals a final record of 8 wins and 3 losses and claim to the city's pro football championship.

7

1923–1924

Eddie Anderson's basketball coaching debut was put on hold while Columbia officials pursued the possibility of a post-season football game in 1922. It was only on December 8, when all hopes of a post-season game faded, that Anderson initiated basketball tryouts. In those halcyon days of two-handed set shots and wooden backboards, college basketball rarely tipped off before January. Scheduling was so casual that contests often weren't contracted until late December. Columbia's 1923 schedule, for example, wasn't finalized until December 30, 1922.

Anderson experienced only a modicum of success in his maiden season, but it wasn't from a lack of effort. Scouring the campus for talent, Anderson required all of his football players to try out for basketball. Some, including Bill Blake, Frank Conlin, Cletus Nockles and Albert Entringer, made the squad. Unfortunately, inexperience and abysmal shooting hampered the team all season.

After a 38 to 20 opening win over Wisconsin Mines on January 10, Columbia dropped its next eight games. Undeterred, Anderson worked diligently at improving his team. Drawing from his gridiron coaching tactics, Anderson was often a zealous participant in his team's scrimmages. Whether by mixing it up underneath the boards or demonstrating how to run the offense, Eddie proved to be a "hands on" coach. Despite overall poor shooting, Columbia gradually improved, winning three of its last four games.

The highlight of the 1923 season came against St. Louis University on February 22. The day before, an uncharacteristically gloomy Anderson watched his team stumble ineptly through practice. Afterward, Anderson confided to a local reporter that Columbia's chances against the highly touted visitors were "slim."[1]

69

Hailed as one of the best teams in the Midwest, St. Louis came to Dubuque sporting a record of 17 wins against 3 losses. Nevertheless, in a cramped gym before 700 raucous fans, Anderson's team showed a complete reversal of form, upsetting the Billikins 41 to 28. It was the most points Columbia had scored in a game all season.

In the spring Anderson served as head track coach. He worked primarily with sprinters and jumpers. Football, however, was Anderson's first love, and when track conflicted with spring football, the coach delegated supervision of track workouts to the team captain Tom Wiley.

Eddie Anderson lost his first football game as a college coach on October 20, 1923, when Wisconsin-LaCrosse shut out Columbia 19 to 0 in Dubuque. The loss snapped Columbia's consecutive winning streak at 16 — a streak that began under Coach Ira Davenport in 1921. What alarmed the school's administration, however, was the poor fan turnout. Only 400 spectators passed through the turnstiles at the Dubuque Athletic Field for both the season opener against Wisconsin Mines and the LaCrosse game. Coming off an undefeated season, school officials were at a loss to explain it.

Scheduling problems now exacerbated Columbia's dismal gate receipts. After plans for an October 13 home game against Morningside College failed to materialize, the *Dubuque Telegraph-Herald* reported on Tuesday, October 23, that "Columbia was slated to play DePaul at Chicago on Saturday, but the Purple and Gold cancelled the game due to DePaul's poor showing this season." No further explanation was provided.

The article suggests that Columbia cancelled the game either because DePaul could not field a competitive team or because the Chicago school could not guarantee Columbia its traveling expenses. In view of Columbia's meager gate receipts, it's possible that the Dubuque school didn't have the cash on hand to pay the team's train fare to the Windy City.

In an attempt to kill two birds with one stone, Anderson phoned Knute Rockne hoping to fill the void in Columbia's schedule by booking a major attraction. Notre Dame football held nationwide appeal and Anderson was confident that even a team comprised of its reserves would draw well in Dubuque. After a frenzied exchange of telegrams and phone calls on October 22, Rockne agreed to send the Notre Dame "reserves" to play at Dubuque on Friday, October 26. Although Rockne and Anderson were friends, Rockne was still a shrewd businessman. The game was a "done deal" only after Columbia guaranteed Notre Dame a payment of $1,000.[2]

With more than 100 players on the Irish roster, the resourceful Rockne occasionally scheduled games for his third- and fourth-string squads against small college teams. These contests were usually scheduled on Fridays before

Notre Dame was playing a formidable opponent (the Irish were hosting Georgia Tech on Saturday, October 27) and the likelihood of third-string reserves seeing action was remote. This practice boosted player morale and kept the Irish football pipeline flowing with talented and experienced personnel.

Despite a steady drizzle that fell throughout the day, a crowd of nearly 1,500 attended the contest. While the weather undoubtedly kept some spectators away, the turnout was considerably larger than what Columbia had enjoyed previously that season. It was a game Anderson fervidly wanted to win and his players sensed it.

Trailing 6 to 0 late in the first quarter, Columbia's Tom Wiley's exciting serpentine 75-yard punt return tied the score. In the second half, Columbia squandered several scoring opportunities and the game ended in a 6 to 6 tie. It was a bitter pill for Eddie to swallow.

As Coach Eddie Anderson and his Columbia squad weathered scheduling snags and anemic game-day attendance, right end Eddie Anderson and his Cardinal teammates breezed past their first five NFL opponents in 1923. The Cardinals' blazing start set the stage for a battle of undefeateds when the Canton Bulldogs visited Comiskey Park on Sunday, November 4. Although the Bulldogs struggled at the gate, Canton was clearly the league's premiere team on the field. The defending NFL champions had defeated the Cardinals twice in 1922. Led by player-coach Guy Chamberlin, the Canton defense was anchored by stellar tackles Roy "Link" Lyman (6'2", 233 lbs.) and Wilbur "Fats" Henry (5'10", 245 lbs.). All three were future NFL Hall of Famers. Half back Lou Smythe and fullback "Doc" Elliot were the linchpins of a solid running game while Harry Robb quarterbacked the team.

After coaching his Columbia lads to victory at the University of Des Moines on Saturday afternoon, Anderson endured an eight-hour train ride to Chicago to join his Cardinal teammates for Sunday's showdown against Canton. A cloudburst accompanied the game's opening kick-off. As field conditions worsened, the momentum swung to Canton, whose line outweighed Chicago's by nearly 25 pounds per man. Early in the fourth quarter Smythe ran three yards for the game's only touchdown to give Canton a 7 to 3 win. The Bulldogs, who would finish the season undefeated, would never look back en route to their second consecutive NFL championship.

In the college and pro football worlds of 1923, the paths of players and coaches often crossed. Nowhere was this more in evidence than on November 9 when Columbia College visited Chicago's Comiskey Park to play St. Viator. Walter Francis Crangle coached St. Viator. The former All-Western Conference end was better known as "Cast Iron" Jack Crangle and was one of the Illinois ringers that had bested Anderson and his Notre Dame teammates in the infamous Taylorville-Carlinville game.[3] It's unlikely the pair reminisced about that 1921 encounter during the customary pre-game coaching banter. Chances are they had already caught up on old times earlier that season as teammates with the Chicago Cardinals. Although coaching rivals on Friday, two days later they would be teammates on that same field when Crangle would score the game's only touchdown to give the Cardinals a 6 to 0 victory over the Hammond (Indiana) Pros.

One of Anderson's former Notre Dame teammates, Roger Kiley, had also joined the Cardinals in 1923. Like Anderson and Crangle, Kiley was also the head coach of a college team — Loyola University of Chicago.

During the twenties it was not uncommon for NFL players to also work as assistant college coaches during the week. Hunk Anderson, for example, assisted at Notre Dame while playing for the Chicago Bears. However, the first head college football coach to simultaneously play in the NFL may have been Luke Urban. Graduating from Boston College in 1921, Urban began playing that fall for the Buffalo All-Americans while simultaneously beginning his 146-game coaching tenure at Canisus College.[4]

To the trained eye the Columbia-Viator contest resembled a lightweight version of Notre Dame playing Illinois. That's because Anderson and Crangle were both disciples of their respective college mentors, Rockne and Bob Zuppke. The contest kept the crowd of 5,000 on edge, with the game's only points coming in the fourth quarter when a kid named McGinnis dropkicked a 30-yard field goal to give Viator a 3 to 0 win.

Losing to Viator precipitated a tailspin for Anderson as Columbia dropped its next two games to St. Thomas College of St. Paul, Minnesota, and Luther College. The nosedive carried over to Eddie's play with the Cardinals when Chicago hosted a pro team from Racine, Wisconsin, on November 16.

Featuring former collegiate stars such as Milt Romney and "Death" Halladay from the University of Chicago and Wisconsin backs Rowdy Elliot and Shorty Barr, Racine attracted the largest crowd of the season to Comiskey Park. The visitors even brought a 45-man drum and bugle corps to entertain the 6,500 fans.

Despite tackling Racine's Shorty Barr for a safety to give the Cardinals a 2 to 0 halftime lead, it was a miserable game for Eddie. Perhaps the worst game he ever played. Seemingly snake-bit, the usually glue-fingered Anderson dropped two "sure" touchdown passes, while teammate Paddy Driscoll missed all four of his field goal tries as Racine rallied to defeat Chicago, 10 to 4.[5] The numbing loss left the Cards with a record of 7 wins and 2 losses. To have any chance of catching the league-leading Canton Bulldogs, the Cardinals had to win all of their remaining games.

Prior to his poor performance against Racine, Anderson was facing a dilemma. His Columbia squad was playing its season finale on Thanksgiving Day against Campion College in Dubuque. A win would give Columbia a .500 record for the season. However, the Cardinals were playing their cross-town rivals, the Bears, at Cub (Wrigley) Field at eleven o'clock that same morning. Obviously, Anderson couldn't be in both cities at once. Should he coach Columbia or play with the Cardinals?

Itching to redeem himself with his Chicago teammates for his poor showing against Racine and believing Campion to be no match for his Columbia squad, Anderson opted to play for the Cards. At mid-week, Anderson informed injured Columbia captain John Aldera that he would pinch-hit for his coach against Campion on Thanksgiving Day. Instructing Aldera to "start the second-team backfield and clear the bench should we get a two touchdown lead," Anderson hopped the train to Chicago.[6]

Following his mentor's instructions, Aldera directed Columbia to a 44 to 0 blanking of the visitors from Prairie du Chien. The shutout gave Columbia a 1923 season record of 4 wins, 4 losses and 1 tie.

It wasn't as pleasant a holiday for Anderson's Cardinals. Playing before 13,500 fans, a new attendance record for a pro football game in the Windy City, the Bears made Ed "Dutch" Sternaman's early 30-yard field goal stand up for a 3 to 0 win. The loss dropped the Cardinals into third place with a record of 7 wins and 3 losses. The grueling contest also exacted a heavy physical toll on the Cards whose next game was only three days away. Eddie Anderson, Roger Kiley, Paddy Driscoll, Jack Crangle and the team's starting center, Nick "Bulldog" McInerney, were now hobbled with injuries or illness and forced to watch in street clothes as their teammates hosted the Oorang Indians on Sunday, December 2.

The Oorang Indians were the league's most unique franchise. Walter Lingo, owner of the Oorang Kennels in LaRue, Ohio, purchased the NFL franchise in 1922. In an attempt to promote his kennels, which bred Airedale terriers, Lingo named his team the Oorang Indians and hired the famed Jim Thorpe as player-coach. Thorpe, a Sac and Fox Indian, had won both the decathlon and pentathlon with record-breaking performances at the 1912 Olympic Games in Stockholm. At the Games' awards ceremony, Sweden's King Gustav V addressed Thorpe as "the greatest athlete in the world."[7] However, when it was discovered that Thorpe had played semi-pro baseball for $25 a week during the summer of 1910, the United States Olympic Committee stripped Thorpe of his medals on charges of professionalism.

With Thorpe's guidance, Lingo filled the Oorang roster with Native-American players, most of whom had played college ball at the United States Indian Industrial School at Carlisle, Pennsylvania. With the exception of

Thorpe, halfback Joe Guyon and end Pete Calac, who were well-known stars, the rest of the squad played under their tribal names. Oorang's starting line-up included Little Twig at left end, Arrow Head at right end, Red Fox at quarterback and Eagle Feather at fullback.

Because the town of LaRue had no football stadium, the team played its home games 15 miles away in Marion. However, the Indians played almost exclusively on the road. Fans initially flocked to see the famous Jim Thorpe and Oorang's acclaimed halftimes that included dog shows (Airedale terriers, what else?) and ceremonial dancing performed by several of the Oorang players.[8] The sizzle was more appealing than the steak, however, as Oorang arrived in Chicago winless in nine games.

In street clothes, the injured Anderson silently agonized on the sidelines over being unable to compete against the Native-American legend. Although Red Grange would soon surpass Thorpe's popularity, in 1923 Jim Thorpe was still the biggest name in football. Eddie's anguish was alleviated, however, upon learning that the aging Thorpe was also sidelined with injuries. Thorpe would only coach, not play, against the Cardinals.[9]

While the injury toll accounted for some sloppy play, the contest was still exciting. A disappointing crowd of only 1,200 enjoyed the fast paced, wide-open action. The highlight was Oorang's Joe Guyon returning an interception 96 yards for a touchdown. Despite Guyon's late game heroics, the injury-riddled Cardinals endured to earn a hard-fought 22 to 19 win.

With Thorpe still sidelined the next week, Oorang managed a 12 to 0 win over the Louisville Brecks in the team's swan song. Banking only 3 wins against 16 losses and besieged with financial burdens during the club's two-year run, Walter Lingo disbanded his colorful franchise after the season.

In the Cardinals' 1923 season finale against the Milwaukee Badgers, Anderson made a leaping end zone catch for a touchdown. It wasn't enough however, as Milwaukee eked out a 14 to 12 win behind the solid play of quarterback Jimmy Conzelman and former Centre College All-American halfback Bo McMillin. The defeat left the Cards with a record of eight wins and four losses.

By the spring of 1924 Egyptologist Howard Carter and his team had bridged a 3,300-year historical gap by discovering the sarcophagus of King Tutankhamen. In Germany, Adolf Hitler was sentenced to five years in prison for his role in the aborted Beer Hall *Putsch*. With good behavior, the Nazi leader would be eligible for parole in six months. In Washington, D.C., Attorney General Harry Daugherty resigned in the wake of the Teapot Dome Scandal and rumors of other fraudulent practices, while Congress passed the Soldiers' Bonus Bill, which would pay veterans of the Great War an annuity in 1945.

The spring zephyrs that thawed Iowa's snow-covered flatlands that year also brought a wave of interest in Eddie Anderson's coaching availability. On April 26, the *Minneapolis Morning Tribune* reported that Anderson had wired his acceptance as freshman football coach and varsity assistant for the University of Minnesota Golden Gophers. In the article, Minnesota Coach Bill Spaulding said of Anderson, "He has a remarkable coaching personality, is a close student of the game and a young man of excellent character."

Spaulding, a close friend of Knute Rockne, had invited Eddie to the Minnesota campus a week earlier. During the visit Anderson met with university president Lotus Coffman. As the two smoked a cigarette in the president's plush office, Coffman assured the 23-year-old that he could pursue his medical studies there while coaching football. With his life-long dream on the verge of becoming a reality, Anderson asked for a few days to think about it.[10]

Back in Dubuque, Anderson was still considering the Minnesota job when Syracuse offered Eddie a coaching position. Syracuse, too, promised he could study medicine while coaching. It's uncertain whether Anderson ever ventured to New York to pursue the offer.[11]

What is certain, however, is that the opportunistic coach traveled to Cleveland in mid–May to interview for the head football job at Case Western Reserve. Case officials initially offered Anderson a contract at an annual salary of $5,500. Asking for a few days to mull it over, Anderson again returned to Iowa. Wanting to seal the deal, Case upped the ante to $6,000. When Anderson remained non-committal, Case offered $6,500 — an incredible salary for that time period.[12]

Then fate intervened when Eddie's 47-year-old mother, Nellie Anderson, passed away in Mason City on May 20, 1924. Grief-stricken, Anderson reassessed his situation. With his 57-year-old father now living alone and his younger brother, Bill, enrolled as a student at Columbia College, Anderson passed on all three offers to remain close to home. (Despite Eddie's best intentions, after attending his mother's funeral it would be 15 years before he again set foot in Mason City.)

Rewarded with a reported "substantial" raise in salary, Anderson looked forward to returning to Columbia for the 1924 season. With an experienced and talented line-up returning, Eddie had reason for optimism. Captain and center Andy Kelly and scatback Tom Wiley were returning for their third season as starters. Albert Entringer had nailed down the quarterback job and in the process acquired the moniker "Cutie." Unfortunately, Cutie had not gained a pound on his 126-pound frame in two years. Pile-driving fullback Joe Ball and two colorfully nicknamed halfbacks, Donald "Jiggs" Noonan and Walter "Scuds" Tschirgi, rounded out the backfield.

Throwing himself into his coaching, Anderson's boys won four of their first five games before heading to Chicago to meet St. Viator on Tuesday,

November 11. The Armistice Day contest was the first college game played at Chicago's new $5 million Grant Park Stadium[13] (today known as Soldier Field). Anderson's former Cardinal teammate and Taylorville nemesis, "Cast Iron" Jack Crangle, had left Viator that season to become the head football coach at the University of Arkansas. His successor was Ralph Glaze.

Glaze had been an All-American at Dartmouth in the early 1900s. After a brief stint as a pitcher with the Boston Red Sox, Glaze coached football at both the University of Southern California and Lake Forest College before taking the reins at St. Viator. Glaze's "rock and sock 'em" style of eastern power football contrasted sharply with Anderson's Notre Dame system that emphasized speed, timing, and deception. The difference in style was also reflected in each team's personnel. Viator's starting line-up averaged 189 pounds while Columbia's averaged only 155.

The game was well publicized in the Chicago area, but torrential rains pelted the city all day on Monday, November 10, and most of Tuesday. As a result, a disappointing crowd of only 3,000 attended. Although weather and turf conditions favored Glaze's squad, the lighter Columbia team withstood two early scoring threats to play Viator to a scoreless tie. For the second consecutive week, Anderson played his starting eleven the entire 60 minutes.

On November 27, Thanksgiving Day, Anderson took a 23-man traveling squad to Decorah, Iowa, to meet Luther College for the Western Interstate Conference Championship. (Other conference teams included St. Viator, LaCrosse, Valparaiso and DePaul.) When injuries forced team captain Andy Kelly to the sidelines in the fourth quarter, Anderson made his first substitution in four games.[14]

The game's big break came in the second quarter when Luther's W. Olson (one of five Olsons in Luther's starting line-up) fumbled Entringer's punt. Frank Conlin recovered for Columbia at Luther's 27-yard line. Seven plays later Joe Ball barreled across the goal line for the game's only score. Columbia's 6 to 0 win gave Anderson's lads a final record of 5 wins, 2 losses and 1 tie and the 1924 Western Interstate Conference Championship. Today, the faded game ball is proudly displayed in a trophy case at Loras College.

Throughout the 1924 season Anderson continued to moonlight at right end for the Chicago Cardinals. With a record of 5 wins, 4 losses and 1 tie, the Cardinals never challenged for the NFL title. Anderson missed a game due to an injury but started the other nine. Making the 350-mile round trip from Dubuque to Chicago every weekend, Anderson took and gave his lumps. He also continued to deposit his weekly game salary into his savings for medical school. Now, financially flush at age 24, Anderson decided to actively pursue his medical studies.

8

THE 1925
NFL CHAMPIONSHIP

Eddie Anderson capped off Columbia's 1924 championship season by procuring Knute Rockne as the main speaker at the Letterman's Banquet scheduled for mid–December. A dynamic speaker, Rockne was in great demand on the banquet circuit — especially after Notre Dame's undefeated 1924 season when renowned sportswriter Grantland Rice immortalized the Irish backfield of Layden, Stuhldreher, Crowley and Miller by dubbing them "The Four Horsemen."

When Notre Dame accepted an invitation to play in the Rose Bowl on New Year's Day, Rockne regretfully wired that the turn of events now prohibited him from attending Columbia's banquet. Knowing that Rock's presence would greatly enhance the affair, Anderson postponed the banquet until mid–January so Rockne could attend.[1]

In appreciation of Anderson's coaching efforts, grateful Columbia players and fans presented Eddie with a round-trip train ticket to Pasadena to see his alma mater play Stanford on January 1, 1925.[2] One of 53,000 spectators sweltering under Pasadena's hot sun, Anderson watched Notre Dame withstand both the blistering heat and the sensational play of Ernie Nevers to defeat Stanford 27 to 10.

Seeking to reap as much publicity as possible from the Rose Bowl win, Rockne took his triumphant Irish on a circuitous victory tour back to South Bend. After spending several days cabareting about Los Angeles, the team visited the California Bay-area and then the Pacific Northwest before heading east through Wyoming and Colorado. At every stop along the way the vibrant Rockne charmed the local citizenry and gave newspapermen colorful copy.[3]

Less enamored with Rockne's whistle stop escapades, however, was the Notre Dame administration. The West Coast excursion had lasted more than a month and resulted in the players missing the first week of spring semester classes. Determined to prevent a recurrence, Notre Dame officials wouldn't accept another bowl invitation for 45 years and only after the advent of commercial air travel.

Because Rockne's celebratory sojourn lasted into mid–January, the Columbia football banquet was again postponed. The much-anticipated event was finally held on Sunday, March 8, 1925, two days after the Notre Dame-Columbia basketball game that served as the formal dedication for Columbia's new $150,000 and 2,200-seat gymnasium. Rockne proved to be a more gracious guest than the Irish basketball team, which stomped the Anderson-coached Columbia squad 44 to 25. Before a packed Elks Club the loquacious Rockne informed the audience, "I can truthfully say that all the time I was

Eddie Anderson poses with his 1925 Columbia (Loras) College basketball team. This squad lost the dedicatory game of the college's new $150,000 and 2,200-seat gymnasium to Notre Dame. In his three years at Columbia, Anderson coached football, basketball and track. Joe Kellogg (seated second from left, second row), Bernard White (holding ball), and Frank Less (far right, second row) also played football for Anderson. (Loras College Archives, Dubuque, Iowa)

at Notre Dame there was never a better end than Eddie Anderson. He was the best not only in football but also in his ability to keep up the morale of the team. He could take a team and make it pull itself up from defeat.

"Those of you who saw the Iowa game [1921] will remember that Notre Dame to the very end was fighting, pulling itself up from defeat. And the cause of that spirit of always refusing to be beaten was Eddie Anderson."[4]

Rockne's praise enhanced Anderson's lofty status on Columbia's campus and around Dubuque. School officials often sought Eddie's opinion regarding matters of student discipline, dormitory regulations and athletic policies. While students viewed Anderson as friendly and accessible, they also saw him as a taskmaster in both the classroom and the athletic arena.

Perhaps a photo and accompanying caption in the 1925 Columbia year-book *Purgold* best captured the student body's reverence for the 24-year-old coach. Grinning broadly from under the brim of a cocked fedora and attired in a three-piece suit, the dapper Anderson stands holding an overcoat in the crook of his arm. The caption below simply reads, "A Champion."

On March 30, 1925, Anderson began spring football practice. Among the 40 gridiron candidates was one Dominic Ameche from Kenosha, Wisconsin. Ameche had captained the Columbia Academy basketball team the previous December. An accelerated student, Ameche amassed enough credits to graduate high school at mid-year. When Ameche matriculated at Columbia College in January, it was too late to try out for basketball. Instead, the freshman plunged into several campus theatrical productions.

While an Academy student in Anderson's class, Ameche grew to admire his mentor and now decided to give football a try. Despite making a creditable showing in spring drills, Ameche opted not to play that fall. However, he continued his theatrical pursuits and through the years stayed in touch with his former mentor. The two became life-long friends. After changing his first name from Dominic, Don Ameche went on to a long and accomplished acting career in Hollywood.

When classes adjourned for summer vacation in 1925, there was no inkling that Columbia's popular young football coach would not return in the fall. As late as July 14, Anderson had met with the Reverends Maurice Sheehy and Nicholas Steffen to discuss spring sports and alumni association matters. Players and fans were therefore stunned when the *Dubuque Telegraph-Herald* announced Anderson's resignation on July 23. The article also reported, "Anderson had accepted a handsome offer from a middle-western university but refused to announce the name of the school with which he has signed..."

The mystery unraveled on July 26 when DePaul University president, the Very Reverend Thomas F. Levan, announced the hiring of Anderson as the school's football, basketball and track coach. The *Telegraph-Herald* also reported, "In addition to his coaching duties Anderson plans on entering business of some kind in Chicago." In fact, Anderson's main business in moving to the Windy City was to begin his medical studies at Loyola University. Shortly after learning of his acceptance at Loyola, Anderson inquired into the vacant head football job at DePaul. DePaul jumped at Anderson's overture like a voracious cutthroat trout snatching a fly upon the water.

With no classroom duties, Anderson was free to attend daytime classes at Loyola Medical School. Believing that the demands of medical school would be partially offset by no more 350-mile weekend round-trips between Dubuque and Chicago, Anderson decided to play football for the Cardinals again in 1925. It was an incredible undertaking — coaching a college team during the week and playing pro football on Sundays, all while coping with the rigors of medical school. Yet, Anderson never doubted that he could master all three. Events would prove him to be correct.

The Vincentians founded DePaul University in 1898. Today it is the largest Catholic university in the United States. In 1925 the school's enrollment hovered at 5,000. Having fielded football teams since 1900, DePaul experienced only moderate success before Anderson's arrival. The program had fallen on hard times in the early 1920s, losing regularly to the likes of Dubuque College, St. Ambrose and St. Viator. In 1925, DePaul football was the stepchild of the Chicago sports scene. Local papers highlighted the squads of Amos Alonzo Stagg at the University of Chicago, Bob Zuppke at Illinois, Coach Thistlethwaite at Northwestern and, of course, the Fighting Irish of media-darling Knute Rockne. Even the city's upstart pro teams, the Bears and the Cardinals, drew significantly more press coverage than DePaul's lowly Blue Demons.

That same year Anderson's former Irish teammate, Roger Kiley, was coaching at Loyola University while finishing his law degree. Although both schools shared the same rung of the college football ladder, Loyola still garnered more media ink than did DePaul.

Anderson's demanding personal schedule did little to improve DePaul's publicity drought. His medical school classes often lasted until 2 p.m. He'd then take the elevated train to the DePaul field where he put the Blue Demons through a two-hour practice. Occasionally a sportswriter would drop by after practice only to discover that Anderson had already bolted the premises either to attend a lecture or to study.

Determined to mold a winner, Anderson welcomed over 60 football candidates to DePaul that fall by holding three-a-day practices. Large doses of scrimmaging soon took their toll on the squad. By September 30, 15 players had sustained season-ending injuries.[5] Mercifully, Anderson halted all live contact the week of the season opener.

On October 3, 1925, the Blue Demons made Anderson's DePaul coaching debut a successful one with a 7 to 6 win over Fort Sheridan. Located on Chicago's North Side, Fort Sheridan was a military reservation for training U.S. Army officers. Although the Chicago papers printed the game's score, none provided a written account of the contest.

The following week DePaul hosted Elmhurst College. While scanning the sparse crowd behind the Blue Demon bench during warm-ups, Anderson spied his former quarterback, Albert "Cutie" Entringer, perched at the top of the grandstand. Columbia College, DePaul's next opponent, had an open date that weekend, and Elmer Layden, Anderson's successor at Columbia, could not scout the game in person. Instead, Layden sent Entringer, Columbia's senior captain, to scout DePaul with instructions to take copious notes.

Quickly assessing why Entringer was in attendance, Anderson flashed his crooked smile and drew the scout's attention with a wave of his arm. "Hey, Cutie," beckoned Anderson, "come down and watch the game with me on the bench!"[6]

Eddie Anderson as he appeared in the faculty section of the 1925 Columbia College yearbook, *Purgold*. Anderson taught physics, English and history at the college's feeder school, Columbia Academy. (Loras College Archives, Dubuque, Iowa)

Thrilled and flattered by his old coach's invitation, Entringer bounded eagerly down the grandstand steps to join Anderson. Watching together from the bench, Anderson charmed his former pupil as DePaul trounced Elmhurst 44 to 10. So engrossed was Entringer with Anderson's commentary and cordial banter that he failed to jot down a single note about DePaul.

"You know what kind of scouting report Entringer gave me upon his return," Layden wrote years later.[7]

The following week DePaul blanked Entringer and Columbia 12 to 0 to remain undefeated. It's doubtful that Anderson harbored any mixed feelings over defeating his ex-employer or former players. According to family members, Eddie rarely reflected on the past, preferring instead to focus on the task at hand or to work towards the future. Anderson's Sunday afternoons with the Cardinals were also productive. After dropping their season opener 10 to 6 to the Hammond Pros, Chicago reeled off four straight wins. The Cardinals' auspicious start was particularly gratifying for Anderson who had been elected the team's captain. Chicago's sportswriters hailed Anderson's yeoman-like play as a major reason for the Cardinals' success.

In the autumn of 1925, France and Germany signed the Locarno Pact, agreeing never to fight each other again and to respect a demilitarized zone along the Rhine. Guzlon Borglum announced he was starting work on Mount Rushmore, and the Pittsburgh Pirates defeated the Washington Senators in the World Series. Almost daily, papers heralded the upcoming court martial trial of Billy Mitchell. Colonel Mitchell accused his superiors of treason for not supporting air power as a cornerstone of national defense.

Eddie Anderson's imposing daily schedule, however, allowed him little time for staying abreast of current events. When not attending class, coaching or playing football, Eddie was burning the midnight oil over his medical books. To facilitate his medical studies, Anderson had a clause inserted in his contract exempting him from practicing with the Cardinals.[8] After spending most evenings studying, the seemingly indefatigable Anderson conditioned for Sundays' gridiron wars by taking late-night runs along Lake Michigan. As he ran in the dark, he'd review the plays he had to remember for Sunday or anticipate the questions he'd be answering the next day on a medical quiz. Fortunately, in 1925, the Cardinals played all of their games in Chicago. With no road trips, the steadfast Anderson spent weekend nights at home poring over an anatomy text instead of struggling to study while fighting the soporiferous swaying of a Rock Island Railroad car.

While playing with the Cards on Sundays afforded Anderson an outlet from his ascetic life as a medical student, the respite was sometimes a painful one. One of Anderson's toughest games in 1925 came in early November against the Duluth Kelleys. Playing opposite Anderson that day was Duluth end Bob "Rube" Marshall. At age 45, Marshall was the oldest player in the league.[9] A former standout at Minnesota in 1906, he became one of the first African-Americans to play professional football when he joined the Rock Island Independents in 1920. After a four-year hiatus from pro ball, the 6' 2" and 195-pound Wisconsin native was now making a comeback. Despite having lost a few steps, Marshall still possessed a sledgehammer-like forearm with which he battered opponents black and blue.

The underdog Kelleys gave Anderson's Cardinals all they could handle. Trailing 6 to 3 in the game's waning moments, Chicago quarterback Red

Dunn lofted a 40-yard touchdown pass to Hal Erickson to give the Cardinals a 10 to 6 win.

Still sporting bumps and bruises from his battle with Marshall, Anderson was back in the line-up the following week when the Cardinals kicked off to the Green Bay Packers in a blizzard. With just over three minutes remaining, quarterback Red Dunn's pass bounced off the hands of intended receiver Paddy Driscoll and into the arms of the opportunistic Anderson. Clutching the slippery pigskin for dear life, Eddie lumbered the final 10 yards through the snow and mud to tie the score at 6.[10] Although Green Bay blocked Driscoll's extra-point attempt, Driscoll, whom Anderson once described as having a "heart like a blowtorch," still emerged as the game's hero by drop-kicking a last-minute 27-yard field goal to give Chicago a 9 to 6 win.[11] The Cardinals' record now stood at 6 wins and 1 loss.

In 1925, Anderson would have more on his Thanksgiving plate than turkey and cranberries. Not only was DePaul hosting St. Viator at 3 p.m. for the Western Interstate Conference (WIC) Championship, but Anderson's Cardinals were also scheduled to play the Bears at Cub Park at eleven o'clock that same morning. With the Bears' recent signing of famed All-American Red Grange, the cross-town rematch took on epic proportions.

Harold "Red" Grange had exploded onto the national scene in the dedicatory game for the University of Illinois Memorial Stadium in 1924. Incredibly, Grange's four touches of the ball in the game's first 12 minutes resulted in scoring runs of 95, 67, 56 and 44 yards. After sitting out the second quarter, Grange scored a fifth touchdown and threw for a sixth in the second half as Illinois clobbered Michigan 39 to 14.

Grange's Herculean feat was splashed across the front page of every sports section in America. Sportswriters dubbed him the "Galloping Ghost," a moniker that fired the imaginations of sports fans everywhere. Grange also earned the appellation, the "Wheaton Iceman," after millions viewed newsreels of the muscular halfback delivering blocks of ice while working a summer job in his hometown of Wheaton.

By early autumn of 1925, speculation was rampant that Grange would quit school and turn pro after his last college game. In fact, Grange had contracted with an agent named C.C. Pyle, a theater owner in local Champaign to manage all of his business affairs. Pro teams, movie companies, vaudeville acts and advertising firms were all wooing the gridiron hero.

On November 21, only hours after the "Galloping Ghost" led Illinois to victory at Ohio State before 85,000 adoring fans, rumor turned to fact. To no one's surprise, Grange announced that he was leaving school to play pro football for the Chicago Bears. The announcement sparked a storm of controversy, with college coaches once again railing against professionalism tainting the purity of college sport. Supposedly, Grange's decision so incensed Illinois coach Bob Zuppke that it would be three years before he again deigned to speak to his former All-American halfback.

The next day, while Anderson and his Cardinal teammates were blanking the Dayton Triangles 14 to 0, across town at Cub Park Red Grange sat on the Bears' bench in street clothes watching his new teammates thump Green Bay. Grange would make his professional debut four days later, on Thanksgiving, against Anderson's Cardinals.

Monday morning's *Chicago Tribune* pictured Grange in cap and raccoon coat next to a story speculating on the Illinois All-American's future paydays. One report had Grange and manager C.C. Pyle splitting the Thanksgiving Day gate 50/50 with the Bears, thus giving credence to gossip that Pyle's initials, C.C., stood for "Cash and Carry." Another rumor claimed Grange was guaranteed $2,000 per game, as well as 10% on the first $5,000 taken in at the gate, 20% on the second $5,000 and 40% of every dollar beyond that.[12]

Sportswriters ballyhooed Grange's pro football debut as the most anticipated sporting event in the city's history. With the exception of Johnny Mohardt, all of Chicago bubbled with excitement. Mohardt, Anderson's former Irish and Cardinal teammate, had signed to play left halfback with the Bears in 1925. The addition of the superstar Grange now relegated Mohardt to the bench.

Anderson, who rarely had time for recreational reading, now perused newspaper accounts of Grange's impending payday. Realizing that the "Galloping Ghost" stood to collect a paycheck nearly 10 times what the entire Cardinal team would earn for the day motivated Anderson and company to stop Grange dead in his tracks.

Over 36,000 fans turned out to see the Thanksgiving Day contest at Cub Park — nearly tripling the attendance of the teams' October meeting at Comiskey Park. It was the largest crowd Eddie Anderson had ever played before and that included his years at Notre Dame. The fans' anticipation in the stands matched the players' intensity on the field. It would be a thrilling game, well played and characterized by precise execution and crisp blocking and tackling.

With Anderson doing his customary yeoman's work at right end, the Cardinal defense stymied Grange on every sweep he ran. Overall, the Cardinals' inspired play held the Illinois All-American to just 36 yards on 13 carries. His longest run from scrimmage was seven yards. Wheaton's Iceman also failed to complete a pass in six attempts. After Grange zigzagged for a 20-yard return on the Cards' first punt of the day, cagey Paddy Driscoll booted his remaining punts where Grange couldn't field them.

Chicago's most ballyhooed sporting event ended in a frustrating scoreless tie. After the game Eddie and Paddy Driscoll were walking off the field several yards behind Grange and his Bear teammates. As the group approached the tunnel leading under the grandstands, disgruntled fans greeted them with a storm of boos. Amidst the jeering, Mrs. Driscoll joined her husband on the field. Believing the fans to be venting their frustration over Grange's mediocre debut, Driscoll remarked, "Boy, those fans sure are mad at Red." To which his wife replied, "Paddy, they're not upset with Red. They're upset with you for consistently punting the ball to Joey Sternaman instead of to Grange!"[13]

"If one of us was going to look bad," Driscoll later explained to reporters, "it wasn't going to be me. Punting to Grange is like grooving a pitch to Babe Ruth."[14]

Anderson had no time to dwell on the historic contest. Showering and dressing quickly, Eddie caught a ride to DePaul Field to coach his Blue Demons against St. Viator. It's unknown if Anderson was on time for the 3 p.m. kick-off. Whether punctual or not, it's interesting to speculate about how much coaching Anderson actually did that day, for playing 60 minutes against the Bears that morning must have left Eddie both physically and emotionally drained.

Whatever Anderson's coaching contributions, they weren't enough, as St. Viator prevailed 13 to 0. Despite the loss, DePaul's final record of 4 wins, 2 losses and 1 tie allowed the Blue Demons to back into a tie for the WIC championship.

When the gate receipts from the Bears-Cardinals' Thanksgiving Day game were tallied and dispersed, Red Grange and manager C.C. Pyle split over $12,000.[15] If there were any lingering doubts as to Grange's marquee value, they vanished three days later when the Bears beat Columbus in a snowstorm before 28,000 fans. Across town, Anderson's first place Cardinals blanked Rock Island 7 to 0 before barely 3,000 fans.

Cardinals' owner Chris O'Brien then scheduled a game against the Pottsville Maroons for December 6 at Comiskey Park. Located in Pennsylvania's anthracite coal country, Dr. J.G. Striegel's Maroons were enjoying tremendous success in their maiden NFL season. With 9 wins and 2 losses, the Maroons sported the best record among the league's eastern entries. At 9 wins, 110ss and 1 tie, a win over the Maroons would seemingly give O'Brien's Cardinals the undisputed league championship. By laying claim to the title, O'Brien hoped to entice George Halas' Grange-led Bears to a rematch on December 20. This time, however, rather than accept a $1,200 guarantee as he had in the teams' Thanksgiving Day meeting, O'Brien held out for a percentage of what surely would be a lucrative gate. To O'Brien, winning the championship was secondary to reaping a hefty payday for his financially strapped Cardinals.

It was 18 degrees and snowing when Anderson's Cardinals took the field against Pottsville. The visitors led 7 to 0 lead in the second quarter when Maroon half back "Hoots" Flannagan sustained a broken collarbone. The mishap proved to be the game's turning point, but not for the reason one might think. As Flannagan staggered to the sidelines, Walter French trotted into the huddle to replace him.

As the *Chicago Tribune* reported on December 7, "It was Mr. French more than anyone else on the Pottsville team who wrecked the Chicago title hopes. He bobbed up in play after play and the yardage he gained would make Red Grange sit up and check back in his notebook."

This was the same Walter French who had given Anderson and his Irish teammates fits at West Point in 1920. It was French whose 60-yard punt return around Anderson's end resulted in Rockne's tongue-lashing of the Mason City youngster at halftime.[16] It must have seemed like déjà vu for Eddie when, only four plays after entering the game, French bolted around Anderson's right end position and broke three tackles en route to a 30-yard touchdown run. Unlike Notre Dame in 1920, the Cardinals had no George Gipp in the line-up to spark a second half comeback, and Pottsville rolled to a 21 to 7 win.

The loss left Cardinals owner Chris O'Brien despondent. With the Cards now apparently denied the league crown, George Halas had no incentive to delay his Bears' post-season exhibition tour to grant the Cards a rematch. Realizing his dreams of netting a financial bonanza hinged on a December 20 rematch, O'Brien set about salvaging his team's title hopes.

As the *Chicago Tribune* reported, the 1925 league rules maintained "that each club must play at least eight games against eight different clubs to be eligible for the championship, but any club can play as many games against other clubs as it desires up to December 20. On that date the team with the highest standing (winning percentage) is declared the champion."[17]

By notching a few more wins before the December 20 deadline, the Cardinals could reclaim the title and restore the marquee value of a rematch with the Bears. O'Brien quickly sought to remedy the situation by scheduling two additional games against teams that had disbanded weeks earlier — the Milwaukee Badgers and the Hammond Pros.

Although Milwaukee had disbanded on November 22, O'Brien telephoned the Badgers' Chicago-based owner, Ambrose McGurk, and persuaded him to field a team against the Cards on Thursday, December 10. Unable to regroup within just four days, Milwaukee resorted to enlisting four 17-year-olds from Chicago's Englewood High School. Cognizant of, and possibly feeling guilty about, the impending mismatch, O'Brien refused to charge admission and limited play to five-minute quarters.[18] He also relegated his star player, Paddy Driscoll, to the bench. Nevertheless, the abbreviated game was still a laugher as the Cardinals coasted to a 59 to 0 victory.

It's undetermined as to whether Anderson broke away from his mid-week medical classes to play in the Milwaukee game. However, Eddie played the entire 60 minutes two days later when the Cards blanked Hammond 13 to 0. Although Hammond scraped together a competitive team, the Pros were but a skeleton of the club that had defeated the Cards 10 to 6 in September.

O'Brien's eleventh-hour machinations to salvage his title hopes proved to be unnecessary. In a bizarre turn of events, the Pottsville Maroons had scheduled an exhibition game against an alumni team of Notre Dame All-Stars at Philadelphia's Shibe Park on December 12. The impending contest, however, drew a shrill outcry from the league's other Pennsylvania franchise, the Frankford Yellow Jackets. As related in *75 Seasons, The Complete Story of the National Football League*, "The Frankford franchise protested to the league,

Souvenir photo of the 1925 NFL Champion Chicago Cardinals. Eddie Anderson, who captained the squad, is pictured left of the football. Pictured inside the football is coach Norm Barry. Barry and Anderson were also teammates at Notre Dame. (Courtesy of the Arizona Cardinals Football Club)

saying the Maroons were violating the Yellow Jackets' territorial rights. League president Joe Carr agreed and ordered the game canceled. But the Maroons, claiming the NFL office had given verbal approval, played the game and posted a 9 to 7 victory."[19]

Carr then suspended the Pottsville franchise, freezing the Maroon's record at 10 wins and 2 losses. Meanwhile, the breaking story that four high school students had played for the Milwaukee Badgers in the December 10 loss to the Cardinals stirred a nationwide scandal.

The students in question were Bill Thompson, Jack Daniels, James Snyder and Charles Richardson. Although the boys received no money for playing, they did willfully play under the assumed names of Blood, Mooney, Mason and Grant. When the Chicago public schools' investigation brought these facts to light, all four boys — high school juniors — were banned from future interscholastic competition.[20] The investigation also revealed that a Cardinal player, Art Folz, had a hand in recruiting the so-called "Englewood Four" to play for Milwaukee.

The ultimate irony in O'Brien's quest for a Bears' rematch occurred on the same day that the Cards were clobbering Milwaukee's makeshift outfit 59 to 0. In the Bears' December 10 exhibition at Pittsburgh's Forbes Field, Red Grange sustained an arm injury that sidelined him for nearly three weeks.[21] Had the December 20 Cards-Bears' rematch materialized, which it did not, Grange, the game's major attraction, would have been unable to play anyway.

On December 29, Joe Carr completed the league's investigation of the Milwaukee game. Acting swiftly, Carr fined Milwaukee owner Ambrose McGurk $500 and expelled him from the league. He then gave McGurk 90 days to divest himself of the team's assets. Cardinals' owner Chris O'Brien was placed on one-year probation and fined $1,000, while quarterback Art Folz was "barred forever from playing in the National Football League."[22] Furthermore, the Cardinals' December win over Milwaukee was to be expunged from the record leaving Chicago with a final 1925 record of 10 wins, 2 losses and 1 tie. (Despite Carr's mandate, the Cardinals' win over Milwaukee was never expunged from the official NFL records and Folz would later play in the league.)

On that same day Carr fined Pottsville $500 and revoked the team's franchise for violating the territorial rights of the Frankford Yellow Jackets. He did, however, agree to allow the Maroons' owner, Dr. J.G. Striegel, to plead his case before a league meeting of team owners on February 6, 1926. At the February meeting Striegel's protest fell on deaf ears and Pottsville remained banned from the league.

In their 1981 co-authored article, "The Discarded Championship," Joe

Horrigan, Bob Braunwart and Bob Carroll describe what happened next: "However, when it came to awarding the 1925 championship, a new snag developed ... word arrived from Chris O'Brien that the Cardinals would not 'accept' the championship. The decision, of course, was the league's to make, not O'Brien's, but the vote was tabled... The NFL never actually went through the formality of awarding the 1925 championship to anyone!

"The distinction is, of course, purely technical. The Cardinals were indisputably the league champs, and later Redbird owners have had no scruples about claiming the 1925 title as part of the Cardinal heritage."[23]

The matter was never an issue for Eddie Anderson, who always maintained that he captained the 1925 NFL Champions.

Eddie Anderson easily made the coaching transition from football to basketball in December of 1925. In only the university's third year of varsity hoops, Anderson guided the "Red and Blue" to the WIC Championship with an overall record of 11 wins and 5 losses.

During his four seasons at DePaul's basketball helm, Anderson's teams won 25 and lost 21. In 1929, the increasing demands of his medical pursuits combined with his responsibilities as a newly married man compelled Anderson to give up coaching basketball.

9

1926: ONE
WHIRLWIND YEAR

The twenties ushered in the "noble experiment" known as prohibition. America's urban areas never embraced the ban on alcoholic beverages. As a result rumrunners smuggled whiskey into the country from Canada and the Caribbean. Resourceful entrepreneurs bootlegged bathtub gin and speakeasies flourished as venal local authorities turned a blind eye. By the mid-twenties Chicago had become a battleground between rival gangs for control of the liquor traffic, with Al "Scarface" Capone eventually emerging as the city's kingpin of crime.

Such was the Windy City on March 17, 1926, when Mary Broderick attended a St. Patrick's Day party on Chicago's North Side. Her date for the evening was a Notre Dame graduate named Mart McNally. Many Notre Dame alumni were in attendance including several of Mart's classmates.

During the course of the evening Mary happened to notice a nattily attired man staring at her from across the room. At second glance, he appeared to be silently mouthing words to her. Although terribly shy, Mary was curious about the handsome stranger's behavior and occasionally cast a stealthy glance his way. Each stolen glance, however, revealed the man repeatedly mouthing the same phrase. After several minutes Mary realized that the man was silently telling her, "You're beautiful!"[1]

The handsome stranger was Eddie Anderson.

Over the next few weeks the young coach and the comely daughter of a Chicago policeman began dating. It was far from a whirlwind romance, however, as Eddie's medical studies and football and Mary's evening classes at the University of Chicago often kept them apart for weeks.

The daughter of Irish immigrants, Mary Broderick was born in Manchester, New Hampshire, in 1903, and moved to Chicago with her family as a teenager. One summer, while vacationing in New England, Mary entered a beauty contest and was crowned Miss Winnipesaukee. Today that would be the equivalent of being voted Miss New Hampshire. With the crown and her natural beauty, Mary procured modeling jobs at several of Chicago's fashionable department stores. Attractive and intelligent, Mary had many suitors. However, after their St. Patrick's Day meeting, Mary soon set her sights on Eddie, who in turn, only had eyes for Mary.

The romance blossomed, and on February 11, 1929, three days before the infamous St. Valentine's Day Massacre on the city's North Side, Eddie and Mary were married in Chicago's Resurrection Church.

In late January of 1926, two months before Eddie met Mary, Chicago Bears owner George Halas met with Red Grange and his business manager, C.C. Pyle, to discuss the "Galloping Ghost's" contract renewal. Touting his client as the nation's hottest box office attraction, Pyle had the *chutzpah* to demand that he and Grange each be allotted one-third of the Bears' 1926 gate receipts, with Halas and co-owner Ed "Dutch" Sternaman sharing the remaining third.

The Bears only survived the league's fly-by-night early years because of Halas' penchant for squeezing a dime from a nickel. The tight-fisted Halas wouldn't become the NFL's equivalent of "The Godfather" by wilting under pressure. Indignant at Pyle's proposal, Halas broke off negotiations.

When NFL team owners convened the following month in Detroit, Grange and Pyle were in attendance. The pair informed the owners that they had secured a lease for New York's Yankee Stadium and were now petitioning for their own NFL franchise. This scenario alarmed Giants owner Tim Mara, who held exclusive territorial rights to the city. Regarding territorial rights as the linchpin of the league's infrastructure, Commissioner Joe Carr perceived the duo's request as a threat to the integrity of the league. He therefore denied Grange and Pyle their bid for a franchise.

Undeterred, the duo soon announced their plans to form a new league. They named it the American Football League (AFL) and envisioned their own New York entry as its flagship franchise. Pyle's plan proved to be more than bluster. By mid-summer the upstart league consisted of nine teams. In addition to New York, clubs sprouted in Boston, Brooklyn, Cleveland, Newark and Philadelphia. Adding insult to injury, the NFL's Rock Island Independents jumped ship to join the new league.

Wilson's Wildcats, a traveling team comprised of West Coast All-Stars, also joined the AFL. With no home field, the team took its name from former

University of Washington All-American halfback George Wilson, who as player-coach ramrodded the nomadic band.

It was the budding league's ninth entry, however, that jolted the NFL. In a master stroke, star Chicago Bear halfback Joey Sternaman secured a lease for Comiskey Park. Armed with his signed lease and the belief that Red Grange's marquee appeal would sell out the South Side stadium, Sternaman traveled to New York where C.C. Pyle granted him the league's Chicago franchise.

The fallout sent Chris O'Brien scurrying to locate a new home for his evicted Cardinals, a home he soon found at Chicago's Normal Park at 61st and Racine. Joey Sternaman's coup also drove a permanent wedge between his brother, Ed "Dutch" Sternaman, and George Halas, co-owners of the Bears. The partners endured an icy relationship until Halas succeeded in buying Dutch out after the 1932 season.[2]

Calling his fledgling team the Bulls, Sternaman immediately set about signing name players. At the top of his recruiting list was Eddie Anderson. Sternaman and Anderson had first crossed paths in the infamous Carlinville-Taylorville game of 1921. As one of nine Illinois ringers playing for Taylorville, Sternaman's three second-half field goals had sealed a 16 to 0 win over a Carlinville team comprised of Anderson and seven other ringers from Notre Dame.

It's uncertain as to why Anderson joined the Bulls in 1926. He probably was enticed by the promise of more money. Perhaps Anderson was leery of spending another season with the financially strapped Chicago Cardinals. It was common knowledge that Cardinals owner Chris O'Brien sold the contract of his star player, Paddy Driscoll, to the cross-town Bears to procure operating funds for the upcoming season.[3] If money was the reason for Anderson jumping ship, little did he know he was leaping from the frying pan into the fire.

It proved to be a year of fateful decisions for Anderson, who changed not only his football allegiance, but also medical schools. That fall he left Loyola to continue his medical studies at Chicago's prestigious Rush Medical School, which had originally denied Eddie admission in 1925.

On September 19, 1926, a week before the Bulls' season opener, the *Chicago Tribune* reported, "the Disabled Veterans of the World War and the Chicago Marines club brought suit in the Superior court of Cook County against William S. "Big Bill" Edwards, Charles C. Pyle and Red Grange, officials of the newly organized American League of Professional football clubs, and Joe Sternaman, manager of the Bulls.

"The plaintiffs charge that Pyle promised the Disabled War Veterans the Chicago franchise in the league for a team known as the Chicago Marines."

The petitioners claimed that they incurred $10,000 in expenses meeting Pyle's request to secure Soldiers' Field as a home stadium, only to have Pyle later grant the franchise to Sternaman. The veterans' group was seeking a restraining order to keep the Chicago Bulls from operating in the city as well as compensatory damages. Although the court denied the restraining order, it was an omen for the Bulls and the ill-fated AFL.

The Bulls opened league play by traveling to New Jersey on Sunday, September 26 to meet Newark at Davids Stadium. Eddie Anderson set up Chicago's only touchdown by hauling in a 38-yard pass from player-coach Joey Sternaman to put the ball at Newark's 2-yard line. The contest then turned into a punting duel until the second half when Doug Wycoff's 1-yard scoring run and extra-point kick earned Newark a 7 to 7 tie.

The following week the Bulls endured another tedious train trip east. To save future travel costs, the frugal Sternaman scheduled two games in two days. On Saturday, October 2, the Philadelphia Quakers hosted the Bulls at Sesquicentennial Field before 8,000 curious spectators. In a brutally played contest, Philadelphia's Al Kruez kicked three second-half field goals to give the Quakers a 9 to 3 win.

Battered and bruised, the Bulls then trudged aboard a train for the 90-mile trip north to New York. The next day over 7,000 fans turned out to see Harry Stuhldreher, one of Notre Dame's famed Four Horsemen, work his gridiron heroics for the Brooklyn Horsemen. Hoping to give his first team a sorely needed rest, Sternaman started only two of Saturday's starting eleven against Brooklyn.[4] After a scoreless first quarter Anderson and the other regulars entered the game and quickly scored on Sternaman's 8-yard run. However, the road-weary Bulls wilted in the second half. Brooklyn's Earl Britton, who had been the blocking back for Red Grange at Illinois, scored on a 1-yard run before a long touchdown pass to Ed Harrison gave the Horsemen a 12 to 7 win.

During the numbing train ride back to Chicago, Anderson doggedly pored over his medical texts. Although grateful for the extra paycheck, Eddie was already being worn down by the young season. Not only were the Bulls winless in three games, but the two consecutive eastern road trips forced Anderson to miss three days of med-school classes. Catching up would require Anderson to burn the late-night oil even longer in the week ahead.

Then there were Anderson's coaching duties at DePaul. His initial optimism about the Blue Demons' impending season suffered a setback when the team's most talented halfback, Howard "Count" Gaffney, was lost for the year with a broken arm.[5] Anderson knew he could bring the young team around, but it would take longer than originally planned.

The Bulls' tailspin continued in Rock Island on October 10. True to form, Chicago scored first when John Mohardt's 25-yard pass to Anderson set up Sternaman's 19-yard field goal. Also true to form, the Bulls' opponents dominated the second half. Behind the thrashing runs of Ed Novak, Rock Island rallied to win 7 to 3.

Unfortunately, the flood of early-season setbacks continued for Anderson as his DePaul squad matched the Bulls' three-game losing streak. The most painful loss occurred on October 16 at Eddie's old stomping grounds — the campus of Columbia College in Dubuque. Richard Carberry, whose older brother, Glenn, succeeded Eddie as Notre Dame's football captain in 1922, accounted for all of Columbia's points in eking out an 8 to 7 win.

One wonders about the mindset of the Bulls' players as they dressed for the kick-off on October 17. Earlier that week the *Chicago Tribune* reported, "When Red Grange and his New York Yankee grid team dash forth at Sox park Sunday afternoon they not only will meet determined players intent on humbling the Redhead but a team with its back to the wall fighting for existence. For Joe Sternaman, quarterback-owner of the Bulls, has told his men to win or expect to be cut off the payroll."

On Saturday, October 16, the *Tribune* echoed the desperate sentiment, referring to "...the Bulls, who are supposed to lose their livelihoods unless they stop Red and his Yanks...."

Playing the first four games on the road had drained Sternaman's financial resources. Any hope of Sternaman seeing his club finish the season now hinged on the ability of Grange's Yankees to draw a healthy gate. It remained to be seen how many fans would pay to see the "Galloping Ghost" play against the winless Bulls when across town that very afternoon the Bears and Cardinals, both undefeated, were renewing their bloody rivalry.

The match was also hyped as a showdown between Sternaman and Grange. Having watched both play as backfield teammates with the Bears in 1925, some Chicago fans now hailed Sternaman as the superior player. As it turned out neither Grange nor Sternaman played a decisive role in the game's outcome. After a scoreless first half, Johnny Mohardt's two touchdown runs and the Bulls' tenacious defense gave Chicago a 14 to 0 upset win. More importantly, over 16,000 paying customers witnessed the Bulls victory — 4,000 more than had attended the Bears-Cardinals game. Although Sternaman had hoped for a bigger crowd, the day's gate receipts nevertheless proved to be a lifeline for the financially beleaguered Bulls.

The hero of the game was Anderson's good friend, Johnny Mohardt, who as the contest's leading rusher scored both Chicago touchdowns.[6] Anderson and Mohardt had been teammates for six years — four at Notre Dame and two with the Cardinals. The act split up when Mohardt signed to play with

Racine in 1924. In 1925 Mohardt joined the Bears and promptly became the team's starting halfback before being benched in favor of Grange late in the season. Blanking Grange's Yankees was payback for Mohardt.

When reunited with the Bulls in 1926, Anderson and Mohardt had more in common than just being teammates. Like Anderson, Mohardt aspired to become a doctor and was now enrolled at Northwestern Medical School. He later received a fellowship from the Mayo Clinic in Rochester and eventually served on the staffs of Northwestern Medical School and Cook County Hospital.[7] During World War II, the Pittsburgh native enlisted in the U.S. Army Medical Corps and served in North Africa and Italy. Before retiring, Mohardt served as the chief surgeon of the Veterans Administration Hospital in Fort Bayard, New Mexico, and as assistant director of the VA's surgical service in Washington, D.C.

Years later in recounting Mohardt's football talents to his sons, Anderson proffered an assessment that many loyal Irish fans would regard as iconoclastic. "Mohardt was outstanding. In fact, he may have been a better football player than George Gipp!"[8]

After defeating New York, the Bulls caught fire, winning four and tying two of their next six games. Unfortunately, the attendance figures at Comiskey Park did not parallel the team's meteoric rise on the field. In successive home victories over Cleveland and Boston, the Bulls drew crowds of only 3,000 and 3,800 respectively. In a 3 to 3 tie with the Wilson Wildcats on November 7, the Comiskey crowd was so sparse that the attendance wasn't even announced.

On November 14, the league-leading Philadelphia Quakers visited the Windy City. Only 2,500 fans endured a steady drizzle to watch the Bulls knock the Quakers out of first place with a 3 to 0 upset win. The free fall in attendance continued the following week when just 1,500 die-hard fans witnessed the Bulls eke out another 3 to 0 win over Rock Island.

The combination of Mohardt's running and passing, solid defense and Joey Sternaman's kicking all factored into Chicago's newfound winning ways. The 5'6" and 162-pound Sternaman honed dropkicking to a fine art. In the Bulls' 19 to 12 win over Cleveland on October 24, Sternaman's two field goal and extra-point kicks provided the margin of victory. The next day the *Chicago Tribune* described why Sternaman's dropkicking was so effective. "Sternaman has a specially constructed shoe for his dropkicking that seems never to miss. It looks a good bit like a cigar box. Twice during the contest Joe [signaled] to the bench to have the shoe rushed into service, and after the three points were made he changed back to his regular boot."

After another Sternaman field goal beat the Philadelphia Quakers, the *Tribune* again extolled Sternaman and his innovative kicking shoe. "Right there was where Little Joe called for his trick shoe. It looks a good deal like a slab of chewing tobacco. He cast away his regular shoe and buckled on the square-toed slab. Then he moved back to the 26-yard line, just about where the pitcher's [mound] is located on the diamond, and booted the ball between the goal posts for victory."

If accurate, the *Tribune's* accounts refute the traditional belief that Ben Agajanian first employed the square-toed kicking shoe in the mid–1940s.[9] The shoe was a necessity for Agajanian, who lost the toes on his kicking foot in an industrial accident. After the mishap, Agajanian had a shoemaker fit him with a square-toed shoe so he could still kick. Before the advent of soccer-style kickers, Agajanian became pro football's first kicking specialist in a career that spanned three decades with over a half-dozen teams.

Unfortunately, the wins that Sternaman and his "miracle boot" provided could not staunch the Bulls' financial bleeding. The league's money woes were not limited to Chicago. Poor weather and low scoring contests hurt attendance everywhere. By mid-season the wheels began to come off the AFL's wagon. In October the Newark franchise ceased operations. The Cleveland Panthers folded on November 5, and the Brooklyn Horsemen quit the league on November 13. In Brooklyn's case, the NFL's Brooklyn Lions absorbed the Horsemen and finished the season as the "Brooklion Horsemen."[10]

Eddie Anderson's pro football career ended mysteriously. He played his last game for the Bulls in a 3 to 0 win over Rock Island on November 21. Four days later at Comiskey Park, Anderson was not suited up when the Bulls kicked off to the Wilson Wildcats on Thanksgiving morning. Instead, he was across town at DePaul Field preparing his Blue Demons to meet St. Viator.

Despite a rough start, Anderson's DePaul squad turned things around behind the quarterbacking of Eddie Hussey. Beginning his collegiate career at Columbia College, Hussey followed Anderson to DePaul to play for the Blue Demons. With Hussey at the controls DePaul developed a potent aerial attack that led to impressive wins over Wisconsin-LaCrosse and Valparaiso. Unfortunately, Hussey was carried from the field late in the Valparaiso game with a fractured ankle and two broken ribs.[11]

With little Eddie Saggau substituting for the fallen Hussey at quarterback, DePaul rolled up 12 first downs and completed 7 of 10 passes in defeating St. Viator 7 to 0. The upset win enabled DePaul to share a three-way tie for the WIC Championship with Columbia College and St. Viator. Anderson had now coached teams to three consecutive WIC titles.

When the Bulls departed for New York on Friday, November 26, Anderson was not aboard the train. Nor did Anderson suit up for the Bulls' two remaining home games in December. The Chicago papers gave no explanation for Anderson's absence and years later his four children had no knowledge that their father had ever played for the Bulls. Could Anderson have been released? It's possible, but unlikely, as Anderson still seemed to be on top of his game. It's possible that Anderson may have sustained an injury that ended his playing days. Perhaps he grew weary of collecting bumps and bruises on Sunday afternoons, or he reached a point where he felt continuing to play would jeopardize his coaching duties at DePaul and/or his medical studies. The Bulls' tenuous financial situation may also have influenced his decision to hang it up. In any case, it's all speculation.

What is known, however, is that after Anderson's departure the Bulls stopped winning. The team lost three and tied one of their four remaining games to finish with a record of 5 wins, 6 losses and 3 ties. Although limping financially, at least the Bulls played out the schedule. In late November, Rock Island became the fourth team to drop out of the moribund league. The Philadelphia Quakers went on to win the league's only championship as the league folded after the 1926 season.

In the NFL's official history, *75 Seasons,* Joey Sternaman reflected on his Chicago Bulls' experience: "It was a big gamble and I got talked into making it. It seemed like a real good thing at the time. We actually had a pretty good team and we beat Red and his New York Yankees. But we didn't get the crowds and we just couldn't make it go. I came out broke ... it was a bum gamble."[12]

10

THE DePAUL YEARS

Several rule changes affected college football in 1927. First, the goal posts were moved from the goal line to the back line of the end zone.[1] The change had mixed results. While moving the goal posts back 10 yards reduced the number of successful extra points and field goals, it also encouraged passing within an opponent's 10-yard line that resulted in more touchdowns being scored. Previously, teams had been reluctant to throw into an opponent's end zone because if a pass struck either goal post or the cross bar, the play was immediately blown dead and ruled a touchback for the defensive team.

Another change that directly impacted DePaul was the so-called "freshman" rule. As cited in Chapter Two, because of the manpower shortage during World War I, freshmen were declared eligible for varsity competition in 1918. Many institutions continued the practice after the war and had grown dependent upon having freshmen bolster their varsity ranks. DePaul was one such school. But freshmen were now again barred from varsity competition and Anderson found himself entering the season with only a 20-man varsity roster.[2]

There would be no WIC Championship for DePaul in 1927. As some consolation, the Blue Demons played well in games that held special significance for Anderson. Sandwiched between an opening loss to St. Viator and a thumping at the hands of Tulsa, DePaul managed a 14 to 14 tie against Eddie's former employer, Columbia College.

The season's most anticipated match-up came against Loyola University at Wrigley Field on October 29. (The name Wrigley Field superseded the stadium's previous moniker of Cub Park.) Billed as the "Championship of Chicago's North Side," the Catholic schools were meeting for the first time since 1922 when DePaul had prevailed 12 to 6. That contest had been so

98

fraught with cursing and fighting that DePaul's Vincentian priests and their Jesuit counterparts at Loyola agreed to a five-year respite from meeting on the gridiron.

Adding spice to the rivalry's renewal was the fact that Anderson would be matching coaching wits with his former teammate, Roger Kiley. As senior ends at Notre Dame, both had earned All-American recognition. South Bend journalists referred to the seemingly inseparable pair as Damon and Pythias.[3] (In classic Greek legend, Damian and Pythias had been so devoted to each other that when Pythias, who had been condemned to death, wanted time to arrange his affairs, Damon pledged his life that his friend would return for the execution.) Kiley, who would eventually become a U.S. Appellate Court Judge for the Seventh District, began coaching at Loyola in 1922 to pay his way through law school. Neither man, however, would allow friendship to interfere with winning.

Seeking yet another human-interest angle on the North Side showdown, the *Chicago Tribune* erroneously reported that Anderson was still a medical student at Loyola, and would be coaching against his own school.[4] In reality, Anderson had departed Loyola the previous year for Rush Medical School.

Over 15,000 fans turned out to witness a hard-fought, clean game. Anderson's Blue Demons drew first blood when a nifty 55-yard pass play from Ed Hussey to Howard Gaffney set up fullback Duke Dolowy's short touchdown run. Dolowy later scored again to give DePaul a 12 to 6 win. It was the identical score of their 1922 game.

There were only salutations and smiles when Anderson and Kiley met at mid-field for the post-game handshake. The moment was the highlight of DePaul's 1927 season, for the Blue Demons lost their last three games to finish with a record of 1 win, 5 losses and 1 tie. It would be the nadir of Anderson's seven-year tenure at DePaul.

The 1927–28 basketball season was no brighter for Eddie. For whatever reason, DePaul played only a seven-game schedule and managed but two wins.

The opponents on DePaul's 1928 football schedule may well have been plucked from a grab bag. Home victories over Crane Junior College and the reserve squads from the Universities of Illinois and Minnesota were offset by road losses at Detroit, Tulsa and St. Mary's of San Antonio, Texas.

On October 13, Anderson's Blue Demons wilted in Oklahoma's 90-degree heat before a relentless Tulsa defense whose two interceptions and blocked punt led to three touchdowns in the Golden Hurricane's 27 to 0 win. The loss left Eddie fuming.

Upon the team's return to Chicago, Anderson sought to toughen his squad by arranging a mid-week scrimmage against the Los Angeles Fire Department football team.[5] Coached by former California star, Bill Blewett, the firemen were in transit east to meet the New York City Fire Department's eleven. (Five days later, on October 21, Blewett's club routed the New Yorkers 57 to 0 before 36,000 fans at the Polo Grounds.) Neither squad scored during the 90-minute scrimmage in what proved to be a prelude to DePaul's scoreless tie with the University of Des Moines that Saturday.

The roller coaster 1928 season peaked with DePaul's homecoming game against Niagara University on November 11. Played for charity, the contest's proceeds were earmarked for the Sisters of Mercy to build an addition to the John B. Murphy Memorial Hospital.[6] In anticipation of a big crowd, the game's site was switched to Soldier Field. Many of the city's most prominent citizens embraced the event by purchasing tickets in bunches.

Ensconced in their box seats, Cardinal Mundelin and the Right Reverend Bernard J. Shirl, auxiliary bishop of the Chicago Diocese, beamed with delight while scanning the crowd of 44,000 paying customers, a delight that usually only accompanied the bounty harvested from passing the plate among a parish of generous donors.

DePaul had lost both of its previous meetings with Niagara, but Anderson now had his players primed to kick off before the largest crowd in the school's history. From the start the Blue Demon defense blanketed Niagara's wide-open attack. Not once did Niagara threaten to score. On offense, DePaul quarterback Ed Hussey's play calling kept the visitors off balance all afternoon. The star of the game, however, was Blue Demon halfback Clair "Skeet" Byers. A transfer student from the University of Iowa, Byers consistently scampered for large chunks of yardage.

In the vernacular of the day, *Chicago Tribune* sportswriter Arch Ward wrote: "It was he [Byers] who scooted around their flanks and off the tackles for repeated gains. He was like a ghost, this DePaul flash — a shadowy, intangible something that mocked at Niagara tacklers. When Byers had the ball Niagara hands clutched only to grasp air."

Byers' flashy runs set up both Blue Demon touchdowns in DePaul's 13 to 0 win.

Commenting on Anderson's proclivity for "calling off the dogs" when his team held a comfortable lead, Ward added: "Recalling that yesterday was Armistice Day, Coach Eddie Anderson early in the fourth quarter ordered his men to stop firing and DePaul finished the game with a second string set of backs."[7]

During Anderson's years at DePaul his teams often played charity games. Such contests were usually scheduled on Sundays at Chicago's Soldier Field. The biggest fundraisers came against archrival Loyola. (The rivalry contin-

A kneeling Anderson talks with his 1928 DePaul football squad. The season's highlight was the Blue Demons' 13 to 0 shut out of Niagara University before 44,000 fans at Chicago's Soldier Field. The hero of that game, Clair "Skeets" Byers, is absent from the photo. Today, neither university fields a football team. (Courtesy of DePaul University Archives, Chicago, IL.)

ued, however, without Roger Kiley, who left Loyola in 1928 to practice law full time.) On November 3, 1929, just days after Black Tuesday's infamous stock market crash, Anderson's injury-riddled squad dressed only 17 players in dropping a 13 to 0 decision to the Ramblers before an all-time record crowd of 51,000. The following year, Anderson's lads returned the favor by eking out a 6 to 0 victory before 25,000. (The drop in attendance could undoubtedly be attributed to the increasing depths of the Great Depression.) The games' proceeds were donated to the Sisters of Charity and the Rosary College Building Fund respectively.

As the Catholic rivals lined up to kick off in 1930, they believed that they were again playing for the "Brown Barrel," the so-called coveted victor's trophy. The prize had been in Loyola's possession since 1928. However, at game time Loyola officials had no clue as to the trophy's whereabouts.[8] Unperturbed, DePaul took the opening kick-off and launched a five-minute, 60-yard scoring drive to take a 6 to 0 lead. The Blue Demons dominated the first half, the Ramblers the second. Despite the momentum swing, DePaul prevailed 6 to 0.

Sadly, the afternoon was the last of the Brown Barrel in more ways than one. DePaul fullback Eddie Stafford's first quarter scoring plunge would be the last points scored in the North Side rivalry as Loyola dropped football the next year.

Anderson's DePaul squads also played charity games for Chicago's St.

Vincent's Orphanage. The biggest turnouts came in a 27 to 0 loss to Michigan State Teachers College (today's Eastern Michigan University) before a crowd of 20,000 on October 12, 1929, and in a bizarre 4 to 0 loss to St. John's College of Brooklyn, New York, on November 30, 1930.

On March 26, 1931, Eddie Anderson signed to coach DePaul for a seventh season. Five days later, Anderson shared a shocked nation's grief at news of Knute Rockne's death. The legendary 43-year-old coach was killed when the Fokker Trimotor plane in which he was a passenger crashed in a remote Kansas cornfield. Presidents Hoover and Coolidge, as well as King Haakon VII of Norway, eulogized the beloved coach. Telegrams of condolence poured in from the likes of General Douglas MacArthur, Secretary of War Patrick J. Hurley, Will Rogers, Babe Ruth, Lou Gehrig and Jack Dempsey.[9] A saddened Anderson paid his former mentor the ultimate coaching compliment: "Rock was a molder of men."[10]

With the backfield and line averaging 155 and 185 pounds respectively, Anderson's 1931 squad was bigger than his previous DePaul teams. The roster included the speedy Matty Steffen, the nephew of Chicago judge and Carnegie Tech football coach Walter P. Steffen, and an offensive line anchored by Captain Everett McClane and center Jack Kelly.

The Blue Demons lived up to Anderson's high expectations by upsetting the University of Detroit 13 to 0 in the season opener. The win was especially gratifying for Eddie, who had endured Coach Gus Dorais' pre-game condolences about the unfairness of Anderson's youngsters starting the season against his powerhouse Detroit squad. The upset proved to be a Pyrrhic victory, however, as five of Anderson's starters emerged from the contest too crippled to travel to North Dakota the following week.[11]

Several other DePaul players were still hobbling when they boarded the train to Grand Forks on October 1. The University of North Dakota had lost only once in three years, and that was to powerful Army at West Point. Scoring in every quarter, the "Fighting Sioux" continued their winning ways by pummeling their Catholic visitors 41 to 7.

Bruised, but determined, Anderson's gritty bunch rebounded by winning their next five games. The streak included a 46 to 0 win at Louisville and a 34 to 20 victory over South Dakota State. DePaul would end its 1931 season with a western swing to the University of Arizona followed by a West Coast visit to the University of San Francisco.

A sense of adventure and excitement permeated the air as the DePaul team boarded a westbound train on the night of November 18. The official DePaul party consisted of 28 players; a trainer and a manager; Father Corcoran, president of the university; Father Blechle, faculty supervisor of athletics; athletic director and assistant coach James Kelly; Anderson; and assistant coach Ben Connors.[12] To his wife's delight, Eddie also arranged for Mary to accompany him on the 13-day journey.

When recalling the trip years later Mary reminisced: "It was wonderful! It was like a second honeymoon."[13]

Mary Anderson's romantic memories of the Southwest's spectacular sunsets and her first visit to the City by the Bay were more pleasant than the football fortunes DePaul experienced along the way. Playing Arizona in Tucson's blistering heat on November 21, DePaul suffered a heartbreaking 14 to 13 loss when Matty Steffen missed an extra-point kick. The western swing concluded at San Francisco's Kezar Stadium before 25,000 fans on November 28. Halfback Bob Kleckner proved to be DePaul's nemesis by scoring three touchdowns as the "Riders of the Grey Fog" scored early and often in trouncing DePaul 38 to 7.

The loss gave the 1931 DePaul team a final record of 6 wins and 3 losses. It was the most games DePaul had ever won in a single season. The team's western swing also brought the curtain down on Anderson's coaching tenure at DePaul. Anderson had brought the program to new heights and had the Blue Demons flirting with the "big time." Although DePaul managed a few winning seasons after Anderson's departure, the student body grew apathetic. The Chicago school could never attract the top local football prospects. Attendance and revenues dwindled, while the cost of fielding a team continued to soar. After several abysmal seasons under Coach Ben Connors and student interest on the wane, DePaul dropped the sport after the 1938 season.[14]

Over the years DePaul somehow lost or tossed records documenting much of the school's football history — including the 1931 season. As a result, Anderson's seven-year record at DePaul has been erroneously reported as 21 wins, 22 losses and 3 ties. Data discovered while researching this book, however, confirms that Anderson actually won 24, lost 24 and tied 4 during his tenure at DePaul. The NCAA officially lists Eddie Anderson's overall career record at 201 wins, 128 losses and 15 ties. After reconciling the DePaul discrepancy, however, Anderson's overall career record actually stands at 204 wins, 130 losses and 16 ties.

In the spring of 1932, Anderson quietly resigned as football coach at DePaul to finish his medical internship at St. Joseph's Hospital in Chicago. Throughout his career Anderson periodically wrestled with thoughts of giving up coaching to concentrate on medicine. This may have been one of those times.

With the country in the throes of the depression, it has been hinted that Anderson's resignation may have stemmed from the economic realities of the times. On November 13, 1939, *Chicago Herald-American* sportswriter Jim Gallagher would write: "Times grew tough for football in 1932, and when Eddie couldn't see eye-to-eye about accepting one of the then fashionable salary trims he came to an amicable parting of the ways with DePaul. He did no coaching that fall."

Dr. Jerry Anderson, Eddie's son, refutes Gallagher's version: "No. The reason Dad left DePaul in 1932 was to finish his medical internship."[15]

In any case, Anderson would not stay out of coaching for long.

11

HOLY CROSS

Founded by the Society of Jesus in 1843, Holy Cross was New England's first Catholic college. Built on Pakachoag Hill in Worcester, Massachusetts, the all-male Jesuit institution reached an enrollment of 1,000 by the fall of 1932. That year boarders comprised approximately 75% of the student body. Tuition, room and board totaled $700 annually. Campus life revolved around religion and sports, with baseball being far and away the most popular varsity sport. Under Coach Jack Barry the Crusader baseball team had experienced phenomenal success since 1921 and would continue to fare well throughout Barry's 40-year reign.

By 1932, football had begun shouldering its way into the athletic spotlight. Basketball, however, was dropped as a cost-cutting measure in 1931. It was re-instituted as a varsity sport for the 1934 season, only to be dropped again before being reinstated permanently under Coach Edward "Moose" Krause in 1939.[1]

The rise in Crusader football fortunes began during the twenties under Coach Cleo A. O'Donnell and continued into the thirties under Captain John J. McEwan. As an All-American center, the colorful McEwan had played on Army's undefeated teams in 1914 and 1916. As team captain in 1916, McEwan was the biggest and fastest man on the squad. His speed and power combined with his zest for tackling made him nearly impossible to block.[2] Commissioned as a second lieutenant in 1917, McEwan returned to West Point as an assistant coach in 1920 before ascending to the head football job in 1923. During his three seasons as head coach, Army never lost to Navy and whitewashed Notre Dame 27 to 0 in 1925.

In those years, coaching football at West Point was not a full-time position. During the off-seasons the Army assigned McEwan to military duty in

Puerto Rico. Bored with barracks life in a semi-tropical climate, McEwan resigned his commission in 1925 and signed a five-year contract to coach football at the University of Oregon. In 1930 he succeeded O'Donnell at Holy Cross.

A giant of a man, the gregarious McEwan was well liked by his players. Continually preaching the need for grace in an athlete's every movement, McEwan occasionally had a player (always a lumbering lineman, never a nimble halfback) stand atop a desk on one leg while attempting to execute a graceful 360-degree turn. Uncertain as to how seriously Captain McEwan regarded the exercise, players muffled their laughter when observing a burly teammate stagger under flailing arms to exhibit grace.[3]

Although a fierce competitor who loved to win, McEwan wasn't ruthless in his quest for victory. McEwan's compassionate side was humorously demonstrated in a 1932 game against the University of Maine. Accompanying the Black Bears to Worcester that autumn afternoon was the popular crooner, Rudy Vallee. While an undergraduate at Maine, Vallee had composed the school's fight song. Still a devout Maine fan, the entertainer had graciously agreed to perform for the Fitton Field crowd at halftime.

Unfortunately, the visitor's gridiron performance paled in comparison to Vallee's lively halftime show. Trailing by four touchdowns in the fourth quarter, it was unlikely that any "steins were going to be raised in victory for dear old Maine" that afternoon.

Appreciative of Vallee's halftime serenade, Captain McEwan decided to give the gloomy Maine faithful something to cheer about. With Maine in possession at its own 25-yard line, McEwan sent a substitute into Holy Cross' huddle with the message, "Captain says to let Maine score on this play, but make it look good![4]

On the next play Maine ran a sweep to the right. Several Crusaders crumpled before Maine blockers while would-be tacklers dove in vain at the ball carrier. Turning the corner, the halfback raced downfield. At the Maine 35-yard line, Holy Cross safety Tony Rovinski drew a bead on the scatback. Although a talented football player, Rovinski was not the "brightest bulb in the box."[5] As Rovinski got within striking distance, rather than attempt to tackle the runner, he merely ran alongside the Maine man, escorting the stunned runner down the sidelines. The crowd's initial gasp turned to laughter when Rovinski seemingly waved the ball carrier on at the Holy Cross 25.[6] To the delirium of Maine fans, the dutiful Rovinski ran stride for stride with the Maine halfback into the end zone. Thanks to McEwan and Rovinski, Maine rooters had a reason to hoist a stein that night.

McEwan's coaching tenure at Worcester started auspiciously. In 1930, the Crusaders won 8 and lost 2 and enjoyed a record of 7 wins, 2 losses and

1 tie in 1931. After winning their first six games in 1932, the Crusaders were on track for another stellar season when calamity struck. It began innocently enough. With Holy Cross leading Brown 7 to 3 late in the game, the Bruins were driving when Captain McEwan called for Bob O'Brien to substitute at guard.

"But I just came out," challenged O'Brien. (The rules of the day prohibited a player from leaving and re-entering the game in the same quarter.)

"Get in there!" roared McEwan.[7]

Realizing the situation, Trainer Bart Sullivan grabbed O'Brien by the arm to keep him from entering the game. Incensed at what he perceived to be Sullivan's defiance, the powerfully built McEwan merely brushed the trainer aside and sent O'Brien into the fray. Spying the infraction, the referee ejected O'Brien and flagged Holy Cross. Unfortunately, it had been fourth-and-four when O'Brien had re-entered. The 5-yard penalty gave Brown a first down, and the Bruins capitalized on McEwan's blunder by scoring the game-winning touchdown on the drive.

Upset over the series of events that cost the team an undefeated season, the Holy Cross coaches hotly exchanged recriminations. During the quarrel it became obvious that McEwan had been drinking.[8] When the team returned from Providence, school officials suspended McEwan and named assistant Arthur "Bunny" Corcoran as the team's interim coach. Under Corcoran the team lost to Harvard and played scoreless ties against Manhattan and Boston College. McEwan was fired at the end of the season, and Holy Cross began looking for a new coach.

With a nationwide unemployment rate of 25%, the country was in the trough of the Great Depression by 1933. In his inaugural address on March 4, President Franklin D. Roosevelt confidently told Americans that the country had "nothing to fear but fear itself."

Throughout his life Eddie Anderson was never afraid of taking a calculated risk, and perhaps heeding the president's words, he took another one later that month. On the evening of March 28, 1933, Holy Cross issued the following succinct press release: "Dr. Anderson has been named head coach at Holy Cross. He is a graduate of Notre Dame."

The announcement ended the school's four-month search for a coach and left Boston sportswriters scratching their heads. None had ever heard of a Dr. Eddie Anderson. Some reasoned that Holy Cross must have signed Hunk Anderson who was reportedly on his way out as coach at Notre Dame. When that theory fizzled, sportswriters futilely tapped into their information networks seeking a line on Holy Cross' new mystery coach.

By contacting Charles Crowley, a local man who had lettered at tackle for Notre Dame in 1918 and 1919 before transferring to Boston College, the

The 1933 Holy Cross College football staff. From left to right: Hop Riopel, Joe Locke, Eddie Anderson, Joe Sheeketski and Bart Sullivan. It would be Joe Locke's only year at Holy Cross as the 24-year-old would die of complications from pneumonia in 1934. (College of the Holy Cross Archives)

Boston Post scooped the rest of New England in providing accurate details on Anderson's background. Crowley recalled: "The Eddie Anderson I knew left football coaching to study medicine. This must be the same one."[9] Crowley then shared anecdotes about his teammate. (When Anderson got settled in Massachusetts, the two renewed their friendship. In fact, Crowley became godfather to Eddie's youngest son, Jim.)[10]

On March 31, 1933, Eddie Anderson arrived in Boston to speak at a Notre Dame alumni meeting and to sign a contract with Holy Cross. Writing for the *Post* 17 years later, sports columnist Gerry Hern recalled Anderson's first visit to New England: "The day Dr. Anderson was introduced to the Boston press at a local hotel, the most embarrassed spectators present were the Holy Cross athletic officials, who, when asked a question about Eddie's background, would walk over, beg his pardon for the intrusion and ask if he would please tell again the name of that college where he had coached. The doctor would shove his cowlick back a bit and solemnly spell out the name.

Then he would be quiet again... The big question was the one even Holy Cross officials present couldn't answer: How had he gotten the job?"[11]

It's a question that has never been definitively answered. The putative frontrunners for the job were Harry Stuhldreher and Al "Dutch" Bergman, who were then coaching at Villanova and Catholic University respectively.[12] How Anderson, who had neither played nor coached against Holy Cross, nor previously worked with anyone in the school's administration, got the job remains a mystery.

When Dr. Anderson returned to Chicago in early April, he not only had the Holy Cross job at a reported annual salary of $5,000, but also a staff position as an eye, ear, nose and throat specialist at Massachusetts General Hospital. The Anderson family (which now included two sons: four-year-old Nick and one-year-old Jerry) would establish residence in Worcester for a year before moving to Brookline. Anderson would make the arduous 40-mile commute from the Boston suburb to Worcester along Route 20 each football season between 1934 and 1938.

On April 11, Anderson announced that former Golden Domers Joe Sheeketski and Joe Locke would round out the Holy Cross coaching staff. Sheeketski, who was finishing his last semester at Notre Dame, had played quarterback for the Irish from 1930 to 1932, and Locke had won varsity letters as a guard in 1927 and 1929. Since graduating in 1930, Locke had been coaching at Wichita University.

The Crusaders had averaged seven wins a season during the previous three years. Upon arriving in Worcester the new staff found the talent cupboard well stocked. Big, experienced linemen returned including tackles Charles "Buzz" Harvey (6', 218 lbs.), Pete Lingua (6'2", 238 lbs.), Thomas Kelly (6'3", 210 lbs.), Joseph Murphy (6', 216 lbs.) and center Anthony Morandos (5'11", 180 lbs.). The speedy Nick Morris, James Hobin, John O'Connor and lightweight Walter Janiak (5'7", 152 lbs.) provided depth in the backfield, while team captain Charles Reiss and Edward Britt manned the end posts.

Anderson immediately set to work installing the Notre Dame system during spring practice. "Within a couple of months he had scrapped our old Warner system and had us prancing and shifting like ballet dancers," recalled Tommy Callan, Class of '35.

The new coaching staff drove the team relentlessly throughout spring drills. "The 1933 spring practice was so hard that most of the team were ready to go on strike by Memorial Day," laughed Callan. "Luckily, Anderson showed his sympathetic side by calling off practice for the holiday weekend."[13]

Aside from inheriting a talented team, Anderson also benefited from the appointment of Father Francis J. Dolan, S.J., as president of Holy Cross in

July of 1933. A former three-sport athlete at both Boston College High School and Boston College, the 40-year-old Dolan loved sports, especially football.[14] During late afternoons in the fall Dolan often shelved his administrative chores and meandered to the athletic fields to watch the football team practice. Faculty members privately groused about the propriety of a college president attending football practice "almost daily." To Anderson, of course, Father Dolan was always a welcomed visitor.

After opening the 1933 season with convincing home wins over St. Michael's of Vermont, Catholic University and Providence, the local pundits hailed the October 21 showdown at undefeated Harvard as Anderson's first real coaching challenge. By coincidence, on the day of the game, the *Harvard A.A. News* published an article that Eddie Anderson had authored on the Notre Dame system. In it Anderson elaborated on the very offense Harvard would be defending that afternoon. Anderson explained that the Notre Dame *shift* was the key to the system: "The purpose of *the shift*, in short, is deception and concentrated power. The idea is to get the right man in the right place at the right time and in so doing to throw the opposing players, the line especially, off balance. In the early days there were many of the opinion that *the shift* was intended merely to beat the gun, to get off to a flying start without taking a penalty, an attempt to get the jump on the opposition...

"The basic formation of the Notre Dame system is the balanced line... From this so-called *T formation*, the *shift* is accomplished... The most common *shift* is into a *box formation*, from which the opposing line is raked with spinners, reverses, cross bucks, and an occasional pass. The opposing line, unless it is especially clever, is thrown off balance by *the shift*; and, more than that, cannot tell [what play is developing.]"

Interestingly enough, it was Holy Cross' defense, not its offense, which would pose the biggest obstacle for Harvard. With a first-and-goal for Harvard at the Holy Cross 6-yard line, the gutsy Crusaders overcame three consecutive offsides penalties to keep the favored Crimson from scoring on seven successive running plays. Buzz Harvey's tackle of Harvard captain Johnny Dean for a one-yard loss before 43,000 fans culminated what may have been the most courageous goal line stand ever witnessed at Harvard Stadium.[15] Inspired by its heroic defense, Holy Cross went on to earn it first-ever win over Harvard, 10 to 7.

Anderson downplayed the victory's significance: "Personally, I don't see why the boys should consider it something out of the ordinary to beat Harvard. The Crimson had a good football team, but it was by no means unbeatable."[16] Years later, however, Anderson would rank the 1933 Harvard win as one of the greatest in his coaching career.[17]

The next week, before 20,000 fans, the largest crowd ever to see a football game in Worcester, Eddie Anderson had a special visitor.[18] His father, Edward Martinius Anderson, rode the train east from Iowa to see the Crusaders beat Brown 19 to 7. It was a trip the "old gent" would make annually during Eddie's first stint at Holy Cross.

The following week players and coaches flashed big grins while posing proudly in new fedoras for a team picture before boarding a train to Detroit. A New Haven hat company had provided the hats *gratis* as part of a publicity campaign.[19] However, Doug Nott's pin-point passing turned those smiles to frowns as Coach Gus Dorais' Detroit Titans blanked Holy Cross 24 to 0. It was the Crusaders' first loss of the season.

A pair of Jim Hobin-to-Tom Callan touchdown passes propelled Holy Cross to a 27 to 6 victory over Manhattan the next week. The Crusaders then hosted a surprisingly stubborn Springfield College team. With Springfield fullback Joe Shields bowling over Crusader tacklers as if they were alley pins, Holy Cross had to rally for two late fourth-quarter touchdowns to escape with a 19 to 6 win.

The stage was now set for an Eddie Anderson-coached squad's first meeting with Boston College. Despite both teams entering the fray with identical 7 and 1 records and playing before a sell-out crowd of 24,000 at Boston College's new Alumni Stadium, Holy Cross was favored to win.

With Holy Cross leading 7 to 0 shortly before the half, B.C. had the ball third-and-goal on the Crusader 9-yard line when Eagle quarterback John Freitas pitched to a kid named Killeles on a well-conceived end around play. Killeles scored untouched to cut the Holy Cross lead to 7 to 6 at the half.

Tommy Callan recounted, "We got stuck on the old end around (the Statue of Liberty play). I was on the backside of the play and could have cried when that guy went around the other end [to score]."[20]

The contest briefly turned ugly in the third quarter when Holy Cross' Phil Flanagan and the Eagle's Bob Ott were ejected for fighting. Shortly thereafter, the scrambling Freitas somehow eluded a pack of Crusader tacklers to hurl a 38-yard touchdown pass to end Eddie Furbush. Late in the game, with the ball on its own 7-yard line, the Eagles took an intentional safety rather than risk having a punt blocked to make the final score Boston College 13, Holy Cross 9.

Eddie Anderson's first taste of Jesuit rivalry was bitter. It would not be the last heartache Boston College caused him.

In his first year at the helm, Anderson guided Holy Cross to a record of 7 wins and 2 losses. Thanks to an exceptionally talented freshman squad, the school's football future loomed bright. The Class of '37 included future standouts such as Hipolet Moncevicz, Rexford Kidd, Ecio Luciano, Joseph Yablonski, Vince Dougherty, Dave Gavin and future captain, Bob Curley. Anderson's first inkling of how good these freshmen were came early in the season when he summoned freshman coach Hop Riopel to bring his starting eleven over to scrimmage the varsity.

"We beat the hell out of 'em!" remembered freshman tackle Hipolet "Hip" Moncevicz. "The varsity offense couldn't move the ball against us. But Eddie Anderson was a master psychologist. He knew he couldn't end the scrimmage without his varsity scoring a couple of touchdowns. So he kept our defense on the field until we were so worn down that the varsity finally scored."[21]

That year the Crusader freshmen traveled to New Haven to take its customary pounding at the hands of the Yale frosh — only this year wasn't business as usual. Riopel's bunch clobbered the Eli by 40 points. Even with future Heisman Trophy winner Larry Kelley in its line-up, Yale couldn't score. "Hop [Riopel] was doing everything he could to keep the score down," laughed Moncevicz. "He was playing linemen in the backfield and backs on the line. He kept shaking his head and fretting over the fact that Yale would never consent to play us again after being beaten so badly!"[22]

The 1934 season began under a cloud of gloom. Assistant coach Joe Locke had been hospitalized with pneumonia before the team's 1933 season finale against Boston College. In December, he returned to his family home in Chicago to recuperate. Although not fully recovered, the devoted coach returned to Mount St. James the following March for spring drills. When spring football ended he again returned home to convalesce. Unfortunately, Locke's health continued to deteriorate and in late summer he wired Anderson his resignation. On September 4, 1934, the popular 24-year-old coach passed away in Chicago's Mercy Hospital.[23]

Doctor Anderson replaced Locke with Jim Harris. A native of Bellaire, Ohio, Harris was also an ex–Golden Domer, who had spent a year on "Moon" Mullins' staff at St. Benedict's in Kansas.

Eddie Anderson held the honor of being the first player Knute Rockne had ever substituted into a game. By a strange quirk of fate, Anderson was now hiring the man that was the last player Rockne ever substituted.[24] (Rockne had substituted Anderson against Case Tech in 1918 and Harris against Southern Cal in 1930.) Harris would coach with Anderson for many years; in the words of one former Holy Cross player: "Harris probably owed his entire professional career to Doc."[25]

Reflecting on the 1934 season, ex-quarterback Tommy Callan recalled: "Doc had some great underclassmen that he could see as a better team in the

OFF TO CONQUER THE CHALK-LINED PRAIRIES

For many years Brother Francis X. Horweedle worked a small farm on the Holy Cross campus that provided the school's dinning hall with fresh produce and milk. Among the equipment on that farm was this hay wagon, on which the Crusader football team posed to kick-off the 1934 season. Eddie Anderson is on the far left. (Courtesy of Tommy and Virginia Callan)

future. All they needed was experience. Therefore, he inserted the sophomores frequently, even starting a second team if the opponent was inferior. It worked out fine for him as the '35 team went undefeated.

"But we seniors liked to play. I can remember us first stringers smiling when substituting for the second team after they couldn't move the ball."[26]

Regardless of who was in the line-up, the Crusaders reeled off five straight wins (including a 26 to 6 pasting of Harvard) to start the 1934 season before losing to Andy Kerr's Colgate squad and Temple on successive Saturdays.

The Temple trip was a nightmare from start to finish. En route to Philadelphia, Holy Cross Athletic Director Tom McCabe, irked by the previous week's loss to Colgate, announced that no complimentary tickets would be issued. Players were accustomed to receiving two free tickets per game and McCabe's announcement angered those who had family and friends coming to the game. Although the players did receive complimentary tickets at the last minute, the episode left some hard feelings.[27] Certainly, the distraction didn't help Anderson ready his team to play football.

To compound matters, after losing the game 14 to 0, quarterback Tommy Callan decided to drive the family DeSoto back to Worcester with his aunt and uncle, who had journeyed to Philadelphia for the game. It was innocent enough. However, by failing to inform either Anderson or school officials that he would not be returning home with the team, Callan violated school policy. On Monday morning Callan was summoned to Athletic Director Tom

The 1934 Crusader starting line-up is shown in one of the flamboyant poses characteristic of the era. Quarterback Tommy Callan is second from the right in the row of
leaping ball carriers. (Courtesy of Tommy and Virginia Callan)

McCabe's office. With the approval of the Moderator of Athletics, Father
Gerald Phelan, McCabe summarily dismissed the quarterback from the team.[28]
However, McCabe acted without consulting Anderson, who only learned of
the decision at Monday's practice. While Anderson understood the need for
complying with school rules, he fumed over what he considered to be a usurpa-
tion of his coaching authority.

Upon learning the reasons for Callan's dismissal, local sportswriters Joe
Keblinsky and Mike Shea lambasted Holy Cross and McCabe in both
newsprint and over the radio waves on Tuesday.[29] On Wednesday morning,
Callan received an unsigned, typed note on college stationery to report to football practice that afternoon.[30] Whether prompted by the fireworks sparked
by Keblinsky and Shea or the result of Anderson's private Tuesday meeting
with McCabe, Callan was back in the Crusader fold.

The Crusaders rebounded from the Temple fiasco with wins at Manhattan and Brown to enter the season's finale at Boston College with a record of
7 wins and 2 losses.

Anderson shook up the Crusader lineup by starting sophomores Rex
Kidd, Joe Yablonski and Vince Daugherty for upper classmen Callan, Britt
and Hobin. Only Nick Morris retained his starting backfield slot. Playing in
a quagmire at Newton's Alumni Field, the teams were mired in a scoreless tie
at the half. In the third quarter the Crusaders mounted a 50-yard scoring drive.

Morris' three-yard touchdown run and Harvey's extra-point kick gave Holy Cross a 7 to 0 lead.

While Boston College substituted freely throughout the contest, Eddie Anderson, perhaps reverting to his days at Columbia College, made only one substitution — replacing Leonard Avery at end with Red Daughters.

"Doc was really structuring his future team," recalled the benched Tommy Callan. "God bless him! With about five minutes remaining Doc turned to me and told me to substitute for Kidd. I looked at him and quietly said, 'Kidd is doing okay. He doesn't need me to substitute for him.' With that I walked away and Doc never said any more about it. I'm sure he understood how I felt."[31]

Taking a page from Boston College in their previous meeting, Holy Cross also took an intentional safety late in the game rather than risk having a punt blocked in its own end zone. The safety accounted for the Eagles' only points in Holy Cross' 7 to 2 victory. The win gave the Crusaders a final 1934 record of 8 wins and 2 losses and Eddie Anderson his first triumph over Boston College.

Taking an instructional knee, Eddie Anderson makes a teaching point to the front seven of the 1934 Holy Cross squad. From left to right the players are Anthony Morandos, Charles "Buzz" Harvey (captain), Thomas Kelley, Phil Flanagan, Paul Brogan, Peter Lingua and James Moran. (College of the Holy Cross Archives)

Words like structured, rigid, abstemious and even "police state" have been used to describe student life at Holy Cross during the thirties. A typical day began with a 7 a.m. wakeup and mandatory mass at 7:15. (Absentees were restricted to campus the following Saturday.) After breakfast at 7:45, classes ran from 9 to 3, and each began and ended with a prayer. Lunch was served at noon with supper at 6 p.m. Chapel was available at 6:25 p.m. and followed by three hours of mandatory study with lights out at 10 p.m.[32]

Students were periodically required to attend vespers, a time set aside for prayer in the late afternoon or evening. Student-athletes were not exempt from attending. Hip Moncevicz, a first-generation American, always felt more comfortable reciting prayers in his family's native Lithuanian than in English. To assure the piety of Moncevicz's offerings, the Jesuits assigned a Lithuanian-speaking priest to monitor the tackle's supplications.[33]

At 6'3" and 205 pounds, Moncevicz's aggressive play quickly caught the eye of teammates and coaches. During a scrimmage in his sophomore year, the wiry tackle created havoc against the first team by repeatedly tackling ball carriers for no gain. Was the Brockton youngster that good or were first-string players merely taking it easy on him? Eddie Anderson decided to find out first-hand by playing the position opposite Moncevicz.

"Take me on," Anderson challenged while assuming his stance.

"Sure, I'll be glad to," replied Moncevicz.

Giving away 40 pounds and 5 inches, Anderson gamely charged on the snap of the ball only to be knocked back several yards. Landing in a heap, Anderson had his answer. The coach later informed Moncevicz: "You're definitely a Saturday player, but you fool around too much during practice."[34] As a result, Anderson often had the wiry tackle running laps during intra-squad scrimmages, but Moncewicz always saw plenty of action on game days.

"Eddie Anderson was one of the cagiest men there was," Moncevicz recounted. "As a coach he knew exactly where he wanted to place his men and exactly how he was going to attack every team's offense.

"Anderson knew opponents were scouting us closely. For several weeks prior to my final game against B.C, Anderson instructed me on defense to 'penetrate two steps into the offensive backfield and no further. When it comes time for the B.C. game, you'll be able to walk in and block a kick.' Sure enough, that's exactly what happened."[35]

The Crusaders began the 1935 season with shutouts over their first four opponents, which included a third straight win over Harvard. In the fifth game against Manhattan College at Brooklyn's Ebbets Field, Holy Cross held a 13 to 0 lead early in the third quarter when Hip Moncevicz broke his nose. Time was called, and Anderson was summoned from the sideline to tend to the bloodied tackle. Placing his hands on the patient, Anderson positioned his thumbs on each side of Moncevicz's crooked nose and squeezed, skillfully resetting the bone. Still smarting from the pain, Moncevicz held his head back as Anderson stuffed his nostrils with cotton all the while instructing: "You do what I tell you and you'll be all right. Spit the blood out. Don't swallow it. Spit it out and you'll do fine."[36] Following the doctor's advice, Moncevicz played the rest of the game without missing a play. Unfortunately, Manhattan rallied for two fourth-quarter touchdowns, and the game ended tied at 13.

Lou King, who played quarterback for Anderson at Iowa, recounts a similar experience from the 1946 season. "He was a medical doctor, so he told everyone that he was the one to decide if any player was hurt. That meant very few got hurt badly enough to come out of a game. In one game I had three front teeth knocked out, got two aspirin, but was not even taken out of the game. During my years at Iowa I had my nose broken nine times and played every minute after each of them with cotton up my nose. Dr. Eddie could not stand a coward, and if you played for him, you had to go all out every minute."[37]

Anderson may have administered tough love, but on one occasion his medical skills saved a player's life. In a game against St. Anselm, a Saints player took a knee to the head while making a tackle. The shock of the blow caused the tackler to swallow his tongue, blocking his air supply and making suffocation imminent. Quickly assessing the situation, Anderson grabbed a referee's metal whistle and used it to pry open the victim's mouth that had seized shut. He then reached in and pulled the tongue up, freeing the airway.[38] While opposing coaches may have dreaded matching coaching wits with Anderson, they took comfort in knowing that his sideline presence guaranteed a doctor in the house.

After the tie with Manhattan, Holy Cross shut out Colgate 3 to 0 at Worcester's Fitton Field. The Crusaders' Rex Kidd put on virtually a one-man show by intercepting two passes, returning a punt 50 yards, making a diving catch for his team's only first down, and for the *coup de grace*, dropkicking the game-winning 23-yard field goal.

Holy Cross blanked its next three opponents that included a 7 to 0 win over mighty Carnegie Tech. Sporting the unorthodox moniker "the Skibos," Carnegie Tech was nationally ranked when they visited Worcester on November 9. Just as it had against Colgate, Anderson's defense played brilliantly. This time, however, Walter Janiak provided the individual heroics. A former sprinter on Poland's national team, Janiak ran 12 yards for a touchdown only three minutes into the game. Then, just before the half, Tech's Jerry Matelin intercepted Vince Daugherty's pass on the Skibo 11-yard line. With only green grass in front of him, Matelin took off for the Crusader goal line and what looked like a sure touchdown. It was the speedy Janiak, however, who denied Tech a score by catching Matelin from behind at the Crusader 26-yard line.[39]

Before a sellout crowd in the season's finale at Boston College, the Crusaders ended the suspense early by scoring three touchdowns in the game's first six minutes. The Crusaders held on for a 20 to 6 win to finish the season with a record of 9 wins and 1 tie. It was the first undefeated football season in the school's history. It was also Anderson's first undefeated team since his rookie year at Columbia College in 1922.

12

1936—1937

The 1936 season began with the customary dollops of conditioning and scrimmaging. Before the advent of Olympic lifting and weight training, Anderson implemented his own unorthodox methods of strength training. To increase handgrip strength, Anderson advocated finger-tip pushups and often made his players squeeze stones. When he spied a player trekking empty-handed to practice Anderson would urge: "Take some stones up with you!"[1]

Anderson, who years later tore a New York City phone book in half, occasionally brought a broomstick to practice and amazed his players by lifting it horizontally at arm's length between his index and middle fingers. (If it sounds easy, try it some time.)

The 1936 campaign began with easy wins over Bates and Providence. Anderson started the second team in both contests. On October 10, the Crusaders ventured to Hanover, New Hampshire, to meet rugged Dartmouth. The two schools had played 10 games since 1903, and Dartmouth had won them all. The "Big Green" was coached by Earl "Red" Blaik, who was destined to lead Army to greatness in the forties.

A heavy rain stopped only minutes before the kick-off making for sloppy conditions and treacherous footing. Although Dartmouth controlled the game's tempo, the contest remained scoreless after three quarters. When Crusader halfback Joe Yablonski left the game with an injury in the fourth quarter, the stage was set for the heroics of Bill Osmanski. Substituting for Yablonski, the 5'10", 190-pound sophomore from Providence, Rhode Island, would arguably go on to become the greatest football player in Holy Cross history.

With about seven minutes remaining Dartmouth mounted a serious drive. The Dartmouth center was Carl Ray. To several Holy Cross players he was dubitably referred to as "Mutt" Ray. After picking up a first down at the Crusader 30-yard line, Ray bent over the ball and announced to the purple-clad defenders: "Okay, you Catholic bastards, now pray. Because we're going to kick your ass!"[2]

Ray snapped the ball to quarterback Freddie Hollingworth who dropped back to pass. Throwing to his right, Holy Cross lineman Ecio Luciano tipped the ball slightly, slowing its flight. At the 22-yard line Osmanski stepped in front of the Dartmouth receiver to make the interception in full stride. Running interference for Osmanski along the sideline, Moncevicz took out Hollingworth with a crushing cross-body block. Picking up another block from John O'Donnell, Osmanski ran 78 yards untouched for a score. Rex Kidd's extra-point kick made the final score 7 to 0 and gave Holy Cross its first win over Dartmouth.[3]

Osmanski turned in another heroic performance the following week against Coach Chick Meehan's Manhattan Jaspars. Seemingly stopped at the line of scrimmage on one carry, Osmanski brought the home fans to their feet by bouncing the play outside and sprinting 76 yards for a touchdown en route to a 13 to 7 Crusader win.

Anderson's Crusaders earned their second consecutive 7 to 0 win over Carnegie Tech the following week and the New England papers began touting Holy Cross as a legitimate Rose Bowl contender.

On October 31, Holy Cross journeyed to Philadelphia to meet Temple. Coached by the legendary Glenn S. "Pop" Warner, the Owls had a few Halloween tricks awaiting the visitors. The 65-year-old Warner was truly one of football's pioneer coaches. Credited with devising the body block, the reverse play and both the single and double wing formations, Warner was one of the first coaches to envision the possibilities of the forward pass. At both the Carlisle Indian School and Stanford, Warner had coached two of college football's greatest players: Jim Thorpe and Ernie Nevers. Perhaps it was an omen that Anderson's Crusaders, who hadn't lost in 18 games, suffered their last setback at the hands of Warner and Temple in 1934.

In 1936, fullback Augie Macali was Temple's most potent offensive weapon. At 214 pounds, Macali was a punishing runner and accurate passer. Against Holy Cross, he accounted for most of Temple's 217 yards of total offense. As described by the *Worcester Telegram*'s Walter Kiley, the game's key play was "as sparkling and as perfectly executed as any seen on an Eastern gridiron this season.

"With the ball on the Holy Cross 38-yard line, Macali faded back and tossed a pass to end Ed Walker who lateraled to halfback Horace Mowrey as he was tackled. Mowrey then lateraled to tackle Stan Gurzynski who tossed back to Walker, who was finally downed on the 9-yard line."[4]

The Crusader defense then stiffened, and Bill Docherty kicked a 19-yard field goal to give Temple a 3 to 0 lead. Just before the half Holy Cross drove the ball to the Temple 2-yard line. "We opened a tremendous hole," recalled Hip Moncevicz. "Kuziora was supposed to follow behind my block. He could have walked through, but Kuziora left the ball on the ground." Temple's Mowrey recovered the fumble to kill the Crusaders' best scoring chance of the day. Temple held on to win 3 to 0.

"All of those reporters and newspapers touting us for the Rose Bowl, and we went down the drain," lamented Moncevicz.[5]

Monday practices were usually light workouts. However, the Monday following the Temple game Anderson put his squad through a grueling two-hour scrimmage before finishing practice with a series of deadening 100-yard sprints.

"Anderson was really mad," recounted Moncevicz. "On Monday he worked the hell out of us! Many of the guys got angry and decided to go on strike. On Tuesday only a handful of players showed up to practice."

While several players were in the school's infirmary with legitimate injuries, most were rebelling at what they considered to be Anderson's draconian measures during Monday's practice. Although no player stepped forward to voice the team's concerns, Anderson quickly sized up the situation and decided to put a different spin on things. After running the few attendees through a light workout, Anderson assembled his depleted squad. "You better take the rest of today and tomorrow off," Eddie told his boys. "Go to a show or do anything you want. But rest, relax, and don't do anything strenuous. Come on out for practice on Thursday."[6] Anderson then phoned several local reporters to say that he was canceling practice for a few days. He explained that many of his players were injured and now needed rest.

Although still seething, most of the squad returned to practice on Thursday, November 5. Assembling his disgruntled troops Anderson candidly confessed: "I don't know how well we'll do this Saturday. We haven't practiced in a few days. In fact, I wonder what's going to happen to this squad for the rest of the season."[7] Forgoing any drills or conditioning, Anderson merely read off a starting team and asked those players to take their positions on the field. He then put a scout team opposite them and conducted a walk-through of the plays they could expect to see against heavily favored Colgate on Saturday.

Colgate was a major power in the thirties under their innovative coach, Andy Kerr. Kerr's famed 1932 Colgate squad had been "undefeated, untied, unscored-on and uninvited" to any bowl game. Many had hailed the craggy-faced Scotsman's squad as that year's true national champions. By mastering deceptive ball handling and downfield laterals, Colgate played a wide-open, razzle-dazzle style of football that had won Kerr national repute.

With the Red Raiders coming off an impressive win over Army and the shaky state of the Crusaders' morale, Anderson and his staff were not optimistic about the game's outcome. Unaware of the turmoil behind the scenes, a record crowd of 25,000 jammed into Fitton Field hoping to see an upset.[8] Colgate scored first on their trademark razzle-dazzle hook and ladder play. Holy Cross tied the game when Ecio Luciano, recently discharged from the infirmary, out-hustled a trio of Red Raiders to recover Osmanski's fumble in the end zone.

If missing a couple of days of practice hurt Anderson's squad, it didn't show. The two teams battled hammer and tongs throughout the second half before Bill Osmanski's punishing runs wore down Colgate's defense and Holy Cross emerged with a 20 to 13 win. Winning cures many ailments, and the following week there was no lingering animosity between coach and players as the Crusaders steam-rolled over Brown 32 to 0.

For one of the few times in Anderson's tenure at Mount St. James, Holy Cross found itself cast in the role of Goliath when it entertained tiny St. Anselm from Manchester, New Hampshire, on November 21. Being the last game before the annual Boston College showdown, Anderson opted to give his starters a breather by starting the second team. Sporting two nicknames — the Saints and Hawks (take your pick) — St. Anselm was coached by Cleo O'Donnell. O'Donnell had served as the head football coach at Holy Cross from 1919 to 1929, during which time he compiled a record of 69 wins against 27 losses. After the 1929 season he gave up coaching to become the school's athletic director. O'Donnell served in that position until resigning in 1934 to enter the restaurant business. In 1935 he took the St. Anselm job.

O'Donnell's Saints (or Hawks) came to town undefeated. However, they had previously faced no team as formidable as Holy Cross. To the New England press, St. Anselm had as much chance of beating Holy Cross as one had of bringing down a B-17 with a well-aimed rock.

With the customary starters muffled in blankets on the bench, the Crusader second team generated three long drives within the game's first 17 minutes. However, tenacious St. Anselm held on each occasion taking over on downs twice at its own 2-yard line and once on the 13. The underdogs grew more confident with each successive defensive stand. "Anderson put us [the first team] in early in the second quarter," recalled Moncevicz, "but by then St. Anselm was so hopped up that it didn't make a difference."[9]

Convinced they could now win, the inspired visitors played like men possessed. Led by fullback Joe Butchka and fiery 146-pound center Ed Hartung, the scrappy visitors put on a vitalized display of precision blocking and tackling. In the second half, the enheartened Saints dominated the action and drove to the Crusader 14-yard line before turning the ball over on downs.

The Crusaders were spared a humiliating loss when Anselm quarterback Johnny Spirada missed a desperate 40-yard field goal attempt on the last play of the game. The scoreless tie preserved St. Anselm's undefeated season.

As if the embarrassing tie wasn't bad enough for Holy Cross, star halfback Bill Osmanski emerged from the contest with a sore shoulder. When he was still unable to lift his arm by mid-week, Osmanski was scratched from the Boston College game.

The Boston College Eagles were in their first year under Coach Gilmour "Gloomy Gil" Dobie. Dobie had first gained coaching prominence at the University of Washington. During nine seasons at the Northwest school Dobie never lost a game while amassing 58 wins and 3 ties. Nicknamed "Gloomy Gil" because of his pessimistic outlook and dour personality, Dobie was extremely unpopular with his players. At home games he was often booed and occasionally pelted with rotten fruit and vegetables.

In 1917, Dobie began a three-year stint at Navy where his acerbic personality did not endear him to the Middies. According to Jack Clary, in *Navy Football: Gridiron Legends and Fighting Heroes,* "Ernest Von Heimberg, a great Navy end and captain of the 1917 team, reportedly had to be restrained many times from physically assaulting Dobie after being scorched by his demeaning comments."

Charley Hunt, an Annapolis tackle who later became a rear admiral, said: "Dobie was no leader — only a slave driver."[10] Nevertheless, Dobie's Navy teams only lost three games in three seasons.

In 1920, Dobie moved to Cornell where he immediately turned the "Big Red" into winners. During 16 seasons at Ithaca, Gloomy Gil's outlook never brightened. He continually alienated students and alumni by refusing to let either attend practices. He also boarded up the field house to keep spies out. After amassing a record of 82 wins, 36 losses and 7 ties, Dobie resigned under pressure after a winless 1935 season. He took over at Boston College in 1936.

Playing in snow flurries before 25,000 fans at Boston's Fenway Park, Holy Cross held an early 6 to 0 lead when Hip Moncevicz blocked Tony DiNatale's punt (as Anderson had predicted) and Dave Gavin fell on it in the end zone to boost the Crusaders' lead to 12.

In the second quarter Holy Cross center Bob Mautner and Moncevicz both left the game with injuries. "I could tell Anderson was angry with me," recalled Moncevicz, who limped to the sidelines. "He figured there was nothing seriously wrong with me and I knew I was one of the guys he was counting on."[11] Moncevicz's injury was later diagnosed as a fractured ankle.

With Mautner and Moncevicz sidelined, and Holy Cross' erratic passing game, the momentum swung to Boston College. Refusing to lose to their Jesuit rival for a third straight year, the Eagles clawed back on Fella Gintoff's short touchdown runs in the second and fourth quarters. Tony DiNatale's extra-point kick was the difference in the Eagles' 13 to 12 come-from-behind win. The distressing one-point loss left Holy Cross with a final 1936 record of 7 wins, 2 losses and 1 tie.

The 1937 squad was more confident and talented than any of Anderson's earlier Holy Cross teams. Sure of his best players, Dr. Anderson conducted fewer pre-season scrimmages than in previous years and none during the regular season.[12] His strategy had a two-prong effect. First, it reduced the risk of injuries and second, it prevented his team from leaving the game on the practice field. Mid-week scrimmages sometimes left players without sufficient stamina to meet the physical demands of Saturday's game. From 1937 on, Anderson rarely scrimmaged his teams during the season.

The Crusaders were "four deep" in talent at certain positions. The backfield especially was loaded with tough and skilled athletes such as Bill Osmanski, Paul Bartolomeo, Hillary Renz, Charlie Brucato, Arigo LaTanzi and quarterback Henry Ouellette. The bashful Ouellette was so soft-spoken that his signal calling was sometimes inaudible. "Ouellete was so quiet," recalled teammate Hank Giardi, "that he wouldn't say crap if he had a mouth full."[13]

Two promising sophomores also graced the roster: Ronnie Cahill and Hank Giardi. Cahill hailed from nearby Leominster. Weighing only 155 pounds, the taciturn Cahill was a talented runner who would prove to be one of the finest passers in the history of the school. An avid outdoorsman, Cahill often arrived at home games wearing hunting gear and wielding a rifle only minutes before the team was to take the field.

A native of East Hartford, Connecticut, Hank Giardi actually began his collegiate career at the University of Alabama. In a scrimmage during his freshman year the hard-hitting Connecticut Yankee earned a reputation for himself by tackling a popular varsity end so hard that he broke two of his ribs. The varsity end was one Paul "Bear" Bryant.[14]

At the start of fall practice during his sophomore year, Giardi grew disenchanted with Alabama's social climate and hitchhiked back to New England where he promptly enrolled at Holy Cross.

The 1937 season opened with a much-ballyhooed rematch against St. Anselm. Still buzzing over the previous year's scoreless tie, New England sportswriters billed the game as a grudge match between Anselm's David and Holy Cross' Goliath. Anselm's slingshot would hurl the running of Joe Butchka and the passing of Raymer "Scooter" McLean against the Crusaders. (After playing six seasons with the Chicago Bears, McLean would coach the Green Bay Packers in 1958 before being replaced by a relatively unknown coach named Vince Lombardi.) Despite the pre-game hype and numerous Holy Cross fumbles, the rematch was never close. Behind Bill Osmanski's two touchdowns the Crusaders dominated the action and blanked Cleo O'Donnell's gritty 23-man squad 21 to 0.

After successive wins over Providence and Georgetown, the Crusaders met the nationally ranked University of Georgia at Boston's Fenway Park on October 16. How did a small New England Catholic college come to schedule a major southern state university in the thirties? The schools' respective coaches arranged it. Coaching the Bulldogs was Anderson's former Notre Dame teammate and fellow Carlinville Eight conspirator, Harry Mehre.

Hipolet Moncevicz was a star tackle at Holy Cross from 1934 to 1936. During required late afternoon or evening vespers, Moncevicz recited prayers in his native Lithuanian. To assure the piety of Moncevicz's offerings, the Jesuits assigned a Lithuanian-speaking priest to monitor the tackle's supplications. (College of the Holy Cross Archives)

With no other college games scheduled in Boston that weekend, the schools' officials switched the game site from Worcester to Fenway Park in hopes of drawing a lucrative gate. With the country still reeling from the Great Depression, many of the local citizenry opted to listen to a radio broadcast of the game at home rather than pay the exorbitant $3.30 price of admission. A disappointing crowd of 20,000 attended the intersectional contest.

Big and ornery, the red-clad visitors possessed better backfield speed than their New England hosts. Playing for "Southern pride," Mehre's Bulldogs believed that stopping Osmanski was the key to victory. When Georgia assigned three men to shadow Osmanski, the fullback from Providence became a marked man.

Late in the first quarter, Georgia center Quinton Lumpkin knocked Osmanski out of bounds with a vicious tackle. As he lay splayed on the ground, Bulldog quarterback Lew Young jumped knees first onto Osmanski. The flagrant act drew a 15-yard penalty. It also left Osmanski dazed and hurting. He continued to play, but his effectiveness was limited, and Anderson removed him in the fourth quarter. (After the game Osmanski collapsed in the locker room and remained unconscious for three minutes. Complaining of lower back pain, the fullback was hospitalized overnight. His sore back forced him to miss the team's next two games.)

Holy Cross scored first on Ronnie Cahill's 20-yard touchdown pass to fellow-sophomore Bill Histen. With both teams hitting at high velocity, the contest was a continuum of vicious blocking and tackling. Anderson, angered by Georgia's repeated late hitting, approached the officials at halftime and accused them of losing control of the game.[15]

Hoping to protect its 7 to 0 lead, Holy Cross kept the ball on the ground for most of the second half. Down but not out, Georgia took to the air with four minutes remaining and completed a half-dozen passes en route to an 85-yard scoring drive. The drive culminated in a 16-yard touchdown pass from Billy Mims to Otis Maffet. To better focus on kicking the tying extra point, both the Georgia holder and kicker Lew Young removed their helmets. It didn't help. A strong rush by Crusader ends Ed O'Melia and Bill Histen forced Young to hurry his kick, and the ball sailed just inches wide of the mark. The game ended three plays later. The thrilling 7 to 6 win catapulted Anderson's Holy Cross squad into national prominence. Several sportswriters hailed it as the greatest football victory in the school's history.

In a post-game press conference Georgia coach Harry Mehre and Anderson bantered before reporters. When informed that his Bulldogs out-gained Holy Cross in first downs 13 to 9, the gregarious Mehre quipped, "I'll take that fact back to the alumni instead of the score."[16] While Anderson remained tight-lipped about the stellar performance of sophomore Ronnie Cahill, Mehre was lavish in his praise: "Cahill impressed me tremendously. He'll get my vote for outstanding halfback in the United States."[17]

Cahill's gridiron accomplishments certainly earn him an exalted status in the pantheon of Holy Cross football. Jim Anderson, Eddie's youngest son, relates, "Whenever Dad talked about his greatest players, he always mentioned Ronnie Cahill in the same breath as Nile Kinnick."[18] (Kinnick, of course, won the Heisman Trophy while playing for Anderson at Iowa in 1939.)

Over the next five weeks Holy Cross defeated Western Maryland, Colgate and Brown, while earning hard-fought scoreless ties against Pop Warner's Temple Owls and Carnegie Tech. Even though his squad was undefeated in seven games, Dr. Anderson was not without his detractors.

One of his harshest critics was the *Worcester Telegram's* F.E. Whitmarsh. After the 1937 tie with Carnegie Tech, Whitmarsh wrote an open letter to Anderson in his daily column, "Sports and Sportsmen." "Why do we always have to be so staid, solid and conventional... Why must our side always be so conservative?"[19] Whitmarsh then took Anderson to task for eschewing field goal attempts in the first and third quarters and for refusing to substitute fresh players against Tech.

Whitmarsh's second criticism reverberated in certain Worcester neighborhoods, where local high school athletes were said to be balking at playing

On the eve of the 1937 Boston College game, Anderson's starting eleven posed for the camera at Fitton Field. Front Row (L-R): Eddie O'Melia #61, Bill Shields #30, James Turner #48, Jim Bowman #62, John Carr #40, Walter Walewski #50 and Bill Histen #44. Back Row (L-R): Hank Giardi #23, Henry Ouellette #24, Bill Osmanski #25 and Ronnie Cahill #20. The Crusaders defeated Boston College 20 to 0 to finish the season undefeated with 8 wins and 2 ties. (College of the Holly Cross Archives)

for Holy Cross because of Anderson's reputed reluctance to develop second- and third-team players.

While some critics may not have cared for Anderson's game strategies, no one could argue with his coaching results. At the time of Whitmarsh's attack, Anderson's record at Holy Cross stood at 38 wins, 6 losses and 4 ties.

Anderson's squad had won 7 and tied 2 entering the 1937 season finale against Boston College. Boston College came into the contest with 3 losses and 1 tie, and the honeymoon between the school and Coach Gloomy Gil Dobie was over. Disgruntled with Dobie's dour personality and his so-called "antiquated emphasis on sheer power football," many B.C. alumni were hollering for Gloomy Gil's scalp. To make matters worse, the Eagles' football budget was supposedly $40,000 in the red.[20] Nevertheless, an upset win over the Cross would go a long way towards smoothing the ruffled feathers of B.C. alumni.

There'd be no upset in 1937. Playing on a balmy afternoon before 34,000 at Boston's Fenway Park, Anderson's Crusaders controlled the action from start to finish. Ronnie Cahill bootlegged five yards for the game's first score, and "Bullet" Bill Osmanski's two second-half touchdowns gave Holy Cross a 20 to 0 win and a season record of 8 wins and 2 ties. It was Eddie Anderson's second undefeated season in three years.

After the game, Holy Cross athletic director Tom McCabe publicly announced that the Crusaders would welcome any and all bowl invitations.[21] None came.

13

Iowa Comes Calling

By 1938 Eddie Anderson was also carving his niche in the medical profession. Although still affiliated with Massachusetts General Hospital, Anderson had also been selected to head the ear, nose and throat clinic at Boston's Veterans Hospital. The Veterans Administration position enhanced Anderson's professional status, and the job's annual $4,000 salary provided a boon for the growing Anderson family. Eddie and Mary now had three sons: nine-year-old Nick, six-year-old Jerry and Jim, age two.

That spring Eddie attended a medical conference on obstructions of the throat and airway in Philadelphia. As fate would have it, on the eve of Eddie's scheduled return, two-year-old Jimmy Anderson swallowed a safety pin. Mary Anderson rushed her son to a local hospital where she learned that, while the pin was not blocking the youngster's airway, it was firmly lodged in his throat. Doctors feared that manual attempts to extract it might inadvertently move it to a position where it might block Jimmy's airway. Such a mishap could have fatal consequences. As Jimmy was not in immediate danger, Mary refused to consent to surgery for her son. Instead, she opted to wait for Eddie's return to discuss their next course of action.

The next morning the hospital had a car waiting at the train station. Upon his arrival, Anderson was apprised of his son's condition and whisked to the hospital. After examining Jimmy, Anderson removed his jacket, rolled up his sleeves, washed his hands and then calmly reached his hand into the boy's throat. Extracting his hand a moment later, Anderson winked at his wide-eyed son as he revealed the shiny safety pin between his index and middle fingers.[1]

129

At the dawn of the 1938 season Anderson again had the Crusaders poised on the brink of national prominence. Behind team captain Bill Osmanski, the team possessed even more talent and depth than the previous year's squad. With seven of its nine games at home, another banner year seemed imminent.

The Crusaders started strongly with home wins over Providence, Rhode Island and Manhattan before traveling to Pittsburgh to meet Carnegie Tech. Like Holy Cross, Coach Bill Kern's Skibos were loaded with talent. Chet Grant, Anderson's former Irish teammate who was now scouting for Notre Dame, told the good doctor that Tech was the best team he had scouted all season.[2]

The game was a bruising contest that saw Carnegie Tech take a 7 to 0 halftime lead. Holy Cross retaliated when Osmanski returned the second-half

Bill Osmanski may have been the greatest football player ever to don the Royal Purple for Holy Cross. As a sophomore in 1936 he burst onto the scene with a 78-yard interception return for a touchdown to give the Crusaders their first ever win over Dartmouth, 7 to 0. Here, Osmanski strikes a Heisman pose in front of Alumni Hall. (College of the Holy Cross Archives)

kick-off 92 yards for a score. Unfortunately for the Crusaders, Jim Turner then missed his only extra point of the season. Although repeatedly threatening to score, Holy Cross could muster no more points and Carnegie Tech prevailed 7 to 6. In the end, Tech's superior blocking and tackling made the difference. It was Holy Cross' first loss in 14 games and would ultimately cost the Crusaders a trip to the Sugar Bowl.

It was a melancholic train ride back to Massachusetts. However, the gloom lifted when the train pulled into Worcester's Union Station on Sunday morning to reveal the entire Holy Cross student body cheering on the platform.[3] Most of the players were speechless at their classmates' spirited show of support. The astonished players detrained to blaring music, handshakes and congratulatory slaps on the back. Several, like Osmanski, were limping. It was a touching and unforgettable experience for the emotionally overwhelmed players as they posed for a picture before a throng of cheering classmates. The photo appeared in the next day's *Worcester Telegram*.

Above the loud music Anderson shouted to *Telegram* sportswriter Roy Mumpton: "We no longer have an unbeaten record to worry about. There is nothing but tough opposition ahead of us, but I'm now hoping that this defeat may be just the thing to fire our boys to better football than we have played thus far."[4]

Anderson needn't have worried.

The following week Georgia's Bulldogs invaded Fitton Field before a crowd of 20,000. Dignitaries in attendance included the Peach State's governor, I.D. Rivers, and Massachusetts Senator David I. Walsh. Georgia was loaded with returning veterans from its 1937 squad. However, Anderson would no longer be pitting his football acuity against his good friend and former Notre Dame teammate, Harry Mehre. After winning 59 games in a decade at Georgia, Mehre flew the coop for the University of Mississippi in 1938. Joe Hunt was now coaching the Bulldogs.

With Arigo LaTanzi substituting for the injured Henry Ouellette, and Gus Gerasimas and Hillary Renz alternating at fullback for the ailing Bill Osmanski, the Crusaders scored in each quarter en route to an impressive 29 to 6 win.

Anderson spoke glowingly of his team's performance: "Everything we did was right. We just couldn't make a mistake.

"Georgia was a good team, but it just happened to play us when everything was working."[5]

"This is the best Holy Cross team yet," remarked Colgate scout Les Hart after watching the Crusaders cruise past Georgia.[6]

The Crusaders did nothing to change Hart's mind the following week. With Osmanski back in the lineup Holy Cross shut out Colgate 21 to 0. It

was Anderson's fourth-straight win over Andy Kerr's Red Raiders. On November 5, after a scoreless first half, the Crusaders exploded to steam-roll over visiting Temple 33 to 0.

Perhaps the most exciting game of 1938 came against DeOrmond "Tuss" McLaughry's Brown University squad during a rare Friday afternoon contest at Fitton Field. The gentlemanly McLaughry had taken over the coaching reins at Brown in 1926. That year McLaughry's Bruins went undefeated. The only blemish on their record was a season-ending tie against Colgate. When all 11 starters played 60 minutes in successive wins over Yale and Dartmouth, New England sportswriters tabbed McLaughry's Bruins the "Iron Men." (It was a moniker that Anderson would later apply to his 1939 Iowa squad.) Universally respected by his coaching colleagues, the mild-mannered McLaughry never complained about the limited material he often had to work with and never criticized his players publicly.

A raucous crowd of 27,000 turned out to see the inspired and underdog Bruins give Holy Cross all it could handle. The spark plug for Brown was John McLaughry, the coach's son. McLaughry was a gifted passer and runner, a devastating tackler and blocker, and a skilled punter and place-kicker. Brown took the opening kick-off and marched 71 yards to take a 6 to 0 lead. There was no further scoring until the third quarter when McLaughry broke a 30-yard run up the middle. Bill Histen's jarring tackle forced McLaughry to fumble on the Crusader 5-yard line, but the Bruins' George Mahwinney alertly recovered it in the end zone to give Brown a 12 to 0 lead.

Late in the third quarter the Crusaders seemed snake-bit when a penalty nullified Hillary Renz's one-yard scoring plunge and placed the ball at the Brown 6-yard line with a fourth-and-goal. Ronnie Cahill then swept around end but was bounced out of bounds at the 2-yard line. Knocked woozy from landing on his head, Cahill had to be helped to the bench.

With Brown taking over on downs and the dazed Cahill now sidelined, a team of lesser mettle might have folded, but not Anderson's Holy Cross bunch. They were gutsy kids, talented and tough, who found ways to win. Two plays later Brown's Shine Hall punted and Arigo LaTanzi returned it to the Brown 33. Hank Giardi then connected on a 14-yard pass to Jack Reardon as the third quarter closed. Osmanski opened the fourth by plowing 14 yards off-tackle to the 5-yard line. Three plays later Osmanski scored from a yard out. Turner's extra-point kick narrowed the score to Brown 12, Holy Cross 7.

Opposite: A superstar on the gridiron, Osmanski was also a big man on campus. Attired in top hat and tails, Osmanski enters a limousine en route to one of many formal affairs he attended during his years at Holy Cross. (College of the Holy Cross Archives)

In the game's waning minutes Holy Cross launched a 68-yard, 13-play drive to break Brown's heart. Absorbing several punishing tackles during the drive, Osmanski was nearly "out on his feet" as the Crusaders neared the Bruin goal line.[7] Yet, with only 43 seconds remaining, he somehow found the resolve to plow two yards through a wall of tacklers for the winning touchdown. Turner added the extra point and the game ended five plays later with the final score Holy Cross 14, Brown 12.

In the post-game locker room, concerned teammates peeled a grass-stained jersey off Osmanski, who was too exhausted to undress himself. As he slumped on a bench, Osmanski began to shed tears of joy. The fact that this kid from Providence, Rhode Island, ever got to play college football, let alone become an All-American, is a stirring story in itself. At age 10, Osmanski's father died. While playing sandlot football during his early teens, he twice sustained injuries that required life-threatening operations followed by lengthy periods of convalescence. In high school, with six brothers and sisters at home, Osmanski washed dishes at a local restaurant every night after practice until 11 p.m. As a high school senior Osmanski endured another setback when he broke his leg in mid-season.

"I was proud of every boy on the team today," declared a beaming Eddie Anderson after the game. "That was one of the most gratifying victories I have ever seen. I would far rather win like that than win by 50 to 0, especially when we got all the bad breaks, dropped passes and took those penalties on touchdown plays."[8]

With two weeks until their season finale against Boston College, Anderson gave his team a well-earned weekend off.

While Anderson's Crusaders were reveling in their come-from-behind win over Brown, the football picture at the University of Iowa was mired in the depths of despair. The Great Depression had been financially devastating for the state. With the precipitous drop in agricultural prices, thousands of Iowa farmers went broke. Many lost their farms and homes to foreclosure. Hundreds of financial institutions statewide declared insolvency and closed their doors forever. The thirties dragged on with no economic silver lining in sight. Mirroring the state's economic woes was the University of Iowa athletic program. The school's football picture was especially abysmal.

Like the depression itself, Iowa's football problems began in 1929 when the university was rocked by a slush fund scandal. During their investigation, Big Ten officials found Iowa's illegal payments to be so egregious that they banned the Hawkeyes from conference play in 1930. Although re-admitted in 1931, Iowa had difficulty attracting quality student-athletes in the wake of the scandal.

A new 53,000-seat stadium had been completed in 1929, but game day attendance rarely approached 20,000 over the next decade. Iowa won only six Big Ten games in eight years. In 1938, Iowa's lone win came against the University of Chicago's lowly Maroons. (The once proud Maroons of Amos Alonzo Stagg would drop football after 1939.)

On the weekend that the Crusaders were savoring their win over Brown, the University of Iowa's athletic board fired football coach Irl Tubbs. Tired of being shellacked on the gridiron and operating in the red financially, Iowa hoped to replace Tubbs with a renowned coach. University officials sought a proven winner, perhaps a Rockne disciple well versed in the Notre Dame system and, most importantly, a native of Iowa.

Walter "Stub" Stewart was an alumni member of Iowa's athletic board and a prominent Des Moines lawyer. As a 120-pound halfback, Stewart had played football for Iowa from 1907 through 1909. He now longed to see his beloved Hawkeyes return to the national spotlight they had enjoyed under Coach Howard Jones in the early twenties. For several years Stewart had been quietly tracking Anderson's success at Holy Cross. He supposedly recommended Anderson's hiring to the athletic board after the 1937 season, but the board failed to act.[9] Iowa's athletic board now gave Stewart its blessing in procuring Anderson's services.

Sometime during the week of November 13, 1938, Stewart boarded a train for Boston to meet with Anderson. Exactly where and when the two met has never been ascertained, but when they did, Stewart offered Anderson a deal he couldn't refuse. It included a three-year contract at an annual salary of $10,000 plus a staff position at the eye, ear, nose and throat clinic at the University of Iowa Hospital. The salary Iowa offered was a $3,000 raise over what he was making at Holy Cross. Coaching at Iowa also meant no more 80-mile round-trip commute during the football season. While those were reasons enough for Anderson to accept the job, there was still a more compelling reason. The chance to return to his native Iowa and ply his coaching skills in what at the time was the most prestigious football conference in the country was a challenge the competitive Anderson couldn't pass up.

At no time before or during the negotiations did any Iowa official contact Holy Cross seeking permission to talk with Anderson. Playing his cards close to the vest, Anderson also kept his employer in the dark regarding the talks with Iowa. Both parties agreed that no formal announcement would be made until after the Crusaders' season finale with Boston College. The agreement also stipulated that Iowa officials would permit Eddie to coach Holy Cross in a bowl game should such an invitation be forthcoming.[10]

Despite the clandestine efforts of both parties, reports soon began appearing in Boston and Chicago newspapers that Anderson would succeed Tubbs

Nattily attired and smoking a cigar, Dr. Anderson intently watches the action during the 1938 Boston College–Holy Cross game at Fenway Park. Team trainer Bart Sullivan is seated in front of Anderson. The 29 to 7 Crusader victory gave Anderson's teams a record of 47 wins, 7 losses and 4 ties during his first six-year coaching stint at Holy Cross. (College of the Holy cross Archives)

at Iowa. With rumors of Anderson's imminent departure swirling like late November snowflakes, the two Catholic rivals squared off again.

The 1938 edition of New England's Jesuit rivalry had all the makings of a typical Holy Cross-Boston College clash — a hard-fought, thrilling contest to be decided in the game's waning moments. Boston College coach Gloomy Gil Dobie entered the fray as obdurate as ever. His dour personality and acrid remarks continued to alienate players and alumni. Yet, his coaching trademark of winning games was still very much in evidence as the Eagles came into the contest undefeated.

The game was played in sub-freezing temperatures (inclement weather was often another feature of the Jesuit rivalry) before a bundled, but spirited, crowd of 38,000 at Fenway Park. Remnants of a Thanksgiving Day snowstorm had been plowed into giant snow banks surrounding the field, but the playing surface itself was relatively dry. The Crusaders jumped to a 14 to 0 halftime lead, but the Eagles narrowed the score to 14 to 7 by marching 50 yards on their first possession in the second half. From that point on, however, the game belonged to Holy Cross. Later in the quarter Osmanski sprinted around right end for a 5-yard gain. While being tackled, Osmanski alertly pitched to teammate Johnny Kelley who sprinted 45 yards untouched down the sidelines for the third Crusader touchdown.

Whenever Holy Cross needed a first down, Osmanski sliced through tacklers for the required yardage. Late in the game with the ball inside B.C.'s 5-yard line, Anderson subbed for all of the starters except Bullet Bill. With 30 seconds left, the indomitable Osmanski plunged over for the game's final touchdown. Ecstatic Holy Cross fans poured into the end zone, engulfing the senior fullback in a wave of hugs and backslapping. Boston's "finest" had to rescue Osmanski from the swarming celebrants and escort him back to the bench.

Holy Cross' impressive 29 to 7 win convinced those in attendance that the Crusaders were worthy of anybody's bowl bid. The austere Gil Dobie turned gracious in their post-game meeting and proffered the following advice: "Eddie, you're a young man in this business. I'm an old man. Let me give you a piece of advice. Never lose the final game of the season.

"First of all, you're losing it to a traditional rival and around here the traditional rival is right in the same neighborhood. You'll spend a very unhappy winter, spring and summer explaining what happened. No matter where you go, you'll run into alumni. In this section there are alumni and parents and friends."[11]

Later, both coaches lauded Osmanski's play. "Bill Osmanski is the best back I have ever seen," professed Anderson. "He was the one who made the team go today... He is the finest back in the country."

Dobie, who praised a player as often as a miser tipped a silver dollar, trumpeted, "I think that Osmanski is the best back I have ever seen in all my life."[12]

Anderson's coaching career was on a meteoric rise while Dobie's was drawing to a close. Anderson's six-year run at Holy Cross had produced an overall record of 47 wins, 7 losses and 4 ties. Despite losing only one game in 1938, Boston College officials had had enough of Gloomy Gil and his sullen demeanor. The school refused to renew his contract. Independently wealthy from a series of shrewd stockmarket investments, the 59-year-old Dobie never coached again.

On Sunday evening, November 27, Anderson telephoned Holy Cross Athletic Director Tom McCabe to inform him that he was resigning as football coach. Although McCabe had heard rumors of Iowa's interest in Anderson, Eddie's announcement still came as a shock. In an eleventh-hour attempt to keep the coach on board, McCabe began negotiating with Anderson over the phone. McCabe must have been persuasive, for according to an article later written by Bert McGrane in the *Des Moines Register*, "As late as 8 p.m. on Sunday [November 27, 1938] Holy Cross was still trying to keep Anderson... Anderson supposedly made one phone call to ask Iowa whether it mattered much whether he came or not..."

After realizing that he could not dissuade Anderson, McCabe issued the following news release at 9 p.m.: "Dr. Edward Anderson notified me tonight ... that he wished to resign as coach at the college. He gave me no reason for his action which comes as a direct shock to me... I have read the accounts in the newspapers during the past week, but I felt Dr. Anderson would consult with me before he did anything about accepting such propositions as have been carried in the press.

"We wish to make clear that Dr. Anderson has made the decision without consulting the officials of Holy Cross. He is going because he wishes to go himself. We wish him success in his new field."[13]

The next morning, when Iowa athletic director, E.G. "Dad" Schroeder, was officially announcing Anderson's hiring, Eddie and Mary Anderson, along with assistant coaches Joe Sheeketski and Jim Harris, were boarding the New England Limited at Trinity Station. Several photographers and *Boston Post* sportswriter Gerry Hern were there to see them off. "He left," wrote Hern, "the same way he came, without fanfare."[14]

While Anderson's departure lacked fanfare, Eddie did leave with regrets.

On the morning the Andersons left Boston, Roy Mumpton quoted the departing coach in the *Worcester Telegram*: "I have thoroughly enjoyed my work and associations at Holy Cross with players, athletic officials, faculty and student body. I shall always cherish the six years I have spent in Worcester and it is with regrets that I am leaving. But I feel that there is a greater opportunity in the position which I am considering and that I would not be honest with myself if I did not accept it."[15]

14

A COACHING MOSES COMES TO IOWA

It was cloudy with a light mist when the train carrying Anderson pulled into Iowa City's Rock Island station on Tuesday afternoon, November 29, 1938. A glance out the window revealed a multitude of cheering fans on the station's platform eagerly awaiting the arrival of Iowa's new football coach. Reaching for his hat and overcoat, Anderson nodded approvingly at the two men sitting across from him. Taking their boss' cue, Joe Sheeketski and Jim Harris followed Anderson down the aisle to exit the train; a third man, John Mooney, scurried closely behind.

The editor of *The Daily Iowan*, Mooney had left Iowa the previous day to meet Anderson in Chicago and accompany him on the last leg of his trip to Iowa City. By doing so, the enterprising Mooney hoped to scoop other newspapers by interviewing the state's newest celebrity. Mooney found the well-dressed Anderson to be accommodating, articulate and poised.

Stepping onto the station platform, Anderson was greeted warmly by both Iowa athletic director, E.G. "Dad" Shroeder, and Myron J. Walker, Iowa City's mayor. After exchanging pleasantries, the coaches were whisked to a local hotel only long enough to register and deposit their luggage before being ushered into a waiting convertible for a parade ride to the Iowa campus. Arriving at the Old Capitol building, Anderson attended a brief closed-door meeting with the university's board in control of athletics, headed by Professor Karl E. Lieb.

At four o'clock the newcomers were guided into the Old Capitol's east portico where over 1,500 students and fans anxiously waited. After a half-dozen administrators and prominent alumni lavished praise on the new coach, Anderson was asked to address the crowd. Relaxed and confident, Anderson approached the microphone stationed behind a banner-covered railing that read, "Welcome Home, Eddie." He then set about charming the Hawkeye faithful.

"Display this same spirit," implored Anderson, "and we'll play winning football next fall!"[1]

Anderson's entreaty met with booming applause peppered with vehement pledges of support. The crowd grew ecstatic and the atmosphere electric. Could this native son, this man of medicine, who learned his football from America's greatest coaching legend, heal the ailing Iowa program? Previous skeptics and zealots alike now sensed that perhaps this disciple of Rockne could indeed lead the Hawkeyes to football's Promised Land. Dr. Eddie Anderson never doubted it.

Casting a critical eye on the afternoon's festivities were Iowa football players Nile Kinnick and captain-elect Erwin Prasse. Only weeks before in a letter to his parents, Kinnick, a Christian Scientist, expressed concerns over rumors that "some Notre Dame man" would be Iowa's next coach. "The consensus of opinion," wrote Kinnick on November 14, 1938, "seems to point to Buck Shaw of Santa Clara — a former Stuart (Iowa) boy and player at Notre Dame."[2] The halfback had hoped that either of Iowa's assistant coaches, Ernie Nevers or Pat Boland, would succeed the outgoing Irl Tubbs as head coach.

Kinnick's doubts, however, evaporated upon meeting the charismatic Anderson. The next day, November 30, Kinnick wrote home, "Yesterday afternoon the coaches arrived amid much fanfare and enthusiasm... I met and talked with them briefly. Head coach Anderson impressed me favorably. Both he and I took an immediate like and respect for each other... He has a lot of fire and enthusiasm and looks to be a determined man — in actuality he isn't as tough looking as the newspaper photographs would indicate."[3]

Nile Kinnick's words proved to be prophetic. The player-coach relationship between Kinnick and Anderson would be unique to team sports, and it's doubtful that in just a single season any player ever had a greater impact on his coach's career or vice versa. In 1939, Kinnick's gridiron heroics would help Anderson garner "Coach of the Year" honors. Conversely, by exploiting Kinnick's many talents, Anderson put his halfback in the national spotlight that allowed him to win the Heisman Trophy.

The dynamic Anderson also made an immediate impact on quarterback Al Couppee. On Wednesday night, November 30, city and university officials held a function for Anderson and his staff at the Jefferson Hotel. Couppee was one of several Iowa players in attendance. Couppee recalled, "When introduced to Dr. Eddie Anderson, I first got the Anderson handshake. Eddie damn near broke my hand, but I squeezed back as hard as I could. Anderson's handshake became famous in just a few introductions.

"I became a believer in Dr. Eddie Anderson. He was leadership defined. My thinking turned around drastically after one meeting with Eddie."[4]

On Thursday, December 1, Anderson, Sheeketski and Harris boarded the Rock Island Rocket to Chicago where Mary Anderson, who had spent the last few days visiting family, rejoined Eddie for the trip back to Boston. On December 18 Anderson found himself in need of a backfield coach when Holy Cross hired Joe Sheeketski to succeed Eddie as the school's head coach.

The position was still vacant in mid–February when Anderson and Harris returned to Iowa City to prepare for spring football. First on the pair's agenda, however, was a goodwill tour throughout the Hawkeye State to promote Iowa football. The barnstorming began in Eddie's hometown of Mason City on Monday night, February 13, 1939. It was Anderson's first visit to Mason City since attending his mother's funeral 15 years earlier.

The Mason City Chamber of Commerce, in cooperation with the local chapters of the Lions, Rotary and Kiwanis clubs, honored Anderson with a dinner at the Hotel Hanford. Over 750 people from 30 different cities turned out to hear the new Hawkeye coach. Mason City's Harvey J. Bryant was the toastmaster for the evening with Emmettsburg attorney James Fay as one of the featured speakers. An avid Iowa fan, the hunchback Fay was a motivational speaker whose resonant voice captivated audiences. In 1938, a desperate Irl Tubbs had asked Fay to deliver a pep talk to the downtrodden Hawkeyes before the Purdue game.[5] Inspired by Fay's fiery speech, Iowa played its best game of the season by holding the Big Ten's second-place Boilermakers to a scoreless tie.

Beaming proudly in spats and a three-piece suit from his seat on the dais was 72-year-old Edward Martinius Anderson, Eddie's father. Seated next to him was Eddie's high school coach at Mason City, C.A. "Jack" West. It was West who had first persuaded the elder Anderson to allow his son to play football. Like Anderson, West also went on to considerable success coaching college football. While coaching at South Dakota State University from 1919 to 1927, West's teams compiled an overall record of 44 wins, 17 losses and 9 ties. Also taking in the evening's activities were Iowa halfback Nile Kinnick and tackle Mike Enich.

The after-dinner talk was moved from the hotel to the Mason City High School auditorium to accommodate the crowd. There, Iowa's assistant athletic director, Glen Devine, concluded his introduction of Anderson by stating: "You can't lick an elephant with a feather duster. That's why we got Eddie. We'll meet big time coaching with a big time coach."[6]

In his first formal talk to his fellow Iowans Anderson spoke with both confidence and humility. He concluded his remarks by declaring: "Nobody is barred. Color, creed and race make no difference. If a boy is one of the 11 best players he'll be out there on Saturday afternoons. I don't care if the 11 are all tackles, guards, centers, ends or backs, they'll be playing football."[7]

(Before Anderson's arrival Iowa had been one of the few major state universities where African-Americans starred on the gridiron. Fred "Duke" Slater had been an All-American tackle in 1921 and scatback Ossie Simmons, known as the "Ebony Eel," had awed Iowa fans with his slithering running style in the mid-thirties. Homer Harris of the 1937 squad was the first black to captain a major college football team. Anderson too would prove to be colorblind when it came to putting his best team on the field. The list of black athletes who starred for the Hawkeyes during Anderson's tenure included tackle Jim Walker, who played from 1939 to 1941, as well as Emlen Tunnell and guard Earl Banks, who both played after the war. Walker and Banks would go on to prominent coaching careers at Ohio's Central State University and Morgan State University respectively. Tunnell would be voted into the NFL's Hall of Fame after a brilliant 13-year career with both the New York Giants and Green Bay Packers. When Anderson's coaching drew harsh criticism in 1947, Tunnell and Banks were among his staunchest defenders.)

Anderson's barnstorming trip ended in the state capital on Friday, February 24. At a Des Moines Chamber of Commerce luncheon Anderson shared the dais with U.S. Secretary of Commerce Harry Hopkins. While introducing the new coach, Iowa athletic director, Dad Shroeder, explained that the university was giving Anderson a "blank check" in overseeing the football program. "There will be no interference with Dr. Anderson's football program," declared Shroeder. "He will schedule games, buy the equipment, supervise training and handle everything else connected with football. Dr. Anderson holds the chair as head of the department of football and any reports to the contrary are erroneous."[8]

When his turn to speak came, Anderson echoed his earlier remarks at Mason City. "There will be no political appointments on Iowa's 1939 football team. If a boy doesn't get into a game, it will be because he is not good enough. That's the only test we will require, and no other qualification is necessary."[9]

Later that afternoon Eddie Anderson told a joint session of the Iowa state legislature. "It's your state — your football team. I'll try to do my part to give you a team worthy of your support."[10]

That same day university officials announced the hiring of Frank Carideo as Iowa's backfield coach. A native of Mount Vernon, New York, Carideo had quarterbacked Notre Dame to undefeated seasons in 1929 and 1930. At 5' 7" and 175 pounds, the two-time All-American was known as Knute Rockne's "coach on the field." Besides being an excellent runner, passer and defensive back, Carideo was also an outstanding punter. A master of the coffin corner kick, Carideo once nailed four punts inside the 1-yard line in a game against Northwestern.

In 1931 Carideo served as an assistant coach at Purdue where he often ran scout team halfback against the Boilermaker's first-team defense. Only a year out of college, Carideo hadn't lost a step. The scuttlebutt among Purdue tacklers was, "If Coach Carideo liked you he just ran by you. If he didn't, he ran over you."[11]

In 1932, the 23-year-old Carideo became Missouri's head coach. Although capable of articulating his vast knowledge of the game, Carideo's three-year tenure at Missouri was a nightmare. In the early thirties, several pockets of the "Show Me State" were Ku Klux Klan strongholds, and the embers of Civil War animosities still smoldered. Many Missourians were unwilling to accept an Italian-Catholic "Yankee" as head coach of the state's major university. Had his Tiger teams matched the gridiron success of those he had quarterbacked at Notre Dame perhaps things would have been different for Carideo, but they weren't.

On November 30, 1934, Carideo resigned as Missouri's coach after his teams managed only two wins in three seasons. Carideo then served as both assistant football coach and head basketball coach at Mississippi State University, where he met and married his lovely wife, Vera. Bringing Carideo's knowledge and technical expertise to Iowa City would prove to be a boon for the Hawkeye football program.

Wherever Anderson traveled that spring, Iowans rolled out the red carpet. With university officials giving him *carte blanche* in administering the football program and the enthusiastic support of Iowa fans, Anderson hoped to make the Hawkeyes competitive immediately. To realize that aim, Anderson decided to delay starting his medical affiliation at the University of Iowa Hospital until after the 1939 season, thus freeing him to focus all of his energies on reviving the ailing football program.

Marshaling his resources, Anderson took out ads in *The Daily Iowan* announcing open tryouts for spring football. Wanting all of his football hands on deck for spring drills, Anderson tried to prevail upon captain-elect Erwin Prasse to forgo playing shortstop for the Iowa baseball team in order to participate in spring football.

"Are you going to be with us for spring drills?" Anderson asked his senior end.

Prasse, who batted cleanup for the two-time defending Big Ten Champion Hawkeyes and entertained hopes of one day playing big league baseball, replied, "Coach, I can't let my baseball buddies down. We want to win another Big Ten Championship this spring."

"He looked at me like I was crazy," recalled Prasse. "From that time on Dr. Eddie was pretty chilly towards me. Yet, I knew that I could show him in the fall."[12]

A gifted three-sport athlete who won nine varsity letters during his Iowa career, Prasse again cracked Iowa's starting lineup in 1939.

In late February, Anderson held his first team meeting in University Hall. While diagramming the T-formation on the blackboard Anderson announced, "Okay, men, let's select an All-Opponent Team from the Big Ten. Who's the best left end in the conference?"[13] As the players exchanged quizzical glances, the new coach solicited reluctant responses from around the room.

"Okay," spouted Anderson, "now, who's the best left tackle?"

Getting into the spirit of things, several of the Hawkeyes chirped players' names until arriving at a consensus. Anderson continued the process until all 11 positions were filled. Giving the squad a minute to survey its handiwork, the good doctor then directed a question at captain-elect Erwin Prasse. "Prasse," Anderson asked while pointing to a name on the board, "are you better than this guy?"

Caught by surprise, but confident in his own abilities, Prasse responded emphatically, "Yes. I am!"

"Good!" snapped Eddie, who then wrote Prasse's name next to the left end's name already on the board.

Pointing to another name Anderson asked, "Enich, is this guy a better football player than you?"

"No, Coach," replied tackle Mike Enich.

"All right, then," Eddie responded as he wrote Enich's name next to that of the All-Big Ten tackle's.

Calling on select returning veterans, the cagey Anderson worked his way through the lineup getting an affirmative response from each player he quizzed. When he finished, Anderson put the chalk down, wiped the chalk dust off his hands and calmly stated, "Well, if we feel we can match up with the All-Conference team, there's no reason why we can't pursue the Big Ten Championship this year."

"Listening to Anderson at that first meeting, many of us thought that his expectations were out of bounds — maybe even crazy," recalled Prasse, "but yet, he inspired us!"

Sophomore Bill Diehl from Cedar Rapids also remembers Anderson's first team meeting. "I thought to myself, this guy walks like a coach and he talks like a coach. He was so different from Irl Tubbs. Anderson exuded confidence. Everyone in the room could feel it, and we all left believing in both him and in ourselves."[14]

Believing was only a start. It needed to be coupled with hard work and

The University of Iowa football team is pictured during spring practice in 1939. Under Dr. Eddie Anderson's leadership, the squad established a legacy as Iowa's "Iron Men" and restored Hawkeye football to national prominence. Anderson, in Iowa sweatshirt, stands at far right of second row. Standing with hands in pockets beside Anderson is assistant coach Frank Carideo. Assistant Jim Harris is standing on far left. To the right of Harris with hands crossed is Nile Kinnick. George "Red" Frye holds football in front row. Team captain Erwin Prasse is seated in second row; one player to left of Frye. The African American in the third row is Jim Walker, who went on to a lengthy coaching career at Central State University in Ohio. Bill Diehl is the second player to the left of Walker. Papers of Nile C. Kinnick, Dept. of Special Collections, University of Iowa Libraries, Iowa City, Iowa.

intense preparation. Anderson provided both by conducting 10 grueling weeks of spring drills.

As previously mentioned, Anderson had run ads in *The Daily Iowan* inviting students to try out for football. One of the 125 candidates who reported was 6' 2", 205-pound Wally Bergstrom. Because his high school at Olds, Iowa, lacked enough boys to field a team, he had never played football. He had, however, developed exceptional hand strength from milking cows on his family's farm. On the first day of spring drills Bergstrom walked onto the practice field and introduced himself. Bergstrom's vise-like handshake so impressed Anderson that the coach barked to a nearby manager, "Get Wally suited up!"[15]

The neophyte returned a half-hour later with his helmet on backwards and his shoulder pads all askew. Although he was a project for line coach Jim Harris, Bergstrom soon proved to be a formidable player.

Initially, the Iowa boys experienced difficulty adapting to Anderson's

Notre Dame system. Eddie rarely allowed his team to huddle on offense. Instead, the Hawkeyes lined up in a T-formation with the quarterback directly under center. The quarterback then called out three single digit numbers followed by three double-digit numbers. The numbers told the direction the team would shift, the play to be run and the snap count.

Once the team shifted from the T-formation to the Notre Dame Box, the quarterback became primarily a blocker. Nevertheless, he still called the plays and was expected to know each player's assignment on every play. By the end of spring drills, sophomore Al Couppee had emerged as Iowa's starting quarterback and the team's offensive repertoire consisted of 100 plays.[16]

The team scrimmaged every other day during spring drills. On non-scrimmage days the coaches ran them relentlessly. Each practice concluded with a series of 50-, 80- or 100-yard sprints. The punishing practice sessions soon took their toll. After a few weeks many of the remaining 80 players were injured. The mounting injury toll prompted sophomore Red Frye to ask, "What kind of physician is Dr. Anderson anyway? No matter what the injury, he always prescribes the same treatment — run it off!"[17]

Tackle Wally Bergstrom once wrote of Iowa's 1939 coaching staff, "They all had one-track minds, drive, drive, drive!"[18]

Because of his stern and business-like demeanor at practice, players soon came to refer to assistant coach Frank Carideo as "Markoff," after the martinet character portrayed by actor Brian Dunleavy in the popular movie of the day, *Beau Geste*.[19] All the coaches, including Carideo, had a good laugh over the moniker.

Line coach Jim Harris had his own idiosyncrasies. He always referred to his linemen as "athletes" and carried a specially marked ball that only his "athletes" could handle. Backs were forbidden to touch it. Prior to intra-squad scrimmages Harris liked to quip, "Now we'll separate the sheep from the goats."[20] Harris frequently signaled the end of water breaks by barking, "Let's go — off and on, off and on!" When players didn't respond quickly enough, Harris gleefully elaborated, "Let's go — off your asses and on your feet!"[21]

Harris' off-color use of the word "ass" was the closest thing to profanity ever uttered by the coaches. Anderson prohibited coaches and players alike from cursing. According to Al Couppee in his book, *1939: One Magic Year*, Anderson continually preached, "Swearing is a lazy man's excuse for lack of vocabulary." He also extolled, "Football is a rough game to be played by rugged and tough men, but always remember that no man is tougher than a tough gentleman."

Anderson could be tough and even ungentlemanly when dealing with indolent players. Believing a classroom setting to be more conducive to learning than a drab locker room, Eddie often conducted team meetings in a class-

Iowa's Nile Kinnick punts under the watchful eye of Coach Frank Carideo. Under Carideo's tutelage, Kinnick developed into an exceptional punter and drop-kicker. Papers of Nile C. Kinnick, Dept. of Special Collections, University of Iowa Libraries, Iowa City, Iowa.

room in the old Commerce Building. As Anderson approached the lectern to start one meeting, he spied a player sprawled out with his hands behind his head and his feet resting on a chair drawn up in front of him. "You," growled Anderson, "get your feet off that chair and get the hell out of here! You don't belong with this football team."[22] Shaken, the slacker left and never returned.

"It was an experience playing for Dr. Eddie," recalled Wally Bergstrom. "He was a fine individual, a hard-boiled guy but all man. He fought hard, and he felt hard, but he had a great understanding of human nature. He could motivate you."[23]

Sometimes his motivational techniques took interesting twists. During one spring practice a guard named Ham Snider repeatedly missed his block on a particular play. Each time Snider missed his block, the ball carrier, Ray Murphy, was smeared. Unable to bear it any longer, Anderson ordered, "Run it again! This time, Snider, you get at fullback and run with the ball. See what it's like to carry the ball without any blocking."[24] With no one manning his guard spot, Snider carried the ball and was immediately plowed under by several tacklers. Snider got the point. His blocking improved considerably from then on.

Although the Hawkeyes respected Anderson and sought his approval, many also found him to be intimidating. "I liked talking with him," recalls Red Frye, "but I always felt it was better to let him break the ice."[25]

"I know I had more fear for him than liking," said Al Couppee. "He was on my case more than most, I guess, because I was a quarterback and probably too cocky for even Eddie's tastes. However, when he said 'jump,' I leaped. I learned to stay far away from him at times. Most of the other guys went through this trauma in varying degrees. Eddie was an extremely likeable man, however, and in later years we became good friends."[26]

In late April, Bill Osmanski spent a week in Iowa City helping Anderson coach. When he returned to New England, the Holy Cross All-American told several local sportswriters, "Among the 5,000 male students at the University of Iowa there are only five real football players."[27] Despite the squad's lack of depth, Anderson was optimistic about the upcoming season.

Of special interest was the way Frank Carideo had taken halfback Nile Kinnick under his wing. After a strong sophomore season in 1937, Kinnick's performance in 1938 was hindered by a chronic ankle sprain. One reason the injury lingered was because, as a devout Christian Scientist, Kinnick's religious beliefs prohibited him from receiving most types of medical treatment. Kinnick had handled Iowa's punting chores for two seasons. But now, under Carideo's tutelage, Kinnick was about to become one of the country's premier punters. Carideo taught Kinnick certain nuances that significantly enhanced the senior's accuracy and distance. Kinnick's punts now seemed to explode off his foot. By the end of spring drills the two could stand 50 yards apart and punt the ball back and forth to one another. Rarely did either man have to move more than a few steps to field the other's punt. It was like two baseball players playing catch.

Because Iowa lacked a consistent place-kicker, Carideo also honed Kinnick's skills as a dropkicker. Dropkicking had nearly disappeared from the gridiron scene several years earlier when a rule change narrowed the football's dimensions. Under Carideo's watchful eye, however, Kinnick soon mastered the vanishing art. Teacher and pupil often spent an hour before practice drop-kicking balls through the goal posts from numerous angles and distances. Kinnick's mastery of the archaic craft would pay handsome dividends for the Hawkeyes that fall.

15

1939
ONE MAGIC SEASON

Nearly 60 candidates reported for the start of fall practice on Monday, September 11. When two-a-day practices ended with the start of classes on September 21, only about 45 remained. A new face at practice was that of Willard "Bill" Hofer, who had been hired by Anderson to replace Bill Osmanski as Iowa's freshman coach. Over the summer Osmanski had signed a contract to play pro football for the Chicago Bears. Like fellow assistants Carideo and Harris, Hofer was also a Notre Dame graduate. The 22-year-old Montana native had quarterbacked Elmer Layden's Irish squads from 1936 through 1938. Aside from coaching the Iowa freshmen, Hofer would provide an invaluable service by quarterbacking the scout team once or twice a week against the varsity. A tremendous athlete, Hofer often assumed the role of the upcoming opponent's biggest star, thus affording Iowa's defense a realistic look at what to expect on Saturday. Over the course of the 1939 season Hofer portrayed Hal Hursh of Indiana, Tom Harmon of Michigan, Lou Brock of Purdue, Harry Stevenson of Notre Dame and Bruce Smith of Minnesota.

Called "Hofe" by the varsity players, the fun-loving bachelor drove a sporty two-toned Buick Roadmaster that was the envy of the campus. On Sundays Hofer often drove a carload of senior players to his parents' tavern in Rock Island, Illinois, for delectable fried chicken dinners. On the practice field, however, Coach Hofer always maintained discipline and kept a professional distance from his players.[1]

Although the fall practices were rigorous, Anderson, hoping to avoid injuries, virtually eliminated scrimmaging and contact drills. "We had very little contact during the fall," remembered Iowa captain Erwin Prasse. "We players appreciated that. Who likes to beat the hell out of your friends all the time?"

Nevertheless, Prasse claimed, "Eddie Anderson had us in the best shape of our lives!"[2]

As the opening game approached, the squad's confidence grew. A sense of camaraderie permeated the practice field and locker room. The coaches worked well together and seemed to possess a special chemistry. Center Red Frye remembers, "Sometimes a coach would really give you hell. You'd be so hurt you just felt like quitting. But then another coach would come along, pat you on the back and offer a word of encouragement to pick you right up again."[3]

When Nazi Germany unleashed its *blitzkrieg* against unsuspecting Poland on September 1, 1939, the state of Iowa was still staggering under the weight of the depression. Hitler's naked aggression provided beleaguered Iowans with a brief diversion from their own economic woes. Newspapers statewide furnished detailed accounts of Poland's heroic struggle. Poland's mounted lancers, however, were no match for mechanized *Panzer* tanks and strafing *Stukas*. Polish units that had escaped encirclement retreated east to make a stand in the wooded and marshy terrain there. But this strategy collapsed on September 17 when Soviet troops invaded eastern Poland to seize territories secretly promised to Russia in the nonaggression pact signed with Germany earlier that summer. By the time Iowa hosted South Dakota for the season-opener on September 30, Poland had ceased to exist as a political entity.

The specter of Carlinville may well have flashed through Anderson's mind as he approached mid-field to shake hands with visiting coach Harry Gamage. Eighteen years earlier Gamage had been one of the nine Illinois ringers that played for Taylorville against a Carlinville team whose own ringers had included Anderson and seven of his Irish teammates. As detailed in Chapter Five, when the scandal broke it resulted in Anderson, Gamage and 15 others being banned from future intercollegiate competition. Neither Gamage nor Anderson now wanted to stir up memories of Taylorville.

Iowa had been favored to win, but both Anderson and the crowd of 17,000 were surprised at the margin of victory. In a rousing performance, Nile Kinnick scored three touchdowns, passed for two more and dropkicked five extra points as the Hawkeyes dismantled South Dakota 41 to 0.

The team's morale soared as Iowa prepared for its Big Ten opener against the Indiana Hoosiers. Hawkeye fans, however, remained dubious. Beating South Dakota was one thing, but the Coyotes were tiers below Big Ten competition on the football food chain. Furthermore, Bo McMillin, the former All-American halfback from Centre College, coached the Hoosiers. During their playing days in the NFL, Anderson had battled against McMillin's Milwaukee Badgers in 1923. Regarding McMillin to be one of the country's leading experts on the passing game, Anderson drilled his team extensively on pass defense that week.

To afford his players a quiet night's rest before the game, Anderson cloistered the team in an isolated ward at the University of Iowa Hospital. Anderson had his own theory about proper rest. Believing that most players were too keyed up on the eve of a game to get a good night's rest, Dr. Anderson maintained that football players needed their best sleep two nights before a game. It was a theory Anderson would advocate throughout his coaching career.[4]

With the temperature hovering at 95 degrees and a steady breeze at kickoff, the game was played in blast furnace conditions. Trailing the Hoosiers 10 to 0 late in the first quarter, Nile Kinnick's 73-yard quick kick changed the game's momentum. Kinnick's scoring passes of 30 and 50 yards to Erwin Prasse sandwiched around his own three-yard touchdown run gave Iowa a 20 to 17 halftime lead.

Resting in what was called a "ready room," the Hawkeyes stretched out on blankets spread across the room's cement floor or sat with their backs against the wall while imbibing cold ginger ale, Dr. Anderson's prescribed halftime drink.[5]

Lying on the floor, Iowa captain Erwin Prasse watched a fuming Eddie Anderson trudge into the room. Believing Anderson was peeved over Indiana scoring just before the half, Prasse thought, some of the guys are really going to get it now! Little did he know.

Prasse, who had caught two touchdown passes in the first half, remembered, "I thought I had played pretty well, but Eddie made a beeline for me and started reaming me out."

Although he didn't understand Anderson's behavior at the time, years later Prasse theorized: "I think Eddie did it as a psychological ploy for the other guys. It started them thinking: If Coach can chew out our captain like that [after catching two touchdown passes], just what could he say to me?"[6]

The insufferable heat continued to sap each team's strength in the second half. Broiling in their long-sleeved jerseys, players moved like men encumbered by armor. Both squads wilted but neither would quit. With Indiana leading 29 to 26 in the game's final minutes, Iowa faced a fourth-and-fifteen at the Hoosier 18. As he would do repeatedly that season, Nile Kinnick delivered in the clutch — he calmly lofted a pass to the corner of the end zone where Erwin Prasse made a leaping acrobatic catch to give Iowa a 32 to 29 win.

As sportswriter Tait Cummins wrote in the *Cedar Rapids Gazette* the next day, "...the manner in which Dr. Eddie Anderson's colorful charges came from behind in the closing minutes left a crowd of 17,500 sweating fans prostrate in their seats."[7]

The thrilling win in sweltering conditions exacted a heavy toll on the victors. Late in the game, tackle Mike Enich collapsed on the field from near heat stroke and was hospitalized over the weekend.[8] Having played all 60 minutes in the torrid heat, Nile Kinnick shed 13 pounds and tackle Jim Walker lost 15. The Hawkeyes also lost their biggest man, 266-pound tackle Henry Luebcke, with what turned out to be a hernia in the second quarter. The injury required immediate surgery and ended the giant guard's career at Iowa. Quarterback Al Couppee also sustained a separated shoulder.

On October 14 Iowa traveled to Ann Arbor to do battle with Fritz Crisler's University of Michigan Wolverines. The visitors drew first blood when Nile Kinnick tossed a 70-yard scoring bomb to half back Buzz Dean. Kinnick then dropkicked the extra point to give Iowa a 7 to 0 lead. After that, however, the afternoon belonged to the Wolverines. To be more precise, the afternoon belonged to half back Tom Harmon, whose four touchdowns and three extra points accounted for all of Michigan's scoring. Harmon also excelled as a defender, intercepting two passes and returning one 90 yards for the game's last touchdown in Michigan's 27 to 7 win.

Dressing out what seemed like a cast of thousands, the Maize of Michigan just had too much depth, strength and talent for the visitors. With just 19 of its players seeing action, Iowa's lack of depth was exacerbated when center Bill Diehl and tackle Jim Walker suffered knee injuries. Bruno Andruska replaced Diehl while Wally Bergstrom replaced Walker. (It was quite a baptism for Bergstrom, who, with less than 10 minutes of lifetime football experience, now found himself pitted against one of the best lines in the country.)

Iowa had played its heart out and never quit. The one-sided loss could have devastated the team's morale, but Eddie Anderson wasn't about to let that happen. He and Jim Harris walked through the locker room patting deserving players on the back and playing down the loss while stressing the importance of future games.

In his book, *1939: One Magic Year*, Al Couppee relates the scene as Anderson gathered his lads about him in the post-game locker room. "All right, men," Anderson said, "we're going to leave the game here in Ann Arbor. It's over. We've got two weeks to get ready for Wisconsin. I had planned to switch trains in Chicago, and make it back into Iowa City late tonight. It's going to take some doing, but we're going to stay over in Chicago tonight, and we're going to see the Bears-Cardinals game at Wrigley Field tomorrow. Forget this game and let's have some fun tonight."[9]

Later in Chicago, Anderson offered a cigarette to several players he knew to be smokers before again addressing the team. "There's no curfew tonight.

We're staying downtown in the loop at the Hotel Morrison. There'll be no room checks. I want to warn you about a couple of things, however. No hard liquor and no strange women — remember that. Remember, also, you're representatives of a great state and a great university; don't do something to embarrass yourself, your team, your state or your school... After the game tomorrow, when we board the train home, I want all cigarettes tossed away, no more playing around, and we start getting ready for Wisconsin."

The players relished their night on the town. It was the first time many of them had either visited a major city or attended a professional sporting event. When the Hawkeyes boarded the Rock Island Rocket for Iowa City, they were eager to prepare for Wisconsin.

"The whole affair was a masterful piece of football coaching psychology," recalled Couppee. "It really paid off; we never lost another game."[10]

With two weeks to prepare for the Badgers, Anderson deviated from his normal practice routine by spending the first week scrimmaging his first and second teams against the freshmen, and the third-string against the first team in hopes of discovering hidden talent. He changed gears the second week. There was no practice on Monday and all contact work was eliminated while focusing on Wisconsin.

After losing to Michigan, many of Iowa's sportswriters cooled on the Hawkeyes. The unwritten but underlying sentiment seemed to be that the Hawkeyes would revert to their old losing ways. Only 26 Iowa players boarded the train to Madison.

Iowa hadn't won at Madison in a decade, and things didn't look promising at the half when Coach Harry Stuhldreher's Badgers held a 7 to 6 lead. But in the end, Nile Kinnick again emerged as Iowa's hero by throwing touchdown passes to Al Couppee, end Dick Evans and Bill Green in leading the Hawkeyes to a 19 to 13 victory. Only 18 Hawkeyes saw action with five players playing all 60 minutes. Assessing Iowa's lack of depth, Wisconsin sportswriter "Roundy" Coughlin wrote, "The Iowa bench Saturday looked more like a high school squad. I don't believe they had one lineman to put in the game in the last ten minutes."[11]

The Iowa media now began referring to Anderson's contingent as "Iron Men."

Despite every sportswriter in the Midwest picking Purdue to win, the Iron Men legend mushroomed the following week when Iowa played only 14 men in defeating the Boilermakers at West Lafayette, Indiana. The game remained scoreless at the half thanks to Purdue's three goal line stands. Jack Brown twice intercepted Nile Kinnick in the end zone and Purdue later held on downs inside its own 10-yard line. It was quarterback Al Couppee's play calling on the last series of plays that set Anderson off like a rocket in the locker room at halftime.

"Couppee!" bellowed Anderson as he bent over his seated quarterback, "when we get inside the 10-yard line, there's just one man on this football team who should get the football. Do you know Nile Kinnick, Couppee? I want you to shake hands with Nile Kinnick. Nile, this is your quarterback, meet Mr. Couppee. Shake his hand; I want him to know you when we again get inside the 10-yard line."[12]

Seated next to Couppee, an embarrassed Kinnick meekly reached out and the pair sheepishly shook hands. Couppee would never again fail to call Kinnick's number inside an opponent's 10-yard line.

The defensive struggle continued in the second half. In the fourth quarter Iowa's defense scored the game's first points when tackle Mike Enich blocked a Purdue punt in the end zone for a safety. Amazingly, Enich blocked another punt minutes later for yet another safety. Enich's gritty heroics gave the visitors a hard-fought 4 to 0 victory.

"We only scored the second one [safety] to make it decisive," Coach Jim Harris later joked.[13]

That night over 1,500 fans, cheerleaders and band members greeted the victors' train upon its arrival in Iowa City. Pandemonium reigned as the players were carried to automobiles and paraded back to campus. Iowa fans were thrilled that their beloved Hawkeyes now sported a record of 4 wins and 1 loss. The pandemonium was only beginning.

It was ironic that perhaps the biggest game of Anderson's storied coaching career came against his alma mater. Undefeated in six games, Notre Dame was coming to town ranked number one in the nation. Elmer Layden, one of Notre Dame's famed Four Horsemen, now coached the Irish. Layden and Anderson had traveled similar paths in their careers. Both were Iowa natives — Anderson from Mason City and Layden from Davenport — who had been All-Americans under Knute Rockne. Both men also began their coaching careers at Columbia (Loras) College. Layden had succeeded Anderson at the Dubuque school in 1925 when Eddie moved on to DePaul. For the next two years they coached both football and basketball against one another. While Anderson used coaching to earn a medical degree, Layden used it to study law. As coaches, both men adhered to the highest ideals of sportsmanship.

In 1927, Layden had begun a successful coaching stint at Duquesne University before replacing Hunk Anderson at Notre Dame in 1934. In his first four seasons at South Bend, Layden's teams never finished worse than 6 wins and 3 losses.

At the start of a team meeting during the week of the Notre Dame game, Anderson casually lit a cigarette as he leaned back against his desk. Calmly surveying the room, his gaze fell upon second-string quarterback, Bill Gallagher.

"Gallagher," the smiling coach asked, "how badly do you want to beat Notre Dame?"

"Coach," snapped Gallagher, "I want to beat them 40 to 0!"

Amused, Anderson laughed softly before responding, "Well, why don't we just beat them 7 to 6. That way we'll all remember it for the rest of our lives."[14]

The coach's words would prove to be prophetic.

For the first time in years Hawkeye football was the talk of the campus. The excitement over the upcoming game heightened during the week until it reached a crescendo Friday evening when nearly 10,000 exuberant fans amassed on the sloping green west of the Old Capitol building for a pep rally.[15] The crowd was so raucous that the remarks of team captain Erwin Prasse and teammate Mike Enich were barely audible over the public address system. To insure a quiet night's rest, the team once again spent the night in a secluded ward of the University of Iowa Hospital.

On game day, stores throughout Iowa City closed at 1 p.m. so that the merchants could make it to the stadium for the two o'clock kick-off. Five different radio stations were to broadcast the game. The play-by-play man for Des Moines station WHO was Bill Brown, who only a few years earlier had replaced Ronald "Dutch" Reagan when the latter ventured off to Hollywood.[16] Another celebrity in attendance was screen and stage star Don Ameche. Ameche, Anderson's former pupil at Columbia Academy, was in town as the weekend guest of Eddie and Mary Anderson.[17]

Before 47,000 fans Notre Dame won the toss and elected to defend the South goal. After a scoreless first quarter, Notre Dame substituted an entirely new team while all 11 of Iowa's starters remained on the field.

The first break of the contest came shortly before the half when Nile Kinnick intercepted Harry Stevenson's pass at mid-field and returned it to Notre Dame's 35-yard line. On the next play, Kinnick lofted a deep pass intended for Bill Green. Notre Dame's Steve Sitko intercepted the ball in his own end zone and decided to run it out. It proved to be a costly mistake—Bruno Andruska's bone-jarring tackle caused Sitko to fumble, and Ken Pettit recovered for the Hawkeyes on the Irish 5-yard line.

Kinnick's two carries off right tackle barely netted a yard. Believing that running to the left might be more productive, Iowa quarterback Al Couppee called a huddle for only the second time all season. With Anderson's blistering instructions still ringing in his ears from the Purdue game, Couppee ordered, "Kinnick, you go to right half, Dean to left half. We're going to run 31-left. Got that, 31-left?" (It was the same play, only this time Kinnick would carry the ball to the left.)

When several teammates began to object Couppee snapped, "Damn it, we're going to run it just like I said — Kinnick to right half, Dean to the left. Now get the hell out of this huddle and go to work!"[18]

On the snap of the ball, Prasse and Dean blocked down on the tackle, Couppee kicked out the end, and a thunderous ovation exploded throughout the stadium as Kinnick plowed into the end zone for a touchdown. The fans emitted a collective gasp 30 seconds later, however, when Kinnick struggled to field a poor snap from center and then hustled to dropkick the extra point to give Iowa a 7 to 0 lead.

"Who made that shift of Nile [Kinnick] to right half down on the goal line?" yelled Anderson as he entered the ready room at halftime.

"I did," answered Couppee.

"Well, that was the smartest thing I've ever had a quarterback do," replied Anderson, who quickly went on to other business.[19]

Anderson addressed the team as it readied to take the field for the second half. "You men realize you're leading Notre Dame, unbeaten Notre Dame, by seven points, and you've got 30 minutes of football to play. Every team in the United States would like right now to be in your position. Thirty minutes left, and the greatest moment in your football lives is within your grasp. Now let's go out that door and finish this job."[20]

However, Notre Dame was Notre Dame for a reason. In a stratagem to be employed with varying degrees of success in later years by Notre Dame coaches, the Irish burst onto the field in the second half wearing the green of Old Erin. In a psychological ploy to fire up his troops, Elmer Layden had had his players remove their customary blue jerseys for the emerald green of Ireland.

The Hawkeyes, however, were oblivious to Notre Dame's histrionics, and most of the third quarter turned into a punting duel between Kinnick and Notre Dame's Harry Stevenson. Late in the third quarter, the Irish began to mount a drive behind the punishing running of fullback Milt Piepul. Two plays into the final period Piepul scored from six yards out. However, the luck of the Irish failed the green-clad visitors when Lou Zontini's extra-point try sailed wide of the mark.

With Iowa now leading 7 to 6, the punting duel resumed. Iowa tried to burn as much time off the clock as possible. With just over two minutes remaining in the game, Iowa was forced to punt from its own 29-yard line. The ball boomed off Kinnick's foot, sailing well over the head of Notre Dame's Steve Sitko before rolling out of bounds at the Irish 6-yard line — a 65-yard punt.

"That punt epitomized the type of player Kinnick was," recalls Bill Diehl. "Nile usually punted a ball about 40 or 42 yards beyond the line of scrimmage. But here we were, playing in the biggest game of our lives and in desperate need of a good punt to preserve the lead, and Nile punts the ball 65 yards! That was Nile. Whenever we needed a big play, Nile somehow went beyond his physical abilities to make one."[21]

Five plays later the clock ran out, and Iowa had stunned the football world with a 7 to 6 win over previously undefeated Notre Dame. The Irish had played 33 men, while Iowa, in an amazing display of stamina, had played only 15 (eight of whom played the entire 60 minutes).

Ecstatic Hawkeye fans flooded onto the gridiron and carried the elated Iowa players off the field. Within hours after the game Iowa City's Western Union office had received over 600 congratulatory telegrams for Dr. Anderson.[22] Revelers endlessly honked their car horns as they cruised downtown into the wee hours of the morning.

The celebration carried over to Monday morning when approximately

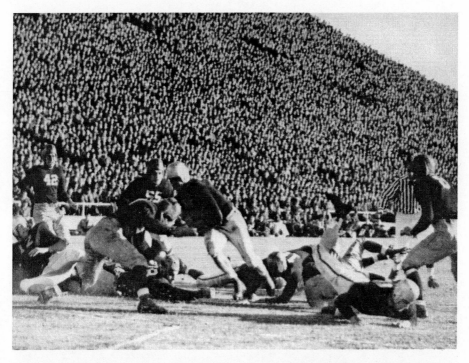

Nile Kinnick scores the winning touchdown in Iowa's 7 to 6 upset win of previously unbeaten Notre Dame before 47,000 fans at Iowa Stadium on November 11, 1939. Papers of Nile C. Kinnick, Dept. of Special Collections, University of Iowa Libraries, Iowa City, Iowa.

5,000 students walked out of classes to attend a spontaneous football rally at the Old Capitol building. A fraction of the celebrants then marched to the Anderson house on East Fairchild to hear from their coach. Eddie, who had already left for the field house, hurried home when Mary telephoned.

Holding his three-year-old son, Jimmy, in his arms, a delighted Anderson addressed the students from his front porch, "You're the greatest student body in the world. You think that I'm going to send you back to classes. Well, I'm not!"[23]

The coach's remarks drew a resounding cheer. The students then drifted back to campus where they learned that the university president, Eugene Gilmore, had declared a moratorium on classes for the day and arranged for a victory dance that afternoon in the Iowa Memorial Union.

A fact of football life is that during the season players have only about 24 hours, and coaches even less, to relish a big win before undertaking the arduous preparation for the next opponent. Next up for Iowa: the dreaded University of Minnesota Golden Gophers.

Eddie and Mary Anderson read the headlines of Iowa's 7 to 6 upset of Notre Dame the morning after. (Courtesy of Dr. Jerry Anderson)

Coach Bernie Bierman's invaders from the North were comprised of the strapping sons and grandsons of Scandinavian immigrants who now farmed the vast prairies of western Minnesota or worked the mines of the state's iron range. Big, powerful and hard working, these muscular youths were well-suited for Bierman's ball-control, single-wing offense. With the coming of the autumn harvest, Minnesota would annually pulverize the Hawkeyes throughout the thirties, winning games by scores of 34 to 0, 48 to 12, 52 to 0, 35 to 10 and 28 to 0. Since taking over the reins at his alma mater in 1932, Bierman saw his squads gain national prominence, if not outright dominance.

In 1935, Governor Floyd Olson of Minnesota donated an 85-pound bronze pig, "Floyd of Rosedale," as a traveling trophy for the winner of the annual Gopher-Hawkeye contest. "Floyd will be retired from old age before Iowa ever wins the trophy," boasted Olson.[24] Many were beginning to wonder if Olson's prediction was prophetic, as the prized statue had remained in Minnesota's possession since its inception. However, Iowa's stunning upset of Notre Dame had given Hawkeye fans genuine hope that this would be the year Floyd stayed in Iowa. The contest was also Iowa's 1939 homecoming game. To commemorate the event, the university sold over 16,000 homecoming buttons that featured an artist's rendition of the Iowa coach. Anderson's celebrity status was also enhanced when the United Press honored him as its Coach of the Week after Iowa's upset of Notre Dame.

In a humbling moment before practice on Monday, November 13, the Iowa players presented Anderson with a birthday gift of a gold cigarette case bearing the simple inscription, "To Eddie, from the team."[25]

The touching scene served as a prelude to Friday night's pep rally where before 10,000 ebullient fans, Professor Karl Lieb, chairman of the university's athletic committee, handed the keys to a 1940 Buick sedan to an overwhelmed Anderson.[26] The gift was the brainchild of Erling Larson, president of the Davenport alumni club. (Assistant coaches Frank Carideo and Jim Harris weren't forgotten. The Des Moines alumni club presented each with a new Chevrolet after the season.)

If accepting such an extravagant gift placed additional pressure on Anderson to defeat Minnesota, it didn't show the next day when Anderson exhibited his customary calm demeanor during his pre-game remarks.

Kicking off in an air of exhilaration before a record-breaking crowd of 50,000 irrepressible fans, Iowa quarterback Al Couppee sustained a separated shoulder while tackling Minnesota's Joe Mernik. Shrugging off the pain, the gutsy Couppee played the entire first half before leaving the game in the third quarter when he could no longer lift his arm.

In a game characterized by vicious blocking and tackling, Nile Kinnick kept punting Iowa out of trouble in the first quarter. However, Minnesota's

Mernik made one of two field goal tries to give the Gophers a 3 to 0 halftime lead.

Early in the third quarter, Minnesota's Harold Van Avery fielded a Kinnick punt at mid-field and returned it to the Iowa 28. With the visitors wielding a 25-pound per man weight advantage over Iowa's line, Minnesota methodically pounded the ball to Iowa's 7-yard line for a first-and-goal. Iowa's defense stiffened, but on fourth-and-goal from the 6-yard line Minnesota's speedy Sonny Franck ran a reverse around left end. A host of Iowa tacklers hammered Franck out of bounds at the goal line. The officials, however, ruled that the ball had broken the plane of the end zone and awarded Minnesota a touchdown. Iowa blocked the extra point and Minnesota led 9 to 0.

Catching their second wind, the beleaguered Hawkeyes embarked on their customary fourth-quarter heroics. With Bill Gallagher now at quarterback for Couppee, center Bruno Andruska snapping the ball with a broken wrist, and Kinnick's bruised passing hand swollen to nearly twice its normal size, the resolute Hawkeyes covered 80 yards in four plays to score. The scoring strike came on a 50-yard pass from Kinnick to Erwin Prasse. Kinnick's dropkick extra point narrowed the score to 9 to 7.

With just over five minutes remaining, Iowa took possession on its own 21. Four plays and a Minnesota penalty put the ball on the Gopher 28-yard line. From there Kinnick connected on a beautiful pass to a streaking Bill Green for a touchdown. Elated Hawkeye fans engulfed Green in the end zone. When order was restored, no one seemed to notice that Kinnick missed the extra point. Iowa now led 13 to 9.

Minnesota fielded the ensuing kick-off with only 3 minutes and 25 seconds remaining and pounded the ball out to mid-field. In the game's waning seconds, Kinnick intercepted Van Avery's deep pass and returned it to mid-field. Iowa then ran out the clock and over 50,000 jubilant fans poured onto the field. For the second week in a row, ecstatic Iowa fans carried their underdog Hawkeyes off the field as victors.

In the euphoric Iowa locker room Eddie Anderson praised his team to reporters. "They played like demons. You can't lick a team like that."[27]

When asked by a Minnesota sportswriter, "Do you think there are any better than Kinnick?" Eddie, with a wave of the hand responded, "You tell me who is better than Kinnick. That boy is one of the greatest ball players I've ever seen."[28]

Sportswriters throughout the Midwest trumpeted Iowa's tremendous upset. Dick McCallum of the *Minneapolis Tribune* wrote, "Iowa's men of iron fought a courageous battle here today, and by their courage, their refusal to be discouraged when things went against them, their ability to come from behind with poise and fire, they worked out a 13 to 9 victory over Minnesota's Gophers."[29]

The *Chicago Herald-American*'s Jim Gallagher acclaimed, "Iowa's Iron Men did it again. Crushed for three quarters by Minnesota's juggernaut, the doughty little band of Hawkeyes came back in the fourth quarter to score a 13 to 9 victory over the powerful Gophers, while a homecoming crowd of more than 50,000 went near-hysterical."[30]

George Edmond of the *St. Paul Pioneer Press* gushed, "Iowa's team of destiny and its man of the hour, Nile Kinnick, are still marching forward in the most amazing bid for the Western Conference championship in memory. The Hawkeye iron men, more truly men of steel, grabbed a sensational 13 to 9 triumph over Minnesota here Saturday, the fifth major triumph of the season for a team that has been a Big Ten doormat for the greater part of a decade and was not expected to be greatly different this year."[31]

The delirium inundating the university town was captured in the *Des Moines Register* headline: "Iowa City Goes Mad with Joy."[32] Taverns and nightclubs were jammed with revelers. Ecstatic fans stood for hours on street corners singing and cheering. Motorists paraded through downtown endlessly honking their car horns. Placards sprouted all over campus hailing "Anderson for President" and "Nile for Governor." Unlike so many campus celebrations today, the festivities at Iowa never turned violent or destructive.

The celebrating carried over to Monday when university president, Eugene Gilmore, once again declared a moratorium on classes and called for administration officials to arrange another pep rally in front of the Old Capitol building on Monday afternoon to be followed by a victory dance.

College football didn't get any better than that.

Iowa's dramatic onfield turn-around also yielded financial benefits. The university's gross football receipts increased from $51,000 in 1938 to $190,000 in 1939. A bond issue had financed construction of Iowa Stadium in 1929. However, with athletic revenues slumping throughout the thirties, the university had not made an interest payment to bondholders in five years. After the successful 1939 season, the university resumed the interest payments throughout Anderson's reign until the debt was satisfied in 1947. These facts led to an amusing anecdote years later involving Doctor Anderson's son, Jerry.

While a medical intern at New York City's Veterans Hospital in the early sixties, Jerry Anderson received a phone call from the hospital's chief administrator. "Jerry, there's a Mr. Belting here from Iowa who would like to meet you. Can you see him?"

Eager to talk with someone from his teenage stomping grounds, Jerry replied, "Sure, I have a few minutes."

The visitor turned out to be the son of Paul Belting, Iowa's athletic director during the twenties. After being introduced, the two spent several minutes fondly discussing life in Iowa City and reminiscing about Hawkeye football. As he was taking his leave, young Belting added, "Jerry, did you know that my father built Iowa Stadium?"

To which Jerry Anderson quipped, "Yes, and my father paid for it."[33]

On Thursday, November 23, university officials announced that Eddie Anderson was being rewarded with a new six-year contract at an annual salary of $12,000. The lucrative deal resulted in Anderson being the school's highest paid employee. Since state law mandated that no university employee could be paid more than the school's president, the trustees raised President Eugene Gilmore's salary to keep in compliance. Several days later Gilmore scribbled Anderson a note that read, "Eddie, thanks for the raise!"[34]

A win at Northwestern on November 25 would have given Iowa a share of the Big Ten championship with Ohio State. Facing the formidable Wildcats of Coach Lynn "Pappy" Waldorf, with a line revamped due to injuries, Iowa suffered more misfortune late in the third quarter when all-everything Nile Kinnick, who had played 402 consecutive minutes of football, every minute of six straight games, left the field with a separated shoulder.

Trailing 7 to 0 in the fourth quarter, Iowa caught a break when Mike Enich recovered a fumble on the Northwestern 22. The determined Hawkeyes capitalized on the turnover six plays later on Ray Murphy's 1-yard touchdown plunge. Looking on from the sidelines with bated breath and crossed fingers, Kinnick stood shivering with teammates as his replacement, Buzz Dean, attempting his first-ever extra point in a game, heroically booted the ball through the upright to knot the score at 7.

Like a hurt boxer on the ropes weathering a storm of punches until the final bell, Iowa's battered Iron Men gamely withstood several more Northwestern scoring threats, including a dramatic goal line stand, to earn a gallant and bitterly contested 7 to 7 tie.

While denied a share of the Big Ten championship, Iowa still enjoyed a Cinderella season. Rising from the depths of the depression, few teams in the history of college football ever captured the hearts or impacted the hopes of an entire region of the country as did Eddie Anderson's 1939 Iowa Iron Men. Today, whenever the Iron Men are mentioned, the conversation always echoes with all that is right about college football and the young men who play it.

At the post-season team banquet, each varsity coach expressed his feelings regarding this exceptional group of young men. Backfield coach Frank Carideo told the audience, "I've seen a lot of teams and I've played with good teams, but this one had it on all of them."[35] Considering that the stoical Carideo had quarterbacked two national championship teams at Notre Dame, it was quite a compliment.

Gravel-voiced assistant coach Jim Harris lauded, "This was the greatest bunch of kids I've ever worked with. Sometimes, you could kill them on Thursday, but you always wanted to kiss them on Saturday!"[36]

During his turn at the podium Eddie Anderson, who had caught a long touchdown pass from the dying George Gipp in the last game the Gipper ever played, declared, "No team ever graced a football field with more spirit, more determination or more courage."[37]

16

NILE KINNICK

On November 28, 1939, Willard B. Prince, chairman of the Heisman Trophy committee, announced that Iowa's Nile Kinnick had won the award. Since 1935 the trophy has been awarded annually to the best college football player in America. The announcement spawned a whirlwind two months for both Kinnick and Anderson during which they traveled the country accepting numerous awards and honors. Kinnick had received 651 Heisman votes to 405 for Michigan's Tom Harmon. (Only a junior, Harmon, who had scored all 27 of Michigan's points in handing Iowa its only loss of the season, would win the Heisman Trophy in 1940.)

Post-season honors continued to pour in for the halfback the Iowa media had labeled "The Cornbelt Comet." On November 30, it was announced that Kinnick had won the Robert Maxwell Trophy, which was to be presented in Philadelphia in January. Kinnick's stellar performance also won him the Walter Camp Memorial Trophy, the Chicago Silver Football Award (given to the Big Ten Conference's Most Valuable Player) and berths on several All-American teams. His teammates voted him "Most Valuable Player" and Iowa's student body voted Kinnick "Athlete of the Year." The Iowa halfback also edged out Yankee slugger Joe DiMaggio and heavyweight champion Joe Louis to win the Outstanding Male Athlete of the Year.

Kinnick and Anderson shared a special rapport as player and coach. In his book, *The Iron Men*, Scott Fisher touches on that relationship. "Anderson, a good judge of character, knew that Kinnick never had to be driven or pressured — he did enough of that to himself. On the practice field, Anderson would call each player by his last name, whether in praise or criticism — except Kinnick. With him it was always Nile."[1]

Erwin Prasse, a great three-sport athlete at Iowa, remembered, "Every day after practice Dr. Anderson walked off the field with his arm around Nile. Nile was a heck of a guy, but as team captain there were times I just wanted to shout, 'Hey, Coach, you've got two arms!'"[2]

Kinnick, in turn, idolized Anderson. In his correspondence home he often lauded "Dr. Eddie" as both a man and a coach. Writing to his mother after Iowa's loss to Michigan, Kinnick wrote, "I wish we could play it over ... it breaks my heart to sort of let him [Anderson] down."[3]

Thirty-seven years after his son won the Heisman, Nile C. Kinnick, Sr. wrote to Eddie's son, Dr. Jerry Anderson, "Nile's first letter home after meeting Eddie Anderson expressed full confidence in him as a man and a coach. And each succeeding letter confirmed and expanded that confidence. As you know, those bonds grew during that astonishing season into a friendship and an affection that could not have been more real."[4]

At a December 4 luncheon, Frank L. Mott, head of the Iowa University School of Journalism, on behalf of the Midwest Sportswriters Association, presented Dr. Anderson with a pure platinum, diamond-studded watch valued at $1,000.[5] (Several years later young Jimmy Anderson, wanting to see what made the shiny watch tick, dismantled it with a screwdriver. Discovering the watch's inner workings scattered over the living room floor, Mary Anderson frantically scooped them up and hurried to a local jeweler who painstakingly restored the timepiece to working order. Mary never informed Eddie of the mishap.)[6] Kinnick and teammate Erwin Prasse were also presented with handsome, but considerably less expensive, Bulova watches. (The Bulovas retailed at $49.50 each.)[7]

The next morning, Kinnick and Anderson boarded the Rock Island Rocket to Chicago where they took the Twentieth Century to New York City for the Heisman Trophy presentation. Arriving in New York on Wednesday, December 6, the pair was treated to an aerial tour over Manhattan and Brooklyn in a Navy transport plane. Accompanied by a dirigible and two-dozen smaller aircraft, Kinnick consented to a live radio broadcast from the skies above Manhattan. In an attempt to boost Navy recruiting, Kinnick agreed to ask questions previously prepared by military personnel about naval aviation on the air. Then, he and Anderson fielded football questions posed by Dave Driscoll, sports announcer for WOR radio.

Later that night, Anderson and Kinnick attended the Heisman Dinner at Manhattan's fashionable Downtown Athletic Club. Upon receiving the prestigious award, Kinnick, speaking without a prepared text or notes, delivered the following acceptance speech.

"I thank you very, very much, Mr. Holcomb. It seems to me that everyone is letting his superlatives run away with him tonight.

A beaming Nile Kinnick accepts the Heisman Trophy at New York City's Downtown Athletic Club on December 6, 1939. Papers of Nile C. Kinnick, Dept. of Special Collections, University of Iowa Libraries, Iowa City, Iowa.

"Every football player in the United States dreams of winning this trophy. The fact that I am actually receiving it overwhelms me, and I feel what those who have received the Heisman Award before me must have felt.

"From my personal viewpoint I consider this a tribute to the coaching staff at the University of Iowa, headed by Dr. Eddie Anderson, and to my teammates sitting back in Iowa City. A finer man and a better coach never hit these United States, and a finer team never performed on any gridiron than the Iowa team of 1939. I wish they might all be with me tonight to receive this trophy.

"I want to take this grand opportunity to thank the sportswriters all over the country who saw fit, saw their way clear, to cast their votes for me. I also want to thank Mr. Pierce and all those connected with the Downtown Athletic Club for making this trophy available to football players of the nation.

"And I would like, if I may, to make a comment which I think is appropriate at this time.

"I thank God that I was born to the gridirons of the middle-west and not to the battlefields of Europe. I can say confidently and positively that the football players of this country would much rather fight for the Heisman Award than for the *Croix de Guerre*."[8]

Broadcast live by WOR radio, Kinnick's heartfelt speech drew an overwhelming ovation from those in attendance. Within days, newspapers across America carried Kinnick's speech.

On December 7, Anderson and Kinnick were flown to Washington, D.C., for a tour of the Anacostia Naval Air Station and the Naval Academy at Annapolis. Accompanying the pair on the flight were Navy football coach, Swede Larson, and Navy team captain, A.A. Bergner. By late afternoon official word arrived that Dr. Eddie Anderson had been selected Coach of the Year by the *New York World Telegram*.[9]

The trip took on a somber tone on Friday, December 8, when the sojourners visited 18-year-old Edward Collins at St. Michael's Hospital in Newark, New Jersey. Collins, a tackle at St. Benedict's Prep School, had had his gangrenous leg amputated after severely breaking it in a game against the Villanova freshmen. Offering words of encouragement, Kinnick gave Collins his All-American sweater as a gift.

Three nights earlier Anderson watched proudly as Kinnick accepted the most coveted award in college sports. Now, on December 9, with renowned cartoonist Rube Goldberg presiding as toastmaster at New York's Ruppert Brewery, Kinnick watched as Anderson accepted the Coach of the Year award. After thanking the presenters and the University of Iowa for the splendid cooperation he had received at every level, Anderson concluded by saying, "We must remember that a winning football team rises or falls with the boys on that team. I was very fortunate in having an exceptional fine lot to work with. One of the finest was Nile Kinnick."[10]

Later in the program, Ray McCarthy, director of football operations at New York's Yankee Stadium and the Polo Grounds, also presented Eddie with the Jacob Ruppert Memorial Trophy. At age 39, Dr. Eddie Anderson had scaled the summit of the coaching profession.

When the pair returned to Iowa City on December 11 bearing their prestigious hardware, they were greeted by over 4,000 well-wishers. With speaking engagements almost nightly over the next two weeks, Anderson relished a quiet Christmas at home with Mary and the boys. On December 26 Anderson boarded a train to California with Iowa athletic director Dad Shroeder for the annual NCAA Convention. Eddie attended the Rose Bowl on New Year's Day before returning home on January 4.

Three days later Anderson and Kinnick were on a train east, this time to Philadelphia, where Kinnick received the Maxwell Trophy at Philadelphia's Warwick Hotel on January 9. The next day the two were ringside at New York's Madison Square Garden when Iowan Lee Savold knocked out Jim Robinson. On January 13, coach and player attended the Iowa alumni dinner at New York's Western Club, where Kinnick received the Captain of the All-Americas Award. After the ceremony Anderson accompanied Kinnick and his lovely date, Delaware heiress Virginia Eskridge, to Manhattan's posh Kit Kat Club. Attired in a tuxedo and seated between Anderson and Eskridge, the Heisman Trophy winner posed for a photo while holding a glass of milk. The *New York Daily News* ran the picture two days later providing fodder for local gossip columnists.[11]

Anderson and Kinnick then traveled to Washington, D.C., where Kinnick was presented with the Walter Camp Trophy, and returned to Iowa City on the evening of January 17.

If a movie producer wanted to cast someone in the role of the All-American boy in 1939, he'd only need to visit the University of Iowa campus to find Nile Clarke Kinnick, Jr. Handsome, intelligent and industrious, Kinnick personified Jack Armstrong and Frank Meriwell rolled into one. His wholesome image could have graced the front of a box of Corn Flakes. Kinnick would have been an extraordinary young man in any era.

Born in Adel, Iowa, in 1918, Kinnick was the oldest of three sons born to Nile Kinnick, Sr. and Frances Clarke. He was 13 months older than his brother, Ben, and eight years older than his brother, George. Kinnick's maternal grandfather, George W. Clarke, had served as Iowa's governor from 1913 to 1917 and may have spawned Nile's eventual interest in politics and public service.

Growing up on the family farm, young Nile enjoyed playing baseball, shooting baskets and kicking a football. As an eighth-grader playing on a junior American Legion baseball team, Kinnick was the battery mate of a pitcher from nearby Van Meter named Bob Feller. Feller, of course, would go on to become a Hall of Fame hurler for the Cleveland Indians. Kinnick attended Adel High School, but the depression forced the Kinnick family off the farm and to Omaha, Nebraska, in 1934, where Nile Senior procured employment with the Federal Land Bank. At Benson High, Kinnick earned all-state honors in both football and basketball while maintaining straight A's in the classroom. With 16-year-old Nile scheduled to graduate in 1935, Mr. Kinnick arranged with school officials for his son to miss a required course so Nile could attend high school for another year and better prepare himself for college by taking classes in electives, such as trigonometry, accounting, chemistry and literature. During this "extra" year of high school, Nile concentrated solely on academics and did not participate in interscholastic sports.[12]

On July 11, 1935, Nile and his brother Ben loaded the family's 1929 rumble-seat Ford coupe with camping gear and drove off to adventure. Over the next two months the Kinnick boys traveled through Sterling and Estes Park, Colorado, down through Raton Pass to the Gene Hayward Ranch in Cimarron, New Mexico (Hayward had been Nile Senior's roommate at Iowa State), over to Taos and then the Philmont Ranch. Belching steam, the old Ford rattled across the Painted Desert to the majestic Grand Canyon and on to Los Angeles. From there, the brothers drove north to Berkeley and up to Seattle for a two-week stay at Uncle Fred Clarke's home. The last leg of the journey took the adventurers to Grand Coulee Dam, Yellowstone Park, the Grand Tetons and Ogallala, Nebraska, before returning home to Omaha. During the journey's last leg, the boys stopped nearly every 50 miles to patch one of the Ford's now threadbare tires.[13]

Enrolling at the University of Iowa in the fall of 1936, Kinnick played football, basketball and baseball his freshman year. By the end of his sophomore year, Kinnick had given up the latter two sports to focus on football and his studies. He rationalized his decision in the following diary entry: "The athlete learns to evaluate — to evaluate between athletics and studies, between playing for fun and playing as a business, between playing clean and playing dirty, between being conventional and being true to one's convictions. He is facing the identical conditions [that] will confront him after college — the same dimensions and circumstances. But how many football players realize this?"[14]

Throughout his college years and beyond, Kinnick steadfastly recorded his thoughts and experiences in a series of diaries and journals. A prolific letter writer, he maintained a steady correspondence with family and friends. Affable and out-going, Kinnick enjoyed the company of pretty women and dated frequently. He was also elected the class president in his senior year at Iowa.

When Kinnick sustained a separated shoulder in the '39 Northwestern game, several doctors advised that the injury required surgery. As a devout Christian Scientist, Kinnick's religious beliefs ruled out such an operation. When a local wrestling coach named Mike Howard learned of Kinnick's quandary, he paid a visit to the Heisman Trophy recipient.

"Nile," offered Howard, "if you'll do what I say, you'll get full use of your arm and shoulder back." Kinnick agreed to give it a try.

Howard devised a demanding exercise rehabilitation program that Nile diligently followed. After several weeks the plan called for Kinnick to start playing handball. "So, Nile went out and played handball," recalled teammate Erwin Prasse. "That spring Kinnick played for the handball championship of the University of Iowa. The point being that whatever Kinnick pursued, he went after it with everything that he had."[15]

Kinnick didn't win the university's handball championship, but only months after the injury he had regained full use of his shoulder and arm without surgery.

An excellent student, Kinnick was one of 30 Iowa students elected to membership in Phi Beta Kappa on May 3, 1940. A month later he won the John P. Laffey law scholarship given annually to a first-year law student.

That summer the *Des Moines Register* hired the Heisman winner to write a series of articles. Kinnick's best piece had nothing to do with football, but it clearly demonstrated his compassion for others. One day he picked up a hitchhiker north of Ames. The middle-aged woman was named Alice Dogwell. Her children were raised and gone and her husband was too ill to work. Unable to find steady employment during the depression, Alice began making kitchen curtains, towels and potholders. Several mornings a week she would fill shopping bags with merchandise and hitchhike to a neighboring town to sell what she could. Later that day she would hitchhike back to Des Moines to tend her ailing husband.

Touched by the woman's plight, Kinnick highlighted Alice Dogwell in his article that appeared in the *Register* on August 4. In it he praised the woman's plucky resolve and spirit of "rugged individualism."[16] Although Kinnick had not given Dogwell his name, he received a letter from her on September 28 in which she thanked him for the kind article that had provided such a boon for her business.

While much has already been written about the Cornbelt Comet's football prowess, it needs to be added that Kinnick also received over a million votes to play for the College All-Stars against the World Champion Green Bay Packers at Chicago's Soldier Field on August 29, 1940. It was 100,000 more than the nearest candidate. (In a landslide vote of sports fans, America also elected Eddie Anderson to coach the All-Stars.) Before 85,000 fans,

Green Bay's passing combination of Cecil Isbell to Don Hutson proved to be too much for the All-Stars and Anderson's collegians fell 45 to 28. It should be noted, however, that when Kinnick was in the game the All-Stars scored four touchdowns, and when he was on the bench they could make only one first down and couldn't move the ball past mid-field. In a losing effort, Kinnick threw two touchdown passes and dropkicked three extra points.

The summer classic was the last football game Kinnick ever played. The NFL's Brooklyn Dodgers offered Kinnick an exorbitant $10,000 a year to play pro football. The Heisman winner declined, stating, "My football career is over. Law is now my first priority."[17]

In September of 1940, Kinnick began his studies at the University of Iowa Law School while serving as an assistant coach for the freshman football team. Despite his demanding schedule, Kinnick still found time to participate in politics.

On September 27, 1940, the football hero was asked to introduce Republican presidential candidate Wendell Wilkie to a crowd of 10,000 at Iowa Falls.[18] Later that afternoon, Kinnick gave his first political speech at a meeting of the Young Republicans. In it he praised the blessings of democracy and stressed the importance of being involved in the political process.

In his first year of law school Kinnick earned a 3.8 cumulative grade point average and ranked third among 103 students. With much of the world at war and the United States inching toward involvement, Kinnick joined the Naval Air Corps Reserves at Fairfax Airfield in Kansas City in the summer of 1941. Classes were so full that Nile couldn't report until December.

He returned to Iowa City in the fall to help coach football but because of his impending enlistment, he did not return to law school. On December 4, 1941, just three days before the Japanese attack on Pearl Harbor, Kinnick was called to active duty. On the eve before reporting Kinnick wrote in his diary, "May God give me the courage and ability to so conduct myself in every situation that my country, my family and my friends will be proud of me."[19]

Over the next 18 months Kinnick kept a diary of his thoughts and his flight training experience. His last entry was recorded on Tuesday, June 1, 1943. It reads: "How I wish I could sing and play the piano!

"It is a sad mistake to try to be headman in everything you attempt. The axiom: 'If it is worth doing at all it is worth doing well' has its limitations. Stay on the ball most of the time, but learn to coast between moments of all-out effort.

"People must come before profits!"[20]

The next day, June 2, 1943, the Navy Grumman F-4 Wildcat that Kinnick was piloting during a routine training mission developed a serious oil leak. When the controller aboard the USS *Lexington* asked him to stay in the

Nile Kinnick poses in flight gear while training to become a Navy pilot. Papers of Nile C. Kinnick, Dept. of Special Collections, University of Iowa Libraries, Iowa City, Iowa.

air 10 more minutes so the carrier's decks could be cleared of other aircraft, Kinnick responded, "I'll try."[21] Unfortunately, Kinnick didn't have 10 more minutes. He made a perfect wheels-up landing in the water approximately four miles off the *Lexington*'s starboard bow in the Gulf of Paria, off the coast of Venezuela.

A fellow pilot, Ensign Bill Reiter, flew over the floating aircraft and observed a seemingly dazed Kinnick climb out of the cockpit and wave. Radioing the carrier with the downed plane's location, Reiter then turned back to the carrier to lead rescue vessels to the site.[22] By the time rescuers arrived at the scene, both Kinnick and the plane had vanished beneath the waves. Kinnick's body was never recovered. Naval authorities speculated that "he was knocked unconscious by the impact through failure of his safety belt and was drowned."[23]

As biographer Scott Fisher writes, "He was 24 — the same number he had worn with such grit and grace during the Hawkeyes' dream season of 1939."[24]

Gene Corbett played end on Eddie Anderson's Holy Cross teams during the early sixties. After a 30-year career as an officer in the United States Air Force, Corbett reflects on his playing days for the good doctor. "Doc said many times that Nile Kinnick was the greatest player he ever coached... What I found particularly interesting and inspiring was that twenty-some years later, Doc always was emotional when he spoke of him. It's my recollection that he almost teared up whenever he told a Nile Kinnick story... To this day I feel the same way my self whenever I talk about Kinnick. Several years ago my wife and I were driving I-80 through Iowa City and saw a sign for Kinnick Stadium. And years after Doc Anderson went to his grave, there I was clutching up while telling her who Nile Kinnick was."[25]

17

THE FORTIES AT IOWA

In 1940 Dr. Eddie Anderson began his affiliation with the University of Iowa Hospital. During spring practice and the regular season Anderson started medical rounds at 6 a.m. and practiced medicine until early afternoon when he headed to the field house to prepare for practice. For whatever reason, Anderson and the head of the hospital's eye, ear, nose and throat clinic didn't hit it off. As a result, Anderson gradually came to spend time working with the eminent Dr. N.G. Alcock, head of the hospital's urology department. Under Alcock's guidance, Anderson eventually became well versed in urology. When Anderson entered the service in 1943, it was as a urologist in the U.S. Army Medical Corps.

On August 11, 1940, Eddie Anderson welcomed 67 of the previous fall's best college football players to the All-Star training camp in Evanston, Illinois. In a national poll, over four million Americans had elected Eddie to coach the All-Stars against the World Champion Green Bay Packers. Anderson had garnered a million votes more than the runner-up, Missouri's Don Faurot.

The brainchild of *Chicago Tribune* sports editor, Arch Ward, the late-summer clash between the College All-Stars and the National Football League Champions had gained wide acceptance since its inception in 1934. In the thirties, college football was immensely more popular than the professional game. When Ward first proposed the idea to benefit the Chicago Tribune Charities, Inc., NFL team owners, seeing it as a chance to grab national exposure, enthusiastically embraced the proposal. Often played before crowds of 90,000, the game was an unqualified success that heralded the start of every football season for over 40 years. The annual event was a catalyst to pro football's burgeoning into a billion dollar industry.

By the late sixties, however, NFL team owners felt they had bigger fish to fry. They came to view the August event as a hindrance to the league's profitable pre-season exhibition schedule. Owners also dreaded their top draft picks risking injury while playing for the All-Stars. The NFL Players' Union also objected to the world champions having to report to training camp earlier than other league teams to prepare for the game.[1] Many believed that the series had become too one-sided, that a bunch of 22-year-olds practicing for three weeks had no chance against seasoned pros. As the grumbling swirled, the last College All-Star game was played in 1976, two decades after the death of the game's founder, Arch Ward. With 1:22 remaining in the third quarter and the Pittsburgh Steelers leading 24 to 0, the contest was unceremoniously aborted due to a severe lightning storm. As fans dashed for cover from the pelting rain, booming thunder above the light stands of Soldier Field rang the death knell for the annual event.

The official end came on December 21, 1976. Citing uncertainties in recruiting player personnel and increasing insurance costs, Robert Hunt, the president of Chicago Tribune Charities, Inc., pulled the plug on the College All-Star game after 43 years.

In 1940, however, the game was a premier attraction that held special significance for millions of Americans. Winning it was serious business for both the collegians and the pros. Green Bay coach Curly Lambeau, whose Packers had endured a humiliating loss to the All-Stars in 1937, was now bent on revenge. Dr. Anderson was also determined to win. In an unprecedented move to prepare the All-Stars, he contacted Jimmy Conzelman, head coach of Eddie's old pro team, the Chicago Cardinals, and arranged scrimmages on August 22 and 24.

Lambeau, however, had also arranged for the Packers to scrimmage the Cards on August 19 and 20. Learning that Conzelman planned to scrimmage the All-Stars, the temperamental Lambeau became irate. He immediately cancelled his workouts with the Cardinals and wired Anderson, his former Notre Dame teammate, suggesting that he do the same. Anderson refused.

As Joe Ziemba writes in his history of the Chicago Cardinals, *When Football Was Football,* "Finally, Arch Ward of the *Tribune* stepped in and announced that henceforth, neither the pros nor the All-Stars would be allowed to scrimmage another pro team prior to the All-Star game. The Cardinals would now face neither opponent."[2]

Serving as assistants on Anderson's All-Star staff were Don Faurot of Missouri, Princeton's Tod Wieman, Tulane's Lowell Dawson and Buck Shaw of Santa Clara. Shaw, of course, had played tackle next to Anderson at Notre Dame. Before one practice a local cub reporter spied Shaw walking through the locker room.

"Coach Shaw," the reporter eagerly asked, "how does it feel to be reunited with your old Notre Dame teammate, Eddie Anderson?"

"Hell," replied Shaw, "I had to carry that guy for three years at Notre Dame. Now, look at him!" With that, Shaw smiled, waved and exited the room. No sooner had Shaw departed than Anderson entered from another doorway.

Still looking for a human-interest angle, the rookie reporter asked: "Doctor Anderson, how does it feel to be working with Buck Shaw again after all of these years?"

Cracking his famous crooked smile, Anderson explained: "Do you know that I carried that guy for three years at Notre Dame? I guess I can carry him for a few more weeks."[3]

Anderson was pleased to have four members of his 1939 Iron Men squad with him in Evanston. Hawkeye ends Erwin Prasse and Dick Evans, halfback Floyd "Buzz" Dean and, of course, Nile Kinnick, were on the All-Star roster. Other players of note included Ken Kavanaugh (LSU); Lou Brock (Purdue); Kenny Washington (UCLA); Joe Thesing (Notre Dame); Ambrose Schindler (USC); Frank "Pop" Ivy (Oklahoma); and Clyde "Bulldog" Turner of Hardin Simmons. (Bulldog Turner was such a vicious tackler that Anderson refused to let him participate in intra-squad scrimmages for fear of his crippling someone.)

The contest briefly reunited Anderson with former Holy Cross star, Bill Osmanski, who was honored at halftime with the Most Valuable Player Trophy for his performance in the 1939 College All-Star game.

As mentioned in Chapter Sixteen, Green Bay's dynamic passing duo of Cecil Isbell to Don Hutson proved to be too much for the All-Stars. Kinnick, however, was brilliant in throwing touchdown passes of 52 and 43 yards respectively to Ken Kavanaugh and Clemson's Banks McFadden and converting on three of three extra-point dropkicks. In a wide-open and exciting contest Green Bay prevailed 45 to 28. (Curly Lambeau would later tell *Milwaukee Journal* sportswriter Oliver Kuechle that Green Bay's 1940 win over the All-Stars was the most satisfying of his coaching career, because with it pro football caught the fancy of the American public.)[4]

Iowa fans and administrators held high hopes for Anderson's 1940 Hawkeye squad. Tackle and team captain, Mike Enich, led a solid core of returning lettermen that included quarterback Al Couppee; linemen Bill Diehl, Red Frye, Ken Pettit and Jim Walker; and running backs Bill Green and Ray Murphy. There were also talented newcomers and returning non-lettermen like Burdell "Oops" Gilleard.

An orphan, Gilleard was a speed-burner from New London, Iowa. In his senior year in high school, Gilleard led the nation in scoring. In 1939 he acquired the moniker "Oops" because his voice would suddenly rise an octave or two while barking out the signals.[5]

The 1940 season began with a 46 to 0 thrashing of visiting South Dakota. The next week, Iowa beat Wisconsin 30 to 12 before hitting a tailspin with four straight losses to Indiana, Minnesota, Purdue and Nebraska.

The fact is that Dr. Eddie Anderson might have become a victim of his own success. He had enjoyed phenomenal success during his six years at Holy Cross and then a wondrous 1939 season at Iowa. As a result, fans and administrators now expected Anderson's teams to win, and win often. After the Wisconsin game, Dr. Karl Lieb, chairman of the Iowa athletic board, decreed that schools like South Dakota were no longer satisfactory competition and that scheduling tougher rivals was now essential for both the team and the fans. Somehow forgetting that before Anderson's arrival Iowa had won only two games in two years, Lieb declared, "We tried our best to open with Michigan (with eventual Heisman winner, Tom Harmon), but couldn't. No one else was available so we had to take South Dakota."[6] (With friends like Lieb, Anderson didn't need any enemies.)

Although still possessing some talented players in 1940, Iowa had lost the incomparable triple-threat halfback Nile Kinnick to graduation. Anderson employed half a dozen players at left halfback trying to find a suitable replacement for Kinnick but never came close to finding one. Assistant coach Frank Carideo worked with place-kickers who could make 40 straight extra points in practice, but none could successfully kick an extra point in five consecutive games.

Anderson and his staff had accomplished incredible things with a team that melded uniquely behind Kinnick in 1939. During his remaining years at Iowa, however, Eddie never again approached the success of that magical year. Yet, playing in the best football conference in America against teams that usually possessed more talent and depth, Anderson's teams remained competitive and even managed to engineer several major upsets. One such upset occurred in 1940.

Sporting a 2 and 4 record the Hawkeyes were expected to be sacrificial lambs for Elmer Layden's Fighting Irish, who were bent on avenging their upset loss at Iowa in 1939. For the second year in a row, Iowa would meet an undefeated 6 and 0 Notre Dame football team. Although given little chance of beating Notre Dame, Anderson was guardedly optimistic. He told assistants Carideo and Harris that the Irish running game had been slipping in recent weeks, and if they didn't solve the problem, he was certain that the Hawkeyes could take them.[7]

While the Irish controlled the game's tempo, the contest was still score-less in the fourth quarter. With about six minutes remaining, Iowa's Ken Pet-tit recovered a Notre Dame fumble on the Irish 24-yard line. Four plays later Bill Green plunged two yards for a touchdown. Bill Gallagher's extra-point kick gave Iowa a 7 to 0 lead. On Notre Dame's next possession, Red Frye's interception sealed the win for Iowa.

Twice in two years Anderson's Iowa teams had shocked the nation by upsetting mighty Notre Dame. Back in Iowa City, Hawkeye fans who had listened to the radio broadcast of the game were now beside themselves, while on the Iowa campus the engineering building's whistle blew its victory shrill well into the night.

Determined to end the season on a winning note, Anderson warned his team against a letdown the following week. Although Bob Zuppke's Illini were winless in the Big Ten, Anderson cautioned, "What can we get overconfident about? This Zuppke, he throws everything in the book at you, including the footnotes."[8]

Zuppke's Illinois team lived up to Anderson's advance billing by jump-ing out to a 7 to 0 lead before the gritty Hawkeyes fought back to win 18 to 7 and finish the 1940 season with a record of 4 wins and 4 losses.

In February of 1941 Elmer Layden resigned as football coach at Notre Dame to become the Commissioner of the National Football League. As a Notre Dame alumnus who had engineered upsets of undefeated Irish squads in both 1940 and 1941, Anderson seemed a logical choice to succeed Layden. As rumors swirled that Eddie was bound for South Bend, the local Monsignor visited the parish school and summoned young Jerry Anderson from class.

"Is your father going to take the Notre Dame job?" inquired the Mon-signor.

"I don't know," answered eight-year-old Jerry.

"Find out and let me know tomorrow," instructed the priest.

That night the boy dutifully put the question to his father. Eddie Ander-son chuckled before responding, "I hope they ask me. I'd like to be the first one to turn them down."[9]

A month later Notre Dame hired Frank Leahy as coach. Anderson was never offered the position nor did he interview for it. "I don't think my father would have taken the Notre Dame job had it been offered in 1941," explains Jerry Anderson. "However, I think he would have taken it had it been offered in 1954.[10] (That year the Irish hired 25-year-old Terry Brennan to replace Leahy.)

"I would imagine that Dad would have wanted to be the coach at Notre Dame," says Eddie's daughter, Judy Anderson. "While Dad never said anything about it, Mom said not getting the Notre Dame job when it became available may have been one of the few disappointments in Eddie's life.

"Dad was not political at all," adds Judy. "He would have never politicked for the job nor have others campaign for it on his behalf."[11]

Anderson disliked recruiting. Perhaps he never considered it to be an inherent part of coaching, or perhaps practicing medicine while coaching drained him of both the energy and desire to actively pursue potential players. His distaste for it only intensified over the years, until he eventually delegated all recruiting to his assistants.

Nevertheless, Anderson employed every trick in his coaching bag to give the talent on hand a competitive edge. Believing that running plays on a slight uphill grade made players quicker, Anderson often had his teams run plays from the sidelines to the crown in the middle of the field. To insure his starting players a comfortable sleep on overnight trips, he assigned them sleeping berths in the middle of the railroad car, while second-teamers had to endure a bumpy night in berths situated directly above the train's wheels. At times, Anderson could resort to subtle intimidation as he did in 1941 when captain-elect Bill Diehl informed him that he would be missing spring football to play baseball for the Hawkeyes. "Gee," asked Anderson, "how is it going to look if the team captain sits on the bench this fall?"[12]

Iowa stumbled to a 3 and 5 record in 1941 but rebounded the next year to win 6 while losing 4. The highlight of the 1942 season came when Anderson's Hawkeyes upset previously unbeaten Wisconsin 6 to 0. It was Wisconsin's only loss of the season and probably cost the Badgers the national championship.

By 1942 America's war effort was in full swing. Every day thousands of young men entered the U.S. Armed Services. As a medical doctor, Eddie wanted to do his part. Should he enlist or wait to be drafted? A colonel in the U.S. Army Medical Corps helped Anderson make that decision.

That fall Colonel Lester Dyke and his family rented a house in Anderson's neighborhood while Dyke was taking classes at the university's hospital. The colonel and the coach soon became friends. Dyke persuaded Anderson that, rather than wait to be drafted and sent to God knows where, he should enlist in the Army Medical Corps. If he did, Dyke would make sure that Anderson would be assigned to his command. "Eddie," promised Dyke, "wherever I'm assigned, I'll take you with me."[13]

On February 11, 1943, which was also Eddie and Mary's 14th wedding anniversary, Anderson was inducted into the U.S. Army Medical Corps. True to his word, Colonel Dyke had Major Edward N. Anderson assigned to his staff at the Schick Veterans Hospital in Clinton, Iowa. When Dyke was ordered to Churchill Hospital in England in 1944, he again arranged to have Anderson on his staff.

Taking a long drag on a cigarette while he waited to board ship in Brooklyn's Naval Yard, Major Anderson wistfully thought of his beloved wife, Mary, who was now pregnant with their fourth child. Years later Anderson recalled, "The loneliest time in my life was carrying a duffel bag up the gangplank of that troop ship to Europe."[14]

On February 16, 1943, five days after Anderson's military induction, the University of Iowa named Jim Harris as its new football coach. With spring drills scheduled to start soon, the anticipation apparently became too much for the son of a coal mine superintendent from Bellaire, Ohio. While celebrating one weekend, Harris had a few too many drinks at Iowa City's Depot Lunch, the infamous barroom that Notre Dame's Hunk Anderson had cleaned-out after the 1921 Iowa game. It's unknown whether Harris' outburst was premeditated or spontaneous but, in either case, that night he set about duplicating Hunk Anderson's legendary house-cleaning feat.

When police arrived they found a well-lubricated Harris defiantly challenging all comers. Rather than risk further bloodshed, the police chief placed a call to Dr. Anderson's residence. Fortunately, Eddie was home on a weekend pass. After driving to the scene and conferring with police, Anderson entered the bar alone to reason with his good friend. Several minutes later, Anderson emerged with a contrite Harris in tow.[15]

Although the incident never made the papers, university officials washed their hands of Harris by quietly firing him on Monday. Shortly thereafter, Harris enlisted as a private in the Army Air Corps.

Because Frank Carideo was soon leaving for the Navy, the university reached off campus to hire Slip Madigan as its football coach. A former Notre Dame teammate of Eddie Anderson, Madigan had previously enjoyed a successful coaching stint at St. Mary's College in California. However, with the nation's war effort siphoning off most of Iowa's able-bodied athletes, Madigan entered the season woefully undermanned. In his two seasons at the Hawkeye helm, Madigan managed only two wins. Madigan's last game at Iowa was a 30 to 6 loss to Iowa Pre-Flight.

In 1942, the U.S. Navy established pre-flight programs at four college campuses, one of which was the University of Iowa. Popularly called "V-5 training," these programs were to provide aviation cadets with introductory training to prepare them for naval flight schools at Pensacola, Corpus Christi or Jacksonville. Regarding athletic competition as an integral part of leadership training, every pre-flight cadet was required to participate in either a varsity or inter-squadron sport.[16]

Iowa Pre-Flight fielded intercollegiate football teams from 1942 through 1944 with a different, but proven, coach at the helm each year. Minnesota's Bernie Bierman coached the "Seahawks" in 1942, Missouri's Don Faurot in 1943 and Auburn's Jack Meagher in 1944. (In early 1943, naval authorities offered Eddie Anderson the job. Had Anderson accepted, he could have fulfilled his military obligation without leaving home. However tempting the offer, Anderson declined, opting instead to honor his commitment to Colonel Dyke and the Army Medical Corps.)[17]

Half a world away from the killing on the beaches of Normandy and the volcanic ash of Iwo Jima, growing up

Major Edward N. Anderson served in the United States Army Medical Corps during World War II. This picture was taken in a London photo studio. Anderson served in England and later in field hospitals in both France and Germany. (Courtesy of Judy Anderson Moore)

in Iowa City during the war years could be a marvelous experience for a young boy with a bicycle. It was for Jimmy Anderson. To help train its aviation cadets, Iowa Pre-Flight used a long row of continuous tennis courts on the Iowa campus to simulate a carrier deck. From a three-story wooden bridge constructed alongside the courts, eight-year-old Jimmy Anderson often observed simulated flight operations along with the pre-flight school's top naval brass. The boy grew adept at returning snappy salutes from the cadets below. As long as the kid stayed out of the way, no one seemed to mind.

When the war ended in August of 1945, the Navy closed its pre-flight schools. One late summer afternoon Jimmy rode his bike to the pre-flight grounds to find a lone sailor emptying a storage building of all types of athletic equipment. What started as a small pile soon turned into a veritable mountain of baseball bats, catcher's mitts, boxing gloves and assorted game balls.

The wide-eyed youngster finally screwed up the courage to ask, "What are you going to do with all that stuff?"

"I'm going to destroy it," replied the sailor.

"Wow!" exclaimed Jimmy. "Can I have some of it?"

"No, kid. This is surplus government property. We can't give it away," explained the sailor. Then with a wink he added, "But I'm going to lunch now and when I get back in an hour I'm going to have to destroy whatever is left."[18]

No one had to wink twice at Jimmy Anderson. As soon as the sailor disappeared over the hill the boy crammed his pockets with baseballs, loaded what he could onto his bike and pedaled madly for the nearby woods. Like a squirrel gathering nuts for winter, the boy made a half-dozen hectic trips to the woods to stash his prized booty.

Christmas had come in August for young Jimmy Anderson.

Unfortunately, the complete military records of Eddie Anderson and thousands of other U.S. veterans were destroyed in a fire at the National Personnel Records Center in St. Louis, Missouri, on July 12, 1973. The mishap makes it impossible to retrace exactly where the good doctor was stationed overseas and for how long. However, family members claim that Anderson was assigned to various hospitals throughout England. Promoted to the rank of lieutenant colonel, he later served at field hospitals in both France and Germany.

Although Anderson rarely spoke of his overseas experiences, it's likely that his medical duties extended well beyond the field of urology. Judy Anderson remembers seeing several photos of her surgically gowned father in the operating room of an Army hospital in England. Carlin Lynch, the leading receiver on Anderson's 1955 Holy Cross team, recalls a conversation he once had with his former coach. "One day Dr. Anderson sat next to me on the team bus traveling to a game. I think it was during my sophomore year. We had a lengthy talk and I remember how pained he looked upon learning that my two older brothers were killed in the war. He told me that [during the war] he used to assess the physical disabilities of wounded GIs for the purpose of determining veterans' disability payments and pensions."[19]

One wounded veteran who heard from Anderson during the war was the 1939 Hawkeye captain, Erwin Prasse. While leading a night reconnaissance mission to determine a major crossing of the Roer River on January 13, 1945, Prasse suffered major shrapnel wounds in his right arm. Realizing his dreams of a major league career were now over, Prasse was understandably depressed while recuperating in a hospital in England. His gloom lifted when he received a letter from his former coach. "He wrote me a very kind and caring letter saying that he was stationed in a hospital only 80 miles away. He wanted to get together for a few drinks to talk over the old days at Iowa. Unfortunately, I was transferred to a distant hospital before we could meet. To this day, I still don't know how he ever knew I was there. I was always grateful to Dr. Anderson for that. He was one hell of a person."[20]

Incredibly, every player and coach from Iowa's 1939 Iron Men team served in the armed forces during World War II. Former assistant coach Bill Hofer suffered severe wounds while serving as a Marine officer in the Pacific. Ex-tackle and Marine Major Mike Enich survived a sniper's bullet to the lung on Okinawa.

Burdell "Oops" Gilleard, the orphan from New London, Iowa, was killed on November 23, 1944, on Leyte in the Philippines. Gilleard was 26.

And, of course, there was the tragic tale of Nile Kinnick, who died in the Gulf of Paria on June 2, 1943. Unfortunately, the Kinnick family had to endure yet another heartbreak. Marine pilot Ben Kinnick, Nile's younger brother, was killed when the B-25 Mitchell Bomber he was flying was shot down over Kavieng Peninsula on September 17, 1944.

Immediately after the war there was a groundswell movement to change the name of Iowa Stadium to Kinnick Stadium. Nile Kinnick, Sr., however, believed it would be unfair to honor just one fallen veteran when Iowa had sacrificed so many of her finest sons in the war. He therefore humbly declined the honor. After rebuffing repeated campaigns to adopt the name Kinnick Stadium, the elder Kinnick finally relented and agreed to the name change in 1972.

18

THE POST-WAR
YEARS AT IOWA

Lieutenant Colonel Eddie Anderson returned stateside just as Iowa was ending its 1945 season under interim coach, Clem Crowe. Captain of the 1925 Notre Dame team, the embattled Crowe had endured lopsided losses to Ohio State (42 to 0), Purdue (40 to 0), Indiana (52 to 20), Notre Dame (56 to 0) and Illinois (48 to 7) in guiding the outmanned Hawkeyes to a season record of 2 wins and 7 losses. After being discharged from the Army on December 17, Anderson announced his intention to coach full time. Within a year, however, he would again be practicing medicine while coaching football.

During spring drills in 1946, Anderson was reunited with Frank Carideo, back from three years of active duty as a U.S. Navy officer, and former Holy Cross assistant, Joe Sheeketski. Sheeketski had succeeded Anderson as head coach at Holy Cross, only to resign after the 1941 season. Now, the ex–Notre Dame halfback would replace the exiled Jim Harris as Iowa's line coach. Reunited with his old coaching friends, Eddie looked forward to building another football team.

That summer, however, Eddie's health took a turn for the worse. Feeling poorly and tiring easily, Anderson underwent an appendectomy at University of Iowa Hospital on August 23. While the operation was deemed a success, Anderson continued to run a fever and felt no better after a week. Hospitalized when fall practice began, Anderson underwent another battery of tests that proved to be inconclusive. Carideo and Sheeketski conducted the team's two-a-day practices around visits to Anderson to confer on football matters. Anderson's physician, Willis Fowler, grew more perplexed as his

186

patient's health continued to deteriorate. Finally, a young hospital intern correctly diagnosed Anderson to be suffering from amoebic dysentery, a bug he probably picked up while stationed in Europe.[1] With the life-threatening ailment now identified and being properly treated, Anderson's condition improved rapidly. Nevertheless, he remained hospitalized until September 17, just four days before Iowa's 1946 home opener against North Dakota State.

With a gaunt Dr. Anderson joining his team on the sidelines, Iowa trounced the visitors 39 to 0. Comprised primarily of incoming transfer students, the Hawkeye backfield looked especially strong. The speedy Emlen Tunnell, a transfer student from Toledo University, started at left halfback, while two transfers from Tulsa University, Lou King and Bob Smith, manned the quarterback and right halfback positions respectively. The starting fullback was Dick Hoerner. Hoerner, who had starred for the Hawkeyes in 1942 before spending the next three years in the Army, would earn All-American honors.

The Hawkeyes' 78-man roster included 70 men who had served in the armed forces during the war. Anderson had a special fondness for the World War II veterans. "A lot of us were married and Dr. Eddie always called the wives by their married names like Mrs. King," recalls ex-quarterback Lou King. "He let us bring our wives to the training table on Sundays. He always helped us out on medical bills, usually through the university hospital. As an example, the head of Iowa's OB Department delivered our first son. There was no hospital bill and no delivery fee. He even gave me my new front teeth at no charge! (King had lost several teeth playing for Iowa.) Dr. Eddie and the other coaches also gave us tickets to sell to help with money."[2]

Other players of note on the '46 squad included the Schoener twins, Hal and Herb; backs Ronnie Headington and Bob Sullivan; center Dick Lassiter; guard Earl Banks; and ends Tony Guzowski and Jack Dittmer.

In their second game Iowa played only 15 men in a 16 to 0 shutout of Purdue before traveling to Ann Arbor to do battle with Fritz Crisler's Michigan Wolverines. Before 54,000 fans, the home team jumped out to a 14 to 0 lead on Bob Chappius' two touchdowns. Anderson's Hawkeyes came roaring back in the second half. Iowa's fourth-quarter drive to win the game ended on the Wolverine 14-yard line when halfback Bob Smith was thrown for a loss on fourth down and a foot.

Shaking hands after the game, the Michigan coach, Fritz Crisler, told Anderson, "I should be congratulating you. You brought those kids a long ways and they will go a long ways yet."[3]

Crisler was right. In the next two weeks Iowa defeated Nebraska and upset defending conference champion Indiana 13 to 0 in Bloomington. On October 26 the Hawkeyes hosted Frank Leahy's Fighting Irish before 53,000

The Anderson family on the steps of their Iowa City home in the late fall of 1945. Major Anderson had just returned from overseas duty with the U.S. Army Medical Corps. [Top step (L-R): Nick Anderson, age 15; Mary Anderson and Eddie holding baby Judy. Bottom step (L-R) Jerry, age 13; and Jim, age 9. (Courtesy of Dr. Jerry Anderson)]

upset-minded fans. Iowa had won all three of the schools' previous meetings. However, Leahy was bringing a virtual juggernaut to town. The Irish roster read like a future roll call for the College Football Hall of Fame with players like Terry Brennan, George Connor, Bill Fischer, Leon Hart, Johnny Lujack, Jim Martin, George Ratterman, Emil Sitko, George Strohmeyer, Frank Tripucka and Jack Zilly. If Anderson entertained hopes of working another upset against his alma mater, they were quickly squashed as the Irish made it look easy en route to a 41 to 6 win. (Two weeks later Notre Dame played West Point to a scoreless tie at Yankee Stadium finishing the season undefeated and edging out West Point for the national championship.)

Iowa's record fell to 4 wins and 3 losses the following week when Illinois scored a fourth-quarter touchdown to defeat Anderson's lads 7 to 0. Unfortunately, the loss provoked a maelstrom of acrimony involving Iowa's coach. At the vortex of the controversy was the following letter that appeared in *The Daily Iowan* on November 8, 1946.

To The Daily Iowan:

> The composition of this letter was stimulated by the widespread condemnation of the quarterback on Iowa's 1946 football team. I would like first of all a fixation of responsibility for the distasteful showing of a potentially great football team. This responsibility can be laid at only one door — that of Dr. Eddie Anderson's.
>
> It is well known to anyone who has competed in football under Dr. Anderson that his quarterbacks are, for the most part, pre-directed and trained as to the strategy of "play calling." Dr. Anderson's responsibility in the Illinois fiasco was illustrated by the fact that Louis King spent most of the defensive time on the sidelines, re-entering when Iowa took the offensive — with Dr. Anderson's instructions. That fixes this responsibility.
>
> I believe also we have very strong proof that Dr. Anderson not only doesn't know how to use the T-formation but doesn't even know the theory behind it. First, all advocates of the T-formation recognize that it is an offense of deception and of "power." In all Iowa's efforts to date the T has been used for power. The forward pass has to date been only a weapon of frustration when, not only the opposing team, but the entire stadium knew Iowa would pass. Contrast this with the Notre Dame T-formation where passes are thrown on first down and any time. In fact, passing must be an integral part of any T-formation as well as the use of the lateral pass, the man in motion, and wide end sweeps of which we saw very few Saturday.
>
> ... If it's power football Dr. Anderson chooses to play, let him return to the Notre Dame box or the single wingback formation where it can be effectively used rather than, through stupidity, allow a great squad to be humiliated. I speak of a great squad in terms of two fine teams, not just the one team that Dr. Anderson plays "till it drops."
>
> How long will Dr. Anderson ride on the laurels Nile Kinnick won for him?
>
> B.F.

This scathing letter was actually written by two former Iowa football players, Bill Barbour and Harry Frey. Barbour hailed from Anderson's hometown of Mason City, and both had played as sophomores on Anderson's 1942 team and then for Slip Madigan in 1943. They passed up playing in 1944 to concentrate on their studies. Now enrolled in the university's medical school, both asked that their names be withheld and the letter simply be signed with their initials "B.F." This request was in accordance with *The Daily Iowan*'s stated policy to withhold names upon the author's request.

The following Monday, November 11, Dr. N.G. Alcock, a close friend and professional colleague of Dr. Anderson, telephoned Gene Goodwin, editor of *The Daily Iowan*, to try to learn the names of the authors. Goodwin declined to reveal the names.

Not content to let Iowa's recent 21 to 7 win over Wisconsin answer his critics, an irate Eddie Anderson called *The Daily Iowan* several minutes later. As Goodwin was no longer in the office, he spoke with the paper's sports editor, Chad Brooks. Brooks also refused to divulge the authors' names, but he agreed to meet with Anderson later that afternoon.

When Brooks arrived at the football coach's office, he had the original (and signed) letter with him. During the course of their conversation Brooks handed the letter to Dr. Anderson. In doing so, of course, Brooks violated the newspaper's ethics by revealing the authors' identities. Brooks later explained that he only did so with the understanding that the authors would not be harassed in any way. He attempted to justify this breach of ethics by saying that, as head football coach, Dr. Anderson could make his own position as sports editor untenable.[4]

A seething Anderson then had Brooks wait while he wrote a rebuttal letter to the editor. Brooks delivered it to Gene Goodwin. Realizing that publishing Anderson's letter would be yet another violation of the paper's ethical duty to protect the identities of Barbour and Frey, Goodwin attempted to consult the paper's publisher, Fred Pownall. Unable to contact Pownall, Goodwin took his dilemma to Dr. Wilbur Schramm, director of Iowa's School of Journalism. Schramm advised Goodwin to persuade Anderson to either withdraw his letter or at least agree to print it without making reference to either Barbour or Frey.

Goodwin, Brooks and assistant sports editor Don Sulhoff then set off to change Anderson's mind. They caught up with the coach at the team's nightly training table. Goodwin explained the paper's ethical dilemma to Anderson, but Eddie wouldn't budge.

Leaving the dining hall, Frank Carideo took Mr. Goodwin aside and threatened him with bodily harm if Dr. Anderson's letter was not printed intact.

At nine o'clock that evening, Mr. Pownall and Dr. Schramm visited Dr. N.G. Alcock's home hoping that they could prevail upon him to persuade Anderson to withdraw his letter. They also offered to publish an apology to Dr. Anderson for publishing the original letter if Anderson would agree to withdraw his letter. Alcock then visited Anderson's home to present the proposal.

Anderson agreed to the paper's withholding his letter for one day, pending the appropriateness of the apology. After a late night meeting between Pownall, Schramm, Goodwin and three of the paper's board members, it was decided that an apology should be discarded in favor of an editorial expressing *The Daily Iowan*'s regret over publishing Friday's letter. The editorial published on Tuesday, November 12, appears below.

Our Mistake, Dr. Eddie

Last Friday morning, *The Daily Iowan* did something for which we are now deeply sorry.

We published a letter which hurt and offended a fine gentleman who has been a part of Iowa's greatest athletic tradition, and which also hurt and offended the friends of that man who have come to number almost as many as there are people in Iowa.

This letter was a criticism of Dr. Eddie Anderson. It was without justice; it was unfair; it was in bad taste. We did not agree with the sentiments expressed in the letter, but that is beside the point. We printed it without the signatures of the authors. That made it our responsibility. The letter in question was written by two former Iowa football players and signed with the initials "B.F."

We shouldn't have published the letter without requiring the signatures of the authors. That was a mistake, a mistake for which we are now offering humble apologies.

It seems to us that persons who write letters to the editor of the *Iowan* should be willing to stand up and be counted. We don't think that will make for less criticism, but for less irresponsible criticism.

Again we say, sorry, Dr. Anderson

Although the apology was effusive, if not downright groveling, it didn't satisfy Anderson's fiercely loyal assistant, Frank Carideo. Iowa's backfield coach phoned editor Gene Goodwin that afternoon castigating the editorial as ridiculous. He again threatened Goodwin with bodily harm if Anderson's letter was not printed.[5] That afternoon, *The Daily Iowan*'s publisher, Mr. Pownall, met privately with Anderson. He informed him of Carideo's second threat against Goodwin and raised the possibility of initiating legal action against his assistant coach. Pownall emerged from the conference with a revised letter from Anderson. It was published in *The Daily Iowan* on Wednesday, November 13, which was also Anderson's 46th birthday. It appears below.

Editor, *Daily Iowan*
Dear Sirs:

I would like to reply to a letter published in *The Daily Iowan* last Friday morning, November 8, in regard to myself, and I wish to reply through the same channels responsible for publication of the original.

The letter was signed in the paper by the initials "B.F." However, I think it is only fair that the faculty, student body, and other readers of *The Daily Iowan* should know who those initials stand for. The letter written to *The Daily Iowan* was signed by Bill Barbour and Harry Frey, so people can see that the "B.F." was for Barbour and Frey who I understand are students in the Medical School at the present time.

I had Bill Barbour and Harry Frey out for the football squad before the war, and I guess they were fortunate enough to be regulars during the war years of 1943 or 1944.

I feel that my record as a coach, both before and after coming to the University of Iowa, makes it unnecessary for me to discuss the technical aspects of coaching with relatively inexperienced detractors. However, I do resent uninformed attacks, especially when the would-be critics attempt to hide their identity behind a cloak of anonymity and jumbled initials.

I am very sorry that they had to mention the name of such a great hero as Nile Kinnick in an article like this, and I only wish that Nile were here to answer their last sentence.

Sincerely,
E. N. Anderson

In a private memo dated November 16, 1946, Dr. Wilbur Schramm expressed his regrets that *The Daily Iowan* printed Anderson's letter revealing the names of Barbour and Frey. However, he saw no other alternative.[6]

Anderson's letter resulted in an outcry from sportswriters and state legislators rallying around the coach. Some legislators, previously irked at what they considered to be the paper's liberal bent, now urged an investigation into the finances of what they called the university's "pinko" newspaper. Conversely, many students and journalists expressed outrage at what they viewed to be *The Daily Iowan*'s "coerced" apology to Anderson. To them, the episode violated the principle of freedom of the press.

The imbroglio also involved an ugly incident that occurred on November 12 when Frank Carideo called Harry Frey's wife saying that he wanted to meet with her husband for Harry's own good. Later that afternoon, Frey, accompanied by Barbour, went to the practice field to talk with Carideo. In a written statement submitted to *The Daily Iowan* officials on November 13, Barbour gives his version of what happened next.

Dr. Anderson and Carideo, upon seeing us, rushed down the field. Dr. A said, "Frank, I told you these two would come crawling over after talking behind my back."

Barbour: "We haven't come to apologize. Our sentiments are still the same."

Then Anderson went on to say, "I'm going to see you two out of medical school. And if I don't get you out of here, I'm ready to go to the American Medical Association and testify to your character so that you will never become a member of that organization.

"There's to be a letter in the paper tomorrow that will follow you two for the rest of your lives.

"Now, get out of here before I throw you out!"

Carideo added, "And I'll help you!"

As the two students left, Frey called out, "You've shown what you are Anderson."[7]

After reading Barbour's statement, the head of the school's Journalism Department, Dr. Wilbur Schramm, spent the next 48 hours discussing the matter with the university president, the athletic director, the dean of liberal arts, the dean of the graduate college and the faculty representative on the board of athletics. Schramm informed all parties that he would do everything within his power to make sure that no recriminations were made against either Barbour or Frey, and that he would tolerate no further threats against members of *The Daily Iowan* staff.[8]

University officials agreed. The head of the athletic board said that he would calm down Anderson while the athletic director promised to rein in Carideo. In a journalistic age far different from today's, neither Anderson's threats against Barbour and Frey, nor Carideo's against *The Daily Iowan* editor Gene Goodwin, ever appeared in any newspapers.

It's difficult to assess why Anderson reacted so vituperatively to Frey and Barbour's letter. Yes, the letter was stinging in its criticism, but Anderson's coaching strategies and tactics had been criticized in print before. His behavior in this instance was very much out of character. Anderson knew and appreciated the value of maintaining a working relationship with the press and had managed to do so throughout his coaching career. Perhaps Anderson was angered by the letter's reference to Nile Kinnick, which was in bad taste by any yardstick of decency. Perhaps his acrimony was fanned by the memory of all the maimed and wounded brave young men he had treated during the war, men who had demonstrated their courage on the battlefields of Europe, not in criticizing another's work behind a guarantee of anonymity.

The flap over the "B.F." letter did have one positive outcome. *The Daily Iowan* announced that in the future it would no longer publish unsigned letters.

The turmoil certainly didn't help Iowa prepare for the season finale against Minnesota. The Golden Gophers handed the Hawkeyes a 16 to 6 loss, and Iowa finished the year with a record of 5 wins and 4 losses. It would be Anderson's last winning season at Iowa.

The 1947 season was even more trying for Anderson. After an opening-day 59 to 0 rout of North Dakota State, the Hawkeyes dropped two straight to UCLA (22 to 7) and Illinois (35 to 12). Even though these losses came at the hands of quality teams who had been the previous season's Rose Bowl contestants, Anderson, for one of the few times in his career, was not optimistic about the season's outcome.

"Dad wouldn't let us (the Anderson family) go to the homecoming game against Indiana because he was afraid we might lose," recalls Anderson's oldest son, Nick.[9] Despite Anderson's premonition, the Hawkeyes upset Indiana 27 to 14 behind quarterback Al DeMarco's three touchdown passes to Emlen Tunnell.

The following week, before 72,000 fans at Columbus, the Hawkeyes dominated Ohio State for three quarters before yielding two touchdowns in the game's last nine minutes for a frustrating 13 to 13 tie.

Bob Smith and Emlen Tunnell, who would go on to lengthy pro careers with the Detroit Lions and the New York Giants respectively, were standouts on an Iowa squad that lacked depth and overall speed. Lou King was shifted from quarterback to safety to make way for Al DeMarco, who was the better passer. Certainly the Hawkeyes missed the power running of 6' 4," 220-pound fullback Dick Hoerner, who had by-passed his senior year to play with the NFL's Los Angeles Rams.

Over the next two weeks, powerhouse Notre Dame and Purdue both blanked Iowa by identical scores of 21 to 0. As is often the case with struggling teams, when it rains it pours. More trouble erupted on Monday after the Purdue game when a frustrated Emlen Tunnell quit the team during a tackling drill after Coach Carideo reprimanded him for a half-hearted effort. Although Tunnell had a quick change of heart and was allowed back on the squad after meeting privately with Anderson on Wednesday, the story generated negative publicity statewide. Tunnell's penance came that Saturday when the benched halfback watched Wisconsin's Badgers pummel his teammates 46 to 14.

The Wisconsin game was the nadir of the 1947 season for Iowa. Alumni grumbling, which had surfaced after the Purdue game, now rose to new heights. Sportswriter Tait Cummins blamed Iowa's woes on the many returning veterans not living up to their pre-war billing. "Approximately 16 of the first 20 men are married now and experiencing problems they didn't have to face before the war."

Cummins' observation rang true. The aftermath of World War II had dramatically changed the landscape of college football. Veterans who had experienced the horrors of Tarawa and Anzio were no longer starry-eyed teenagers motivated by pep talks or college fight songs. They now viewed football differently than they did before the war. To those who had lived in foxholes or stormed machine gun nests, football was merely a game or perhaps a means to a college diploma, but certainly not the ultimate test of one's manhood or self-worth. Veterans with families could not or would not make the personal or emotional sacrifices to the sport that they had as bachelors before the war.

Not only did coaches have to deal with the phenomenon of veteran-laden rosters, but from Columbus to Iowa City, Big Ten coaches now felt more pressured to win. It seemed that the mentality adopted in mobilizing America's economy to win a total war was now being applied to the gridiron by fans, sportswriters and administrators. Major college football was indeed becoming a big business whose bottom line was measured in wins.

On Wednesday, November 12, *The Daily Iowan*'s Chad Brooks lambasted Iowa for not playing more substitutes. Others, like Pat Harmon of the *Cedar Rapids Gazette*, predicted that Minnesota would paste the Hawkeyes in their season finale to give Anderson his worst conference record since coming to Iowa.

At the team's evening meal on November 13, Anderson, pained over his squad's predicament, confided to several sportswriters, "I feel like walking down alleyways ... avoiding people on the streets. I wonder how the kids feel?"[10] It was Anderson's 47th birthday and later that night he made a gutsy decision.

Knowing that he would be losing key players to graduation and that talent was limited in the freshman pipeline, Anderson decided to roll the dice on his future at Iowa. As the state's third-highest paid employee at an annual salary of $12,500 and with over two years remaining on his contract, Anderson decided to tender his resignation as football coach. If the athletic board rejected his resignation, it would be a strong vote of confidence in the job Anderson was doing. If his resignation were accepted, Anderson would still make a fine living practicing medicine.

On Friday, the eve of the Minnesota game, Anderson paid a visit to the home of university president Virgil Hancher and submitted his resignation. The shocked president asked Eddie if he was sure of his decision. Anderson said he was. Hancher then informed the coach that his resignation would be presented to the university's athletic board on Monday evening, November 17. After phoning several board members, Hancher released Anderson's decision to the press shortly before midnight.

"I only learned about Dad's decision early Saturday afternoon from a friend who showed me the headlines in the paper," recalls Anderson's youngest son, Jim.[11]

Anderson's resignation stunned his players. On the morning of the game Emlen Tunnell told reporters, "This is a great surprise to me. I believe that fellows will go all out to beat Minnesota. I know I will."[12]

Minnesota entered the contest a two-touchdown favorite. Although squandering several early scoring opportunities, the Gophers still took a 7 to 0 halftime lead. The second half, however, would be all Iowa's. Playing with their embattled coach's job on the line, the Hawkeyes drove 66 yards on their first possession to score on Al DeMarco's pass to Herb Schoener. Ron Headington later ran three yards for a touchdown to provide the 50,000 hometown fans with a marvelous 13 to 7 upset win.

In the jubilant post-game locker room, halfback Bob Smith yelled, "This one was for Eddie! I don't know what those people say, but I know our fellows want Eddie back." Anderson, in turn, told reporters, "I told them to go out and win it for themselves. I wanted them to prove themselves before the home crowd."[13]

When asked to speculate on his pending resignation Anderson replied, "No comment. I haven't thought about anything except the Minnesota game all day. I haven't even talked to my wife about what I would do."[14]

On Sunday, November 16, Anderson addressed a high school banquet in Edgerton, Wisconsin. Afterwards he told local reporters it seemed unlikely that Iowa's upset win over Minnesota would result in the athletic board refusing to accept his resignation.[15]

As Anderson attended a luncheon in Chicago the next day, Iowa's Bob Smith was at the Iowa City Quarterback Club luncheon circulating a petition to convince Iowa's athletic board to retain "the best coach in the world." However, when the petition failed to get unanimous backing from the players, Smith dropped it.[16]

That morning the Iowa student council held a campus vote on whether Anderson should be retained as football coach. The results did not bode well for Dr. Eddie. Of the 2,738 students that voted, 1,347 voted against him and 683 favored his retention. The remaining 708 participants felt unqualified to express an opinion.

Anderson supporters saw a glimmer of hope that night when the university's board of athletics adjourned without voting on Anderson's resignation. Saying they wanted to meet privately with the coach first, the board announced it would decide the issue later in the week. After meeting for over four hours on Thursday, November 20, the board announced its recommendation that, "the resignation of Dr. Anderson be not accepted."

"I am glad we got things straightened out," a relieved Anderson told reporters. "I am very grateful to Paul Brechler (Iowa's athletic director), the board in control of athletics, alumni in and out of state, and all loyal supporters."[17]

The vast majority of Hawkeye players were thrilled at the outcome. Guard Earl Banks, who would later go on to a lengthy coaching career at Morgan State, declared, "I think the board made a wise decision. I don't think there could be a better coach in the country."[18]

An appreciative Emlen Tunnell offered, "I think the board did the right thing. The board is a lot closer to the players than a lot of the students who have been doing so much talking."[19]

"The board's decision is a great victory of Iowa," echoed a beaming Bob Smith. "I hope everyone will get behind Eddie and make him realize that we really want him here."[20]

In addition to giving Anderson a vote of confidence, the board also agreed to increase the size of Anderson's coaching staff and promised to employ a full-time recruiter to work with prospective Iowa athletes. As a result, Anderson entered the 1948 season with some breathing room. With only four returning starters, he would need it. Although the Hawkeyes finished the 1948 season with a record of 4 wins and 5 losses, they were competitive in every game. The team's widest margin of defeat was a 15-point loss to Notre Dame that was ranked number two in the nation. Iowa lost three conference games by a touchdown while posting wins over Marquette, Ohio State, Wisconsin and Boston University.

While Anderson's football team struggled on the gridiron, his personal financial dealings were about to make a quantum leap.

Situated in a rustic valley 20 miles west of Iowa City are the Amana Colonies. Comprised of seven villages, the colonies were organized by a German religious sect in the mid-nineteenth century. Practicing self-sufficiency and piety, these industrious people came to be called Amanaites. They lived under a communal system until 1932 when they adopted cooperative capitalism.

In 1934, a 26-year-old Amanaite named George Foerstner accepted a challenge from a local businessman to build a dependable beverage cooler. Using his own hands, Foerstner did just that. He then founded the Electrical Equipment Company to produce them commercially. In 1936 Foerstner sold his company to the Amana Church society, which renamed it Amana Refrigeration but wisely retained Foerstner to oversee its operations. During World War II it became the Navy's chief supplier of walk-in coolers and refrigeration systems.

In 1949 the Amanaites decided to sell the company. Cognizant of Amana's vast lucrative potential, Foerstner wanted to buy it. He needed investors but was uncertain of how to attract them. One day, business took Foerstner to the University of Iowa where he noticed a large crowd watching football practice. It then dawned on him that Iowa's football coach was perhaps the most popular man in the state and certainly knew other influential people. If Foerstner could convince Anderson to invest in Amana, surely Anderson could introduce him to other potential investors.

A shy man with a thick German accent and a sixth-grade formal education, Foerstner was too self-conscious to approach the famous coach in public. Instead, he decided to deliver a gift of a frozen turkey to Anderson's home. Losing his nerve at the last minute, Foerstner left the bundle at the door and fled without ringing the bell.[21] After several other aborted attempts, the timid entrepreneur finally did meet Anderson and pitched him on Amana.

Knowing a good deal when he heard one, Anderson wanted in. As Foerstner had hoped, Anderson helped assemble a small circle of co-investors, each venturing a minimum of $10,000. As a result, Foerstner was able to buy Amana Refrigeration as a closed corporation. Under Foerstner's direction the company continued to prosper.

Not only were Foerstner and Anderson business associates, but they also became close friends whose families vacationed together. When Anderson retired from coaching in 1964, he netted a small fortune by liquidating his Amana stock — over 16,000 shares.[22]

Anderson's young but spirited Hawkeyes started strongly in 1949. Trailing Oregon 31 to 7, Bill Reichardt's 99-yard kick-off return for a touchdown sparked a miraculous second-half comeback resulting in a 34 to 31 win to give Iowa a record of 4 wins and 2 losses entering November. Because of the running of Reichardt and Bob Longley and the pass catching of Jack Dittmer and Bob McKenzie, Iowa was tied for first place in the Big Nine Conference when it entered the Minnesota game on November 5. (The conference was called the "Big Nine" because it had not yet admitted a replacement for the University of Chicago, which had dropped football in 1939.)

Unfortunately, the Hawkeyes ran into a buzz saw in Minneapolis. Trailing 28 to 7 with 12 minutes remaining, Iowa resorted to passing on every down. Under a relentless pass rush from Clayton Tonnenmaker, Leo Nomellini and Bud Grant, the Hawkeyes suffered two interceptions that were returned for touchdowns. (Nomellini and Grant both went on to the NFL Hall of Fame, Nomellini as a tackle for San Francisco's 49ers and Grant as head coach of the Minnesota Vikings.) When the smoke cleared, Minnesota had scored 27 fourth-quarter points to trounce Iowa 55 to 7.

"Forget about this one," Anderson told his bruised and battered players afterwards. "It was just one of those days and the best thing to do when something like this happens is to just wipe it out of your mind."[23]

Unfortunately, the physical punishment Iowa endured that afternoon left many players hobbling, and the schedule provided no rest for Iowa's walking wounded. After dropping a 35 to 13 decision to Wisconsin at Madison, Anderson's lads traveled to South Bend to battle Frank Leahy's Fighting Irish. Riding a 35-game winning streak, the Irish were en route to winning their third national championship in four years. After battling to a 7 to 7 halftime tie, Notre Dame pulled away to a 28 to 7 win. The loss left Iowa with a final record of 4 wins and 5 losses — Anderson's third consecutive losing season at Iowa.

The next weekend was Thanksgiving weekend and Eddie's old coaching crony, Jim Harris, was visiting. Over a martini in the Anderson living room the two were listening to the day's college football scores when the radio blared: Boston College 76, Holy Cross 0.

"Wow!" exclaimed Harris, almost leaping out of his chair. "If Osmanski has any more games like that, he'll be pulling teeth full time!"[24]

During the off-season, Holy Cross coach Bill Osmanski practiced dentistry in Chicago, where he had enjoyed a prominent playing career with Chicago's Bears. Harris' animated outburst was a foreshadowing of things to come.

Although his Iowa teams had now experienced three consecutive losing seasons, Anderson remained a highly desired commodity in the coaching world. According to Nick Anderson, Eddie's oldest son, both Harvard and Yale had sent Anderson feelers about coaching at their respective universities after the 1947 season.[25] (Harvard eventually hired Arthur Valpey; Yale, Herman Hickman.) Prior to the 1949 season, Eddie's former pupil and movie-star friend, Don Ameche, courted Anderson to coach his Los Angeles Dons of the All-American Football Conference (AAFC). Ameche was the team's majority owner and thus named the team after himself. Knowing the AAFC's financial status was shaky at best, Anderson declined.

"I know that Dad traveled to Los Angeles in 1949 to interview for the head job with the Rams," recalls his son, Jerry Anderson. "It wasn't offered to him, but he interviewed for it."[26]

There was also rampant speculation that the Bidwell family would offer Anderson the job of coaching the Chicago Cardinals in 1950.[27] (The Cardinals eventually hired Curley Lambeau, Anderson's former Notre Dame teammate.)

Believing that he had numerous coaching options available to him and that he could always practice medicine, Anderson judged the time was ripe for him to "batten down" some job security at Iowa. With a year still remaining on his contract, Anderson approached the university's athletic board in mid–January to renegotiate.

A few weeks earlier, in an attempt to retain their Rose Bowl-winning coach, Ohio State had granted Wes Fesler lifetime tenure as a professor of physical education whenever he decided to bow out of coaching. Now, perhaps influenced by Fesler's deal, Anderson asked that his next contract include a promise of professional rank and tenure at the University of Iowa Hospital should he step down as Iowa's head football coach. The good doctor asked for an answer by January 27.

Anderson had another reason to believe that he was negotiating from a positon of strength. Since buying out Coach Bill Osmanski's contract on January 6, Holy Cross College officials had been relentlessly wooing Anderson to return to Worcester.

On January 27 Iowa's athletic board offered Anderson a four-year contract extension at an annual salary of $13,000. However, the board denied Anderson's request for tenure by explaining, "University and state board of education regulations specifically do not provide for tenure for coaches of intercollegiate teams."[28]

Several members of the athletic council were sympathetic to Anderson's request. However, the decision to grant tenure to a coach would have to be made at a much higher level, and it would take time. It's possible the athletic board considered that Anderson had already played his trump card by tendering his resignation in 1947 and was now unwilling to make any further concessions.

With the ball in his court, Eddie Anderson submitted his resignation as football coach at Iowa on Saturday, January 28.

"I don't know how happy Dad was about leaving Iowa," muses Nick Anderson. "He felt that he put his neck on the line by requesting tenure, and his ego wouldn't let him stay when it was denied."[29]

During his eight years at the Iowa helm, Dr. Eddie Anderson compiled a record of 35 wins, 33 losses and 2 ties. However, his coaching legacy extends well beyond his actual record. No team in the annals of Iowa football ever captured the hearts and imaginations of the Iowa citizenry as did Anderson's 1939 Iron Men. When Anderson arrived, the university had an abysmal football program with a $450,000 cloud of debt shrouding Iowa Stadium. During his reign he made Iowa competitive, masterminding several unforgettable upsets along the way. His teams drew the largest crowds in the school's history. When Anderson left a decade later, Iowa Stadium was paid for and the university's athletic program was a quarter of a million dollars in the black.

19

RETURN TO MOUNT ST. JAMES

During the 11-year interval between Dr. Anderson's coaching stints at Mount St. James, Holy Cross football actually experienced considerable success. Between 1939 and 1949 the Crusaders compiled an overall record of 54 wins, 43 losses and 8 ties, while winning 5 of 10 games against archrival Boston College. (The teams did not meet in 1943.) The school also made its only bowl appearance in 1945, a 13 to 6 loss to Miami in the Orange Bowl. However, the 1949 season was a debacle. Suffering their worst record in 55 seasons of football, the Crusaders won only 1 game while losing 9. The once proud program hit rock bottom when Boston College humiliated the Crusaders 76 to 0 in the season's finale. After the game, Coach Bill Osmanski sat in bewilderment over his team's fate.

By many accounts, Osmanski had been the greatest player ever to don the Royal Purple of Holy Cross. With no real coaching experience, the former All-American assumed the coaching reins at his alma mater in 1948. However, superstars seldom make good coaches. In his rookie season Holy Cross won 5 and lost 5, before slipping to 1 and 9 in 1949. The abysmal 1949 season brought college administrators to the embarrassing and painful realization that Bullet Bill was not the man for the job and opted to buy out the remaining three years of Osmanski's contract.

On February 8, 1950, the day before Wisconsin Senator Joe McCarthy would accuse the U.S. State Department of being infested with communists during an address in Wheeling, West Virginia, the rakishly attired Eddie Anderson smiled for the camera as he signed a five-year contract to coach football at Holy Cross at an annual salary of $15,000. Beaming proudly over the coach's right shoulder were the Very Reverend John O'Brien, S.J., the president of the college, and Gene Flynn, the school's athletic director. The signing marked the first time a college football coach ever returned to a coaching position he had previously resigned.

"You know, it's a nice feeling to be back here," Anderson told reporters. "This was my first big time job. I was happy here and I know I'll be happy again."[1]

Did Anderson really believe that he could lead Holy Cross back to national prominence or had he merely grown weary of the pressure to win in the Big Ten Conference? The Jesuit fathers had made no significant physical improvements to the college since Anderson's departure a decade earlier. Both the facilities and athletic budget were spartan compared to what Anderson had enjoyed at Iowa. Yet, Anderson seemed genuinely happy to be back at Mount St. James.

When Anderson signed on for a second coaching stint at Holy Cross, he and Mary kept their home in Iowa City. The Anderson house was so lovely that *Better Homes and Gardens* magazine featured it in its October 1941 issue. Between 1951 and 1955, Anderson spent the off-seasons practicing medicine in Iowa. It was only when Eddie accepted a staff position at the Rutland Veterans Hospital outside of Worcester that his seasonal migrations between Massachusetts and Iowa ceased.

"My mother and I stayed in Iowa in 1950," recalls Judy Anderson, "but after that we would go back with him every season. I'd start the school year in Worcester while my brothers stayed in Iowa.

"When the season was over we would drive to Iowa and I'd enroll in school there. Those trips would take three days. We'd drive from 5 a.m. until it was dark. My mother never drove, so Dad did all the driving."[2]

Judy was the baby in the family by eight years. Due to her father's unique situation in the early fifties, the dad Judy knew growing up was different from the one her brothers had known. "When Dad was coaching in Worcester, he wouldn't get home at night until nine o'clock, but during much of the winter and summer he was always there," remembers Judy. "He drove me to and from school every day. He'd take me to the pool in the summer, not to play, but for swimming lessons. I'm sure my brothers didn't have that kind of time with him.

"Because I'd go back and forth from school between Massachusetts and Iowa, I'd sometimes fall behind in math or reading, and Dad would spend nights teaching me and bringing me up to speed."

Anderson became more devout in his Catholic faith as he grew older. In 1950 while driving in Worcester, Eddie narrowly escaped a head-on collision

On February 8, 1950, Eddie Anderson signed a five-year contract at an annual salary of $15,000 to return to coach football at Holy Cross. Standing behind Anderson are athletic director Gene Flynn and the Very Reverend John O'Brien, S.J., president of the college. (College of the Holy Cross Archives)

with another auto. Perhaps shaken by the close call, Eddie would pray aloud every time he got behind the wheel. "When we got in the car Dad would turn the ignition key and begin reciting the 'Our Father,' and I'd have to finish it as well as add a 'Hail Mary' or a 'Glory Be.' We did it every time we got in the car. I was so used to it that I never realized how bizarre that must have been for my friends who sometimes rode with us."

Eddie also taught his athletic daughter how to swing a golf club. Although Judy developed a near-perfect swing, the good doctor never deemed it good enough to take her out on the links with him. At age 12, Anderson tried to teach her how to throw a baseball. As Judy struggled to master the nuances of delivering an overhand fastball, her frustrated father's instructions grew increasingly acerbic until drawing a stern rebuke from his wife, Mary. "Eddie, she's a girl!"

"I can never remember going to bed at night without my father giving me a kiss on the cheek," reminisces Judy. "I always felt protected. It was certainly a nice way to grow up. I never felt that my father didn't love me.[3]

While Eddie doted on his only daughter, he could sometimes be austere and aloof with his sons. For example, when Eddie's 84-year-old father died in 1951, Anderson flew to Iowa for the funeral. On his 51st birthday, Anderson stood at the gravesite as his father was buried in Mason City's St. Joseph Cemetery. At the time, his son, Jerry, was a student at the University of Iowa, while 15-year-old Jim was attending Loras Academy in Dubuque. Anderson came and went without ever informing either son. Young Jim eventually learned of his grandfather's death from a classmate.

Jim Anderson later attended St. Peter's High School in Worcester where he played end on the football team. St. Peter's annual big game was against archrival St. John's on Thanksgiving morning at Fitton Field. In his last game as a senior, Jim was walking off the field tired and forlorn after suffering a heart-breaking loss when his father walked up beside him. Putting his arm around his disappointed son, Dr. Anderson asked, "Have you ever thought about playing college ball?"

Slightly taken aback by what seemed like his father's invitation, young Jim confessed, "Well, no, not really."

"Good, because you don't have it," replied the senior Anderson.

Recalling the incident over 45 years later Jim Anderson laughs, "That was Dad. He didn't mean anything by it. He was just stating his opinion."[4]

Yet, there were special times when Eddie made it a point to take his son under his wing and give Jim memories he would carry with him the rest of his life. For example, after Eddie coached in the 1952 East-West Shrine game, the coaches and their families were provided with tickets for the Rose Bowl game on New Year's Day. After making sure that Mary and Judy Anderson were comfortably settled inside the stadium's press box, Eddie told his teenage son, "Jim, let's leave the girls here. You need to come with me."

Jim then accompanied his father to the 50-yard line, where they took seats next to coaching greats Bernie Bierman and Andy Kerr as well as Michigan State's Biggie Munn and Ray Elliot of Illinois. "I felt so honored that Dad had asked me to sit with him while he talked with those coaching legends," recalls Jim Anderson. "Dad knew what a unique experience it would be for me. It was reminiscent of a scene from Edwin O'Connor's novel, *The Last Hurrah*, when Mayor Skeffington invited his nephew to accompany him behind the scenes to witness how the political world really worked."[5]

"When it came to buying something for our mother or sister, the sky was the limit with Dad," reflects Jim Anderson. "Yet, he was a little different when it came to my brothers and me. He wanted us to understand the value of a dollar." To make his point, Jim cites his junior year in high school when his father noticed him writing in a pocket-size spiral notebook the day of a game. Intrigued, Eddie asked to see it and began flipping through the pages.

"How much did you pay for this?" the good doctor inquired.

"Ten cents," replied Jim.

"What!" yelped Anderson. "How could you pay 10 cents for this?"

Later that afternoon Jim watched his dad coach the Crusaders to victory at Fitton Field, after which he stopped by the locker room to congratulate his father.

"Nice game, Dad!" said Jim, patting his father on the back.

"Thanks," replied the victorious coach. "But I'll tell you what. It took me a long time to get my mind on that game knowing that my son paid 10 cents for that little notebook!"

"Now I know Dad didn't give that notebook a thought during the game," recalls Jim. "That was just his way of driving home a lesson that we needed to be careful about how we spent our money."[6]

One of Eddie Anderson's passions in life was shopping for bargains. His favorite shopping spot in Massachusetts was a place called Spag's. Located on Route 9 near Shrewsbury, Spag's was a forerunner of the giant wholesale discount stores that permeate America today. Advertising "there are no bags at Spag's," customers carried out their purchases in cardboard boxes.

On Friday afternoons before home games, with the game plan already put to bed, the Holy Cross coaching staff had a few hours to kill before the team's light afternoon workout. Anderson would use this lull to marshal his coaches for a run to Spag's.

"Actually, I think shopping was a catharsis for Eddie," speculated assistant coach Mel Massucco. "It was something he did to clear his mind of the pressures of medicine and coaching. It relaxed him."[7]

Much to his dismay, while a student at Holy Cross, Jim Anderson often found himself chauffeuring his father on many of his shopping safaris. "Dad would ask me to run him over to Spag's for ten minutes. Then, three hours later, he'd want me to run him over to a sale at Caldor's!"[8]

During these years Jim jokingly began referring to his father as "Economy Ed."

Judy Anderson rolls her eyes and laughs when she hears her brother refer to their father as "Economy Ed." "None of us, including Jim, ever lacked for anything when we were growing up," stresses Judy. "Whether it was toys, bikes or an education, Dad was extremely generous with all of us. When the time came for us to drive, Dad made sure we all had cars. That was back in the fifties and early sixties when most American households were still one-car families."[9]

Both the Holy Cross community and New England's press corps welcomed Anderson back with open arms. The most zealous of Anderson's supporters were alumni who had played for Eddie in the thirties. "This is just what the Cross needed — the best," exclaimed Buzz Harvey, captain of the 1934 Holy Cross team. "Anderson was always the best. He worked the devil out of us, but it paid off on Saturdays."[10]

"Under Anderson," recalled Dave Gavin '37, "it was almost a survival of the fittest. If you survived, you started on Saturday."[11]

Hop Riopel, who had stayed on as the school's freshman coach after Anderson's departure in 1938, declared, "Now the fur will fly up on the hill."[12]

Anderson's reputation as a taskmaster, a needler and a strict disciplinarian raised eyebrows among the returning squad members. "The old timers had told us, 'Oh, geez, Anderson's back. You guys are in for it now!'" recalled half back Mel Massucco. "We had heard stories of Anderson practicing the team on the hill immediately after losing a home game in the thirties. But I didn't find it to be that way under Eddie. Now, don't get me wrong, he worked us hard, but he always had the knack of knowing when to back off."[13]

Determined to restore Holy Cross football to its thirties' heyday, Anderson announced his intention to put the squad through six weeks of spring drills. However, he'd first have to assemble a coaching staff. His long-time, devoted assistant, Frank Carideo, had remained in Iowa with aspirations of becoming Eddie's successor. When the Hawkeye job was awarded to Leonard Raffensberger, Carideo left coaching to enter the insurance business in Des Moines.

With Hop Riopel already on board as freshman coach, Anderson telephoned his old friend, Jim Harris, who was serving as an assistant coach at Dayton University.

"How would you like to come back to Worcester with me?" asked Anderson.

"The car's packed!" replied Harris.[14]

When spring drills began on Monday, March 20, former Boston College quarterback-great Charlie O'Rourke had joined Anderson's staff. O'Rourke had played with the Chicago Bears in 1942 before spending the next three years in the armed forces. After the war, O'Rourke played four seasons in the All-American Football Conference (AAFC).

Shortly thereafter, Anderson completed his staff by hiring Elmer Mader. Mader had played at Michigan before joining the Army Air Corps in March of 1943. After 17 months in England assigned to the Eighth Army Air Force, Mader returned to Michigan where he earned honors as an All-American end in 1946. The following year Mader caught passes for the AAFC's Baltimore Colts before spending two years as an assistant on Arthur Valpey's staff at Harvard.

During his four years at Holy Cross, Mader ramrodded "Mader's Marauders," a scout team comprised of second-string players. During the week the Marauders battled the first team in bloody scrimmages as fierce as most action they encountered on game days. "We probably played some better games on Tuesdays against the Marauders than we did on Saturdays," recalls Chet Millett, a consensus All-American tackle in 1952.[15]

Anderson's former players are nearly unanimous in the opinion that Eddie was not a "rah-rah" coach who delivered fiery pre-game and halftime talks. Yet, through his professorial demeanor, he cogently made his points. During one meeting at the start of spring practice in 1950 Anderson asked a young tackle, "Sweeney, what is the most important position on a football team?"

"Left tackle," replied Sweeney.

"What position do you play, Sweeney?" Dr. Anderson inquired.

"Left tackle," answered Sweeney.

"That's right," Anderson instructed, "and I want each of you to remember that the position you play on the team is the most important."[16]

It was a question Anderson would put to his new players each season.

At another early meeting Anderson informed his squad, "You guys are as good as any team I've ever coached. You just have to put it together."

"Our attitude changed almost immediately," professed Mel Massucco. "That's when we started becoming a team instead of just a bunch of individual players."[17]

Bent on his team's mastering the game's fundamentals Anderson drilled his troops in the basics for nearly 40 consecutive days during the spring of 1950. They even practiced on Sundays. When Vic Rimkus, a handsome Lithuanian kid from the nearby town of Hudson, was an hour late for a Sunday afternoon practice, the freshman experienced his first real encounter with Dr. Anderson.

"I had started every game for the freshman squad that year," relates Rimkus. "Yet, I felt like I was getting lost in the shuffle during spring drills. For whatever reason, I was late for Sunday's practice. The next day Dr. Anderson called me into his office and read me the riot act in front of the entire coaching staff. As a scholarship player, [I knew] he held my whole future in his hands that afternoon."[18]

When satisfied that the frazzled freshman had gotten the message, Anderson informed Rimkus that he wanted to move him to end. Rimkus easily made the switch and started nine games at end in 1950. The next year Rimkus was switched back to tackle where, along with teammate Chet Millett, he became one of the finest tackles in Holy Cross history.

"Eddie Anderson had an aura about him," lauds Rimkus. "He was a man above men and a tremendous role model."[19]

Chet Millett was also a freshman when Anderson returned to Holy Cross. His first meeting with Dr. Eddie was far different than the one that Rimkus had experienced. Millett was playing basketball at the Navy surplus Quonset hut, which then served as the school's field house, when a well-dressed man watching from the balcony yelled down, "Hey, I'm Dr. Anderson. I'm the new football coach."

"We just hit it off immediately," reminisces Millett. "There was almost a oneness there. I understood what he was trying to do as a coach, and he understood that I was always giving my best as a player. I'd have run through a wall for him!"[20]

His teammates observed the affinity between player and coach and soon began calling Millett "Little Doc." Baby-faced and pudgy, Millett's physical appearance belied the future All-American's athleticism. When the innocuous-looking freshman from Brockton first set foot on the practice field a varsity player quipped, "Somebody ought to get that kid out of here before he gets hurt."

On the snap of the ball, however, Millet became, in the words of ex-teammate Mel Massucco, "a baby-faced killer." Possessing a love for contact and explosive quickness, Millett wrought havoc in opposing backfields.

Although two-platoon football was in vogue in the early fifties, both Millett and Rimkus often played 58 or 59 minutes in a game. If the duo was catching a breather on the bench when an opposing team neared the Crusader goal line, the home fans shouted for Millett and Rimkus to enter the game to snuff out the opponent's scoring threat. Anderson once remarked of Rimkus and Millet, "Those guys are so tough they could free Poland!"[21]

Holy Cross' 1950 spring football concluded with a practice game against the University of Massachusetts. The schools had not met on the gridiron since 1915 and, when Anderson left Worcester in 1938, UMass was still a small state school competing against other small colleges. In private conversations with his staff, Anderson disdainfully referred to UMass as "the Aggies." He was incensed that UMass had the gall to think that it could now play on the same field with the Cross. He shared these sentiments with the team during the days leading up to the event. "Let's show these guys what we can do," Anderson implored. "This team isn't up to our caliber. They have a heck of a nerve asking us to scrimmage."

The teams squared off on a soggy practice field atop Mount St. James on Saturday, April 29. Holy Cross dominated the action from the start and jumped to a 20 to 0 lead. While his own players were enjoying a much needed halftime rest, UMass Coach Tommy Eck did a doubletake when he saw Holy Cross engaging in an intra-squad scrimmage during halftime.

"The Doc had a great ego," offers Chet Millett, "and he wanted to send a message to UMass that they were not in our league."[22]

The Crusaders went on to blank the upstarts 34 to 0.

"I think we accomplished some good things here this spring," Anderson confided to reporters after the game, "but we aren't too deep — not too deep at all."[23]

On May 2, 1950, Anderson learned that he had again been selected to coach the College All-Stars in the annual summer classic. This time the opponent would be the world champion Philadelphia Eagles. The game would be played against the backdrop of alarming events in the Far East, where communist North Koreans had swarmed across the 38th Parallel to invade South Korea in late June. By mid–August the invaders had rolled back UN and Republic of Korea troops to the Pusan perimeter in the southeast corner of the peninsula.

In an attempt to halt the recent string of shellackings the collegians had absorbed at the hands of the pros, Anderson opted to train the All-Stars at St. John's Military Academy in Delafield, Wisconsin. By isolating the team 100 miles from Chicago, Anderson hoped to keep his players focused on the upcoming game and not on the Windy City's attractive nightlife.

Anderson's experiment was only partially successful, for many of the All-Stars were steely World War II veterans with no qualms about reconnoitering Wisconsin's remote woods to locate and frequent inviting watering holes and nightspots. On humid summer mornings following those nightly excursions, the scent of alcohol mixed with sweat was so strong on the All-Stars' practice field that it smelled like a brewery. Nevertheless, the hardbitten collegians worked through the heat and the hangovers, and by August 11 they were more than ready to meet the world champions.

Before a Soldier Field crowd of 89,000, the All-Stars dominated every aspect of play in upsetting the Eagles 17 to 7. The key to the victory was the collegians' unveiling of the "belly" series. From a straight T-formation, All-Star quarterback Eddie LeBaron would "ride" the fullback into the line, either giving him the ball or keeping it himself and running off-tackle. Sometimes after faking to the fullback, LeBaron would either pitch to a halfback running wide or drop back to pass. Behind the 5'8", 165-pound LeBaron's masterful ballhandling and passing, and "Choo Choo" Charlie Justice's 122 rushing yards on eight carries, the Stars kept Philadelphia off balance all night. It was only the All-Stars' fifth victory in 17 outings against the pros.

Bobby Dodd, one of Anderson's assistant coaches for the game, later implemented the belly series at Georgia Tech and won a national championship with it. This turn of events sparked a minor controversy among fans and football historians. Many credited Dodd with developing the belly series. Others claimed it was a brainchild of Eddie Anderson. In actuality, Coach

Larry Siemering of the College of the Pacific devised the offense in 1947. After fine-tuning it for two years, and with Eddie LeBaron as his triggerman, Siemering's Pacific team ran the belly to perfection en route to an undefeated 11 and 0 season in 1949.[24]

Eddie LeBaron relates how Anderson came to use the belly series against the Eagles. "One of our assistant coaches for the game was Stanford's Marchie Schwartz. Schwartz had seen me run it at Pacific and asked me to show it to Dr. Anderson. We ran it for a couple of days before Anderson said he didn't want to run it anymore. Bobby Dodd, however, used to keep me out after practice so I could show it (the belly series) to him in greater detail.

"About three days before the game, Dr. Anderson approached me saying that he had liked the belly series very much and wanted to run it against the Eagles. The only reason we had stopped practicing it was because he didn't want the Eagles to get wind of it and have a chance to prepare for it. He said that he would start Baylor's Adrian Burk at quarterback for our first offensive series and then put me in to run the belly. That's what we did. Except for the game's first and last offensive series when Burk played, I played quarterback the whole game and ran the belly."

LeBaron recalls, "Anderson wasn't a warm and fuzzy guy. Yet, he was a good football man who certainly understood the passing game. I think he would have made a fine coach in the pros."[25]

A week after his stellar performance in the All-Star game, LeBaron began his Marine Corps officer training. Shipped to Korea that December, LeBaron spent 1951 leading a rifle platoon on the front lines where he earned a Bronze Star and Purple Heart.

Anderson's coaching victory over the Philadelphia Eagles only elevated the high regard his Holy Cross players already held for his coaching skills. The 47 candidates who reported for fall practice were confident that under Anderson's guidance they could reverse their losing ways of 1949.

The Second Anderson Era at Holy Cross began on September 30 when the Crusaders traveled to Hanover, New Hampshire, for the 1950 season opener against Dartmouth. It may have been a new era for Anderson, but he found himself facing an old friend and coaching adversary in Tuss McLaughry. McLaughry had left Brown University in 1941 to succeed Earl Blaik at Dartmouth. Like Anderson, McLaughry had also answered his country's call during World War II. As a lieutenant colonel in the Marines, the 50-year-old McLaughry directed the physical conditioning of recruits at Parris Island for two years. Having earned a law degree from Northeastern University in 1932, McLaughry was later appointed judge advocate of general courts martial at the South Carolina base before returning to Dartmouth in 1945.

During his years at Brown, McLaughry's Bruins had been winless against Anderson's Holy Cross squads in five outings. With an experienced team led by quarterback Johnny Clayton, a bona fide All-American candidate, 1950 seemed like the year Tuss would chalk up his first win against Anderson. The prognosticators thought so too, making Dartmouth a 13-point favorite.

In an exciting and well-played game, Dartmouth's Johnny Clayton and Holy Cross quarterback Charlie Maloy both enjoyed exceptional passing performances. Maloy, a sophomore from Rochester, New York, would go on to arguably become the greatest passer in Holy Cross history.

With the score tied at 21, victory again eluded McLaughry when Dartmouth's Charles Daly's 37-yard field goal try fell short as time expired. Although it wasn't a win, Worcester sportswriters hailed it as the finest game a Holy Cross team had played in two years.

"I'm proud of these boys," Anderson told reporters after the game.[26]

The city of Worcester was also proud of them. To celebrate the season's home opener against Brown University the following week, Worcester's mayor, Andrew B. Holmstrom, proclaimed Friday, October 6, 1950, to be Eddie Anderson Day. The festivities began at 6:30 p.m. with a student rally on campus. A torchlight parade of 3,000 students and fans led by the college's 80-piece band and three official cars then headed down Southbridge Street to the steps of City Hall where Eddie was presented with the key to the city.

An enthused Anderson told the spirited crowd, "I am accepting this honor with the intention of doing all in my power to give Holy Cross and the people of Worcester the kind of team they'd like to have."[27]

The rally's final speaker was team captain, Thomas "Tex" Donnalley, who promised the fans a victory over Brown. Donnalley made the promise, but it was halfback Johnny Turco who kept it the next day. Before a crowd of 20,000, the speedy Turco scored five touchdowns, four on passes from Charlie Maloy, in the Crusaders 41 to 21 win. A blond-haired Italian from Walpole, Turco had great speed and balance. In the figurative words of ex-teammate Chet Millett, Turco was so shifty that "he would hand you your jock" in the open field. A genuine major league prospect, the 160-pound outfielder also had a flair for public speaking and often wowed the student body with his orations at pep rallies.

Holy Cross' bubble burst the following week in a 35 to 28 loss to Colgate in Hamilton, New York, where the power running of the Red Raiders' Al Egler and Fred Totten proved to be too much for the Crusaders.

Sitting among the 8,000 spectators scouting Holy Cross was Syracuse head coach, Floyd "Ben" Schwartzwalder. The following week Schwartzwalder would lead his Orangemen into Worcester's Fitton Field. After playing his collegiate ball at West Virginia, Schwartzwalder began coaching high school football. Enlisting as a paratrooper in World War II, the West Virginia native made four combat jumps in Europe, winning the Silver Star, the Bronze Star and the Purple Heart, while rising to the rank of major.

In 1946 he became the head coach at Muhlenberg College where his teams won 25 games in three years. Taking the Syracuse job in 1949, Schwartzwalder implemented a T-formation with an unbalanced line. It would be his trademark offense over the next two decades while cranking out powerhouse teams spearheaded by great running backs like Art Baker, Ernie Davis, Floyd Little, Larry Czonka and perhaps the greatest runner of all-time, Jim Brown.

During Anderson's second stint at Holy Cross, his Crusaders would meet Schwartzwalder's Orangemen 14 times. While Syracuse was perennially bigger, faster and stronger, the match-ups often resulted in epic struggles with Anderson at his coaching best. The rivalry spawned a friendship and mutual respect between the two men. Over the years, Anderson, Schwartzwalder and their respective coaching staffs took to meeting on the eve of their annual showdown for a drink and some good-natured kidding.

Now they locked coaching horns for the first time on a perfect Indian summer afternoon. Holy Cross' Jack Cullity shocked the visitors with an 80-yard punt return for a touchdown on the fifth play of the game. Syracuse responded with 27 unanswered points. After being totally dominated for 50 minutes, the Crusaders went on a tear. Trailing 27 to 7 with eight minutes remaining, the Crusaders stormed back to tie the game at 27.

Mighty Syracuse was stunned but not dispirited. With less than three minutes remaining, a Holy Cross penalty on the ensuing kick-off moved the ball to the Crusader 44-yard line. From there it took Syracuse quarterback Benjamin Custis just three plays to find the end zone and give the Orangemen a 34 to 27 win.

The next week Anderson's bunch suffered a heart-breaking 14 to 13 loss before 30,000 fans in New Haven's Yale Bowl. Victories over Harvard and Temple sandwiched around losses to Marquette and Georgetown gave Holy Cross a record of 3 wins, 5 losses and 1 tie entering the season's finale against Boston College. Despite being plagued by turnovers all season, Holy Cross had been competitive in every game, with its widest margin of defeat being only seven points. Although a winning season was no longer possible, beating B.C. would go a long way to atoning for the 76 to 0 drubbing the Eagles had inflicted upon Holy Cross the previous year.

The horrors of the gridiron wars that had befallen Holy Cross in 1949 had descended upon Boston College in 1950. Winless in eight games, beleaguered Eagle coach, Denny Myers, had already submitted his resignation after nearly a decade on the job. Although plagued by a lack of team speed and an erratic passing game, the Eagles were big and strong and determined to send the beloved Myers out a winner.

The adage, "One can throw the record books out when these two teams meet," is often used to preface archrivals meeting on the gridiron. Never did the proverb seem more appropriate then on December 2, 1950, at Braves Field when winless Boston College exploited penalties and Crusader miscues to a build a 14 to 0 lead.

Brimming with a newfound confidence, Boston College kicked off at the nine-minute mark of the second quarter. Waiting at the Holy Cross goal line with his right shoulder taped and heavily padded was Johnny Turco. The scatback had injured his shoulder 10 days before, resulting in Anderson's decision to play him only sparingly in the previous week's win over Temple. Peeved at what he considered to be a benching, Turco was now determined to make something happen.[28] He did. Catching the ball at the goal line, the fleet-footed Turco picked up a great block from teammate Bill DeChard and streaked down the right sideline 97 yards for a touchdown. Turco's electrifying run immediately deflated Boston College's morale. On Holy Cross' next two possessions, the inspired speedster from Walpole scored on a 23-yard pass from Charlie Maloy and a six-yard run to give the Crusaders a 20 to 14 half-time lead. Turco added a four-yard scoring run in the second half and Mel Massucco galloped 36 yards for another score en route to a 32 to 14 Holy Cross victory.

For his four-touchdown performance, Johnny Turco was named the recipient of the sixth annual Eddie O'Melia Award as outstanding player in the annual Holy Cross–Boston College football game. From 1935 through 1937, Ed O'Melia had been an outstanding end on Dr. Anderson's Holy Cross teams. When World War II broke out, the handsome O'Melia enlisted as a private in the U.S. Army. Rising to the rank of captain, O'Melia was killed while leading a rifle company in Schwampaneul, Holland, during the last days of the war.

Having played the last game of his career, an emotional Bill DeChard sat in the locker room and praised Dr. Anderson to reporters. "I've said this all year. But I'll have to say it again. The coach is a marvelous man. He's the best coach in the world. And I'm broken up because I can't come back to [play for] him again."[29]

Anderson's predecessor, Bill Osmanski, may not have been a great football coach, but he was one high-powered recruiter. When he assumed the coaching reins at Holy Cross in 1948, the former All-American and Chicago Bear was well remembered for his gridiron heroics on both Fitton and Wrigley fields. Idolized by schoolboys across New England and the Midwest, the

Mel Massucco, captain of the 1951 Holy Cross squad, holds a football while talking with head coach Eddie Anderson. Massucco would later serve as an assistant on Anderson's staff before succeeding him as head coach in 1965. (Courtesy of Mel Massucco)

affable Osmanski didn't have to twist any arms to persuade a youngster to attend Holy Cross.

Thus, when Dr. Anderson returned to Holy Cross, he found the talent cupboard far from bare. Osmanski bequeathed Anderson such talented players as Johnny Turco, Charlie Maloy, Owen Coogan, Chet Millett, Vic Rimkus and halfback Mel Massucco.

Elected captain of the 1951 Holy Cross squad, the 25-year-old Massucco had been one of the greatest athletes ever to come out of Massachusetts' Arlington High School. He quit school to join the Merchant Marines in 1943. After two years Massucco grew weary of life at sea aboard smelly oil tankers. Hoping to garner some veterans' benefits, Massucco joined the Army and spent most of 1945 and '46 serving with the 350th Infantry in Italy. Discharged in 1947, he enrolled at Brewster Academy where he starred in football, hockey and baseball.

In the spring of 1948 Dartmouth was doggedly recruiting the former GI when Osmanski invited Massucco to Worcester for a tryout. (Such tryouts were permissible at the time, and they were a standard practice at many colleges.) Over 100 candidates were divided into two groups. The first group reported in the morning. They were issued sweatsuits and then timed in the 100-yard dash and tested in various drills. As Holy Cross only had 50 sweatsuits on hand, they were collected and re-issued unlaundered to the afternoon's participants. The sweatsuit Massucco received was soaked with perspiration. The 5'9", 180-pound halfback was so impressive that Osmanski offered him a scholarship that very afternoon. Since Massucco still hoped to play for Coach Tuss McLaughry at Dartmouth, he asked Osmanski for a few days to think about it.

"Sure," replied Osmanski, "but we have to have your answer by five o'clock this Friday."[30]

When Massucco didn't hear from Dartmouth by Friday afternoon, he called the Dartmouth football office only to be told that the coaches were out. At 4:50 p.m. Massucco telegrammed Osmanski accepting the scholarship to Holy Cross. Returning home, Massucco discovered that Dartmouth assistant coach Milt Piepul had called with a scholarship offer while he was at the telegram office. Massucco then called Dartmouth to say that he had given his word to Osmanski and was now honor-bound to attend Holy Cross. Anderson was delighted that he did.

With his legs churning like pistons, the 180-pound Massucco ran with the power of a 220-pound fullback, and customarily ran over would-be tacklers. All-American Chet Millett remembers, "Mel was as tough as nails and a great leader. He had several teeth knocked out in one game, but he continued to play. It didn't affect him at all."[31]

A fine runner, receiver and blocker, Massucco was also an excellent punter. In 1950, Massucco set the school's single season rushing record by running for 723 yards. The record stood until broken by Jack Lentz in 1964. After a fling with the NFL's Chicago Cardinals and two years as an assistant coach at the University of Massachusetts, Massucco joined Dr. Anderson's coaching staff in 1954 — eventually succeeding him as head coach in 1965.

Due to the military draft siphoning off young men for the Korean War, the NCAA ruled freshmen eligible for varsity competition in 1951. While the added depth would help, Anderson wasn't counting on any freshmen cracking his talented line-up.

The Crusaders opened the season with a 33 to 6 win at Harvard. The following week, with Massucco and Turco each scoring two first-half touchdowns, and Charlie Maloy completing 16 of 19 passes for 193 yards, Holy Cross trounced Fordham 54 to 20 before 23,000 fans at Fitton Field. In both wins Anderson played the reserves throughout the second half.

After two games Holy Cross was leading the nation in total offense (1,150 yards) and rushing offense (797 yards). The pundits, however, said the country would see just how good Holy Cross was in its upcoming game at Tulane on October 13. Many felt that if the Purple could get by the Green Wave, the rest of the schedule would be a cake-walk until the season's finale at Boston College.

Coach Henry Frnka's Tulane team was bulwarked by 290-pound tackle Jerry Helluin and 6'3", 193-pound end Max McGee, who later experienced a prolific and colorful pro career with the Green Bay Packers.

Aided by Jim Buonopane's fumble recovery on the first play from scrimmage, Holy Cross jumped to a 12 to 0 lead. Then, however, the game officials began dolloping out some southern home cooking for the northern visitors. "After getting a 12 to 0 lead," recalled Crusader captain Mel Massucco, "every time we ran for a 10- or 12-yard gain, out came the [officials'] flags to take it away from us."[32]

A questionable call early in the second quarter sent Anderson into orbit and may have ultimately cost his team the game. It would be the only time in his 39-year coaching career that Eddie lost his composure on the sidelines. The outburst was sparked when a trio of Crusaders tackled Tulane's Ronnie Kent at the Holy Cross 27-yard line. Kent, who appeared to be fumbling on the play, was saved by referee M.J. Bullock's quick whistle. Bullock then flagged the Crusaders 15 yards on the play for a late hit.

An irate Anderson, who thought he had the permission of head linesman James Armistead to enter the field, made a beeline for Bullock.[33] Field judge Charles Tucker immediately intercepted Anderson and ordered him off

One of Dr. Anderson's finest football squads during his second stint at Holy Cross was the 1951 team. Captained by Mel Massucco, the squad won 8 games while losing only to Tulane and Boston College. Top row (L-R): Mel Massucco #15, Charlie Maloy #37, Bobby Doyle #41, and Johnny Turco #30. Bottom row (L-R): Tom McCann #81, Mike Cooney #70, George Foley #65, Joe Gleason #54, Chet Millett #61, John Feltch #71 and Joe Mikutowicz #82. (College of the Holy Cross Archives)

the field as Bullock stepped off 15 yards against the Crusaders for the late hit. He then walked off an additional 15 for Anderson for being illegally on the field. With the ball now on the Holy Cross 1-yard line, Roy Bailey slashed across for a touchdown to make the score Tulane 13, Holy Cross 12.

The Crusaders' passing game was hindered by quarterback Charlie Maloy's subpar performance. The gutsy Maloy, however, was seriously ill. Although he told no one, Maloy had lost 12 pounds during the week, and for several days leading up to the game his only source of nourishment had been glasses of milk. It wasn't until he checked into the school's infirmary after the game on Monday that he was diagnosed to be suffering from a duodenal ulcer.[34]

Nevertheless, Tulane clearly outplayed the Crusaders in the second half and scored again to make the final score Tulane 20, Holy Cross 14.

In his column "Looking 'Em Over," sportswriter Hap Glandi of the *New Orleans Item* took Anderson to task for his costly outburst. "The good medico from Worcester, Mass., Dr. Edward N. Anderson, was just what the Wave ordered Saturday on the Sugar Bowl green.

"It is my humble opinion, with no buts, and ifs attached, that Dr. Anderson won the game for Tulane and lost it for his school, Holy Cross... For some unexplained reason, Dr. Anderson's colossal blunder has been soft-pedaled."[35]

The mood was somber and tense when Anderson boarded his team's chartered flight back to Worcester that night. "Eddie felt terrible," recalled Mel Massucco, "and he knew everyone else did too."

Knowing that the 25-year-old World War II veteran enjoyed a good cigar, Anderson walked up to his team captain and with a big smile and a slap on the back handed Massucco an expensive cigar, saying, "Here, have a smoke!"

"The team saw it," explained Massucco, "and the whole mood on the plane instantly lightened. He knew how to break the tension."[36]

"In fact," adds former center Joe Gleason, "I seem to remember the coaches having some cases of beer brought on board so the guys could relax with a beer or two on the long flight home."[37]

Despite quarterback Charlie Maloy being sidelined for two games with an ulcer, the Crusaders rolled up lopsided wins over their next six opponents. The victims were NYU (53–6), Brown (41–6), Colgate (34–6), Marquette (39–13), Quantico Marines (39–14) and Temple (41–7).

When Boston College and Holy Cross took the field before 40,000 fans crammed into Braves Field on December 1, the Crusaders were a 13-point favorite. Anderson's lads entered the fray with a record of 8 wins and 1 loss, while Boston College managed 2 wins against 6 losses under rookie coach Mike Holovak. In the opinion of many, what was supposed to be a walk-over for Holy Cross turned out to be the most exciting contest ever in the schools' storied rivalry.

Trailing 12 to 7 mid-way through the fourth quarter the Crusaders engineered an 84-yard drive to take a 14 to 12 lead. With less than three minutes remaining, John Irwin returned the ensuing kick-off to the Boston College 31. After picking up a first down on the B.C. 43-yard line, Eagle quarterback Jimmy Kane unleashed a pass to Tommy Joe Sullivan who was wide open behind the Crusader secondary for a 56-yard gain. With no timeouts, less than a minute remaining and the ball on the Holy Cross 1-yard line, B.C. quickly ran two plays but failed to score. With 40,000 sphincter muscles tightening in the stands and only 11 seconds remaining, the third time proved to be the charm as Joe Johnson carried two Crusaders into the end zone with him. The extra point made the final score Boston College 19, Holy Cross 14.

Among the ecstatic Boston College fans spilling onto the field, a composed Dr. Anderson weaved his way through the mob scene to congratulate winning coach Mike Holovak. Over 50 years later, Holovak remembers the moment. "Needless to say, this rookie coach was in another world, but I had only admiration and praise for the veteran coach (Anderson) who showed his greatness in accepting defeat in a truly first-class manner."

Mel Massucco leaps toward the goal line in Holy Cross' 34 to 6 victory over Colgate before a full house at Fitton Field in 1951. Massucco scored on the next play. (Courtesy of Mel Massucco)

Holovak adds, "I have always felt that the growth and popularity of college football was mainly because of men like Dr. Eddie Anderson."[38]

"In Dad's 39 years of coaching," attests Nick Anderson, "the '51 B.C. game was his most heart-breaking loss."[39]

Having anticipated a Holy Cross victory, sportswriter Dave Egan of the *Boston Record* wanted to enjoy the game merely as a spectator. Therefore, he wrote his column in advance, hailing the genius of Dr. Eddie Anderson as a teacher of football. Egan's column stood magnificently for 59 minutes, but when Boston College scored in the game's waning seconds, Egan hastily tore up his original column ("The best one I ever wrote," Egan later told Anderson), borrowed a typewriter and pounded out a new story.[40]

The following Monday Anderson watched the game film with his squad. As they relived the heartbreak and agony of B.C. scrambling frantically to beat the clock and score the game winner, Anderson sardonically commented, "Instead of taking your time getting off the pile, you knuckleheads couldn't jump off fast enough to give them another crack at making it!"[41]

Bill Samko was an athletic trainer at Holy Cross from 1947 until 1967. He remembers first meeting Dr. Anderson in 1950. "My first impression was that this fellow came out of the clouds. He was sartorially dressed, and his mannerisms had a radiance about them that greatly impressed people."[42]

One of Anderson's more striking mannerisms was his use of a cigarette holder. A chain smoker for most of his coaching career, Anderson began using a cigarette holder upon his return to Holy Cross in 1950. "It seems to make smoking easier," he told reporters.

It also enhanced his stately demeanor. "With that long cigarette holder," recalls former Crusader Carlin Lynch, "he resembled F.D.R [President Franklin D. Roosevelt]."[43]

A man of tremendous resolve, Anderson quit smoking cold turkey during a game in 1957. "It was just before the half," recalled assistant coach Mel Massucco, "when Eddie suddenly said aloud, 'I don't know why I'm doing this. I know that smoking isn't good for me.' And with that Eddie dropped the cigarette to the ground and snuffed it out with his foot. He then put the holder in his pocket and never smoked again."[44]

Unbeknownst to Massucco, Anderson had received a letter earlier that week from his son, Jim, who was stationed in Germany with the Army. When he read that Jim had given up smoking, Anderson promptly wrote back that he wouldn't be outdone by his son and promised to quit smoking soon.

Mary Anderson saw her husband cry only once. That was in May of 1952 while Eddie was reading a letter from their oldest son, Nick, informing them that his military unit was being shipped to Korea. Like thousands of other American families, the Korean War hit home for the Andersons.

"That would have been the worst scenario for Dad," professes Judy Anderson, "because he always took care of everyone else, and now here was a situation he couldn't control. That's just the way he was. He paid my uncle's way (Bill Anderson) through college and law school. He took care of my mother's mother near the end of her life. He used to send $100 to $200 a month to The Little Sisters of the Poor in Canada. Every spring he filled up the nuns' freezer at St. Mary's with ice cream. He was a caretaker.

"I can remember too, that my father felt that perhaps by his serving in World War II, that would keep his sons from having to serve somewhere later on, but it didn't."[45]

Lieutenant Nick Anderson led a rifle platoon in Korea from June of 1952 until May of 1953, winning both the Silver Star and the Purple Heart. Today, all Nick will say about his time in Korea is that "it was a miserable experience, something I wouldn't recommend for anyone."[46]

However, Nick Anderson's combat heroics were detailed in Worcester's

Evening Gazette on March 18, 1953. "He led his men up the precipitous slopes, and was twice knocked to the ground by the concussion of incoming rounds. Undismayed by the intensity of the barrage, he maintained superb control over his men and they converged on the objective and routed the foe from the trenches.

"Lieutenant Anderson conducted an orderly withdrawal despite painful wounds received in vicious fire. As the unit disengaged he carried a comrade to the safety of Allied lines. Reaching the main line of resistance he was informed that one of the casualties still remained in the battle area.

"Refusing medical assistance he returned to the scene of the encounter, rendered aid to the seriously wounded soldier and single-handedly evacuated him to safety through an unrelenting spray of Communist fire.

"The gallantry, leadership and spirited devotion to the welfare of his men displayed by Lieutenant Anderson in the face of severe hostile fire reflect the highest credit on himself and the U.S. Army."

Upon his return from Korea, Nick would earn an M.B.A from Harvard and go on to a successful business career. Today, Nick Anderson is retired and living in Florida with his wife, Pam.

Despite the loss of three-quarters of his starting backfield (Massucco, Turco and fullback Bobby Doyle) to graduation, Anderson knew he had a powerhouse team returning in 1952. In fact, Anderson even had Athletic Director Gene Flynn attempt to schedule Ohio State at Columbus because he felt his Crusaders could handle them.[47] To Anderson's dismay, however, the contest couldn't be arranged.

With only a 43-man varsity and the NCAA reinstituting a ban on freshmen competing on varsity teams, the squad could not afford injuries. Thus, Anderson eliminated much of the customary contact work and held only one pre-season intra-squad scrimmage.

The '52 Crusaders lived up to Anderson's expectations by beginning the season with successive wins over Dartmouth, Fordham, NYU and Brown. After an open date gave Anderson's lads two weeks to prepare, the undefeated Crusaders traveled to Syracuse's Archbold Stadium on October 25. Quarterback Charlie Maloy was brilliant, completing 24 of 48 passes for 252 yards and two touchdowns. Midway through the fourth quarter Holy Cross led 19 to 13. However, as would be the case throughout most of the series rivalry, the depth and talent of the Orangemen would prevail in the end. Syracuse culminated a winning 72-yard drive on quarterback Pat Stark's 10-yard touchdown pass to Don Ronan with only 40 seconds remaining in the game. Syracuse's 20 to 19 win resulted in the Orangemen and not the Crusaders being invited to the Orange Bowl.

After the tortuous loss, a seething Anderson remained tight-lipped. He fumed silently on the bus ride to the airport. When the bus arrived, however, Anderson jumped out and made a beeline for the airport bar where he ordered a double martini. The whole time, he never said a word.[48]

After close wins over Marquette and Colgate, the Crusaders prepared to do battle with the Quantico Marines on November 16. The Holy Cross-Quantico games were unique match-ups for several reasons. First, Quantico was comprised of both enlisted personnel and Marine Corps officers, many being former All-Americans and future or ex-pros. As a result, the Leathernecks were both more experienced and physically mature than Anderson's Crusaders. Some of the more renowned football-playing Marines included Rice's Weldon Humble (Cleveland Browns, 1947–50); Northwestern's Ray Wietecha (New York Giants, 1953–62); Alabama's Ken MacAfee (New York Giants, 1954–58); Villanova's Gene Filipski (Giants, 1956–57); Orville Trask (the first captain of the Houston Oilers, 1960–61); and Holy Cross' own Bob Dee (Washington Redskins, 1957–58 and Boston Patriots, 1960–67). Second, several Holy Cross players who had belonged to the college's Naval ROTC unit were later commissioned as Marine officers and found themselves playing football for Quantico against their old Crusader teammates. In addition to Bob Dee ('55), who played for Quantico against Holy Cross in both 1955 and 1956, the list includes Class of '63 Crusaders Dennis Golden, Pat McCarthy, Hank Cutting and John Whalen, who all returned to Worcester the following autumn to help Quantico eke out a 7 to 6 win over their alma mater.

Now, on November 16, 1952, five Holy Cross graduates stood at Fitton Field's 50-yard line as Quantico game captains waiting for the coin toss with their former Crusader teammate, Joe Gleason. The five were George Foley, John Feltch, John Cullity, Richard Murphy and Bill DeChard. (All except DeChard were Class of '52.)

The Fitton Field fans were treated to an aerial circus as 89 passes were thrown that afternoon. Charlie Maloy set an individual game passing record for the Crusaders by completing 24 of 56 passes for 291 yards. Ex-Northwestern and Rose Bowl star, Dick Flowers, was even more impressive for Quantico. The Marine completed 20 of 32 passes for 251 yards and four touchdowns. Three of those were to ex-Notre Dame star Jim Mutscheller, who would go on to a prominent career catching passes from Johnny Unitas with the world champion Baltimore Colts. An exciting and wide-open affair, the Leathernecks finally pulled away in the fourth quarter for a 27 to 18 victory.

Between 1951 and 1964 Anderson's Crusaders won five of eight meetings with the Leathernecks. The teams never met after 1964 and Quantico gave up football in the early seventies. All of the contests were played in Worcester, and the six played during the fifties were all Sunday games. Because Sunday games were more conducive to the Marines' duty schedule, Quantico enticed Holy Cross to play on the Sabbath by asking for neither a financial guarantee nor a percentage of the gate. Thus, nearly 100% of the gate went into the college's athletic coffers.

In the mid-fifties Nick Anderson asked his father, "Why do you keep scheduling Quantico? They're tough as nails and when you do beat them your team never gets the recognition it deserves in the polls."

"This is a game we have to play for the financial good of the school," Anderson explained.[49]

In 1956, Holy Cross upset talent-laden Quantico 13 to 0 in yet another ferocious battle. With both teams teeing off at high velocity, ball carriers and receivers paid dearly for every yard gained and each pass caught.

After the game Dr. Anderson told his son, Jim, "I never saw two teams hit as hard. We could have beaten any team in the country today. I don't know if the crowd appreciated what they witnessed out there. Maybe one has to be a pro to see it, but that was probably the finest game a Holy Cross team ever played."[50]

After losing to Quantico in '52, the Crusaders blanked Temple 28 to 0 to enter the season finale against archrival Boston College with a record of 7 wins and 2 losses. For the second year in a row, the Crusaders were a 13-point favorite. Boston College, sporting a record of 4 wins, 3 losses and 1 tie, was out to prove that the previous year's upset of the Jesuit rival was no fluke.

Both coaches engaged in the usual psychological sparring the week of the game. Boston College coach Mike Holovak told reporters, "Holy Cross should beat us by something like 60 to 0."[51]

Not to be outdone by Holovak's palaver, and with teeth clenched on his cigarette holder, Dr. Anderson parried, "Boston College should be the favorite. We lost 27 lettermen from last year while B.C. lost only Mike Roarke and T.J. Sullivan. They have practically the same team as last year."[52]

As was customary for the late fall classic, the frigid weather turned the Braves Field infield rock hard. The Crusaders' Gerry O'Leary brought the bundled 38,000 spectators to their feet when he returned a punt 55 yards for a touchdown behind great blocks from teammates Hank Lemire and Owen Coogan. In the third quarter Boston College tied the score at 7 on Joe Johnson's 1-yard run and Dick Zotti's extra-point kick. The upset-minded Eagles had the momentum early in the fourth quarter until Crusader George Blair alertly intercepted a Jimmy Kane pass. Behind a great block by Vic Rimkus, Blair returned it 53 yards to the Eagle 10-yard line. Two plays later, Lou Hettinger ran seven yards for a touchdown to give Holy Cross a 14 to 7 lead.

Hettinger later ran three yards for another score to give Holy Cross a 21 to 7 win.

The 1952 Crusaders finished with a record of 8 wins and 2 losses. In three years Anderson had returned Holy Cross to national prominence. Could he keep them there?

20

A NEW DEAL
AT HOLY CROSS

Anderson's Crusaders kicked off their 1953 season with a nationally televised contest against Dartmouth, played before a disappointing crowd of 10,000 at the Manning Bowl in Lynn, Massachusetts. John Carroll's two touchdown receptions sparked Holy Cross to a 28 to 6 victory. Unfortunately, the injury bug that had hampered the Crusaders throughout the preseason continued to plague Anderson's squad as fullback Gerry O'Leary broke his leg in the fourth quarter. O'Leary was replaced by Warren O'Donnell, whose father, Cleo O'Donnell, had been football coach at Holy Cross from 1919 through 1929. Making the most of his opportunity, O'Donnell scored a touchdown and kicked two extra points.

With wins over Bucknell and Colgate in successive weeks, Holy Cross was undefeated when Quantico's Marines invaded Fitton Field on a beautiful Sunday afternoon before 22,000 spectators. Loaded with ex-All-Americans and future pros, the Leathernecks dominated the action. Behind the power running of former Notre Dame star John Petibon, Quantico blanked the Crusaders 17 to 0. So talent-laden were the Marines that, despite the nation's return to single-platoon football, Quantico coach Major Charles E. Walker substituted a new team mid-way through each quarter. Playing 38 men to Holy Cross' 22, the Marines inflicted a terrific physical pounding on the home team.[1] Several of Anderson's starters were unable to play and others were still nursing injuries when the team traveled to Providence six days later to play Brown University.

Despite a patchwork backfield, Holy Cross entered the fray a three-touchdown favorite. (Brown had won only one game while losing to light-

225

weights Amherst and Rhode Island.) The game's only score came with six minutes remaining and Holy Cross in possession on the Bruin 16-yard line. A
jarring hit popped the ball out of half back Billy Haley's grasp and into the
waiting arms of Brown reserve tackle Bill Klaess. Then, to Anderson's utter
agony, Klaess sprinted down the sideline in front of the Holy Cross bench
with Crusader captain Hank Lemire in desperate pursuit. Klaess' 82-yard
touchdown run gave Brown a 6 to 0 victory.

Dr. Anderson had never lost to the Bruins in eight previous outings and,
next to the last-minute 1951 loss to archrival Boston College, this 1953 loss
to Brown was the most haunting setback in Anderson's 39 years of coaching.[2]

If Anderson was crestfallen, he never revealed it in his post-game comments. As always, he accepted defeat gracefully. "Yes, it's true, we didn't play
well; but give all the credit to that Brown team. They really wanted this one
and they played a fine ball game."[3]

To make matters worse, star receiver John Carroll and running backs
Gene Schiller and Warren O'Donnell all sustained injuries that would sideline them for the homecoming game against Syracuse.

With dim prospects for victory, Dr. Anderson and his staff rolled up their
sleeves to prepare for Ben Schwartzwalder's once-beaten Orangemen. As was
often the case, matching wits with Schwartzwalder brought out the best in
Anderson's coaching. By implementing a slanting 6–2 defense and starting
an unknown senior, Don Jolie, at quarterback, Holy Cross played Syracuse
to a scoreless tie at the half.

The inspired Crusaders continued to stymie the Orange offense until late
in the third quarter when Syracuse quarterback Pat Stark broke an option play
49 yards for a touchdown. The run ignited Syracuse's passing game and in
the fourth quarter the 23-year-old Stark connected on touchdown passes to
Bruce Yancey and Bob Leberman to give Syracuse a 21 to 0 win.

Speaking of Stark's game-breaking run, Schwartzwalder later told
reporters, "But that's one of the few times we fooled the Crusaders. Dr. Anderson had a smartly planned unorthodox defense which was stopping everything we tried until Pat came up with that triple option."[4]

Having been shut out for three consecutive weeks, the Crusaders, with
12 of their top 22 players sidelined with injuries, prepared to meet Boston
University for the first time in 24 years. The Terriers came to Worcester as
the top-ranked team in New England. Trailing 7 to 0 at the half, Anderson
gave one of the few fiery halftime orations in his career. "It was wonderful,"
offered team captain Hank Lemire. "I went back for that second half feeling
I'd never return to the dressing room if we lost this one."[5]

"Me too," added end Bob Dee. "I've never been so fired up since I've
been playing football."

"I just had a heart-to-heart talk with the boys," Anderson later told reporters.

Whatever Anderson said, it worked. The Crusaders dominated the second half. Overcoming several first-half miscues, quarterback Don Jolie scored two touchdowns and tossed a third to Lou Hettinger to give Holy Cross a 21 to 7 win.

"Those kids played a great second half; I've never been more proud of any team I've coached," Anderson said.[6]

Two days later, sportswriter Clif Keane of *The Boston Daily Globe* cast a pall over the coach's lofty praise when he reported that Dr. Anderson was ready to quit Holy Cross. Claiming that Anderson was dissatisfied with the school's football picture because of the lack of material, Keane speculated that Anderson might retire from coaching to concentrate on business interests in his native Iowa.[7]

That same day, Worcester's *Evening Gazette* gave Anderson's response. "You can make it emphatic. I am not considering leaving Holy Cross. Please tell the fans that I am happy here.

"I was as much surprised as you were when I read the story out of Boston and there is absolutely nothing to it... I have no intention of leaving Holy Cross."[8]

The *Gazette* then speculated that Anderson might succeed Frank Leahy at Notre Dame, who was rumored to be retiring due to poor health.

With only a year remaining on his existing contract, it's quite possible that Anderson, always a shrewd businessman, may have exploited the rumor mill to negotiate a new contract for himself.

The rumors, however, didn't help the injury-plagued Crusaders prepare for their upcoming game against a 5 and 2 Marquette team. Behind a pair of seven-yard touchdown runs by Ronald Drzwiecki, the Hilltoppers prevailed 13 to 7.

After rebounding with a win over Fordham, Holy Cross met Boston College before 35,000 at Boston's Fenway Park. On a cold, drab Thanksgiving weekend, the teams may have played the dullest and most inept contest of their 58-year rivalry. Although B.C. dominated the action, the game's only score resulted from the Eagles blocking Hank Lemire's fourth-down punt from the Holy Cross end zone. Taking possession on the Crusader 6-yard line, Dick Charlton scored from a yard out to give Boston College a 6 to 0 win.

Only 19 players saw action for the injury-plagued Crusaders, who finished the 1953 season with a record of 5 wins and 5 losses.

In a tomb-like locker room after the game, sportswriters asked the somber coach for his prognosis on the 1954 season.

"I'm afraid things will get worse before they get better," replied Anderson.[9]

Two events significantly impacted the future of Holy Cross football in early 1954. First, on February 3, Anderson quelled rumors about his imminent departure by signing a new five-year contract to coach at the Jesuit school.[10] The second came a month later when Athletic Director Gene Flynn announced that Holy Cross would drop spring football. In making the announcement, Flynn explained, "In keeping with a general trend among many eastern colleges, Holy Cross has decided not to conduct spring football practice this year. This action is prompted by the fact that our first two opponents — Dartmouth and Colgate — will have no football sessions this spring."[11]

Other factors also influenced Holy Cross' decision to abandon spring football. First, the school was finding it increasingly difficult to schedule games. Several of the Cross' biggest financial guarantees had come from playing at Harvard and Yale. With the newly formed Ivy League scheduled to begin conference play in 1956, those games were now in jeopardy. Comprised of eight schools — Brown, Columbia, Cornell, Dartmouth, Harvard, Pennsylvania, Princeton and Yale — the Ivies agreed to round-robin play within a nine-game schedule. Thus, each Ivy League school was now limited to playing only two non-conference games per season. Surely, the Ivies would seek non-conference opponents whose football policies and practices were most similar to their own and that meant playing schools that had no spring football.

Holy Cross was already beginning to feel the Ivy League pinch, for Brown, Dartmouth, Harvard and Yale had all been on the Crusaders' 1950 schedule. Only Dartmouth remained on the 1954 slate.

A second factor influencing the college's decision was that other eastern independents were also having scheduling problems. As a possible remedy, these schools were discussing forming their own conference. According to Boston College athletic director, John P. Curley, such a conference would be "the lifesaver of New England football."[12] (Boston College's scheduling woes were so serious that school officials had approached Eddie Anderson with a proposal to have the Jesuit rivals meet twice a year.)[13]

Potential conference members included Holy Cross, Boston College, Boston University, Colgate, Fordham, Penn State, Rutgers and Syracuse. If enough independents could adopt similar policies, the conference might become a reality. Spring football was a key topic of concern. Colgate had already jettisoned spring ball, and Fordham and Syracuse were seriously considering doing the same. It's possible that Holy Cross dropped spring football to facilitate unity among the prospective members.

For Eddie Anderson, however, the decision couldn't have come at a worse time. He had been counting on spring drills to prepare his inexperienced squad for the 1954 season. Holy Cross had "beefed up" its schedule by replacing Bucknell with Penn State and Brown (which had dropped the Crusaders) with Miami of Florida. "Had I known we were going to drop spring football," lamented Anderson, "I would have kept the freshmen out for a few extra weeks of work after last season."[14]

Unfortunately, dropping spring football did not immediately result in Holy Cross playing more Ivy League schools. In only three of the next 11 seasons would the Crusaders play more than one Ivy League opponent. Furthermore, the conference of major eastern independents failed to materialize. Boston College, Penn State and Syracuse all retained spring football, while Holy Cross did not — a disparity that gave all three a distinct advantage over Anderson's Crusaders. It would not be until 1971, seven seasons after Anderson's retirement, that Holy Cross would reinstitute spring football.

The 1954 season would also see Mel Massucco join Dr. Anderson's staff. The former Crusader captain would become Anderson's most trusted aide.

In the 1954 season-opener, long time coaching rival "Tuss" McLaughry finally got the better of Anderson as Dartmouth scratched out a last-second 27 to 26 win. It would be their last meeting as friendly foes, for in 1955 Dartmouth relieved the venerable McLaughry of his coaching duties and replaced him with Bob Blackman.

Unfortunately, Anderson's earlier prediction that Holy Cross' football fortunes would "get worse before they got better" materialized when the Crusaders dropped their first four games of 1954.

To prepare for undefeated Miami in week three, the resourceful Anderson jettisoned his unbalanced line, single-wing look and installed a wide-open passing offense in just three days. Behind the passing of unknown sophomore quarterback, Tom Roberts, Anderson's upset-minded Crusaders gave the Hurricanes all they could handle in Miami's Orange Bowl. Despite being a three-touchdown underdog, Holy Cross led Miami 20 to 19 when scatback Mario Bonafiglio scooted 36 yards for a touchdown to give the Hurricanes a 26 to 20 lead. With just three minutes remaining, the inspired Crusaders drove the length of the field only to see their frenzied comeback bid foiled when Miami intercepted a pass in its own end zone with just 15 seconds left in the game.

A relieved Miami coach, Andy Gustafson, later told reporters, "Any time you play a team coached by Eddie Anderson, you play a mighty well-coached team. When Eddie saw he couldn't gain through our line, he turned to the air and got three touchdowns."[15]

Haunted by a lack of depth and a murderous schedule, the Crusaders saw their fourth-quarter lead dissolve in a 25 to 20 loss to Syracuse before suffering a 39 to 7 pummeling at Penn State. With the likes of future NFL

Hall of Famer Lenny Moore, Milt Plum and Rosey Grier in the line up, it was one of Coach Rip Engle's stronger Nittany Lion teams.

"We always had trouble with Penn State," recalled assistant coach Mel Massucco. "Rip Engle (the Penn State Coach) was kind of a lay-it-on-you-guy. Schwarzie (Syracuse's Ben Schwartzwalder) would sometimes let up a little when he had you beat, but not Rip. I guess Rip figured that was part of the game."[16]

Between 1954 and 1963 Anderson's teams were winless in nine meetings against Engle's Nittany Lions. All but the '57 and '63 games were blowouts for Penn State. In 1956 the Lions hammered Holy Cross 43 to 0 before an eastern regional television audience. In 1959 it was worse — Penn State 46, Holy Cross 0. However, Anderson's longest trip to University Park came on the weekend of November 14, 1958. In a steady downpour, Penn State blanked Holy Cross 32 to 0. "Dr. Anderson looked totally devastated after the game," recalls team manager, Terry Wadsworth.[17]

The nightmare continued when the team bused to nearby Bradford for a charter flight back to Worcester. A dense fog rolled in preventing their plane's arrival. Stranded, the team spent the night at a local motel that could best be described as a "dump." With the airport still closed the next morning, the team arranged to return to Worcester via Greyhound Bus. After what seemed like an interminable journey, the bus finally rolled up to Holy Cross' Quonset hut field house 18 hours later, just in time for the comatose players to stumble off to their eight o'clock Monday morning classes.

Being the fiery competitor that he was, the mounting losses to Penn State must have angered and frustrated Dr. Anderson. Yet, he was always gracious in defeat. After one lopsided loss in which Rip Engle had kept his first team in to score a late touchdown, the two coaches met at mid-field.

"Eddie, we really didn't want that last touchdown," protested Engle.

Almost apologetically Anderson replied, "Oh, no! I insist. You should have it."[18]

In the Lions' narrow 14 to 10 win of 1957, a Penn State defender named Walters spoiled Holy Cross' upset bid by tackling Crusader quarterback Tommy Greene six inches short of the goal line in the game's final seconds. Earlier that half, Greene had found his old high school teammate, Charlie Pacunas, open behind Penn State's Dave Kasperian for a 78-yard scoring pass. On the ensuing kick-off, Greene kicked the ball to Kasperian, and the son of a Worcester barber promptly returned it 66 yards to the Holy Cross 23-yard line. Two plays later the Lions hit paydirt to make the score Holy Cross 8, Penn State 7. Without the touchdown set up by Kasperian's lengthy return, the Crusaders might have upset Penn State.

Forty-three years later, Mel Massucco recalled what the good doctor had

Eddie Anderson (right) shakes hands with smiling Penn State coach Rip Engle. Anderson's Holy Cross teams experienced some long afternoons against the Nittany Lions. (Courtesy of Mel Massucco)

told Greene the following Monday. "Tom, you kicked the ball to the worst possible man on the field," explained Anderson. "Only two plays earlier you burned him for a 78-yard touchdown. If anyone out there was determined to make something happen, it was Kasperian."

"That's the way Eddie taught," observed Massucco.[19]

By eking out one-point wins over Boston University and Fordham, Anderson's undermanned squad had managed three wins when it limped into the season's finale against Boston College. It would be a long afternoon for Holy Cross fans among the crowd of 40,000 shoe-horned into Fenway Park, who watched in despair as Boston College's Tom Magnarelli, running behind a scythe-like line that shredded the Purple defense, scored four touchdowns en route to a 31 to 13 win. A superb Boston College team finished the 1954 season with 8 wins and 1 loss. The humiliating defeat left Holy Cross with a final record of 3 wins and 7 losses. It was only Anderson's second losing season in 11 years at Holy Cross.

If the prognosticators thought that playing a demanding schedule without the benefit of spring practice would scuttle the Holy Cross football program, they hadn't reckoned with Dr. Eddie Anderson. With a returning veteran squad that had been hardened by bitter defeats at Miami and Syracuse, Anderson was determined to reverse the school's recent tailspin. The 1955 Purple line-up included three solid performers at quarterback in John Stephans, Billy Smithers and Tom Roberts. Dale Hohl, Dick Surrette and Bob Rosmarino were the runningbacks, with Carlin Lynch and Dick Arcand at ends, while captain Jim Buonopane (who had returned to the Cross in 1954 after two years in military service), Bernie Taracewicz, Jim Allegro, Ray Guerard and Joe Murphy manned the line.

Only about 6,000 fans turned out for the Crusaders' 1955 season-opener against Temple. Surveying the sparse Fitton Field crowd, assistant coach Jim Harris growled, "Hell, there aren't enough fans here to start a fight!"[20] Overcoming a soggy field and steady rain, Holy Cross exploded for 28 fourth-quarter points to defeat the Owls 42 to 7. Over the next four weeks, Anderson's rejuvenated Crusaders reeled off wins against Dartmouth, Colgate, Quantico and Boston University. As usual, the Quantico game was a war. After four grueling quarters, the Crusaders came away with a 7 to 0 win on Billy Smithers' 25-yard pass to Dick Arcand.

Although still undefeated in five games, the Crusaders emerged battered and bruised from the Quantico skirmish. After a close win over Boston University, Anderson's walking wounded hosted Syracuse at Fitton Field. The ex-paratrooper, Ben Schwartzwalder, brought another stellar team to Worcester. This one featured perhaps the greatest running back in football history, the inimitable Jim Brown.

On a beautiful Indian summer afternoon before a homecoming crowd of 25,000, the Crusaders stung the Orangemen early when John Stephans scampered 35 yards untouched for a touchdown on a fake punt. Stephans' chicanery, however, only awakened a sleeping giant. Syracuse retaliated by tallying 49 straight points. Although hampered by a sprained ankle, Jim Brown accounted for 173 yards of total offense while providing the day's most exciting run on a dazzling 48-yard punt return. While Brown didn't score any touchdowns in Syracuse's 49 to 9 win, he did intercept a pass and kick three extra points.

Holy Cross suffered numerous injuries that afternoon, the most serious being a season-ending knee injury sustained by quarterback Billy Smithers. So crippled were the Crusaders that Anderson called off practice until Wednesday.

The resilient Crusaders bounced back the following week with a 13 to 7 win over Hugh Devore's Dayton Flyers. The win, however, was a Pyrrhic victory. Beset by additional injuries and operating with a makeshift backfield, the Crusaders dropped their final three games to Marquette, Connecticut and Boston College.

On November 22, 1955, two days after losing to Connecticut in near blizzard conditions, the *Worcester Telegram*'s Roy Mumpton reported that Marquette University was courting Dr. Anderson to become its next athletic director and football coach.

"I have never talked with anyone connected to Marquette University," said Anderson emphatically. "I'm happy here at Holy Cross."[21]

New England's seasoned sportswriters, however, viewed Anderson's repeated denials with skepticism. Many had remembered the good doctor's fervid disclaimers about neither leaving nor returning to Holy Cross in 1938 and 1950 respectively. The scribes would now wait and see. Concerned over rumors of Anderson's departure, 500 students marched to the practice field that afternoon to persuade their coach to stay and to psyche up the Crusaders for their season-ending showdown with Boston College.[22]

On November 26, before 37,000 fans at Fenway Park, the Crusaders threw six interceptions and Boston College rolled to a 26 to 7 win. After a whirlwind 6 and 1 start, the Crusaders, decimated by injuries, finished the 1955 season with a disappointing record of 6 wins and 4 losses.

Rumors of Anderson going to Marquette proved to be unfounded. According to Anderson's son, Jerry, "My father never had any talks with Marquette. Besides, I don't believe that was a job that would have interested Dad."[23]

21

EDDIE ANDERSON: THE COACH

"Doc Anderson was like a father figure to many of us," professed Mike Ryan, who played for Holy Cross in the early sixties. "In some ways it was like playing for your old man. One wanted to make an impression on him ... not merely make the team or the traveling squad, or crack the starting line-up."[1]

For those who played for him in the early fifties, Anderson was more than a father figure. He was a coaching icon. "We all knew that Dr. Anderson was bigger than the rest of us," recalls ex-tackle Vic Rimkus.[2] Because they were in awe of him, his players viewed Anderson as aloof, stern and austere, and few got close to him. Yet, they all sought his hard-earned praise.

"When Dr. Anderson put his arm around you," reflects Carlin Lynch, "you really knew you were doing something, because that didn't happen very often."[3]

"The only time Dad ever said 'well done' was when you asked him how he liked his steak," laughs his youngest son, Jim Anderson.[4]

Decorous and reserved, Anderson seemed humorless at times. Yet, his occasional witticisms and colorful metaphors (known as Andersonisms) often brought levity to the drudgery of practice and the intense scrutiny of film sessions. A poor offensive showing during practice might lead the coach to declare, "You guys couldn't pick up a first down against a stiff breeze!" A lineman's mental lapse might result in Anderson muttering, "That guy is as strong as an ox and almost as smart."

A player never knew what might spark an Andersonism. Former Crusader Carlin Lynch remembers seeing a well-dressed, cigar-smoking businessman frequently chatting with Dr. Anderson after practice. One day, as Lynch approached, the visitor shook hands with Anderson before jumping into a late-model Cadillac and driving away.

"Dr. Anderson, who was that man?" inquired Lynch.

"He's an alumnus who used to play for me during the thirties," replied Anderson.

"Was he a good football player?" asked Lynch.

While pondering the question, Anderson furrowed his brow and took a long drag on his cigarette holder before responding, "Carlin, that man couldn't have knocked a baby off of a pee-pot with a running start!"[5]

With the advent of air-conditioned domed stadiums and artificial turf, weather impacts the game of football less today than it did when Anderson played and coached. Because the game was played outside, Anderson believed it should be practiced outside. The good doctor never "sanitized" football by moving practices indoors. Former Crusaders are nearly universal in their claims that Anderson never cancelled a practice due to weather.

There were, however, a few exceptions. In 1954 a hurricane clobbered New England for several days, knocking out electricity throughout much of Worcester. When the storm hit, the Crusaders were practicing atop Mount St. James. Black clouds shrouded the practice field and a bone-chilling rain pelted the players. The players were miserable, but Dr. Anderson remained unperturbed. Attired in foul weather gear that would have made a Gloucester fisherman proud, Anderson remained the taskmaster, occasionally braying above the howling wind, "Run that play again!"

Years before construction of the Hogan Campus Center, the site had been an apple orchard. It was only when gale force winds blew two of the orchard's uprooted trees across the field like jet planes catapulted off of a carrier deck that Anderson halted practice.[6]

The storm still raged the next day when the team met in Alumni Hall for its customary noon meeting. Dreading the rain and cold awaiting them at practice later that afternoon, most of the team had already turned a deaf ear to Mel Massucco's scouting report when a loud cracking noise, followed by a tremendous crash, interrupted Massucco's presentation. Shocked players stared in disbelief out the window where the hurricane's violent winds had uprooted a 60-foot evergreen tree. The silence was broken when Dr. Anderson turned slowly in his chair to assistant coach Jim Harris and said matter-of-factly, "Maybe we won't go out today."[7]

Anyone who has ever played at the high school or college level knows that watching game films is an integral part of the football experience. By watching films of one's own play, a player learns from his mistakes and focuses on areas that need improvement. However, it can be an embarrassing and painful process psychologically. At times, the atmosphere inside the film room resembles both an inquisition and an IRS audit. Cloistered in the dark with teammates and coaches, it's a semi-public confessional, where not only are one's sins as a player revealed, but one's manhood is sometimes called into question.

The Holy Cross film sessions were usually conducted in a stark classroom in Alumni Hall. Although Anderson gave up smoking in 1957, several of his assistants were edacious cigar smokers. As a result, after the lights dimmed and the whirring 16-millimeter projector beamed its flickering images, large plumes of tobacco smoke wafted across the screen. During silent pauses, the room took on the ambiance of a Saturday night card game in a fraternity basement.

Although Dr. Anderson could be caustic in his criticisms, he never browbeat a player. Unlike many coaches who assailed a poor play or individual effort with a stream of profanity, Anderson never swore. Yet, Anderson would dissect a game film with the precision of a surgeon's steady hand, subjecting even the most miniscule physical or mental error to microscopic scrutiny.

"I used to go into those film sessions thinking that I had played pretty well," recounts 1952 All-American tackle, Chet Millett. "However, after the film was reviewed, I left thinking that I'd played terribly."[8]

Carlin Lynch vividly remembers those film sessions. "You'd be watching the film, realizing that you had a bad play coming and just dreading it. The play would show on the screen and the coaches would point out the mistakes of others. Then, as the film rolled on to the next play and just when you were beginning to relax because you thought your mistake had gone undetected, Dr. Anderson would pipe up in that high-pitched voice, 'Let's run that back again.'"[9] Inevitably, Anderson would catch Lynch's mistake and magnify it before God and teammates.

"There may have been stars in the Sunday paper," affirms Chet Millett, "but there were no stars in the film room."[10]

Prior to the opening game of the 1956 season, Dr. Anderson told Allison Danzig of the *New York Times*, "There is nobody we play that we can't beat, but there is nobody we play that can't beat us." Anderson's words proved to be prophetic, for in the season-opener heavily favored Holy Cross blew a 13 to 0 halftime lead, and lost to Dayton, 14 to 13.

Despite a tie with Dartmouth and lopsided losses to stalwarts Penn State (43 to 0) and Syracuse (41 to 20), Anderson's squad improved steadily throughout the season. Much of the improvement could be attributed to a gifted and rapidly maturing sophomore class that included ends Dick Berardino and Dave Stecchi; guard Jim Healy; tackles Joe Moore and 235-pound Wally Bavaro (whose son, Mark, would become an All-Pro tight end with the New York Giants); halfbacks Ken Hohl and Ed Hayes; and quarterback Tom Greene. (It would be 1960 before Anderson would again see so many talented sophomores.)

With wins over Colgate, Quantico, Boston University and Marquette, a winning season came down to beating Boston College. On December 1, 1956, the Jesuit rivals squared off in their last meeting at Boston's hallowed Fenway Park. Over 34,000 fans witnessed a classic Holy Cross-Boston College struggle. Both teams played brilliantly on defense, with the Eagles thwarting several Crusader scoring opportunities in the first half. When B.C. tackle Joe Gabis blocked Tony Santaniello's 18-yard field goal try with only three minutes remaining in the contest, a scoreless tie seemed imminent. However, the tenacious Crusaders forced another Eagle punt and took possession at their own 34-yard line with 1:55 showing on the clock.

Crusader quarterback Billy Smithers was determined to make his last college game a memorable one. "In the game's final two minutes Smithers looked like he owned the stadium," recalls Jim Anderson, who was watching nervously from the stands. "His impressive performance that day equaled any of Johnny Unitas' late-game heroics."[11]

On first down, Smithers eluded a fierce pass rush and scampered for a 20-yard gain. He then completed successive passes to Dick Surrette and Dick Berardino for another 26 yards. On the next play, Holy Cross fans groaned in unison when Dick Berardino momentarily hauled in Smithers' pass in the end zone only to have it knocked loose by defender Jim Colclough's jarring hit.

Undeterred, Smithers then called "81 pass, down and out" and lofted a pass to the left corner of the end zone where Paul Toland made a juggling catch to give Holy Cross a heart-stopping 7 to 0 win. In the last college football game ever played at Fenway Park, Toland, wearing number 39, caught a pass that traveled 39 yards in the air to score the winning touchdown with 20 seconds remaining on the clock.

In the victorious post-game locker room, Smithers cried unabashedly and in a barely audible voice said, "I couldn't be happier... Honest to God, it couldn't be better."[12] The quarterback's late-game heroics made Smithers the unanimous choice for the Eddie O'Melia Award as the game's outstanding player. The award was a vindication of sorts for Smithers whose play earlier that season had drawn harsh criticism from local sportswriters.

Captained by end Dick Arcand, the 1956 Crusaders finished the season with 5 wins, 3 losses and 1 tie, and gave Anderson his first win over Boston College since 1952.

When Columbia's venerable Lou Little retired in 1957, Eddie Anderson became the Dean of America's college coaches. The former Notre Dame captain proved he was worthy of the title on November 9 of that year when his Crusaders visited Syracuse's frigid Archbold Stadium. Holy Cross dominated the first half of play, but when Syracuse took a 19 to 14 lead with just 3:30 remaining, it seemed like the Orangemen's depth and strength would prevail once again. With Holy Cross needing to march 80 yards into a howling wind to score, the outcome looked bleak. But junior quarterback Tom Greene thought other-

Eddie Anderson circa 1956. Anderson always felt that the biggest asset to coaching at Holy Cross was the overall character of the school's student-athletes. (College of the Holy Cross Archives)

wise. (As a sophomore the year before, Greene had riddled the Jim Brown–led Orangemen with three touchdown passes in a losing cause.) Against the wind, Greene completed a 29-yard pass to Dick Surrette followed by a 43-yarder to Jack Ringel. After Syracuse smeared two consecutive running plays, Greene rolled out and scooted nine yards for the go-ahead touchdown with only 1:15 remaining. Although Greene missed the extra-point kick, Holy Cross held on for a shocking 20 to 19 win. It was Anderson's first win over Syracuse in seven tries and it re-established Anderson's reputation as a mastermind of major upsets.

The Crusaders so enjoyed the role of giant-killer that they set their sights on Penn State the following week in Worcester. With his team trailing 14 to 8 and only two minutes remaining, Tommy Greene, in what seemed like déjà vu, calmly marched the Crusaders the length of the field. On fourth-and-goal from the Penn State 4-yard line Greene bootlegged only to be stopped six inches shy of the goal line. The visitors then took an intentional safety rather than risk a blocked punt in their own end zone to make the final score Penn State 14, Holy Cross 10.

Because Crusader guard Dave Perini's father owned the world-champion Milwaukee Braves, this season's Marquette game held a special significance for the squad. The game was to be played at Milwaukee's County Stadium where the Braves had recently bested the New York Yankees in a seven-game World Series. There was an air of excitement and anticipation about the trip.

The excitement heightened when the team arrived at the stadium. In contrast to the lavish major league locker rooms of today, the lockers at County Stadium had unpretentious signs over them indicating their inhabitant. "I still remember using first baseman Joe Adcock's locker during our stay there," fondly recalls Tom Henehan.[13] (Perini hung his clothes in the locker of Hall of Fame pitcher Warren Spahn.)

An over-sized refrigerator sporting a giant Braves logo sat in a corner of the locker room. When a curious player opened it he found it to be stocked with cans of beer. "The coaches told us that if we won, we could each take a beer after the game," recalls former Crusader "Scooch" Giargiari. "But team captain Dick Surette made it abundantly clear that no one was going to have one before the game!"[14]

In the wake of the Crusaders' 26 to 7 win, the refrigerator's inventory took a major hit. As the victorious players boarded their plane home, they found that flight attendants had festooned the plane's cabin with purple and white streamers.

Reflecting on his years at Holy Cross, Dave Perini recalls, "I was offered a football scholarship out of high school but declined it because my Dad and I felt that I didn't need one, so why deprive someone else in a less fortunate economic situation from getting the advantage of a Holy Cross education. In effect, I was a 'walk-on.' I didn't start until my senior year. When Vince Promuto was injured against Dartmouth early that year, I stepped into the starting left guard position. I might be wrong, but I always felt that part of my promotion was based on Dr. Eddie's appreciation of my 'walk-on' decision."[15]

The curtain came down on the 1957 season with Holy Cross hosting Boston College in Worcester for the first time in 25 years. A torrential rain turned Fitton Field into a quagmire. By game time the field could have passed for the muddy no-man's land of the World War I's Western Front. Within minutes after the opening kick-off, the players' uniforms were so mud-caked that it was nearly impossible to distinguish between teams. The atrocious field conditions turned the game into a comedy of errors that saw a total of 23 fumbles — 12 for B.C. and 11 for Holy Cross. Holy Cross' Vince Promuto alone recovered eight fumbles.[16]

In one of the game's more amusing moments, Promuto was pass-rushing Boston College quarterback Don Allard when he slipped to the turf. On all fours and several yards away from Allard, Promuto saw the quarterback cock his arm to throw. With no chance of sacking Allard, the quick-thinking Promuto scooped up a fist full of mud and tossed it underhand at the quarterback's face. The flying mud momentarily impeded Allard's vision, causing him to tuck the ball and run. Allard made it back to the line of scrimmage before being dumped unceremoniously in the mud.

Capitalizing on two third-quarter Eagle turnovers, the Crusaders slipped and slid to a 14 to 0 victory. Tom Greene won the Eddie O'Melia Award, and Doctor Anderson recorded his fourth victory in eight outings against Boston College since returning to Mount St. James in 1950.

The horrid game-day weather raised a question that fans had been asking repeatedly since the thirties; namely, why was the Jesuit rivalry held on Thanksgiving weekend? Since the Thanksgiving weekend often fell in early December, it virtually assured harsh weather conditions for the game. Although New England's autumn weather is unpredictable, playing earlier in the fall would certainly reduce the risk of frigid, if not wet, weather. Critics argued that scheduling the game even a week earlier would lessen the weather's impact on the Jesuit classic.

However, both schools remained adamant about playing on Thanksgiving weekend for several reasons. First, scheduling the game a week earlier would conflict with New England's other classic rivalry, the Harvard -Yale game. Playing both games on the same weekend meant sharing the media spotlight and possibly reducing the attendance at each. Second, playing on the long holiday weekend enhanced gross gate receipts. Since many of the schools' boarding students traveled hundreds of miles home for the holiday, they often couldn't attend the game. As a result, fewer discounted student tickets were issued, thus increasing the number of higher-priced tickets available to the general public. In short, neither school wanted to risk the decline in gate receipts that might accompany a date change.

As previously mentioned, Dr. Anderson disliked recruiting. It was rumored that when he returned to Holy Cross in 1950, he made sure his contract exempted him from recruiting. In any case, with Anderson initially spending half the year in Iowa, the bulk of the recruiting fell to assistant coach Hop Riopel and, after 1954, to Mel Massucco.

Before co-education and the advent of the Hogan and Father Hart centers, campus life at Holy Cross could be rather cloistered. Although the promise of a traditional Jesuit education in a semi-pastoral setting was highly valued by parents and sons alike, 18-year-olds often sought additional incentives. Hop Riopel, believing that the way to a football player's heart was through his stomach, took every recruit on a walk-in tour of the meat-locker in Kimball Dining Hall. For one blue-chip prospect in 1956, the meat-locker visit sealed the deal.

"As a young kid I loved to eat," recalls Vince Promuto. "Hop Riopel took me into Kimball Hall and showed me the meat-locker. That really impressed me. There were all of these great steaks hanging everywhere. Of course, we never got to eat any of them during my years there."[17]

The last step of the recruiting process often entailed a meeting with Dr. Anderson. It was said that Anderson recruited by a handshake. As a means of determining a recruit's strength, Anderson had devised a telltale method of shaking hands. While extending his right hand, Anderson placed his left hand on the recruit's bicep and gave it a squeeze. If Anderson liked what he felt, he would announce, "I think this one's got it."

Dr. George Lynch, an oral surgeon from Whitman, Massachusetts, who had scouted local high school talent for Dr. Anderson before becoming a New York Giants scout for 19 years, recalls such an incident in the spring of 1964. Lynch and Jim Cheyunski, a prospect from Bridgewater, were waiting in Kimball Hall to meet Dr. Eddie.

"Jim, when you shake hands with Dr. Anderson," advised Dr. Lynch, "squeeze his hand so hard that you put him on the ground."

A few minutes later Dr. Anderson walked in with Hop Riopel. Anxious, but dutiful, young Cheyunski clasped the coach's hand with all his might. Flashing his crooked grin, the coach turned to Riopel and said, "This is the first player you've brought me today!"[18] (Unfortunately for Holy Cross, Cheyunski would attend Syracuse before enjoying an eight-year career in the NFL.)

While Anderson admired strength in others, he always exhibited considerable pride in his own vise-like handshake. "Dr. Anderson thought I was pretty strong," recalls Vince Promuto, "and one year whenever he was talking with a visitor at the practice field he would call, 'Promuto, come over here and shake this man's hand.' So I would shake the guy's hand while Doc would exclaim, 'Promuto, if I had your strength I could kick a hole in the side of a battleship!'

"In those days they never taped a lineman's hands, and by late season your hands and knuckles were nicked-up, swollen and sore. During the last week of the season Dr. Anderson called me over to meet a visitor. This time, after I shook hands with the guy, Dr. Anderson extended his own hand to me. Well, he had a heckuva handshake, and he beamed that crooked smile of his as he shook my sore hand while I grimaced. Then it dawned on me that he had probably been setting me up for that moment the whole season."[19]

In the spring of 1958 Jim Anderson surprised his father by declaring, "Dad, I think I'd like to go to Holy Cross."

"You know, I still have a pretty good reputation up there," replied Dr. Anderson jokingly. "Are you sure you wouldn't rather return to Iowa?"[20]

Jim Anderson had originally matriculated at the University of Iowa but left school to join the Army. After a stint in the service, Jim applied to Holy Cross and was admitted as a member of the Class of '62.

When college authorities sat down with Eddie in March of 1958 to discuss a new contract, Anderson agreed to a $3,000 paycut in return for four years' tuition for his son. In announcing Anderson's new five-year contract, The Very Reverend William A. Donaghy, S.J., president of Holy Cross, said, "Amidst much discussion about the future of intercollegiate football, with a coach like Dr. Anderson, loyal to the school and cooperative with our academic ideals, I am sure there is no danger of Holy Cross football degenerating into a matter of importing mindless muscle merchants who would be valuable to the school only 8 to 10 hours a year."[21]

Donaghy, who had succeeded the football-loving Father O'Brien as president of the college in 1954, was neither anti-athletics nor anti-football. He was, however, determined to see Holy Cross field intercollegiate teams that were truly indicative of the school's student body. His emphatic comments to that effect after the 1958 season, however, led some sportswriters to speculate that Holy Cross was about to drop football.

The Crusaders opened the 1958 season at the University of Pittsburgh before a crowd of 50,000. One of the best teams in the nation, the Panthers not only had the advantage of spring practice but also had a game under their belts; a 27 to 6 upset win over UCLA. Led by All-American guard John Guzik and a square-jawed tight end named Mike Ditka, Pittsburgh had too much muscle for Anderson's gutsy, but outmanned lads, and pulled away for a hard-earned 17 to 0 win. With revenge-minded Syracuse coming to town the following week, the schedule makers hadn't done Holy Cross any favors.

Assistant coach Mel Massucco once said of Dr. Anderson, "He coached from the end of his nose. He thought and felt things and then he did them. And in all of the years that I worked with him I don't know if he was ever wrong."[22]

As a case in point, on Friday afternoon before the '58 Syracuse game the Crusaders were going through their usual pre-game routine on Fitton Field. Near the end of practice, Eddie called the team together and announced, "I want to put something in for tomorrow."

"We assistant coaches almost died!" recalled Massucco. "Here it was Friday night, the game plan had been set for a week, and now Eddie wanted to put in something new."

Anderson proceeded to put a scout team on the field to duplicate Syracuse's unbalanced line and then lined up his own defense against it. After directing each player where to go and what to do, the scout team ran several of Syracuse's favorite plays. Anderson watched and made corrections when necessary.

"Do you know that the next day we used that defense and beat Syracuse!" exclaimed Massucco.[23]

That evening Anderson met Syracuse coach Ben Schwartzwalder at the old Yankee Drummer Inn to talk football over drinks. "When the hell is that Greene kid going to graduate?" asked Schwartzwalder.[24] The ex-paratrooper had reason for concern; Greene had had a hand in scoring five touchdowns in his previous two meetings against the Orangemen. In 1957 it was Greene who had engineered the last-minute drive to beat Syracuse 20 to 19 in Archbold Stadium.

The next day, Greene confirmed Schwartzwalder's fears by ramrodding a 75-yard drive to give the Crusaders an early 6 to 0 lead. Two Syracuse interceptions led to touchdowns and after three quarters the Orangemen led 13 to 6. Taking possession on their own 7-yard line early in the fourth quarter, the Crusaders drove to mid-field where they were confronted with a fourth-and-one at the Syracuse 44-yard line. With the nerve of a burglar, Greene eschewed the run and completed an eight-yard pass to Dave Stecchi for a first down at the Syracuse 36. The drive culminated when Greene sneaked less than a yard for a touchdown. Trailing 13 to 12, Greene spurned kicking the extra point for the tie and called his own number. Bootlegging to his right, Greene dove into the end zone for two points to give Holy Cross a 14 to 13 win.

It was the Crusaders' second consecutive upset of the Orangemen. Greene was awarded the Edward S. Fraser Trophy as the game's Most Valuable Player. The revered Al Banx, whose cartoons of Crusader football games graced the sports pages of the Sunday *Worcester Telegram* for years, punned the title of his Syracuse cartoon, "How Greene Was Their Rally."[25]

In the wake of their upset of Syracuse, the Crusaders caught fire, rolling up successive victories over Dartmouth, Boston University, Dayton and Colgate before absorbing a 32 to 0 loss at Penn State. The Crusaders rebounded the following week with a win over Marquette before meeting Boston College at Chestnut Hill.

Anderson's hopes of capping off a stellar season with a win over the school's archrival were dashed early. With Johnny Amabile starting at quarterback for the injured Don Allard, Boston College never missed a beat in

Holy Cross quarterback Tom Greene (#18) hands off to halfback Ken Hohl (#15) in the Crusaders' 14 to 8 win over Dartmouth at Hanover in 1958. Greene sparked Holy Cross to two successive upsets of powerhouse Syracuse in 1957 and 1958. (College of the Holy Cross Archives)

controlling the game from start to finish. The bigger Eagles, capitalizing on the absence of injured Crusader linemen Vince Promuto and Wally Bavaro, employed mostly straight ahead power plays in steam-rolling to a 26 to 8 win. With their only losses coming to Pittsburgh, Penn State and Boston College, the Crusaders finished the 1958 season with an admirable record of 6 wins and 3 losses.

Five days later, on December 11, Holy Cross captain Jim Healy presented Boston College fullback Alan Miller with the Eddie O'Melia Award as the game's most valuable player. In the true sportsmanship that characterized those years of the Jesuit rivalry, the captain of the opposing team always presented the award to the recipient at the O'Melia Dinner held annually in Boston. Earlier that evening Father William A. Donaghy, president of Holy Cross, had casually mentioned that his school was finding it increasingly difficult to compete with Boston College in football. Donaghy's informal remarks later appeared in the *Boston Traveler* on December 15: "Holy Cross, with 1,800 students, simply can no longer compete in football with Boston College and its 7,600 students.

"Not unless we bring in the football players," explained Donaghy. "And we will not bring in the horses as long as I am president of Holy Cross."

Donaghy then explained that Holy Cross was looking to schedule more Ivy League opponents. "It may be pantywaist football," declared Donaghy, "but it's the kind we have to play if we want to keep our academic standards up to the Ivy League."[26]

Several sportswriters took Donaghy to mean that Holy Cross was either going to drop football or discontinue its rivalry with Boston College and wrote so in their columns the next day. The Very Reverend Donaghy then spent several days picking up the pieces from the alumni fallout.

On December 12, at the Holy Cross Club of Boston's annual dinner, Donaghy attempted to clarify his earlier remarks. "I said last night, and I repeat, that football at Holy Cross will continue on a sane and academically-controlled basis. And we find no conflict with that policy in our continued rivalry with Boston College.

"We will play football the way we are playing it now. We are not bringing in the horses. We are not going in for hypocrisy. We are pledged to the NCAA code.

"And we will not be known as a football team to which a college is attached!"[27]

Father Donaghy never had to worry about the football team undermining the academic integrity of Holy Cross during Dr. Anderson's watch. Anderson never pressured the school's admissions office to accept a player who was not academically qualified. Neither did he object nor intervene on those rare occasions when Holy Cross dismissed or suspended a football player for disciplinary reasons. According to family members, Anderson always maintained that the greatest benefit to coaching at Holy Cross was the overall caliber of its student-athlete. He found them to be intelligent, dependable, courageous and hard working.

"You didn't get anything handed to you at Holy Cross," states Vince Promuto. "There were originally 30 scholarship football players in our class (Class of '60), but Holy Cross never lowered the academic bar for any of us. By Christmas of our freshman year only 15 of us were left. The rest were dismissed for academic reasons."[28]

One of the finest football players that played for Anderson during his second era at Holy Cross was Vince Promuto. A tough street-kid from the Bronx, New York, Promuto never played football until his junior year at Mount St. Michael's High School. At 6'1" and 220 pounds, and with a 28-

inch waist and a 52-inch chest, Promuto was built like Adonis. He quickly discovered that he loved to hit and did so with great ferocity. By his senior year Promuto had received over 40 football scholarship offers. In an attempt to woo him to West Point, Army sent its 1945 Heisman Trophy winning alumnus, Doc Blanchard, on a recruiting visit to the Promuto home.

"I didn't want to go to Army and have to deal with all of that discipline," recounts Promuto. "Little did I know, however, what was awaiting me at Holy Cross."[29]

Arriving on campus wearing motorcycle boots, blue jeans and a black leather jacket, Promuto soon learned that the Jesuits meant business. During his first week on campus, Promuto signed out to visit downtown Worcester. Enjoying several local nightspots, the freshman returned to his Wheeler Hall dormitory room at 3 a.m. Not wanting to awaken his roommate, Promuto began undressing in the dark when he noticed the silhouette of a person sitting on his bed. Believing he had stumbled upon a burglar, Promuto lunged at the intruder. As they wrestled on the bed, he yelled for his sleeping roommate to turn on the lights. When the lights clicked on, Promuto found himself choking a blue-faced Father Thomas P. "Tank" Donovan, S.J.

After 30 seconds of coughing and gasping for air, Father Donovan was finally able to utter, "Mr. Promuto, do you know what the penalty is for violating curfew?"

"No, Father," replied the contrite Promuto.

As an English instructor, Father Donovan believed in the power of the written word. "Well, why don't you read from your student handbook what it says about violating curfew?"

Promuto, who had blithely tossed the handbook into the trash can several days earlier, now feigned looking for it. Father Donovan waited patiently while the freshman spent nearly 10 minutes hopelessly ransacking his desk and bureau drawers for the jettisoned handbook. Finally spying his roommate's copy, Promuto turned to the page and section per Donovan's instructions and penitently read aloud that "students who violate curfew face possible expulsion."

"Needless to say, I never broke curfew again!" confesses Promuto.[30]

After graduating from Holy Cross, Promuto enjoyed an 11-year pro career with the Washington Redskins. During that time he attended law school and became a U.S. Attorney after his playing days. "I remember Dr. Anderson as being a tough guy, but in a nice way," recalls Promuto. "He had a lot of witty and funny sayings. Most importantly, he cared about you getting the right kind of education. It was providence that I went to Holy Cross. The training and discipline I received there later allowed me to partake in many of life's greatest gifts. Things I would never have experienced otherwise. Dr. Anderson was a big part of that."

Promuto adds, "Holy Cross' great showings against bigger schools like Syracuse were a tribute to Dr. Anderson's coaching.

"Football is a spartan game. It goes against the natural law of things. Someone or something has to touch an emotion within you, anger, pride, or whatever, to make you play beyond your own limits. In my career only two coaches had the ability to reach that emotion. One was Vince Lombardi; the other was Dr. Anderson."[31]

During Anderson's tenure at Holy Cross a football player led a spartan existence. There were neither perks nor frills: no athletic dorms, private tutors

or under-the-table payments. "The closest thing we had to a perk," recalls Vic Rimkus, "was if a coach gave you a couple of extra game tickets. With luck, you might be able to sell them and pick up a few bucks."[32]

In the fifties and sixties, college football players who incurred career-ending injuries were often stripped of their scholarships. Another common practice saw coaches harass and abuse players who didn't live up to expectations until the players quit, thereby surrendering their scholarships. Such practices never occurred under Dr. Anderson.

"When you were awarded a scholarship under Doc Anderson," asserts Gene Corbett, an end at Holy Cross in the early sixties, "you were

One of the greatest football players Dr. Anderson coached during his second stint at Holy Cross was Vince Promuto. A tough kid from the Bronx, Promuto would enjoy an 11-year pro career as a guard for the Washington Redskins. Promuto later went on to become a U.S. Attorney. (College of the Holy Cross Archives) expected to maintain a full academic schedule and when you did, you were on scholarship until you graduated."

Corbett cites several examples of the honorable way in which Anderson treated injured scholarship players. "Tackle John Carroll hurt his knee in our sophomore year. Though he tried to rehabilitate it, the knee never fully responded and John eventually had to drop out of football. But he retained his athletic scholarship for the duration and graduated with the rest of us.

"Then there was the case of Alex Velto — same chapter, different verse. Al entered with us in the fall of 1959. On the first day of practice he was blocked while covering a punt and blew out his knee... Al had surgery right away and worked his tail off to get well. After his freshman year, it still was not ready for football and, though he could have returned on a full scholarship, he was determined to play. So he dropped out of school for a year. There was no such thing as redshirting at Holy Cross. Al came back for the next three years, and his scholarship was reinstated until he graduated with the Class of '64, even though, in a virtual repeat of his freshman year, he tore up his knee on the first day of fall practice."[33]

In 1959 Eddie Anderson was in a quandary as to which of five candidates would replace the graduated Tom Greene at quarterback. One of the candidates was senior Ken Komodzinski. A talented baseball player, Komodzinski had been the leading hitter on the Crusader baseball team that had appeared in that year's College World Series. Spurning a big league contract to finish college, Komodzinski hoped to sign a more lucrative contract after graduation. A scholarship athlete, Komodzinski decided to forgo his senior year of football to concentrate on baseball. While Anderson and Holy Cross were honorable and generous regarding athletic scholarships, they weren't pushovers.[34]

The Crusaders had been in the throes of two-a-day practices for two weeks when Komodzinski returned with the rest of the student body for the start of fall classes. After finding a bill for the first semester's tuition in his campus mailbox, the aspiring big leaguer reported for football practice the next day. The bill went away.

Playing its first 10-game schedule since 1955, the Crusaders opened the 1959 season with three straight wins over Dartmouth, Villanova and Dayton. In the 8 to 0 win over Dayton, senior Dick O'Brien, who had won the quarterback job, sustained an injury that required emergency surgery that night to remove a kidney. It spelled the end of the courageous quarterback's football career.

Although O'Brien would be bedridden for several weeks and unable to attend the games, Dr. Anderson had a quirk about seriously injured players.

"Eddie would take an injured player to the game, but he'd arrange for him to sit in the stadium pressbox," recalled Mel Massucco. "For some reason Eddie didn't want an injured player with the team on the sidelines during a game."[35]

The reason might date back to 1931 when Eddie's DePaul Blue Demons upset a superior Detroit team. In a chance meeting with Detroit coach Gus Dorais after the season, the two discussed the game. Dorais explained that the week before his team played DePaul, one of his Detroit players had sustained a career-ending injury. During the week the player attended several practices on crutches and sat on the team bench during the game. Dorais seemed to think that the injured player's presence somehow affected his team's psyche. Perhaps, he was a reminder of just how dangerous playing football could be. As a result, Dorais felt that his team had lost its nerve and played passively against DePaul, possibly afraid of incurring injuries.

As a doctor who often saw how squeamish family and friends could be around injured loved ones, Anderson may have bought into Dorais' argument. Years later, Anderson occasionally told his son, Jerry, "Sometimes, it's not good for an injured player to spend too much time around the team." He would then refer to Dorais and the Detroit game.[36]

It's doubtful that O'Brien's presence in the line-up the following week could have altered the outcome against the season's eventual national champion, Syracuse. Determined to avenge two successive one-point losses to Holy Cross, and led by future Heisman Trophy winner Ernie Davis, the Orangemen took no prisoners en route to a 42 to 6 pasting of the outmanned Crusaders at Archbold Stadium.

The Crusaders rebounded with successive wins over Columbia (34 to 0), Colgate (14 to 12) and Boston University (17 to 8) before once again taking another shellacking at Penn State. Behind a brilliant performance by quarterback Rich Lucas, the Nittany Lions hammered Holy Cross 46 to 0. The Crusaders then played poorly in a 30 to 12 pounding at the hands of Marquette before returning to Worcester to meet archrival Boston College.

On game day the weather and the field conditions were just as atrocious as they had been two years earlier. Hoping to avert a replay of the 1957 comedy of errors, Boston College coach Mike Holovak asked Holy Cross officials to postpone the contest until the next day.[37] Perhaps Holovak, whose coaching future at his alma mater was in doubt, believed that the adverse field conditions would favor the underdog Crusaders, or perhaps Holovak's request was just a plea to exercise common sense. In any case, Holy Cross refused to postpone the contest.

Neither the weather nor the Crusaders improved as the afternoon wore on, but Boston College did. Eagle halfback Vin Hogan's two fourth-quarter touchdowns would prove to be the difference in Boston College's 14 to 0 win. His performance earned Hogan the O'Melia Award. The win also gave Coach Mike Holovak an overall record of 6 wins and 3 losses against Dr. Anderson and Holy Cross. It was also his last game at Boston College. After the season Holovak departed Chestnut Hill and signed on as an assistant coach with the Boston Patriots of the new American Football League. Holovak later served as the Patriots' head coach from 1961 though 1968.

22

EDDIE ANDERSON:
DOCTOR AND TEACHER

A family dentist once told Mary Anderson that her husband had a higher threshold of pain than anyone he had ever met. Whether this quality was attributable to his rugged Norwegian roots or a trait that Eddie developed during his playing days at Notre Dame, toughness was a property that Anderson cultivated among his players.

As a doctor he understood the human body, how it worked and what it could endure. Like most coaches, Eddie knew when to drive a team physically. However, his medical training provided Anderson with a sixth sense. He knew people's tolerance for pain and strain. As a result, he knew when to ease up so as not to over-train his squads. Anderson worked his teams hard, with large dollops of scrimmaging in spring and pre-season practices. Yet, he limited contact work during the season. For years he ended practices with a series of 100-yard sprints, explaining, "You never know when you may have to run the length of the field to win a game."[1]

Being both a doctor and a coach, Anderson understood pain and the importance of conquering it. He knew the difference between being "hurt" and "hurting." As a coach he wouldn't play a boy that was hurt. However, he expected his boys to play when they were hurting. A football player has to play when he's winded, thirsty, hot, cold and aching. Long before Vince Lombardi bellowed the words, "Fatigue makes cowards of us all," Anderson understood that being in great shape could reduce both fear and pain, but getting into shape could be both a fearful and painful process.

Anderson downplayed injuries whenever possible. When a player nursing a charley horse hobbled onto the practice field, Eddie would tell him,

251

"You're going to have early ambulation today. You're going to run it off."[2] Anderson then had the injured player jog around the field until he was so numb that he forgot about his injury.

This practice was actually part of what Anderson called the "Theory of Counterirritants." Anderson first learned of the theory from a story (probably apocryphal) told to him by Knute Rockne. Supposedly, during a game one of Rockne's toughest players was complaining about a sprained ankle. The griping continued long and loud until Rockne had had enough and withdrew the injured player from the game. While on the sideline, Rockne supposedly yanked on the injured player's other ankle, making it sore too. Because he now had two sprained ankles, the player stopped obsessing over the first sprain and returned to action without another complaint — thus, the Theory of Counterirritants.[3]

In an era before the public's awareness of HIV, players sporting open wounds or hematomas would approach Dr. Anderson, point to their wound and inevitably ask, "Doc, do you think I should see the trainer about this?"

After a perfunctory look, Anderson usually replied, "I wouldn't see the trainer unless I had two of those."[4]

Occasionally, Anderson would enter the training room to find several injured players getting taped. "Hell, men," Anderson would proclaim, "the only thing that tape is good for is to mark the site of injury."[5]

Although an ear, nose and throat man, football sometimes forced Anderson to practice orthopedics on the field. During a road game in the late fifties, halfback Ken Hohl once came to the sidelines with his elbow protruding about eight inches from his arm. With a grab and a tuck, Anderson was able to reduce the dislocation. Hohl returned to action and played the rest of the game. Upon his return to Worcester, however, doctors casted Hohl's arm for a month.[6]

Not all of Dr. Anderson's on-the-field procedures went smoothly. In the early fifties, linebacker Ed "Nero" Walsh sustained a dislocated shoulder at practice. Team trainer Bill Samko escorted Walsh to the showers. As per Anderson's instructions, Samko ran hot water over Walsh's injured shoulder, hoping to relax the muscles enough so that Anderson could realign the shoulder. After several unsuccessful and painful attempts to reduce it Anderson had Walsh transported to a Worcester hospital where the shoulder was realigned.[7]

During a practice in the early sixties, end Bob Hargraves also sustained a dislocated shoulder. Without the use of any muscle relaxers or anesthetic, Anderson repositioned it on the spot by having Hargraves bend over and, with one hand on Hargraves' back and the other underneath, Doc tugged and pulled until the shoulder slid back into place. The process, however, was excruciating.

Despite undergoing off-season surgery to correct the problem, Hargraves dislocated it again at practice the following year. This time, when Doc came over "to help," Hargraves was having none of it. The injured end first sought refuge behind trainer Bill Samko, then nearby teammates, blocking dummies, anything, with Anderson in slow but steady pursuit. Finally, shouting, "Keep Doc away from me!"[8] Hargraves ran down the hill, his arm dangling at his side.

Being a doctor influenced Eddie's coaching in other ways. Years of intense medical training formulated Eddie's lofty standards. In turn, he educated his players to have the highest standards. Anderson was a perfectionist who would accept nothing less. He had a physician's confidence and he projected that confidence to his players.

"Dr. Anderson felt he could out-coach his opponent, which most of the time he could," states long-time football scout, George Lynch. "He was a very bright guy, a defensive genius. He certainly had Schwartzwalder's number.

"As far as I'm concerned," hails Lynch, "a better coach never lived."[9]

"Dr. Anderson had a keen intellect and analytical ability," recalls Dennis Golden, captain of the 1962 Holy Cross team. "He never wore a head-set on the sideline. Yet, he always knew what to do and when to do it. That came from being a doctor. What he was able to accomplish against some of the best football programs in the country with no spring practice and a part-time staff is inconceivable."[10]

His medical background also taught Anderson the importance of preparation and he applied this to his coaching as well. Anderson sometimes prefaced a lengthy team meeting by stating, "Men, an hour-and-a-half of preparation is worth a minute-and-a-half in the operation."

"Think about what Doc meant by that," says former Crusader, Chet Millett. "Who would you rather have operate on you, a doctor who spends 90 minutes beforehand studying a surgical procedure and then actually performs it in a minute-and-a-half, or a doctor who spends a minute-and-a-half studying the procedure and 90 minutes doing it?"[11]

One of the few concessions the Jesuits allowed Anderson was the scheduling of all football players for first lunch in Kimball Hall. This enabled Anderson to meet with his players during second lunch to get his players focused on the day's objectives at practice. Anderson had the game down to a fine science, and he simplified it for his players at these noon meetings.[12]

Being a doctor, Anderson was extremely conscientious about sanitation and hygiene. To fight the spread of germs, he preached to his children the necessity of washing one's hands after peeling a banana. Bringing in milk bottles from the porch or cracking an egg into a frying pan were also acts requiring immediate ablutions. As teenagers the Anderson boys spent many a Saturday morning on hands and knees scrubbing floors and baseboards to keep the kitchen and bathrooms germ-free. Despite his on-going battle against germs, the good doctor sometimes dropped his guard.

Anderson loved ice cream. Most evenings Eddie would pull a carton out of the freezer and ask, "Who wants some?" If there were no takers, Eddie refused to snack alone. First, he'd dollop out a big bowl for himself. Then he'd place a scoop of ice cream onto a paper napkin on the kitchen floor for the family bulldog, Buff, who never declined Eddie's dessert invitation. Once, after Buff rapaciously licked the napkin clean of ice cream, Eddie picked the napkin off the floor and absent-mindedly wiped his own mouth with it. Suddenly, the germ-conscious Anderson's face grew ashen and his eyes widened. "The look on Dad's face when he realized what he had done was just unbelieveable!" laughingly remembers his daughter, Judy.[13]

Eddie Anderson was the ultimate practitioner. He spent evenings at home reading, never novels or historical works, but medical journals. He worked continuously to keep abreast of the latest techniques and trends in medicine. When the team flew to a road game, Anderson usually sat next to Bill Samko, bringing the trainer up to speed on recent breakthroughs in the treatments of injuries.

Coach, teacher and healer, Anderson was also something of a philosopher. Although Anderson may not have regarded himself as such, many of his players certainly did. "He often liked to use little word games to teach us or to make a point," recalls former Crusader Tom Carstens. Carstens remembers one Andersonism in particular: "Your life is like a bank account. Learn to do good things early in life, because as you get older, you might have to draw on those experiences."[14]

Anderson sometimes cautioned against life's more mundane dangers. Most of his former Holy Cross players laughingly recall his warnings that sitting on the cold marble steps in front of Kimball Hall would give them hemorrhoids.

On Monday, October 22, 1962, President Kennedy appeared on national television to inform the American public of the Cuban Missile Crisis. The Holy Cross football team met that night in Alumni Hall to hear a scouting report on its upcoming opponent. Former Crusader Gene Corbett reflects on the tension of the times. "Here we were, a bunch of draft-age guys, wondering if we were going to war. Shortly after Mel Massucco began the scouting report it became clear to Doc, probably before we realized it ourselves, that nobody was paying much attention. He interrupted, said that would be enough football for the day and turned the discussion to world events. I have no specific recollection of what was said; just that coach knew there were more important things than football. I know I left feeling comforted that things would work out."[15]

Corbett, who became a career Air Force officer, remembers arriving early at a team meeting to hear the Doc delivering an impromptu lecture on landing a man on the moon and returning him safely to earth. "He went to the blackboard as if he were diagramming a play. I can still recall his exclamation at the science involved and especially the guts of the then un-named astronauts. As he drew the lines describing the return journey from the smaller to the larger globe he stopped where the spacecraft would have to slow to just the right speed at precisely the correct place to re-enter an orbit around the earth. 'Right here, men,'—the X's and O's were in the practiced hand of a football coach—'if they don't get it exactly right ... hell, men, they're gone!' And his voice trailed off as the chalk dust trailed off the bottom of the blackboard and into eternity. Years before we ever heard of NASA, it's still as good an explanation as I've ever heard."[16]

Another example of Anderson's philosophical bent had surfaced in 1954, Mel Massucco's rookie year on Anderson's staff, a time when the ex-halfback did all of the scouting. Once when presenting a scouting report Massucco enthusiastically declared, "and on third down they always do this!"

Anderson looked up from the scouting sheet, cocked his head slightly and instructed, "Mel, *always* and *never* are two words that you should *always* remember *never* to use!"[17] Massucco did his best to adhere to Eddie's advice.

Through the years Eddie's recommendations helped dozens of his former players get teaching and coaching jobs. Carlin Lynch, who later became a highly successful high school administrator and coach, was one such beneficiary. "Doc advised me not to let coaching football become my only profession because every coach gets fired. He told me that coaching should be an avocation, not a vocation, and he urged me to become a guidance counselor."[18]

Anderson also advised prospective coaches to try and get jobs at schools without archrivals. "A coach can win seven or eight games a year," declared Anderson, "but if you lose to your archrival, many people will consider the season to have been a failure."

During his years at Iowa, the state legislature repeatedly tried to resume the rivalry between the Hawkeyes and Iowa State at Ames. However, Anderson always sidestepped the issue and the two schools never met during his tenure at Iowa.[19]

A reporter once asked Anderson, as the Dean of America's football coaches, "What advice would you give a young coach today?"

The Dean replied, "I'd tell him not to get completely immersed in football, not to lose his perspective on life. Find a vocation, another outlet, something to keep him from taking football home every day of his life."[20]

In the twilight of his coaching career, Anderson speculated upon the future of football coaching. "Coaches are going to kill this game for themselves," Eddie frequently told his staff. "There are going to be all kinds of coaches studying all kinds of film. Yet, there's only so much time you can spend on the game before you become saturated.

"I don't care how many times you look at a film. If a kid can't run, he's not going to get any faster by watching the film 100 times.

"You watch, in the future, you won't be considered to be coaching unless you watch 10 or 12 hours of film a day!"[21]

Anderson's words were prophetic. Today, major college staffs have 10 to 12 assistant coaches, each overseeing a specialized position. During the season staffs work into the early morning hours breaking down game film, often returning at sunrise to resume the laborious process. College teams no longer watch game films collectively but rather by specific position groups.

23

THE SIXTIES

Terry Wadsworth, Class of '60, was a football manager for Holy Cross during the late fifties. Because of his managerial duties, he spent many a Saturday afternoon on the sidelines observing Anderson's coaching mannerisms. "Dr. Anderson was very intense during a game," claims Wadsworth. "He had this penetrating look as he watched the action. You could tell that he genuinely enjoyed what he was doing. Although he wasn't short-tempered, he could be pretty demanding of his assistants and the trainer, Bill Samko. Sometimes, he would yell at them just like he would the players."[1]

Anderson could berate an assistant one minute and praise him the next. In the 1964 Richmond game Anderson barked at assistant coach Oscar Lofton, "Get someone else in there at right end!"

"Well, I sent a kid in and wouldn't you know it," recalls Lofton, "on the first play Richmond sweeps the kid's end for a 20-yard gain. Doc gave me 'that look' and snapped, 'That's the last time I'll ask you to put in an end!'

"I felt pretty bad about it. But in the paper the next day Dr. Anderson praised my scouting report as a major reason for our win over Richmond. He was demanding, but fair."[2]

Occasionally, closed door staff meetings would turn into shouting matches between assistant coaches. When Anderson had heard enough on a point of contention, he prefaced his final judgement on the matter with the words, "Well, R.E. Anderson thinks," which signaled an end to further debate. (The initials R.E. came from his playing days under Knute Rockne, who, in attempting to prevent a case of mistaken identity between Eddie and teammate Hunk Anderson, would refer to Eddie as Right End or R.E. Anderson.)[3]

"Doc worked well with his assistants," recalls former halfback, Ken Hohl.

"But there was never any doubt as to who was in charge. Doc called all the shots."[4]

"Doc controlled everything," confirms Chet Millett. "The assistant coaches were silent partners, but it was a perfect blend."[5]

A great athlete at Holy Cross in the early twenties, Hop Riopel had earned 11 varsity letters. He had played pro football with the Providence Steamrollers in 1925 and turned down repeated offers to sign with the New York Giants baseball organization to coach at Milford High School. In 1933 Riopel returned to his alma mater as a freshman coach of all sports. Dr. Anderson often hailed, "I don't think I ever met anybody who knows more things about more sports than Hop."[6]

During his career Riopel served two separate stints as the school's basketball coach and succeeded the legendary Jack Barry as baseball coach in 1961. He also served a term on the Massachusetts Boxing Commission from 1947 until 1950. Riopel etched his mark in Crusader folklore in 1942 while scouting Boston College. Supposedly, Riopel detected a "key" that actually telegraphed what play the Eagles would run next. Holy Cross practiced against it all week, and sure enough, on game day the Crusaders knew each upcoming play. Riopel's scouting report was instrumental in Holy Cross' 55 to 12 derailment of bowl-bound Boston College.

(The shocking defeat probably saved the lives of many Boston College players and fans. Confident of victory, B.C. officials had planned a celebration that evening at the fashionable Coconut Grove nightclub in downtown Boston. In the wake of the stunning upset, the party was cancelled. Four hours after the game a raging fire engulfed the club's overcrowded ballroom, killing 492 people. The Coconut Grove tragedy still ranks as one of the worst fires in our country's history.)

In Riopel's younger days he dealt with stubborn players by threatening to "knock them over the goal posts." To encourage toughness during blocking and tackling drills he would growl, "It's a dog's game and you gotta' be a dog to play it!"[7] Riopel was universally loved by the players, who often targeted Hop for some good natured kidding. During his glory days as a Crusader baseball player, Riopel made a legendary, but questionable, diving grab of a line drive that saved a game against Boston College. Almost daily some player tried to get Riopel's goat by asking, "Hop, did you really make that catch or did you trap it?"

By the early sixties, however, it was obvious that Riopel had seen better coaching days. During a tight game Dr. Anderson once turned to Hop and barked, "Get me an end!" With that Hop scurried along the bench beseeching, "I need an end! Who's an end?" When his frantic pleas evoked no response, Riopel screamed, "Somebody get me a program!"[8]

Anderson's 1960 squad was bolstered by an exceptionally talented sophomore class that included Pat McCarthy, quarterback; Tom Hennessey and
Al Snyder, halfbacks; and tackle Dennis Golden. They joined with junior
quarterback Bill Joern, guard John Timperio and end Jack Fellin to give the
Crusaders some much-needed depth.

In the week prior to the season-opener at Harvard, Boston sportswriters had been hailing the debut of Holy Cross halfback Tom Hennessey, who
had been a local high school phenom. In a story he later confided to Dr.
Anderson, Harvard coach John Yovicsin used his pre-game pep talk to psyche up the Crimson squad to stop Hennessey. Applying psychological war-
fare, Yovicsin challenged one of his star players by asking, "Do you think we
can shut down Hennessey?"

"Gee, Coach, I don't know," the Ivy-Leaguer candidly replied. "I played
against him in high school and he scored four touchdowns against us!"[9]

Yovicsin's jaw dropped to the floor.

Hennessey lived up to his advance billing by returning the opening kick-
off 85 yards for a touchdown. After Hennessey's opening romp, however,
Harvard settled down and, behind the skillful leadership of quarterback Charlie Ravenel, controlled the next 59 minutes and 47 seconds of football to
upset the Crusaders 13 to 6.

In a joint press conference after the game Harvard coach John Yovicsin
proudly explained, "Our gang was really fired high for this one. We wanted
it very badly, so we opened up with our bag of tricks. We didn't hold a thing
back."

"Well, I certainly hope we did," quipped Anderson.[10]

It was Anderson's first loss against Harvard in six games.

The following week things went from bad to worse when the heavily
favored Crusaders lost at Boston University 20 to 14. After the game Anderson rode back to Worcester with his son, Jim. (The son of a railroader who
grew to manhood during the Golden Age of train travel, Anderson came to
hate riding on buses. Whenever the team traveled by bus, Anderson customarily rode behind in a car driven by an assistant coach. After games he often
rode home with one of his sons.)[11] On the way home he and Jim stopped at
a restaurant along Route 9 to catch the last of the Syracuse-Kansas State game
on television. The defending national champion Orangemen were visiting
Fitton Field the following week. Nursing a martini, Anderson watched as
Syracuse finished steam-rolling over the Wildcats, 38 to 6. "How the heck
are we supposed to stop these guys?" lamented Anderson.[12]

During the season, Anderson spent his mornings making rounds at the
Rutland Veterans Hospital. In-between patients, his mind would drift to football and he'd scribble a play or a defense down on his prescription notepad.

Arriving at the field house at noon, he'd drop these notes on Mel Massucco's desk. Massucco would then enlarge them and take them back to Eddie for his approval or corrections before photocopying them for the other coaches. During the week of the '60 Syracuse game, prescription notes fell like snowflakes across Massucco's desk.

Loaded with future pros such as Al Bemiller, John Mackey, Art Baker, Walt Sweeney, Tom Gilburg and eventual Heisman Trophy winner Ernie Davis, Syracuse rolled into Worcester as a 30-point favorite. Many local sportswriters, however, whispered that the Orangemen might roll up 100 points against the winless Crusaders.

A fumble and a botched fake punt kept Syracuse pinned deep in its own territory early. When Tom Armstead recovered an Ernie Davis fumble on the Orange 25-yard line, the Crusaders were in business. Pat McCarthy completed a pass to Hennessey at the Syracuse 13 before McCarthy himself ran it to the 3-yard line. Two plays later, Bill Joern ran the last yard for the score. The pass for the two-point conversion failed. Playing inspired ball, Holy Cross took a 6 to 0 lead into the locker room at halftime, having held the defending national champs to just 21 yards rushing and 5 passing. The Crusaders kept the Orangemen in check until late in the third quarter when Art Baker broke a 33-yard run to give Syracuse a first down at the Holy Cross 22. With Ernie Davis doing most of the running, the Orangemen picked up a first down at the Crusader 1-yard line. Two dive plays yielded nothing, but on third down the bruising John Mackey plowed into the end zone to tie the score. Ken Ericson's extra-point kick gave Syracuse a 7 to 6 lead.

Unperturbed, Holy Cross then drove 73 yards down the field. On fourth-and-less than a yard at the Syracuse 4-yard line, Anderson, unsure of his kicking game, spurned a field goal try to go for the first down. Crusader John Allen carried but Syracuse held. The missed opportunity cost the gutsy Crusaders the game.

Holy Cross had one last chance, but with a fourth-and-11 from its own 20-yard line and less than 30 seconds remaining in the game, the Crusaders came up five yards short. Taking over on downs, Syracuse could have merely taken a knee to run out the clock, but they didn't. With his team's number one ranking on the line, Coach Schwartzwalder decided to take one more shot at impressing the pollsters. With only 11 seconds remaining, Syracuse quarterback Dick Easterly tossed a pass into the end zone that a Crusader defender deflected into the arms of Ernie Davis, who made the catch while lying flat on his back. Dick Sarrette then tossed to John Mackey for the two-point conversion to make the final score Syracuse 15, Holy Cross 6.

Crusader Gene Corbett remembers, "After the game Doc was truly upset by Syracuse's actions but made no public comment. Privately, he expressed only his disappointment that this is what seems to be necessary when the polls become so important."[13]

Energized by their gallant performance, which toppled Syracuse from its number one ranking, the Crusaders won their next four games. Getting that first win, however, is often the toughest, and it took Bill Joern's last-second 15-yard field goal to defeat Dartmouth the following week in Hanover, 9 to 8.

The streaking Crusaders had won five of their last six when they met Boston College at Chestnut Hill for the 1960 season's finale. Anderson and his staff had brought the Crusaders a long way since losing to Boston University, but they now had their hands full against their Jesuit archrival. The heavily favored Eagles had a senior-laden team, big and talented, with depth at each position. Before 26,000 fans on a beautiful day for football, the Crusaders drew first blood when sophomore quarterback Pat McCarthy spearheaded an impressive 98-yard scoring drive in the first quarter. The touchdown came on McCarthy's 22-yard pass to fellow sophomore Tom Hennessey. The pair then connected for the two-point conversion. When Ed "Mud" Lilly thwarted a Boston College scoring threat with an interception at the Holy Cross 10-yard line just before the half, the Crusaders escaped with a 16 to 6 lead at intermission.

Boston College scored quickly in the second half but again failed on its two-point conversion attempt. The Eagles, who were playing two full teams, hammered away at the Crusader linemen who were playing both ways. On all four of Boston College's last possessions, the tiring but determined Holy Cross defense stopped the Eagles cold. Bill Joern sealed the 16 to 12 Holy Cross win by intercepting George Van Cott's desperation pass and returning it 33 yards to the Eagle 8-yard line as time expired.

The upset win gave Holy Cross a record of 6 wins and 4 losses for 1960. With so many talented underclassmen returning, the football picture at Mount St. James looked rosy for the next few years. Sophomore Pat McCarthy's performance earned him the O'Melia Award.

McCarthy, who hailed from Haverhill, Massachusetts, had originally intended to matriculate at the Naval Academy. However, when told that he would first have to spend a year at the Naval Prep School, McCarthy opted to attend Holy Cross. Although an adequate passer, McCarthy was truly a gifted runner who put defensive ends and linebackers covering the flats in a quandary when he rolled out to pass. If the defenders played the pass, McCarthy ran. If they came up to stop the run, McCarthy passed. A natural athlete, McCarthy also had a knack for improvisation — a trait that annoyed his coach.

"In his sophomore year, McCarthy used to drive Anderson nuts!" laughs

Dr. George Lynch. "Eddie would sometimes stand on the sidelines with his hand on the arm of the second-string quarterback, ready to send him into the game, as if defying McCarthy to deviate from the game plan."[14]

Anderson would learn to love McCarthy.

Although Holy Cross was fielding competitive teams, the effects of not having spring football were apparent early in the season, especially when opening against a team that had benefited from spring drills. Such was the case in 1961 when the Crusaders dropped their season-opener to Villanova, 20 to 6. Holy Cross rebounded with successive wins over Buffalo, Boston University and previously undefeated Dartmouth. Although improved, the Crusaders were still no match for goliaths Syracuse and Penn State and dropped one-sided contests to both. Holy Cross also defeated Dayton and, in its first regular season game against the University of Massachusetts since 1915, the Crusaders pounded the Redmen 44 to 7. A 14 to 3 win over stubborn Connecticut gave Anderson's lads a 6 and 3 record going into their contest with Boston College.

Despite their impressive showing, the Crusaders were still ranked as underdogs against the gold and maroon-clad visitors before a sellout Fitton Field crowd. Anderson had his team primed. Holy Cross scored first on Al Snyder's dazzling 42-yard punt return. Pat McCarthy then scored two of his three touchdowns on the day and tossed a 22-yard touchdown pass to Barry Tyne to give Holy Cross a 24 to 0 lead over the befuddled Eagles.

Possessing greater team speed, the Crusaders could have poured it on their demoralized archrival. True to form, however, Anderson refused to run up the score. With Anderson playing his second and third teams for most of the second half, Holy Cross coasted to a 38 to 26 victory. The upset win gave Holy Cross a record of 7 wins and 3 losses for 1961.

One of Eddie Anderson's greatest attributes as a coach was his ability to constantly wring the most out of his players. How? What did he look for in a player?

According to Mel Massucco, Anderson consistently preached, "I don't want any will-o'-the wisps. I want Dependable Dans." By that he meant he wanted players who gave 100% all of the time — men who would do their jobs every day in any type of weather and against any caliber of opponent. He wasn't interested in any one-game wonders or those who only played when they felt like it.[15]

"Doc could forgive physical mistakes but not mental ones," explains one-time All-American, Chet Millett. "If you made a mental mistake it could cost you your position. If he got down on you, you didn't play very much, even if you might be really good."[16]

Dr. Eddie Anderson listens to Crusader quarterback Pat McCarthy during a game at Fitton Field in the early sixties. A talented rollout passer and runner, McCarthy put tremendous pressure on opposing defenses. (Courtesy of Mel Massucco)

Many ex-players believed that once a player was in Dr. Eddie's doghouse, he might never see game action again. Pat McCarthy remembers an incident during one film session. "It was an early-season game, Villanova, I think, and one of our backs led a sweep out of the backfield. He ran by two separate defenders without blocking either. Eddie ran the play over several times and was not very happy about it. Although the guy was one of the best high school backs to come out of New England, I don't think he ever got to play again that season."[17]

Former Holy Cross great Vic Rimkus explains, "If Doc had confidence in you, he'd play you to the dying end. If you let him down once, he had a long memory, and you might not get to play again." Rimkus quickly adds, "Doc was never nasty or vindictive about it. If he didn't play a guy, he just didn't play him."[18]

Former Holy Cross end Dick Berardino remembers it differently. "Dr. Anderson was a very difficult coach to play for because of his huge ego. To defy him in any way put you on his bad side.

"During my junior year (1957) we lost a game to Boston University. (Official records show that B.U. and Holy Cross actually tied that year.) He was upset with the team and some of us had a very bad day on defense.

"On Monday, he wanted us to be on the field right after our last class for some defensive work. I needed to make up an exam that I had missed because of travel to one of our earlier games. If I did not take the exam, I would fail the class and have to go to summer school. I told that to Dr. Anderson after our noon meeting. His response was, 'Be on the football field!'

"I decided to take the exam and reported late for practice. I was put on the fourth team and never started another game the rest of the year.

"Because of that incident I decided, after the baseball College World Series in which Holy Cross participated, to sign a pro contract. That made me ineligible to play football my senior year. Had I not been treated that way by the good doctor, I would have wanted to play my senior year."[19]

(It should be noted that while Berardino was demoted from the first team, he still played in several remaining games and was a major contributor in clashes against Quantico, Syracuse and Boston College.)

Classmate Ken Hohl, however, found Anderson to be very fair. "Eddie once said that if he went strictly by my performance in practice, he would never have played me. However, he liked the way I played defense and felt that I made things happen when I got into a ball game. As a result, I saw a lot of playing time. In fact, he probably gave me more chances than I deserved."[20]

Like most coaches, Anderson admired and appreciated those who played with courage and through pain. He was particularly impressed with players from the South Boston area, often declaring at coaches' meetings, "Give me those kids from South Boston any day!"[21]

According to Gene Corbett, the team's punter in 1961 and '62, one of Anderson's favorites was Billy Joern. "An undersized guy even for our era, Bill was an Iowa boy (Joern was actually from Nebraska) and rough as a cob. (That description must be said in an imitation Doc Anderson accent... Hell, men, that Joern, rough as a cob.) He played some at quarterback until Pat McCarthy established himself, then, at maybe 170 pounds, he became the designated defensive substitute for the quarterback.

"I know that Doc, as an Iowa guy, was really tickled one year when the paper — scrambling as usual for cute stories during the early fall practices — wrote that Joern hitch-hiked back to Holy Cross from Council Bluffs, and even spent one night sleeping in a haystack or a cornfield. (Hell, men ... that Joern, rough as a cob!)"[22]

In the summer of 1962 Anderson was working at a whirlwind pace as the admitting doctor and personnel executive at the Rutland Veterans Hospital. Eddie often pulled the night shift. Yet, the 61-year-old Anderson was eagerly anticipating the excitement of a new football season. With experienced returning veterans like Pat McCarthy, Tom Hennessey, Al Snyder and Dennis Golden, Anderson had reason to be optimistic.

The Crusaders started fast, winning three of their first four games before bowing to powerful Syracuse 30 to 20. Holy Cross then rebounded with wins over Dayton and VMI before being crushed at home by juggernaut Penn State, 48 to 20. In that game, Penn State had the ball near the Crusader goal line and a 42 to 12 lead with only seconds remaining. Wanting to score again, the Nittany Lions called a time out to stop the clock. When play resumed Penn State tallied to make the score 48 to 12. Wanting to score 50 points, Penn State coach Rip Engle spurned kicking the extra point, and to the anger and disgust of the Fitton Field crowd, went for two points instead. The attempt failed and the score remained 48 to 12. As boos and catcalls rained down on the visitors for their lack of sportsmanship, the Lions kicked off. Crusader scatback Jim Gravel fielded the ball and set off on a spectacular 83-yard touchdown run as time expired to make the final score Penn State 48, Holy Cross 20.

Dr. Jerry Anderson, Eddie's son, witnessed the game. "Gravel's run proved to the Holy Cross fans that there is a God, but like my Dad always said, He spends most of His Saturday afternoons at South Bend."[23]

After defeating Connecticut, the Crusaders hobbled into Chestnut Hill for the season's finale at Boston College. The seniors were hoping to make it a three-year sweep over their archrival, but with numerous first-team players slowed by injuries and sensational Eagle quarterback, Jack Concannon, personally accounting for 278 yards of total offense, it wasn't going to happen. In fact, the game was pretty much a reversal of the 1961 contest. Only this time the score was more indicative of the victor's total domination, Boston College 48, Holy Cross 12. The disappointing loss gave the Crusaders a record of 6 wins and 4 losses for 1962.

In *Thy Honored Name*, Father Kuzniewski writes that by 1960 there was a growing awareness of "a great and urgent need to build up a young and strong faculty" at Holy Cross. Many believed that the faculty needed to be revitalized through the infusion of PhD's who were willing and able to publish and participate in professional scholarly meetings. Some also thought that the college's athletic program could stand an infusion of new blood. One former Crusader recalls, "In the early sixties the Holy Cross athletic department was being run by a bunch of old men."

Experience certainly wasn't a problem. The senior statesman of the athletic department was track coach Bart Sullivan. Sullivan, who had arrived at

Mount St. James in 1912, was also the school's head trainer. By 1960, Sullivan had been on the job for 48 years and would continue to serve the school in an athletic capacity well into his eighties.

Baseball coach Jack Barry had won more than 600 games in his 41 years at Holy Cross before his death in 1961. Hop Riopel, Barry's long-time assistant and friend, succeeded him. As previously mentioned, Riopel had coached numerous sports at Holy Cross since 1933. Even the school's golf coach, Charles Donnelly, had been teeing off with the Crusader squads for over 25 years.

As the 1963 season approached, Anderson was embarking upon his 38th year of coaching and his 20th at Holy Cross. It would be a trying season for Eddie, whose undermanned and over-scheduled Crusaders would once again battle the likes of Villanova, Syracuse, Penn State and, of course, Boston College.

"Let's face it," confesses Dr. Jerry Anderson, "Dad may have stayed too long at the dance. He coached until he was 64. Granted, a young 64, but coaching is a young man's game."[24]

In 1963 George Halas, the 68-year-old owner of the Chicago Bears, was still coaching his Monsters of the Midway. Anderson and Halas had first crossed paths in 1918 when Anderson was a freshman at Notre Dame and Halas was playing for the Great Lakes Naval team. In the twenties, of course, their Cardinal and Bear teams met frequently. "It was the funniest thing," recalls Jim Anderson. "During the early sixties Dad often told me that the Bears were a good team, and that all Halas needed to do to win a championship was to hire a good young guy to coach them. Yet, Dad wasn't ready to follow his own advice."[25] (For the record, senior-citizen Halas coached the Bears to the NFL championship in 1963.)

During the early sixties, it sometimes seemed like a time warp for players sitting through team meetings in old Alumni Hall (built in 1905) while listening to a man that had been George Gipp's teammate while playing for the legendary Knute Rockne. "It was as if time had stood still," recalls Bob Noble, who played for Anderson in 1963 and '64. "I don't say that in a bad way, because Dr. Anderson captured and personified many of the virtues that are absent from sports today."[26]

While many players revered Anderson as a father figure, some had difficulty relating to him. Some now greeted Anderson with a degree of cynicism. "I don't think Eddie had the rapport with some of his later teams that he did with his teams in the fifties," states Dr. George Lynch. "Many of his later players weren't as in awe of him as were his earlier players. The kids were emotionally different."[27]

During his last years at Worcester, the fans were also becoming more vocal in their criticism of the seasoned coach. As a result, Eddie asked his wife, Mary, to stay at home and listen to the games on radio rather than watch from the Fitton Field stands.

"My father was incredibly practical," recalls Judy Anderson. "That was the Norwegian in him. To him life was serious and when it was tough you just had to keep going. Near the end of his coaching career some thought he should retire. I know he didn't like hearing that. But his old pragmatic side kicked in and he just kept going."[28]

At age 63 Eddie may have been slowing down. "While I still have the greatest respect and admiration for Dr. Anderson," states former end Bob Noble, "during those last few seasons he may have fallen a half-step behind in organizational and personnel matters."[29] Furthermore, his duties as chief of outpatient services at the Rutland Veterans Hospital began demanding more of his time. Although never late for practice, there were days when his medical duties prevented Eddie from arriving at the field house as early as he would have liked.

"Because he wasn't around campus very much, the only time Dr. Anderson got to know the kids was on the practice field," recalls assistant coach Oscar Lofton. "As a result, he sometimes had difficulty remembering the players' names." (In fact, Anderson often mistakenly referred to Oscar as "Elmer." This could have stemmed from the fact that the handsome Lofton bore a strong resemblance to Elmer Mader, who had served on Anderson's staff in the early fifties.)

In the 1963 Villanova game, Anderson turned to Lofton and asked his advice on a pass play. "Just throw it to Spike, he'll catch it," reassured Lofton.

"Who in the hell is Spike?" queried Anderson.

"Everybody on the team knew that "Spike" was Dick Kochansky," explains Lofton. "Anyway, we started throwing to Spike. Although we didn't win, Kochansky had a heck of a game, catching 11 passes on the day."[30] (Kochansky's record stood until 1976, when Craig Cerretani caught 13 against Boston College.)

Tom Henehan, Class of '60, matriculated at Holy Cross at his father's urging. Tom, Sr. had played for Anderson at DePaul long before the advent of facemasks or helmet shields. When the good doctor discovered that Tom, Sr. had sight in only one eye, he made the senior Henehan give up the game rather than risk an injury to his one good eye and possible blindness.

"Dr. Anderson was an impressive man," recalls Tom, Jr., who played guard and linebacker at 6'3" and 230 pounds. "He was an older man who commanded real respect. However, it wasn't love at first sight. He was nearing the end of his coaching days. He never gave us a rowdy discourse in the locker room and was always gentlemanly in his actions. As a young man at the time, however, you wanted a little more excitement."[31]

In 1964, Anderson's final season, one Crusader complained to *Newsweek* magazine, "Sometimes, I think he (Anderson) doesn't psyche us up enough. When he talks to us it's usually something about behaving like men, playing like men."

Throughout his career Anderson was never a "rah-rah" or "blood and guts" coach. Rarely did he get emotional at halftime but never before had his players regarded his talks as trite.

Critics felt that the college needed a full-time coach if it was to remain competitive — one who would recruit year-round. Everyone knew where Anderson stood on recruiting and had known since his return in 1950. He disliked recruiting and often found it unsavory. He was unwilling to "bad mouth" another school. "What am I going to do, tell a kid not to go to Notre Dame? Heck, I went there myself!"[32] Nor was he about to promise a recruit the world to sign him.

"Eddie wasn't going to chase after some snotty-nosed kid," states football scout, George Lynch.[33]

"If a boy didn't want to play for Dad, Dad didn't want him," recalls Judy Anderson.[34]

Once Anderson and George Lynch were sitting in Eddie's car in front of Beaven Hall discussing a list of high school recruits. As Lynch opened the door to depart, Eddie added, "George, there's one more thing. Don't bring me any more pre-meds!"

"We were both doctors and yet here was Eddie telling me not to bring him any more pre-meds!" laughs Lynch. "It was ironic."[35]

In reality, Anderson was growing frustrated with the number of pre-med students who missed one or two practices a week to attend afternoon labs or, more alarmingly to Anderson, quit football all together to focus on their studies.

The 1963 season also saw changes on Dr. Anderson's coaching staff. Ecio Luciano, who had played for Anderson at Holy Cross in the thirties, returned to work for his old coach after spending 17 seasons as an assistant at Northeastern University. Luciano would replace long-time aide, Jim Harris, as line coach.

Oscar Lofton was another new addition. Lofton, a Mississippi native who had played his college ball in Louisiana, had been one of the original Boston Patriots. Prior to the start of the 1963 season, Lofton had sustained a knee injury and was released. Patriot coach Mike Holovak, who thought he might one day reactivate Lofton, wanted the big end to remain in the Boston area. Lofton was amenable to Holovak's request but said he needed a job in order to stay in New England.

Hearing that Anderson had an opening on his staff (Hop Riopel had also retired), Holovak called Eddie and set up an interview for Lofton. "I drove up to Holy Cross and met with Eddie," recalls Lofton. "We spoke for a while and then he informed me that I had the job. I was stunned because he really hadn't asked me anything about football. I then asked if he had any football questions for me and he responded, 'No, Mike says that you will make a good coach, and Mike's word is all I need.'"[36]

Holy Cross opened the 1963 season with a 6 to 6 tie against Buffalo. If, as Navy coach Eddie Erdelatz once said, "a tie is like kissing your sister," it was the only kiss the Crusaders would get for a while. After successive losses to Syracuse (48 to 0) and Boston University (16 to 8), the Crusaders traveled to Hanover to battle a Dartmouth team that had won 14 straight. A 13-point underdog, Holy Cross led 8 to 7 with 11 minutes remaining when Dartmouth scored on a 13-yard trick pass play to halfback Bob O'Brien. The gimmick play provided the margin of victory as Dartmouth held on for a 13 to 8 win. (Interestingly enough, O'Brien's dad, Bob O'Brien, Sr., was the Holy Cross player that Captain John McEwan had illegally substituted during the 1932 Brown game that ultimately led to his dismissal as coach.)

Winless, the Crusaders returned home for Parents' Weekend against the Quantico Marines. The undefeated Leathernecks stormed Fitton Field with four ex–Crusaders in their ranks: quarterback Pat McCarthy, halfback Hank Cutting and tackles Dennis Golden and Jack Whalen.

In a surprise move, Anderson started Fran Coughlin, a gutsy kid from South Boston, at quarterback. "Dad really liked Coughlin," recalls Dr. Jerry Anderson. "When Coughlin was at quarterback there was no question as to who was running the club. He made things happen."[37]

Coughlin's six-yard pass to Jim Gravel early in the fourth quarter gave the Crusaders a 6 to 0 lead. The Marines regrouped after the ensuing kickoff and, in what *Worcester Telegram* sportswriter Roy Mumpton described as "horse and buggy" football, marched 70 yards on 17 consecutive running plays to score.[38] Jim Davis' extra-point kick gave Quantico a hard-fought 7 to 6 win.

The following week Eddie Anderson was not happy about traveling to Philadelphia to meet Villanova. Anderson considered Villanova to be like an exposed rusty nail — dangerous and just as dirty. In 15 years of working together, the only time Anderson was irked by Athletic Director Gene Flynn was when Flynn extended the football series with Villanova. As Anderson told his son, Jim, "People expect you to beat them. Yet, they're very good and very capable of beating you. Besides that, they're dirty as hell and your kids come out of the game all beat up!"[39]

The '63 game was an exciting contest that saw no unsportsman-like extra-curricular activity. Yet, Villanova proved to be as tough as ever and, despite Crusader Dick Kochansky's 11 receptions, emerged with a 22 to 14 win.

Holy Cross snapped its five-game losing streak with a 14 to 12 upset of VMI at Fitton Field the following week when halfback Jim Marcellino rushed for 106 yards and Fran Coughlin threw two touchdown passes to Dick Kochansky. The difference in the game was Coughlin's two-point conversion pass to Jim Gravel. Delighted with his team's first win of the season, Anderson boasted of Coughlin afterward, "He's got the guts of 18 burglars."[40]

Unfortunately, the one-game winning streak ended the following week with a 28 to 12 loss at Penn State. Although it was obvious that the Crusaders were improving weekly, fans were frustrated with the team's record of 1 win, 6 losses and 1 tie.

Several days before the Connecticut game, a group of about 50 rowdy students hanged Anderson in effigy in the quadrangle in front of Kimball Hall. When contacted by reporters in his Rutland home, Eddie downplayed the incident. "A thing like this is strictly out of my hands," explained the coach. "Protesting seems to be the order of the day in colleges. It was only a small minority. Let them have their fun."[41]

The symbolic lynching and football itself suddenly seemed inconsequential two days later when, on November 22, President John F. Kennedy was assassinated in Dallas. Holy Cross cancelled its game with Connecticut and joined the nation in grieving the loss of the young and vital Boston-bred president. When Kennedy was laid to rest on Monday, November 25, it was a subdued and shaken squad that began preparing to meet archrival Boston College.

Boston College was coming to Fitton Field with a record of 6 wins and 2 losses. Led by All-American candidate Jack Concannon at quarterback, Boston College was a two-touchdown favorite. Concannon had personally accounted for 278 yards of offense in the Eagles' 48 to 12 pounding of Holy Cross in 1962. Local pundits anticipated another blowout for Boston College.

Yet, as was characteristic of his entire career, Eddie Anderson was at his coaching best when things seemed bleakest. Anderson made two decisions during the week that proved to be beneficial in stemming the Boston College onslaught. First, he allowed assistant coach Ecio Luciano to implement a 5–3 Eagle defense. This defense aligned a nose tackle on the center and positioned or "eagled" the defensive tackles down over the offensive guards, thus leaving the offensive tackles uncovered. The middle linebacker stacked behind the nose tackle and the outside linebackers either stacked behind the defensive ends or over the offensive tackles.

"They didn't know how to block Luciano's old 5–3 Eagle defense," laughs assistant Oscar Lofton. "We beat 'em like a rug with it!"[42]

Second, Anderson enlisted Lofton to quarterback the scout team. The 25-year-old ex–Boston Patriot had Concannon's mannerisms down pat. He stood behind the center like Concannon, rolled-out like Concannon and passed almost as well as Concannon. Anderson was delighted with the realistic look Lofton was giving the Crusader defense. "Lofton looks more like Concannon than Concannon does!"[43]

Trainer Bill Samko also concocted a psychological masterpiece. Hoping to erase the anguish of six previous losses and "pump up" the squad, Samko replaced the team's old purple pants with new silver game pants and gave the players new purple jerseys with silver numerals. He also painted the players' purple helmets silver.[44] As the Crusaders donned their new uniforms on game day, it sparked a fire in their eyes and a hunger in their bellies.

On a windy day before 23,500 fans, the Crusaders got the game's first break late in the first quarter when Eagle punter Steve Murray couldn't handle a high snap from center and the ball rolled through the end zone for a safety. With the Crusaders leading 2 to 0, Eagle fullback Don Moran broke a 45-yard run before Jim Gravel hauled him down on the Crusader 3. Bob Budzinski then plowed to the Crusader 1-yard line. On the next play, however, Concannon rolled out to his left only to be nailed for a five-yard loss by end Tom Butler and tackle Jay Dugan.

Concannon then threw an incompletion before passing to an ineligible receiver on fourth down. The ensuing penalty gave Holy Cross a first down on its own 20.

The defensive stalemate continued until midway through the fourth quarter when the Crusaders marched 54 yards in 14 plays to score. The touchdown came when halfback Jim Marcellino catapulted into the end zone from three yards out. Jim McCarvill then kicked the only extra point of his career to give Holy Cross a 9 to 0 lead.

Boston College responded by marching to the Crusader 26-yard line before the drive fizzled. When the clock expired moments later, the Crusaders had achieved one of the most stunning upsets in the history of the storied Jesuit rivalry.

In the post-game locker room, Anderson graciously credited his assistants, Ecio Luciano, Oscar Lofton, Mel Massucco and Mickey Connolly for their contributions to the victory. To most alumni, students and fans Dr. Eddie Anderson and Holy Cross football were synonymous, and at age 63, the old gent proved he could still win the big one. There remained, however, a small contingent of malcontents who saw Holy Cross' victory over Boston College as proof of what the frustrating season might have been. They regarded concluding a 2 win, 6 loss and 1 tie season with an upset of Boston College as being analogous to garnishing a road apple with a maraschino cherry.

The coterie of critics could be damned, however, for on this day Holy Cross had beaten Boston College and on Mount St. James all was right with the world.

24

THE FINAL CURTAIN

Had Dr. Eddie Anderson decided to retire after the Crusaders' upset of Boston College in the 1963 season finale it would have been a fairy tale ending to a storied career. However, with a year remaining on his contract, Anderson opted to answer the coaching bell again in 1964.

"In fact," offers Jim Anderson, "Dad would have liked to have coached through the 1965 season and his 65th birthday."[1] However, Holy Cross president, the Very Reverend Raymond J. Swords, quietly informed Eddie that there would be no contract extension.

After conferring with his wife, Mary, Anderson called a press conference on August 20, 1964, to announce that the upcoming season would be his last at Holy Cross. "The day had to come sooner or later," a resolved Anderson told reporters. "I've made up my mind. I know there will be many times when I will miss the game and the wonderful people involved, but there are other things I must consider — things equally important to me and my family."[2]

Anderson's announcement came a month after President Lyndon Johnson signed the Civil Rights Act of 1964 into law, the nation's most significant social legislation in 100 years. It also came two weeks after the real and imagined events in the Gulf of Tonkin, which would lead to President Johnson's escalation of the United States' military role in Vietnam. It was a decision that would eventually threaten to shred the fabric of American society through years of mass political demonstrations, campus protests and the deaths of over 50,000 Americans in the jungles of Southeast Asia.

Anderson's resignation would become effective after the Boston College game on November 28. After 38 seasons in the coaching trenches Anderson was officially credited with 196 wins. As the out-going Dean of College

273

Coaches addressed the audience, sportswriters in attendance wondered whether the '64 Crusaders possessed enough talent and depth to send Dr. Eddie into retirement with 200 career wins. As in the late innings when teammates avoid mentioning that their pitcher is hurling a no-hitter for fear of jinxing him, no reporter asked Anderson about his chances of becoming the fourth college coach ever to win 200 games. In the weeks ahead, however, Anderson's race for the coveted milestone would be the grist of sports columns throughout New England.

Unbeknownst to the NCAA, sportswriters and even Anderson himself, the official records were wrong. The fact of the matter was that Anderson actually had 199 wins entering the 1964 season — three more than the 196 officially credited to him. The error may have dated back to the late thirties when DePaul University dropped football and then somehow "lost or tossed" the records from its 1931 season. As near as anyone could remember, DePaul had won at least three games in 1931 and those were included in Anderson's career total of 196. Research later revealed that Eddie's Blue Demons had actually won six games in 1931, thus really giving Anderson 199 wins on the eve of the 1964 season. Impassive about his many distinguished accomplishments, Anderson had never counted his career wins and was unaware of the error.

Although unconcerned about documenting his coaching achievements, Anderson had always been a fierce competitor who hated to lose. With the exception of the Crusaders' upset of Boston College, the 1963 season had been a nightmare for Eddie. In the wake of that poor showing, Anderson was determined to go out a winner in 1964. As a result, Eddie may have put more pressure on himself than in previous years.

Anderson's quest to bow out a winner suffered a severe jolt when starting quarterback Fran Coughlin sustained an off-the-field injury that would cause him to miss the entire 1964 season.

By opening day the 63-year-old Anderson had developed high blood pressure that required his taking a tranquilizer before every game. He needed it on September 26 when Coach Alex Bell's Villanova squad invaded Worcester for the season opener. Behind the steady play of quarterback Dave Connell, the Wildcats thumped the Crusaders 26 to 0. Again handicapped by no spring practice, the anemic Crusader offense gained only 41 yards rushing while suffering six interceptions.

Anderson might have considered doubling his tranquilizer dosage the following week when Holy Cross hosted perennial powerhouse Syracuse. Unsheathing a devastating ground attack in a rout of Kansas the week before, the Syracuse backfield featured 230-pound fullback Jim Nance and sophomore sensation Floyd Little. The Orangemen were so heavily favored that many believed the Crusaders were being offered as sacrificial lambs on the

Impeccably attired as he always was on game days, Dr. Anderson views the action from the sidelines during the '64 Syracuse game at Fitton Field. (Courtesy of Mel Massucco)

altar of the National Broadcasting Company (NBC), which was televising the game live along the eastern seaboard. Long-time New York Yankee broadcaster Mel Allen was to provide the play-by-play for the anticipated slaughter. Perhaps fearing the worst, only 12,000 fans turned out on a gorgeous afternoon to root on the home team.

As in so many previous Holy Cross-Syracuse contests, however, Anderson again had his undermanned troops lying in ambush. After holding the Orangemen on their first possession, halfback Jim Gravel's 36-yard punt return set up sophomore Mike Cunnion's 11-yard touchdown pass to Dick Haley. Cunnion then tossed a two-point conversion to Jim Marcellino to give Holy Cross a surprising 8 to 0 lead. Employing a specially designed defense to counter Syracuse's unbalanced line attack, the Crusader defense played like men possessed, swarming to the ball and limiting the visitors to a mere 16 yards rushing in the first half. After Cunnion's early scoring pass, however, the Syracuse defense stymied the Crusader offense for the rest of the half.

As the two teams left the field at halftime, the opposing coaches walked a parallel path to their respective locker rooms. The night before both men had met at the old Yankee Drummer Inn for their customary round of drinks before their annual gridiron encounter.[3] The talk had been light-hearted and the mood cordial. Now, however, neither coaching war-horse would acknowledge the other.

Two minutes into the second half, Syracuse tackle Jerry Everling intercepted an errant Crusader pass and returned it 18 yards for a touchdown. When the conversion try failed, the plucky Crusaders still clung to an 8 to 6 lead. Shortly thereafter another interception set up Jim Nance's two-yard scoring run to give Syracuse a 14 to 8 lead.

As was so often the case in this rivalry, Syracuse's superior strength and depth emerged in the fourth quarter when its battering ground game led to two more touchdowns. Leading 28 to 8, Syracuse had the ball on the Holy Cross 2-yard line with only 35 seconds remaining in the contest. Ben Schwartzwalder could have paid a gracious salute to the retiring Anderson by merely having his quarterback take a knee and run out the clock. Instead, still seething over his team's poor showing in the first half and with a national ranking at stake, Schwartzwalder elected to run halfback Nat Duckett off tackle for the touchdown. Although Syracuse had successfully kicked extra points following their third and fourth touchdowns, Schwartzwalder now opted to go for the two-point conversion. Schwartzwalder and Anderson may have been friends, but on the gridiron the ex-paratrooper took no prisoners. Asking for no quarter, the Crusaders stuffed the two-point try and the game ended with the final score, Syracuse 34, Holy Cross 8.

Before a disappointing homecoming crowd of 10,000 the following week, Coach Hal Lahar brought his Colgate Red Raiders to Mount St. James. Lahar's coaching career had taken a twist similar to that of Anderson's. The former Oklahoma Sooner had enjoyed a winning run at Colgate from 1952 through 1956 when the lure of coaching in the big time took Lahar to the University of Houston. After accumulating a record of 24 wins and 23 losses in five seasons at the Cougars' helm, Lahar jumped at the chance to return to the Chenango Valley in 1962 and again coach the Red Raiders. After two losing seasons, Lahar now had a formidable team that was en route to a 7 and 2 season. Colgate was good, but certainly not in the class of either Villanova or Syracuse.

Nevertheless, in a game that saw Colgate kick only its second field goal in 22 years, a 38-yarder by left-footed kicker Tom Woltman, Colgate dominated the action in its 10 to 0 win.

Winless in three games and struggling with a languid offense, sportswriters and fans began doubting whether Holy Cross had either the ability or the heart to win four games and procure a 200th win for Anderson. The college newspaper, *The Crusader*, fired the harshest volley of criticism on October 16. In his column, student sports editor Paul Freeman blistered the team's listless performance against Colgate. "The Crusaders don't play their best. They don't try their hardest. They don't care if they win.

"Let's face it," Freeman continued, "Holy Cross stunk against Colgate, and they stunk because they don't give a damn. You can't castigate 'Doc' and the rest of the coaches when a team refuses to block and tackle, when a team at their best can only be described as apathetic and mediocre."

The column also claimed that a "good number of players" seemed more interested in outside activities than football. Freeman than posed the question, "Is the proper name for our football team the Driftwood A.C.?"[4] (The Driftwood was a popular nightspot in the Worcester area.)

Anderson had no comment regarding Freeman's article, but he, too, had been disappointed in his team's lackluster effort against Colgate. In fact, Anderson had already taken steps towards rectifying the situation by deciding to bench his leading halfback for the next two games for disciplinary reasons.

"Winning," said Bob Noble, an end on the '64 squad, "was important to Dr. Anderson, but it was far from being all-important. During my junior year he 'sat down' two of the best players on the team for discipline infractions — and this at a time when victories were less then plentiful and time was running out on his bid to win his 200th game."[5]

When the *Worcester Telegram*'s Roy Mumpton asked Anderson about the validity of Freeman's article on the eve of the Quantico game the good doctor simply replied, "If they're men, they can prove it tomorrow. If we hit, we can make a good show of it."[6]

The Quantico Marines came to town a 14-point favorite over Holy Cross. Three former Crusaders would be in the lineup for the Leathernecks: tackles Dennis Golden and John Whalen and safety Hank Cutting. A fourth alumnus, Pat McCarthy, who was Quantico's starting quarterback, suffered a knee injury during the week and didn't make the trip.

Played in a steady rain before a crowd as abysmal as the weather, the Crusaders played their best football of the season. Whether the catalyst for the team's dramatic improvement was Freeman's stinging criticism in *The Crusader* or Anderson's decision to bench four starting players is unclear. What was readily apparent, however, was that the Crusaders were more energized and determined than the team that had taken the field a week earlier against Colgate. Behind sophomore quarterback Jack Lentz's 155 rushing yards on 29 carries and great blocking by tackle John Mee, the Crusaders upset the Marines 16 to 0.

"That's all I wanted to see ... men out there playing their hearts out for Holy Cross," a relieved Anderson told reporters after the game. Regarding the four "benched" players Anderson declared, "But I want to make it emphatic that I have no personal vendettas against any of my players. I hope we've cleared the air. At the same time I think we found some football players out there today."[7]

Winning is always great, but for Anderson the victory nectar from the Quantico game was especially sweet. The coach had made his point while the Crusaders had earned their first win of the season. In retrospect, the shutout was actually Anderson's 200th career win. Yet, like a shooting star blazing across the sky above a sleeping village, nobody noticed.

Winning breeds confidence and confidence breeds winning. Thus it was a confident Crusader team that defeated Buffalo 20 to 14 in western New York on October 24. Returning to Worcester on Halloween Saturday, Holy Cross hosted the University of Richmond. The revived Crusaders exploded on offense behind quarterback Jack Lentz, who ran for 178 yards on 20 carries and set a new school record for individual game rushing yardage. Leading 36 to 6 early in the fourth quarter, Anderson inserted the reserves and Holy Cross breezed to a 36 to 22 win.

Regarding Anderson's proclivity for calling off the dogs when Holy Cross held a commanding lead former Crusader Pat McCarthy recalls, "If there was a chance of running up the score, he would rather have us punt on first down and give the football back to the opposition instead of keeping the football and piling up unnecessary points."[8]

By the incorrect but official count of the day, Dr. Anderson could pick up his 200th win the following week when the University of Massachusetts visited Fitton Field on November 7. Undoubtedly, Anderson would have relished reaching the 200-win milestone against the Minutemen. For most of his coaching career Anderson had regarded UMass as a small agricultural college that didn't belong on the same field with his beloved Crusaders. However, times were a changing. The Minutemen were rapidly emerging as a legitimate football power in New England and had come a long way since being pounded by Anderson's lads 44 to 7 in 1961.

Over 20,000 — the largest crowd of the year — piled into Fitton Field's wooden bleachers to see if Anderson could notch his 200th win. Many in the stands were UMass fans. They wouldn't be disappointed in their team's performance. Soon after the kick-off it became apparent why UMass was entering the contest with a 6 and 1 record. Behind the stellar play of quarterback Jerry Whelchel, who ran for one touchdown, passed for another and kicked a field goal, the Minutemen dominated every aspect of play in Massachusetts' 25 to 6 win.

On the following Friday, November 13, Eddie Anderson celebrated his 64th birthday. Disregarding the unlucky omen, Eddie felt confident that his team would give him his 200th coaching victory as a birthday present the next day.

Sporting a record of 3 wins and 4 losses, Holy Cross ventured to Boston University's Nickerson Field on the sun-splashed afternoon of November 14. In a class move, Boston University athletic director, Victor Stout, featured an artist's rendition of Dr. Anderson on the cover page of the school's homecoming day program. In the lower left corner of the page a caricature of a Boston terrier stood at attention saluting the legendary coach. The program's cover would be a fitting tribute to the day's events.

The Crusaders came out smoking. On the game's first play from scrimmage halfback Jim Marcellino took a hand-off from Jack Lentz and scooted 63 yards for a touchdown. Lentz later scored to give Holy Cross a 12 to 0 halftime lead. As the splendid autumn afternoon wore on, things only got better for Anderson and his Crusaders. Pete Meehan and Brian Flatly sandwiched scoring runs around a 51-yard touchdown pass from Mike Cunnion to Ray Blake. When the final gun sounded amidst the afternoon's lengthening shadows, the scoreboard read Holy Cross 32, Boston University 0.

As Anderson made his way to mid-field to shake hands with opposing coach Warren Schmakel, Anderson couldn't help but flash his crooked grin as player after player gave him a congratulatory handshake or pat on the back. It was a joyous moment, but one that was restrained compared to the ice water dousings inflicted upon winning coaches today. The players bypassed the custom of carrying Eddie off the field because they felt such a display would have been out of character for the reserved Anderson. Yet, almost to a man, they were thrilled for their coach's success and grateful to have played a role in this historic moment. Only three other major college coaches, Amos Alonzo Stagg, Glenn S. "Pop" Warner and Jess Neely had preceded Anderson in winning 200 games.

In the winner's festive locker room Paul Johnson of *The Worcester*

Telegram asked Eddie if he remembered his first coaching win. Although Anderson couldn't recall the score, he remembered that it came against the Wisconsin School of Mines of Platteville back in 1922. The jubilation subsided momentarily when Holy Cross' injured captain, Jay Dugan, who had watched the game in street clothes, appeared with the game ball. As the team crowded around Anderson, Dugan announced, "We just want you to have the game ball for your 200th victory, Coach. Congratulations."

"Thanks, men," replied Anderson. "Now let's make it 202."[9] (Connecticut and Boston College were the Crusaders' last two opponents.)

As the late afternoon faded into evening it didn't matter that no one could find the light switch in the dim and cramped locker room beneath Nickerson Field for there was plenty of light emanating from the glow of respect, admiration and camaraderie shared by the assistant coaches and players surrounding Eddie Anderson. For the young, virile athletes clad in silver and purple, and for the venerable gentleman who coached them, that golden autumn afternoon captured the essence of all that is right about the game of college football. Nothing could have tarnished that wondrous moment, not even the fact that the 200-win celebration may have come four weeks late.

In his last coaching appearance at Fitton Field the following week, Anderson earned his 201st (actually his 204th) win with a 20 to 6 victory over Connecticut. With his team now clicking on all cylinders, Anderson's 5 and 4 Crusaders prepared for the season's finale at Chestnut Hill against Jim Miller's 5 and 3 Boston College Eagles.

There were several big football stories brewing that week. The annual Army-Navy game was to be played in Philadelphia and a re-vitalized Notre Dame football program under first-year coach Ara Parseghian was taking its undefeated record to the Los Angeles Coliseum where a victory would give the Irish their first National Championship in over a decade. (U.S.C.'s 20 to 17 upset win would shatter the Irish dreams.) However, it was the Quonset hut field house on the campus of Holy Cross that became a beehive of media activity during the Thanksgiving week.

Dr. Eddie Anderson, the legendary Dean of America's College Football Coaches, was preparing for his last game, and that was big news. The athletic office was swamped with phone calls requesting interviews with the retiring coach. Sports journalists and television crews flocked to Worcester to cover team practices atop Mount St. James. As players scrimmaged under portable practice lights and shivered in November's icy winds, a bevy of reporters scurried among team members with pads and pencils seeking "suitable" quotes about the out-going coach. Meanwhile, bundled in a parka and hood that seemed suited for Antarctica, the unflappable Anderson put his team through its weekly paces.

After practice on Thanksgiving morning, the squad gathered in Kimball Hall for a holiday meal of turkey with all the fixings. With players, trainers and coaches in attendance, and surrounded by several family members, Eddie seemed relaxed and genuinely happy. The team's annual Thanksgiving meal at Kimball Hall was a part of coaching that Dr. Anderson was going to sorely miss.

The last practice under the Anderson regime was on the afternoon of November 27 at Fitton Field. It was a light workout with players attired in sweatsuits. Afterwards, a photographer from *The Worcester Telegram* photographed the Crusaders' starting offensive and defensive units for the next day's paper. To give the out-going coach some moral support, Judy Anderson paid her father a surprise visit. She brought the family pet with her, a brindle English bulldog named "Buff."[10]

Jerry and Jim Anderson had bought the bulldog as a pup a couple of years earlier. As is often the case, however, when careers took them to New York where they couldn't have pets, parents Eddie and Mary inherited the animal. The Anderson family had owned many dogs through the years, but Eddie had grown especially fond of Buff. He lavished the dog with attention and enjoyed feeding it jelly on toast at breakfast and a scoop of ice cream nightly.

Recognizing a good human-interest shot when he saw one, *The Telegam's* photographer snapped a picture of Eddie with Judy and the bulldog. Saturday's sports section featured the photo of pretty Judy Anderson next to her father and the family pet. While readers were taken with Judy's beauty, they couldn't agree on whose jaw evinced more bulldog-like determination, Eddie's or Buff's?

Saturday, November 28, was cloudy and cold, typical of so many previous Boston College-Holy Cross battles. Jim Miller's Eagles entered the fray as 13-point favorites. The Eagles had beaten both Villanova and Syracuse during the year, two teams that had handily defeated the Crusaders earlier in the season. Boston College had also been a 13-point favorite in 1963 when Anderson "doctored" up a stunning 9 to 0 upset of the Jack Concannon-led Eagles. However, few thought that upset lightning could strike in back-to-back years. Yet, Anderson had always been at his coaching best when things looked bleakest. One of Anderson's coaching trademarks was his ability to get his team up for "big games." Could Dr. Anderson pull one more upset out of his medical bag?

From the opening kick-off the action was fast-paced and hard-hitting, with few penalties. Playing skillfully and tenaciously against the bigger and stronger Eagles, Holy Cross clung to an 8 to 3 lead after three quarters, and

On November 27, 1964, Judy Anderson brought the family bulldog, Buff, to practice to wish her father luck on the eve of his last game as a head coach. (Courtesy of Dr. Jerry Anderson)

it began to look as if the Crusaders might present their coach with a stunning farewell victory. With 12 minutes remaining, however, the Crusader bubble seemingly burst when Eagle quarterback Ed Foley connected with Jim Whalen on a 16-yard touchdown pass. Marty DiMezza's extra-point kick gave Boston College a 10 to 8 lead.

The Eagles dominated the next eight minutes of play and were on the verge of putting the game away when Holy Cross linebacker Tom Nissi intercepted a deflected pass at the Boston College 44-yard line and returned it to the Eagle's 14. Suddenly, the gutsy Crusaders were again knocking on victory's door. Against a determined B.C. defense, however, three running plays netted Holy Cross only seven yards. On fourth down and three yards to go on the B.C. 7-yard line, with 3:45 remaining, Anderson sent in the field goal team.

With nearly 27,000 spectators holding their collective breath, the stage was set for a stirring and courageous upset. It all came down to a 14-yard field goal attempt — an attempt that failed.

Clawing to stave off defeat, the desperate Crusader defense forced a Boston College punt four plays later. Taking possession at mid-field with less than two minutes remaining, Holy Cross still had time for a miracle. Two successive pass completions kept hopes for an upset alive. However, like the brown leaves of autumn fluttering in the afternoon breeze, Holy Cross' last four passes fell harmlessly to earth. The 10 to 8 defeat brought down the final curtain on Dr. Anderson's brilliant coaching legacy.

The mood in the Crusader locker room was more than somber, it bordered on heart breaking. Yet, true to his style — the same style in which he had coached through the years — Anderson was straightforward and sincere in his last words to his team.

"Let me say sincerely that I was proud of you all ... extremely proud. You played like men... Good luck to all of you."[11]

As Anderson moved to an end of the room his oldest son, Nick, grabbed his father and whispered in his ear, "You're a great father. God bless you."[12]

Then an emotional Jerry Anderson stepped up to shake his father's hand while telling reporters, "I'm glad it's over. We want him home more. He's a great man."[13]

By the time the reporters, alumi, and players were gone, night had fallen. Anderson and his youngest son, Jim, crossed the parking lot and climbed into the car. There Anderson spoke the words that his son would always remember — the words that revealed the depth of his passion for the game and his team: "Boy, I wish I had one more shot at those guys!"[14]

But Anderson would get no more shots at Boston College. However, like everything he did in life, his last shot was also his best shot.

25

LIFE AFTER FOOTBALL

Several days after his resignation Anderson was delighted by the announcement that his long-time assistant and former team captain, Mel Massucco, would succeed him as football coach at Holy Cross. Although Massucco had clearly been Eddie's choice as his successor, the college interviewed several candidates for the position including Holy Cross assistants Ecio Luciano and Mickey Connolly as well as Villanova coach Alex Bell and Maryland's Tom Nugent.[1]

Holy Cross never gave Anderson a retirement dinner. According to his children, Eddie had come to eschew formal affairs and it's unlikely that he would have ever agreed to one, preferring instead to exit quietly.

The day after Christmas Eddie and Mary departed for San Francisco, where Anderson would help coach the East squad in the East-West Shrine game to be played on January 2, 1965. Anderson had coached in the annual event since the early fifties. Once, in 1955, he had served as head coach of the East squad. While Eddie coached, Mary and Judy Anderson spent the week shopping and seeing the sights of the City by the Bay.

Upon his return from the West Coast, Dr. Anderson told his son, Jim, "I may have seen the best lineman in my life this week, a kid from Illinois."[2] The kid in question was Dick Butkus. Butkus, of course, was later inducted into the NFL Hall of Fame, and many experts hail him as the greatest linebacker in the history of the game.

In 1965 the Veterans Administration announced that it would be turning its Rutland facility over to the state of Massachusetts. The hospital had originally been devoted to treating tuberculosis patients. Improved health care and modern drugs had almost wiped out the disease by the early sixties.

284

As a result, the Rutland hospital became chiefly concerned with the general medical and surgical needs of veterans. Since these services were offered at the much larger Veterans Hospital in Boston, the government opted to pull the plug on its Rutland operation as a cost-cutting measure.

Not yet ready for total retirement, Anderson went seeking another medical position. On August 4, 1965, Anderson was named chief doctor at the Mansfield State Training Hospital in Mansfield, Connecticut. The position provided Eddie and Mary with a house on the hospital grounds, a perk that delighted Anderson. The hospital itself primarily served special needs children.

"When Dad took over, there were rumors of employee abuse against patients, even sadism," recalls Jim Anderson.[3] Upon his arrival, Anderson called a general meeting and laid down the law to employees that any such conduct under his watch would be prosecuted to the fullest extent of the law. The abuse stopped.

"Dad was so good with those mentally challenged patients," states Judy Anderson. "He neither looked down on them nor was he afraid of them." To the patients he was known as "Dr. Eddie," and soon many took to following him around the hospital grounds as if he were the pied piper. To accommodate his young followers, Anderson always had the pockets of his lab coat stuffed with candy.

From the start Anderson worked feverishly to upgrade Mansfield's sanitation standards. "To my father, a fly was the worst creature alive," asserts Judy Anderson, "and when he arrived the Mansfield Hospital had no screens on the windows. Dad petitioned the hospital's administrators constantly until screens were installed on every window."[4]

When he retired to Florida in 1971, he left Mansfield Hospital a much better place than he had found it.

In his first year after retiring from coaching, the Hartford Knights of the fledgling Atlantic Coast Pro Football League invited Anderson to watch one of their games. The Knights entertained hopes of the one-time coaching great serving as a goodwill ambassador for the team. Anderson, however, was not impressed with the Knights' operation. When his son, Jim, asked him what he had thought of the Knights, Anderson replied, "Those guys could set football back 50 years!"[5]

After hanging up his coaching whistle, Anderson only saw a couple of Holy Cross games over the next half-dozen years. However, according to Nick Anderson, the University of Connecticut coaching staff often invited his father to the Storrs campus to pick Eddie's brain on football matters. Head Coach John Toner held Anderson in high regard and after Anderson's death in 1974, a memorial service was held for Eddie on the Connecticut campus.

On April 25, 1970, Anderson was enshrined as an honorary member of the Holy Cross College Athletic Hall of Fame. It was especially gratifying for Eddie to be inducted in the same class with two of his former football captains, Buzz Harvey ('35) and Mel Massucco ('52). The evening's other inductees included former Philadelphia Athletics and New York Yankee infielder, Joe Dugan ('20), and Bill Merrit ('58), multiple New England track champion.

Dr. Anderson received an even greater honor on December 7, 1971, when he was voted into the National Football Foundation Hall of Fame. (Dick Lassiter, one of Eddie's former players at Iowa, was the catalyst behind a massive campaign for the good doctor's induction.)[6] The $100-a-plate dinner was held at New York City's Waldorf Astoria. Anderson was one of two coaches and eight players enshrined that night. The other coach inducted was Rice's Jess Neely, who, like Anderson, had also won over 200 games.

As the highlight of the evening, Dr. Anderson addressed the audience on behalf of the 1971 electees. At the moment of his highest acclaim as a coach, Anderson, who was criticized periodically throughout his career for not making greater use of his substitute players, paid tribute to all those players who never cracked the starting line-up or earned a varsity letter, but whose selfless contributions and sacrifices allowed their teams and teammates to succeed.

In 1971, Eddie and Mary decided to retire in Florida. They bought a home in a retirement community in Bellaire Beach and moved there with their bulldog, Buff. When neighbors learned that Eddie was a doctor, they often beat a path to his door seeking medical advice. It gave Eddie something to do and he enjoyed helping people. While he and Mary delighted in playing bridge with friends, retirement was a bitter pill for Anderson to swallow. He had never fished or hunted. Outside of playing a little golf, his hobbies were really his life's work, practicing medicine and coaching football.

"The worst thing for Dad," maintains Judy Anderson, "was moving to a place with just retirees. Dad used to growl, 'If I see one more gray hair!' He liked being around little kids and their absence was disastrous for him. He needed his grandchildren around him. He needed to work."

Yet, when Judy suggested that Eddie become a volunteer coach, Anderson replied in a huff, "What, and not get paid for it?"[7]

During a 1973 visit Dr. Anderson and his son, Jerry, were taking a walk when Eddie suddenly seized his chest. "What's the matter, Dad?" a concerned Jerry asked. Anderson then confided to his son that he had been experiencing coronary problems.

"Why don't you see somebody, Dad?" advised Jerry.

"Why? What can anyone do about it?" replied Anderson.[8] (Bypass surgery was not yet a common medical procedure in 1973.)

Not feeling well, a concerned Anderson drove himself to Morton-Plant Hospital in nearby Clearwater one day in March of 1974. He told the attending physician that he thought he was having a heart attack. The hospital performed some tests before informing Eddie that everything was fine. Anderson then returned home where later that night he did indeed suffer a heart attack.

While Anderson was hospitalized at Morton-Plant, Jerry Anderson, an oral surgeon, examined his father's medical history that had been forwarded from the Veterans Hospital in Boston. It was only then that Jerry learned that Eddie had had rheumatic fever as a boy and had lived with the effects of a rheumatic heart throughout his life, a fact that makes Anderson's athletic accomplishments even more amazing. Eddie's mother, Nellie, had died from complications of a rheumatic heart in 1924.

Over the next few weeks Eddie was discharged from the hospital on several occasions only to be quickly readmitted each time. After nearly four decades of practicing medicine, Dr. Anderson never cottoned to being on the patient's end of the thermometer. "Dad was the world's worst patient," recalls Jerry Anderson. Always the master and commander of his active life, Eddie soon grew frustrated at being bedridden. He became waspish with the hospital's doctors and nurses. When attendants served him dinner he often growled, "You eat it." When a nurse once informed him, "Doctor Anderson, we need to draw blood for some tests," Anderson replied sarcastically, "Oh, yeah, and who around here is going to interpret them?"

At times, Eddie would sit up in bed and launch into tirades against the hospital's daily operating procedures. "Take a look around this place," the former hospital chief would complain to family members and visitors. "Do you believe how they do things around here? As soon as I feel up to it I'm going to fly to Boston and check myself into Massachusetts General Hospital."[9] Unfortunately, Anderson never felt well enough to make good on his promise. He did, however, fire his doctor.

Constantly at Eddie's bedside during his illness was his devoted wife, Mary, who provided continual love and support, and occasionally, a mild rebuke when she thought her husband's behavior went too far.

Several weeks into his hospitalization Eddie developed a gastric ulcer and began vomiting blood. To treat his heart condition, Anderson had been taking a daily dosage of aspirin for over a year. Doctors believed that caused the ulcer. The ulcer, combined with his coronary problems, caused Eddie's health to rapidly deteriorate. He grew frail and his arms turned black and blue from being repeatedly stuck with needles to draw blood. Soon, the man who once astonished his players with the number of finger-tip push-ups he could do, and whose vise-like handshake was legendary, now struggled to hold a spoon.

"Watching Dad die was just awful," reflects Judy Anderson, who spent weeks at her father's bedside. "We watched him go from a strong, erect person who went swimming every day to somebody who could not turn himself over in bed."[10]

On good days, Eddie bragged to the nurses about his daughter, the lawyer. During the last week of his life, his spirits were buoyed by a letter from Al Couppee, the quarterback of Anderson's famed Iowa Iron Men of 1939. Proudly, he struggled to show the letter to family members and hospital staff.[11]

A few days before his death, when Eddie was drifting in and out of consciousness, his son, Jerry, sitting at his father's bedside asked, "What are you thinking, Dad?"

Eddie opened his eyes, looked at his son and said, "This too shall pass."[12]

On April 26, 1974, Dr. Eddie Anderson passed away at age 73.

The news saddened his former players, coaching colleagues, sportswriters and football fans everywhere but especially those in New England and the Midwest. The family received hundreds of cards and letters, and phone calls from the likes of famed composer Meredith Willson, Eddie's boyhood friend in Mason City.

The Reverend John E. Brooks, president of Holy Cross at the time of Eddie's passing, paid Anderson the following tribute. "He was always a gentleman, always a teacher. The hundreds of Holy Cross men who played under him and thousands of students and alumni who came to know him drew from Dr. Anderson the best lessons of Christian dedication and integrity. Dr. Eddie's influence will live as long as one Holy Cross man who knew him survives."[13]

Mary Anderson had held up surprisingly well during her husband's lengthy illness and ultimate passing, certainly better than her children expected. During the last weeks of his life, Eddie had confided to Mary his desire to be cremated in the event of his death. Mary now honored her husband's request. In a private ceremony she had Eddie's ashes laid to rest at St. Stephen's Cemetery near Framingham, Massachusetts. The day of the burial was also their son Jerry's 42nd birthday. As the Anderson family walked to the gravesite, Mary turned to her second oldest and said sadly, "Jerry, I'm sorry we ruined your birthday."[14]

Mary, who had never learned to drive or write a check, now decided to return to live in New England so she could be closer to her children. In June of 1974, just two months after Eddie's passing, Mary sold the Anderson home in Bellaire Beach. She moved into an apartment in Hartford, Connecticut. Her oldest son, Nick, also lived in the building. A year later, Mary bought a house in West Hartford. She lived there briefly with Nick and his wife, Pam, before deciding to rent her own apartment in Framingham, Massachusetts, to be nearer to her son, Jerry, and his family, and her daughter Judy.

Although she had no serious hobbies, Mary was an avid reader. She loved to shop and always enjoyed dining at a fine restaurant. She especially relished the days when her granddaughters came to visit. Because she didn't drive, Mary was dependent upon family and friends to get around.

In 1979, Nick and Pam Anderson bought a home in Framingham. Mary once again accepted Nick's invitation to live with them. When Nick's job required him to relocate to Florida in 1982, Mary moved with them to the Sunshine State. On March 23, 1984, the Andersons were living in Dade City when Mary complained of not feeling well. Pam Anderson immediately drove her to Morton-Plant Hospital, the same hospital where Eddie had died in 1973.

That night Pam called Jerry Anderson in Framingham to tell him that the doctors thought that Mary was okay but had admitted her overnight for observation. At two o'clock on the morning of March 24, 1984, almost ten years after Eddie's passing, Mary Anderson died of heart failure at age 80. As per her instructions, she too was cremated and her ashes were buried next to Eddie's at St. Stephen's Cemetery in Framingham.

To commemorate the legendary coach, the Holy Cross Club of Greater Worcester instituted the Edward N. Anderson Award in 1974. The award is presented annually to the outstanding player in the Family Weekend game as determined by the working press.

In recalling his playing days under Eddie Anderson, Tom Henehan, former Holy Cross linebacker and present-day Maryknoll priest maintains, "Doc valued the principles and values inherent within playing the game of football more than he cared about winning. With each passing year I come to appreciate that more and more."[15]

Doctor Eddie Anderson's football career was a 45-year odyssey across the gridiron landscape of America. During that time he crossed paths with the most influential and colorful personalities of the game. With some he stood shoulder to shoulder as teammates, with others, he went toe to toe as an opponent. For 39 seasons he graced the sidelines of college games in a fedora and three-piece suit. With his jaw set and upper lip rolled over his teeth in determination, his sideline presence could have been the subject of a Norman Rockwell painting.

Perhaps it was both symbolic and appropriate that Anderson left coaching when he did. It was time for him to go. How would Anderson have dealt with the changing athlete, perhaps spawned by the social turbulence of the late sixties and early seventies, who often valued individual self-expression and challenging authority over the selfless spirit of true teamwork and tradition?

As former Crusader Bob Noble reflects years later, "I look back on my days in the company of Dr. Anderson as a period when I was exposed to some genuine Americana. I was exposed to a fine man who simply practiced virtue while most of my generation was still trying to define it."[16]

"As young kids," lauds Dennis Golden, captain of the 1962 Holy Cross squad, who later became president of Fontbonne University, "we didn't realize how absolutely unique it was to have Dr. Anderson as a coach."[17]

Eddie Anderson was unique. There'll never be another like the Good Doctor.

APPENDIX:
ANDERSON'S CAREER
COACHING RECORD

204 Wins, 130 Losses, 16 Ties

Loras (Columbia College) 1922–24 (Won 16, Lost 6, Tied 2)

	Won	Lost	Tied		Won	Lost	Tied
1922	7.	0.	0.	1924	5.	2.	1.
1923	4.	4.	1.				

DePaul University 1925–31 (Won 24, Lost 24, Tied 4)

1925	4.	2.	1.	1929	2.	5.	0.
1926	3.	3.	0.	1930	4.	2.	1.
1927	1.	5.	1.	1931	6.	3.	0.
1928	4.	4.	1.				

Holy Cross College 1933–38 (Won 47, Lost 7, Tied 4)

1933	7.	2.	0.	1936	7.	2.	1.
1934	8.	2.	0.	1937	8.	0.	2.
1935	9.	0.	1.	1938	8.	1.	0.

University of Iowa 1939–42, 1946–49 (Won 35, Lost 33, Tied 2)

1939	6.	1.	1.	1946	5.	4.	0.
1940	4.	4.	0.	1947	3.	5.	1.
1941	3.	5.	0.	1948	4.	5.	0.
1942	6.	4.	0.	1949	4.	5.	0.

(Military Service: 1943 -45)

Holy Cross College 1950–64 (Won 82, Lost 60, Tied 4)

1950	4.	5.	1.	1958	6.	3.	0.
1951	8.	2.	0.	1959	6.	4.	0.
1952	8.	2.	0.	1960	6.	4.	0.
1953	5.	5.	0.	1961	7.	3.	0.
1954	3.	7.	0.	1962	6.	4.	0.
1955	6.	4.	0.	1963	2.	6.	1.
1956	5.	3.	1.	1964	5.	5.	0.
1957	5.	3.	1.				

CHAPTER NOTES

AFS   Anderson Family Scrapbook
CRG   Cedar Rapids Gazette
DTH   Dubuque Telegraph Herald
WT   Worcester Telegram

Introduction

1. Jim Anderson interview, March 20, 2000.
2. Mel Massucco interview, June 15, 2000.
3. For accounts of Anderson's postgame remarks see *Worcester Telegram (WT)* and *Boston Globe*, Nov. 29, 1964.
4. Bob Noble interview, June 14, 2000.
5. Jim Anderson interview.
6. Ibid.

Chapter 1

1. Accounts taken from the Anderson Family Scrapbook (AFS). Compiled by Eddie's parents, Nellie and Edward Martinius Anderson, the scrapbook is in the possession of Dr. Jerry Anderson, Eddie's middle son. Unpaginated, many of the scrapbook's yellowed clippings often contain just the articles themselves, lacking date, byline and even the name of the paper in which they appeared.
2. Jim Anderson interview.
3. Dr. Jerry Anderson interview, June 13, 2000.
4. AFS
5. Dr. Jerry Anderson interview.
6. AFS.
7. Roy Mumpton, "Dr. Eddie Anderson: A True Football Hall of Famer," Worcester's *Evening Gazette*, Dec. 8, 1971.

Chapter 2

1. Tim Cohane, *Great College Football Coaches of the 20s and 30s* (1973), 6.
2. Jim Anderson interview.
3. Anthony J. Kuzniewski, S.J. *Thy Honored Name: A History of the College of the Holy Cross, 1843–1994* (1996), 239.
4. James. S. Kearns, "The Country Doctor," *Chicago Daily News*, Nov. 14, 1939.
5. For a detailed account of the 1918 Influenza outbreak see John M. Barry, *The Great Influenza* (2004).
6. Jim Anderson interview.
7. Ibid.
8. Ray Robinson, *Rockne of Notre Dame* (1999) 184–186.
9. AFS.
10. Alison Danzig, *The History of American Football* (1956), 237.
11. Jim Anderson interview.
12. Heartley Anderson and Emil Klosinski, *Notre Dame, Chicago Bears and Hunk* (1976), 30–31.
13. Ibid., 32.
14. Jim Dent, *Monster of the Midway* (2003), 224.

15. Jim Anderson interview.
16. AFS.
17. Ibid.

Chapter 3

1. Murray Sperber, *Shake Down the Thunder: The Creation of Notre Dame Football* (1993), 100.
2. Robinson, *Rockne of Notre Dame*, 72.
3. Ibid.
4. Anderson and Klosinski, *Notre Dame, Chicago Bears and Hunk*, 44.
5. Sperber, *Shake Down the Thunder*, 107.
6. John Garraty, *The American Nation: A History of the United States* (1966), 806.
7. Sperber, *Shake Down the Thunder*, 99.
8. Jim Beach and Daniel Moore, *The Big Game* (1948), 52.
9. *New York Times*, Oct. 31, 1920.
10. Sperber, *Shake Down the Thunder*, 101.
11. Robinson, *Rockne of Notre Dame*, 84.
12. Beach and Moore, *The Big Game*, 56.
13. Robinson, *Rockne of Notre Dame*, 86–87.
14. Knute Rockne, "The Greatest Football Play I Ever Saw," *The American Legion Weekly*, 1924. Also see *College Football Historical Society* magazine, Vol. XIV, No. II, February, 2001.
15. Robinson, *Rockne of Notre Dame*, 87.
16. Ibid., 88.
17. Anderson and Klosinski, *Notre Dame, Chicago Bears and Hunk*, 40.
18. Robinson, *Rockne of Notre Dame*, 90.
19. Sperber, *Shake Down the Thunder*, 135.
20. Jim Anderson interview.

Chapter 4

1. AFS.
2. Ibid. The original congratulatory telegrams were found intact in the Anderson Family Scrapbook as was the ad for the Stephenson Mills Rockne Training shirt discussed on the last page of this chapter.
3. Dr. Jerry Anderson interview.
4. See *South Bend Tribune*, Sept. 24, 1921.
5. Dr. Jerry Anderson interview.
6. Robinson, *Rockne of Notre Dame*, 105.
7. Edgar Munzel, "Eddie Anderson: The Greatest Game I Ever Saw," *Chicago Tribune*, Fall, 1929.
8. Robinson, *Rockne of Notre Dame*, 105.
9. Ibid.
10. Jim Anderson interview.
11. Robinson, *Rockne of Notre Dame*, 108.
12. AFS. Rockne's relationship with Joe Byrne, Jr., is also detailed on 137–139 of Robinson's *Rockne of Notre Dame* and 203–205 of Sperber's *Shake Down the Thunder*.
13. Robinson, *Rockne of Notre Dame*, 111.
14. AFS.
15. Ibid.

Chapter 5

1. Johanna Tinnea, "The Game That Never Was," *Taylorville Breeze Courier* (Sesquicentennial Issue) June 18, 1989.
2. Ibid.
3. Ibid.
4. Jim Anderson interview.
5. Scott Hoover, *Touchdown Taylorville!* (1967), copyrighted but unpublished manuscript appearing in Sesquicentennial issue of *Taylorville Breeze Courier*, June 18, 1989.
6. See *Chicago Tribune*, Dec. 13, 1921.
7. *Chicago Tribune*, Dec. 8, 1921.
8. *Chicago Tribune*, Dec. 9. 1921.
9. *New York Times*, Jan. 28, 1922.
10. *Chicago Tribune*, Jan. 30, 1922.
11. *Chicago Tribune*, Jan. 31, 1922.
12. Dr. Jerry Anderson interview.

Chapter 6

1. AFS.
2. Tinnea, "The Game That Never Was," E-9.
3. Sperber, *Shake Down the Thunder*, 134.
4. Robinson, *Rockne of Notre Dame*, 102.
5. Cohane, *The Great Football Coaches of the 20s and 30s*, 110. Also see Paul N. Johnson, "Boston University Salutes Dr. Eddie," *Boston University–Holy Cross Game Program*, Nov. 14, 1964, 6.
6. AFS.
7. Robinson, *Rockne of Notre Dame*, 102.
8. *Dubuque Telegraph-Herald* (*DTH*), July 22, 1922.
9. *DTH*, Sept. 17, 1922.
10. *DTH*, Sept. 20, 1922.
11. *DTH*, Sept. 13, 1922.
12. *DTH*, Sept. 27, 1922.
13. *Chicago Tribune*, Sept. 26, 1922.
14. *Chicago Tribune*, Sept. 28, 1922.
15. *DTH*, Sept. 24, 1922.
16. Elmer Layden, *It Was a Different Game* (1969), 42.
17. AFS.
18. Ibid.
19. *DTH*, Nov. 20, 1922.
20. *Chicago Tribune*, Nov. 11, 1922.
21. Joe Ziemba, *When Football Was Football: The Chicago Cardinals and the Birth of the NFL* (1999), 102.
22. *DTH*, Nov. 22, 1922.
23. *DTH*, Nov. 23, 1922.
24. Dr. Jerry Anderson interview.
25. *DTH*, Dec. 5, 1922.
26. Ibid.
27. Dan Daily and Bob O'Donnell, *The Pro Football Chronicle* (1990), 15.
28. *Chicago Tribune*, Dec. 11, 1922.

Chapter 7

1. *DTH*, Feb. 21, 1923.
2. *DTH*, Oct. 24, 1923.
3. See *New York Times*, Jan. 28, 1922.
4. Joe Marren, "Buffalo's Two Sport Guys," *The Coffin Corner*, Vol. 19, No. 4, (1997).
5. See *Chicago Tribune*, Nov. 26, 1923.
6. *DTH*, Nov. 30, 1923.
7. Alison Danzig, *Oh, How They Played the Game* (1971).
8. Chris Willis, "Remembering the Oorang Indians," *The Coffin Corner*, Vol. 24, Nos. 3 & 4 (2002).
9. *Chicago Tribune*, Dec. 3, 1923.
10. AFS.
11. Ibid.
12. Ibid.
13. *DTH*, Nov. 9, 1924.
14. *DTH*, Nov. 28, 1924.

Chapter 8

1. *DTH*, Dec. 12, 1924.
2. AFS.
3. Sperber, *Shake Down the Thunder*, 171.
4. "Rockne Praises Coach Anderson at Grid Banquet," *The Lorian*, March 13, 1925.
5. *Chicago Tribune*, Sept. 30, 1925.
6. Layden, *It Was a Different Game*, 124.
7. Ibid.
8. Paul N. Johnson, Commentary, *WT*, April 28, 1974.
9. AFS.
10. *Chicago Tribune*, Nov. 9, 1925.
11. Dr. Jerry Anderson interview.
12. *Chicago Tribune*, Nov. 23, 1925.
13. Nick Anderson interview, Dec. 14, 2000.
14. Arizona Cardinal Website, "The Legacy of Paddy Driscoll," www.azcardinals.com
15. *Chicago Tribune*, Nov. 27, 1925.
16. Sperber, *Shake Down the Thunder*, 101.
17. See *Chicago Tribune*, Dec. 10, 1925.
18. *Chicago Tribune*, Dec. 11, 1925.
19. Will McDonough, Peter King and others, *75 Seasons: The Complete Story of the National Football League* (1995), 32.
20. Ziemba, *When Football Was Football*, 134.
21. Westbrook Pegler, "Muscle Torn: Red Says He'll Play Sunday," *Chicago Tribune*, Dec. 11, 1925.
22. Ziemba, *When Football Was Football*, 135–139.
23. Joe Horrigan, Bob Braunwart and Bob Carroll, "The Discarded Championship," Professional Football Researchers Assoc., 1981. http://www.footballresearch.com/articles.cfm?topic=potts.25, 14 of 17.

Chapter 9

1. Judy Anderson Moore interview, Dec. 8, 2000.
2. Ziemba, *When Football Was Football*, 146–147.
3. Ibid., 149–150.
4. See *Chicago Tribune*, Oct. 4, 1926.
5. *Chicago Tribune*, Oct. 3, 1926.
6. *Chicago Tribune*, Oct. 18, 1926.
7. Joe Layden, *Notre Dame Football A to Z* (1997), 201–202.
8. Jim Anderson and Dr. Jerry Anderson interviews.
9. Kevin Carroll, *Houston Oilers: The Early Years* (2001), 262.
10. See *Chicago Tribune*, Nov. 13, 1926.
11. *Chicago Tribune*, Nov. 14, 1926.
12. McDonough, King and others, *75 Seasons*, 32–33.

Chapter 10

1. *Chicago Tribune*, Sept. 24, 1927.
2. *Chicago Tribune*, Nov. 3, 1927.
3. Roger Kiley letter to Dr. Jerry Anderson, May 21, 1974.
4. *Chicago Tribune*, Oct. 29, 1927.
5. *Chicago Tribune*, Oct. 17, 1928.
6. *Chicago Tribune*, Nov. 5, 1928.
7. *Chicago Tribune*, Nov. 12, 1928.
8. *Chicago Tribune*, Nov. 3, 1930.
9. Robinson, *Rockne of Notre Dame*, 266.
10. Jim Anderson interview.
11. See *Chicago Tribune*, Oct. 1, 1931.
12. *Chicago Tribune*, Nov. 17, 1931.
13. Nick Anderson interview.
14. Alan F. Kipp, "When Blue Demons Wore Helmets," *DePaul Magazine*, Fall, 1999.
15. Dr. Jerry Anderson interview.

Chapter 11

1. Anthony Kuzniewski, *Thy Honored Name*, 292.
2. Danzig, *The History of American Football*, 212.
3. Tommy Callan interview, April 22, 2003.
4. Ibid.
5. Ibid.
6. *The 1935 Purple Patcher*, 372. (The Holy Cross College Yearbook.)
7. Tommy Callan letter to author, Feb. 18, 2003.
8. Ibid.
9. Gerry Hern, "Dr. Eddie Puzzle When First Hired," *Boston Post*, Jan. 31, 1950.
10. Dr. Jerry Anderson interview.
11. Hern, "Dr. Eddie Puzzle When First Hired."

12. Ibid.
13. Tommy Callan interview.
14. Kuzniewski, *Thy Honored Name*, 274–275.
15. See *The Boston Herald*, Oct. 22, 1933.
16. AFS.
17. Gordon Gilmore, "Calling All Coaches," *Cedar Rapids Gazette*, Nov. 12, 1939.
18. Worcester *Evening Gazette*, Oct. 28, 1933.
19. See *WT*, Nov. 3, 1933.
20. Tommy Callan letter to author, Feb. 14, 2003.
21. Hipolet "Hip" Moncevicz interview, June 13, 2000.
22. Ibid.
23. *The Tomahawk*, the Holy Cross school paper, Oct. 2, 1934.
24. See *Iowa-South Dakota Game Program*, Sept. 30, 1939. Also, *Worcester Telegram (WT)*, Nov. 28, 1938.
25. Gene Corbett letter to author, Jan. 16, 2001.
26. Tommy Callan interview.
27. Joe Keblinsky, "The Lowdown on Sports," *WT* (undated), 1934.
28. Tommy Callan interview.
29. Keblinsky, "The Lowdown on Sports."
30. Tommy Callan interview.
31. Callan letter, Feb. 14, 2003.
32. Kuzniewski, *Thy Honored Name*, 287.
33. Moncevicz interview.
34. Ibid.
35. Ibid.
36. Ibid.
37. Lou King letter to author, Dec. 28, 2001.
38. Ernie Roberts, "Dr. Eddie ... 'Man's Man," *Boston Globe*, May 1, 1974.
39. *WT*, Nov. 9, 1935

Chapter 12

1. Moncevicz interview.
2. Ibid.
3. See *WT*, Oct. 10, 1936.
4. *WT*, Nov. 1, 1936.
5. Moncevicz interview.
6. Ibid.
7. Ibid.
8. *WT*, Nov. 8, 1936.
9. Moncevicz interview.
10. Jack Clary, *Navy Football: Gridiron Legends and Fighting Heroes* (1997), 34.
11. Moncevicz interview.
12. *WT*, Sept. 10, 1937.
13. Hank Giardi interview, April 4, 2003.
14. Ibid.
15. *WT*, Oct. 17, 1937.
16. Ibid.
17. Ibid.
18. Jim Anderson interview.
19. F.E. Whitmarsh, "Sports and Sportsmen," *WT*, Nov. 23, 1937.

20. Ibid.
21. *WT*, Nov. 28, 1937.

Chapter 13

1. Jim Anderson interview.
2. *WT*, Oct. 13, 1938.
3. *WT*, Oct. 17, 1938.
4. Ibid.
5. *WT*, Oct. 29, 1938.
6. Ibid.
7. *WT*, Nov. 12, 1938.
8. Ibid.
9. AFS.
10. Ibid.
11. Arthur Siegel, "Football Is Anderson's 2nd Love," *Boston Globe*, Sept. 20, 1964.
12. *WT*, Nov. 27, 1938.
13. Roy Mumpton, "Anderson Resigns at HC," *WT*, Nov. 28, 1938.
14. Gerry Hern, "Dr. Eddie Puzzle When First Hired."
15. Roy Mumpton, "Anderson Resigns at HC."

Chapter 14

1. *Daily Iowan*, Dec. 3, 1938.
2. Paul Baender, *A Hero Perished: The Diary and Selected Letters of Nile Kinnick* (1991), 13.
3. Ibid., 15.
4. Al Couppee, *One Magic Year: 1939, An Ironman Remembers* (1989), 13.
5. D.W. Stump, *Kinnick: The Man and the Legend* (1974), 46.
6. *Mason City Gazette*, Feb. 14, 1939.
7. Ibid.
8. *Des Moines Register*, Feb. 25, 1939.
9. Ibid.
10. Ibid.
11. Bill Diehl interview, April 7, 2000.
12. Erwin Prasse interview, Dec. 14, 2000.
13. Ibid.
14. Diehl interview.
15. Prasse interview.
16. Couppee, *One Magic Year*, 75.
17. Red Frye interview, Nov. 14, 2000.
18. Coupee, *One Magic Year*, 55.
19. Ibid., 29.
20. Diehl interview.
21. Coupee, *One Magic Year*, 39.
22. Red Frye interview.
23. Maury White, "Ironmen—And Mike Enich Most of All," *Des Moines Register*, Sept. 7, 1969.
24. Coupee, *One Magic Year*, 125.
25. Red Frye interview.
26. Coupee, *One Magic Year*, 23.
27. Cohane, *Great College Football Coaches of the 20s and 30s*, 5.

Chapter 15

1. Couppee, *One Magic Year*, 29–30.
2. Prasse interview.
3. Frye interview.
4. Dr. Dennis C. Golden interview, Feb. 28, 2000.
5. James S. Kearns, "The Country Doctor," *Chicago Daily News*, Nov. 15, 1939.
6. Prasse interview.
7. *Cedar Rapids Gazette* (*CRG*), Oct. 8, 1939.
8. Couppee, *One Magic Year*, 88.
9. Ibid., 92–93.
10. Ibid.
11. Ibid., 94.
12. Scott Fisher, *Ironmen* (1989), 74.
13. Stump, *Kinnick: The Man and the Legend*, 60.
14. Red Frye interview.
15. Couppee, *One Magic Year*, 101.
16. Ibid.
17. *CRG*, Nov. 10, 1939.
18. Couppee, *One Magic Year*, 101.
19. Fisher, *Ironmen*, 85.
20. Couppee, *One Magic Year*, 103.
21. Diehl interview.
22. *CRG*, Nov. 12, 1939.
23. *CRG*, Nov. 14, 1939.
24. *Des Moines Register*, Nov. 12, 1939.
25. *CRG*, Nov. 14, 1939.
26. *CRG*, Nov. 16, 1939.
27. *CRG*, Nov. 19, 1939.
28. Ibid.
29. *Minneapolis Tribune*, Nov. 19, 1939.
30. *Chicago Herald American*, Nov. 19, 1939.
31. *St. Paul Pioneer Press*, Nov. 19, 1939.
32. See *Des MoinesRegister*, Nov. 19, 1939.
33. Dr. Jerry Anderson interview.
34. Jim Anderson interview.
35. AFS (remarks made at 1939 Iowa football banquet).
36. Ibid.
37. Ibid.

Chapter 16

1. Fisher, *Ironmen*, 24.
2. Prasse interview.
3. Fisher, *Ironmen*, 57.
4. Nile C. Kinnick, Sr., letter to Dr. Jerry Anderson, May 30, 1976.
5. Baender, *A Hero Perished*, 32–33.
6. Jim Anderson interview.
7. Baender, *A Hero Perished*, 32–33. Also see Kinnick letter of Dec. 12, 1939.
8. Ibid., 34–36.
9. See *Chicago Tribune*, Dec. 8, 1939.
10. *CRG*, Dec. 10, 1939.
11. Dorothy Kilgallen, "The Voice of Broadway," *New York Journal American*, Jan. 15, 1940.

12. Stump, *Kinnick: The Man and the Legend*, 34.
13. Ibid., 34–35.
14. Ibid., 41.
15. Prasse interview.
16. *Des Moines Register*, Aug. 4, 1940.
17. *CRG*, Sept. 7, 1940.
18. *CRG*, Oct. 1, 1940.
19. Baender, *A Hero Perished*, 147.
20. Ibid., 280–281.
21. Scott Fisher, "Iowa's Ironmen," *Sports History*, Nov. 1989, 6.
22. Bill Pennington, *Great American Stories of the Men Who Won the Heisman* (2004), 32–33.
23. Baender, *A Hero Perished*, 135–137 (Paul Buie letter to Kinnick family, June 6, 1943).
24. Fisher, "Iowa's Ironmen," *Sports History*, 31.
25. Gene Corbett letter to author, Jan. 16, 2001.

Chapter 17

1. Jim Grogan, "The College Football All-Star Classic," *The Coffin Corner*, Vol. 22, No. 2 (2000).
2. Ziemba, *When Football Was Football*, 213–214.
3. *CRG*, Aug. 16, 1940.
4. Dave Zimmerman, *Lambeau: The Man Behind the Myth* (2003), 144–145.
5. Frye interview.
6. *CRG*, Oct. 14, 1940.
7. *CRG*, Nov. 17, 1940.
8. *CRG*, Nov. 21, 1940.
9. Dr. Jerry Anderson interview.
10. Ibid.
11. Judy Anderson Moore interview, Dec. 8, 2000.
12. Diehl interview.
13. Jim Anderson interview.
14. Dr. Jerry Anderson interview.
15. Jim Anderson interview.
16. See Donald W. Rominger, Jr., "From Playing Field to Battleground: The United States Navy V-5 Preflight Program in World War II," *Journal of Sport History*, Vol. 12, No. 3 (Winter, 1985).
17. Jim Anderson interview.
18. Ibid.
19. Carlin Lynch interview, March 22, 2000.
20. Prasse interview.

Chapter 18

1. Dr. Jerry Anderson interview.
2. Lou King letter.
3. *CRG*, Oct. 6, 1946.
4. See the *Daily Iowan* Editorial Board letter to Board of Trustees, Nov. 13, 1946, in the University of Iowa Archives.

5. Ibid.
6. Dr. Wilbur Schramm Memo, Nov. 16, 1946, University of Iowa Archives.
7. Barbour Statement, Nov. 13, 1946, University of Iowa Archives.
8. Schramm Memo, 3.
9. Nick Anderson interview.
10. Pat Harmon, "Showdown on Eddie on Monday at Iowa City," *CRG*, Nov. 14, 1947.
11. Jim Anderson interview.
12. Harmon, "Showdown on Eddie on Monday at Iowa City."
13. *CRG*, Nov. 16, 1947.
14. Ibid.
15. *CRG*, Nov. 17, 1947.
16. *CRG*, Nov. 18, 1947.
17. *CRG*, Nov. 21, 1947.
18. Ibid.
19. Ibid.
20. Ibid.
21. Jim Anderson interview.
22. Ibid.
23. *CRG*, Nov. 6, 1949.
24. Jim Anderson interview.
25. Nick Anderson interview.
26. Dr. Jerry Anderson interview.
27. See *Chicago Sun-Times*, Jan. 14, 1950.
28. *CRG*, Jan. 28, 1950.
29. Nick Anderson interview.

Chapter 19

1. Al Hirshberg, "New H.C. Coach Pulls No Punches," *Boston Post*, Feb. 9, 1950.
2. Judy Anderson Moore interview.
3. Ibid.
4. Jim Anderson interview.
5. Ibid.
6. Ibid.
7. Massucco interview.
8. Jim Anderson interview.
9. Judy Anderson Moore interview.
10. Harold Kaese, "Ex-Players Say Anderson a Taskmaster," *Boston Globe*, Jan. 30, 1950.
11. Ibid.
12. Roy Mumpton, "The Sport Lens," *WT*, Jan. 31, 1950.
13. Massucco interview.
14. Jim Anderson interview.
15. Chet Millett interview, June 13, 2000.
16. Charles Shooshan, "60 Candidates Out for Spring Practice at H.C.," *WT*, March 21, 1950.
17. Massucco interview.
18. Vic Rimkus interview, June 12, 2000.
19. Ibid.
20. Millett interview.
21. Massucco interview.
22. Millett interview.
23. Jack Tubert, "HC Gridders Impressive in Final Spring Scrimmage," *WT*, April 30, 1950.

24. Joe Marvin, "The 1949 College of Pacific Tigers," *College Football Historical Society*, Vol. III, No. 4, August, 1990, 11.
25. Eddie LeBaron interview, June 8, 2001.
26. *WT*, Oct. 1, 1950.
27. *WT*, Oct. 7, 1950.
28. Clif Keane, "Anderson Used Psychology on Turco," *Boston Globe*, Dec. 3, 1950.
29. Ibid.
30. Massucco interview.
31. Millett interview.
32. Massucco interview.
33. See "Purple Patches," *WT*, Oct. 14, 1951.
34. Jack Frost, "HC Has Invalid as Star and Doctor as Coach," Worcester *Evening Gazette*, Nov. 15, 1951.
35. Hap Glaudi, "Looking 'Em Over," *New Orleans Item*, Oct. 14, 1951.
36. Massucco interview.
37. Joe Gleason interview, April, 2000.
38. Mike Holovak letter to author, Feb. 21, 2000.
39. Nick Anderson interview.
40. Jim Anderson interview.
41. Ibid.
42. Bill Samko interview, Nov. 16, 2000.
43. Carlin Lynch interview.
44. Massucco interview.
45. Judy Anderson Moore interview.
46. Nick Anderson interview.
47. Jim Anderson interview.
48. Ernie Roberts, "Dr. Eddie: Man's Man."
49. Nick Anderson interview.
50. Jim Anderson interview.
51. Larry Claflin, "Maloy Give HC Big Edge on BC," *Boston American*, Nov. 23, 1952.
52. Ibid.

Chapter 20

1. *WT*, Oct. 19, 1953.
2. Jim Anderson and Nick Anderson interviews.
3. See "Purple Patches," *WT*, Oct. 28, 1953.
4. *WT*, Nov. 1, 1953.
5. Roy Mumpton, "The Sport Lens," *WT*, Nov. 9, 1953.
6. Ibid.
7. Clif Keane, "Anderson Reported Ready to Quit Holy Cross Berth, "*Boston Globe*, Nov. 9, 1953.
8. Worcester *Evening Gazette*, Nov. 9, 1953.
9. *WT*, Nov. 29, 1953.
10. Paul Hines, Jr., "Anderson Signs," *Boston Globe*, Feb. 4, 1954.
11. *WT*, March 4, 1954.
12. See *Boston Post*, Feb. 4, 1954.
13. Jim Anderson interview.
14. *WT*, March 4, 1954.
15. Norris Anderson, "U-Miami didn't Rush Passes Enough," *Miami Daily News*, Oct. 9, 1954.

16. Massucco interview.
17. Terry Wadsworth interview, December 9, 2000.
18. Massucco interview.
19. Ibid.
20. Ibid.
21. *WT*, Nov. 22, 1955.
22. Worcester *Evening Gazette*, Nov. 22, 1955.
23. Dr. Jerry Anderson interview.

Chapter 21

1. Mike Ryan interview, Nov. 18, 2000.
2. Rimkus interview.
3. Carlin Lynch interview.
4. Jim Anderson interview.
5. Carlin Lynch interview.
6. Massucco interview.
7. Carlin Lynch interview.
8. Millett interview.
9. Carlin Lynch interview.
10. Millett interview.
11. Jim Anderson interview.
12. Alex MacLean, "HC Hero Sheds Tears of Joy," *Boston Record*, Dec. 2, 1956.
13. Tom Henehan interview, Jan. 28, 2001.
14. Scooch Giargiari interview, June 14, 2003.
15. Dave Perini letter to author, June 28, 2003.
16. See *Boston Globe*, Dec. 1, 1957.
17. Vince Promuto interview, March 7, 2000.
18. Dr. George Lynch interview, Nov. 16, 2000.
19. Promuto interview.
20. Jim Anderson interview.
21. *WT*, March 31, 1958.
22. Massucco interview.
23. Ibid.
24. Ibid.
25. *WT*, Oct. 5, 1958.
26. *Boston Traveler*, Dec. 15, 1958.
27. *Boston Record*, Dec. 13, 1958.
28. Promuto interview.
29. Ibid.
30. Ibid.
31. Ibid.
32. Rimkus interview.
33. Gene Corbett letter, Jan. 16, 2001.
34. Ibid.
35. Massucco interview.
36. Dr. Jerry Anderson interview.
37. *Boston Globe*, Nov. 29, 1959.

Chapter 22

1. Carlin Lynch interview.
2. Moncevicz interview.
3. Noble interview.
4. Carlin Lynch interview.
5. Corbett letter.

6. Ken Hohl interview.
7. Bill Samko interview.
8. Corbett letter.
9. Dr. George Lynch interview.
10. Golden interview.
11. Millett interview.
12. Golden interview.
13. Judy Anderson Moore interview.
14. Tom Carstens interview, Dec. 10, 2000.
15. Corbett letter.
16. Ibid.
17. Massucco interview.
18. Carlin Lynch interview.
19. Judy Anderson Moore interview.
20. Ernie Roberts, "Dr. Eddie ... Man's Man."
21. Massucco interview.

Chapter 23

1. Terry Wadsworth interview.
2. Oscar Lofton interview, Nov. 13, 2000.
3. Mel Massucco interview.
4. Ken Hohl interview.
5. Millett interview.
6. Jim Anderson interview.
7. Mel Massucco interview.
8. (This anecdote is part of Holy Cross football lore and has been recalled by numerous former Crusaders including Tom Hennessey, Tom Kiley and others.)
9. Jim Anderson interview.
10. *WT*, Sept. 25, 1960.
11. Jim Anderson and Mel Massucco interviews.
12. Jim Anderson interview.
13. Gene Corbett letter.
14. Dr. George Lynch interview.
15. Massucco interview.
16. Millett interview.
17. Pat McCarthy interview, June 14, 2000.
18. Vic Rimkus interview.
19. Dick Berardino's correspondence with the author, Feb. 5, 2003.
20. Ken Hohl interview.
21. Dr. Jerry Anderson interview.
22. Corbett letter.
23. Dr. Jerry Anderson interview.
24. Ibid.
25. Jim Anderson interview.
26. Noble interview.
27. Dr. George Lynch interview.
28. Judy Anderson Moore interview.
29. Noble interview.
30. Lofton interview.
31. Henehan interview.
32. Dr. Jerry Anderson interview.
33. Dr. George Lynch interview.
34. Judy Anderson Moore interview.
35. Dr. George Lynch interview.
36. Lofton interview.

37. Dr. Jerry Anderson interview.
38. *WT,* Oct. 27, 1963.
39. Jim Anderson interview.
40. Phil Jackman, "Dr. Anderson Lauds Coughlin," *WT,* Nov. 10, 1963.
41. Worcester *Evening Gazette,* Nov. 19, 1963.
42. Lofton interview.
43. Ibid.
44. *WT,* Dec. 1, 1963.

Chapter 24

1. Jim Anderson interview.
2. *South Bend Tribune,* Aug. 21, 1964.
3. Massucco interview.
4. Roy Mumpton, "Student Paper Blast HC," *WT,* Oct. 17, 1964.
5. Cohane, *Coaches of the 20s and 30s,* 7.
6. Roy Mumpton, "Student Paper Blasts HC."
7. *WT,* Oct. 18, 1964.
8. Wally Carew, *A Farewell To Glory: The Rise and Fall of an Epic Football Rivalry* (2003), 158.
9. *WT,* Nov. 15, 1964.
10. See *WT,* Nov. 28, 1964.
11. See *WT* and *Boston Globe,* Nov. 29, 1964.
12. *WT,* Nov. 29, 1964.
13. *Boston Globe,* Nov. 29, 1964.
14. Jim Anderson interview.

Chapter 25

1. See Worcester *Evening Gazette,* Nov. 30, 1964.
2. Jim Anderson interview.
3. Ibid.
4. Judy Anderson Moore interview.
5. Jim Anderson interview.
6. Gus Schrader, "Red Peppers," *CRG,* Aug. 4, 1970.
7. Judy Anderson Moore interview.
8. Dr. Jerry Anderson interview.
9. Ibid.
10. Judy Anderson Moore interview.
11. Couppee, *One Magic Year,* 24.
12. Dr. Jerry Anderson interview.
13. John Ahern, "Dr. Eddie Made Them Believers at Holy Cross," *Boston Globe,* April 28, 1974.
14. Dr. Jerry Anderson interview.
15. Henehan interview.
16. Cohane, *Great College Coaches of the 20s and 30s,* 10.
17. Golden interview.

BIBLIOGRAPHY

Books

Anderson, Heartley, and Emil Klosinski. *Notre Dame, Chicago Bears and Hunk.* Oveido, FL: Sunshine-Gato, 1972.

Baender, Paul. *A Hero Perished: The Diary and Selected Letters of Nile Kinnick.* Iowa City: University of Iowa Press, 1991.

Barry, John M. *The Great Influenza.* New York: Viking Penguin, 2004.

Beach, Jim, and Daniel Moore. *The Big Game.* New York: Random House, 1948.

Bowman, John. *Ivy League Football.* Greenwich CT: Crescent, 1988.

Carew, Wally. *A Farewell to Glory: The Rise and Fall of an Epic Football Rivalry.* Worcester, MA: Ambassador, 2003.

Carroll, Bob; Michael Gershman; David Neft; and John Thorn. *Total Football II.* New York: HarperCollins, 1997.

Carroll, Kevin. *Houston Oilers: The Early Years.* Austin: Eakin, 2001.

Clary, Jack. *Navy Football: Gridiron Legends and Fighting Heroes.* Annapolis: Naval Institute Press, 1997.

Cohane, Tim. *Great College Football Coaches of the 20s and 30s.* New Rochelle: Arlington House, 1973.

Couppee, Al. *One Magic Year: 1939. An Ironman Remembers.* Al Coupee, 1990.

Daly, Dan, and Bob O'Donnell. *The Pro Football Chronicle.* New York: Simon & Schuster, 1990.

Danzig, Allison. *The History of American Football.* Englewood Cliffs, NJ: Prentice-Hall, 1956.

_____. *Oh, How They Played the Game.* New York: Macmillan, 1971.

Dent, Jim. *Monster of the Midway.* New York: St. Martin's, 2003.

Fisher, Scott. *The Ironmen.* Lincoln, NE: Media, 1989.

Garraty, John A. *The American Nation: A History of the United States.* New York: Harper & Row, 1966.

Gildea, William, and Christopher Jennison. *The Fighting Irish: Notre Dame Football Through the Years.* Englewood Cliffs, NJ: Prentice-Hall, 1976.

Klosinski, Emil. *Pro Football in the Days of Rockne.* New York: Carlton, 1970.

Kuzniewski, Anthony J., S.J. *Thy Honored Name: A History of the College of the Holy Cross, 1843–1994.* Washington, D.C.: Catholic University of America Press, 1996.

Layden, Elmer, and Ed Snyder. *It Was a Different Game.* Englewood Cliffs, NJ: Prentice-Hall, 1969.
Layden, Joe. *Notre Dame Football: A to Z.* Dallas: Taylor, 1997.
Littlewood, Thomas. *Arch: A Promoter, Not a Poet.* Ames: Iowa State University Press, 1990.
McDonough, Will, et al. *75 Seasons: The Complete Story of the National Football League.* Atlanta: Turner, 1994.
Moss, Al. *Pac-10 Football.* Greenwich CT: Crescent, 1987.
Pennington, Bill. *Great American Stories of the Men Who Won the Heisman.* New York: Regan, 2004.
Peterson, Robert. *Pigskin: The Early Years of Pro Football.* New York: Oxford University Press, 1997.
Robinson, Ray. *Rockne of Notre Dame.* New York: Oxford University Press, 1999.
Schoor, Gene. *100 Years of Notre Dame Football.* New York: Avon, 1988.
Sperber, Murray. *Shake Down the Thunder.* New York: Holt, 1993.
Stump, D.W. *Kinnick: The Man and the Legend.* Iowa City: University of Iowa Press, 1974.
Vesey, Arthur. *Halas by Halas.* New York: McGraw-Hill, 1979.
Wallace, Francis. *The Notre Dame Story.* New York: Reinart, 1949.
Watterson, John Sayle. *College Football.* Baltimore: Johns Hopkins University Press, 2000.
Ziemba, Joe. *When Football Was Football: The Chicago Cardinals and the Birth of the NFL.* Chicago: Triumph, 1999.
Zimmerman, David. *Lambeau: The Man Behind the Mystique.* Hales Corner, WI: Eagle Books, 2003.

Articles

Fisher, Scott. "Iowa's Ironmen." *Sports History,* November 1989.
Grogan, Jon. "The College All-Star Football Classic." *The Coffin Corner.* Vol. 22, no. 2 (2000).
Horrigan, Joe; Bob Braunwart; and Bob Carroll, "The Discarded Championship," *Professional Football Researchers Association,* 1981. http://www.footballresearch.com/articles.cfm?topic=potts 25, 14 of 17.
Kipp, Alan. "When Blue Demons Wore Helmets." *DePaul Magazine,* Fall 1999.
Marren, Joe. "Buffalo's Two Sport Guys." *The Coffin Corner.* Vol. 19, no. 4 (1997).
Marvin, Joe. "The 1949 College of Pacific Tigers." *College Football Historical Society,* Vol. III, no. 4, August 1990.
Rominger, Donald W., Jr. "From Playing Field to Battleground: The United States Navy V-5 Preflight Program in World War II." *Journal of Sport History,* Vol. 12, no. 3 (Winter 1985).
Tinnea, Johanna. "The Game That Never Was." *The Taylorville Breeze Courier Sesquicentennial Issue,* 1984.
Willis, Chris. "Remembering the Oorang Indians." *The Coffin Corner,* Vol. 24, nos. 3 and 4 (2002).

Periodicals

Boston Globe
Boston Herald
Boston Record
Boston Traveler
Cedar Rapids Gazette

Chicago Herald
Chicago Tribune
The Crusader
The Daily Iowan
Des Moines Register

Dubuque Telegraph-Herald
Miami Daily News
Minneapolis Morning Tribune
New Orleans Item

New York Herald Tribune
New York Times
St. Paul Pioneer Press

Author's Interviews

Dr. Jerry Anderson, Jim Anderson, Nick Anderson, Richard Berardino, Tommy Callan, Thomas Carstens, Colonel Eugene Corbett (USAF, Ret.), Bill Diehl, Jay Dugan, George "Red" Frye, John Gearan, Hank Giardi, Scooch Giargiari, Joe Gleason, Dr. Dennis C. Golden, Reverend Thomas Henehan, M.M., Dick Hoerner, Ken Hohl, Mike Holovak, Bill Joern, Lou King, Eddie LeBaron, Oscar Lofton, Carlin Lynch, Dr. George Lynch, Mel Massucco, Pat McCarthy, Chester Millett, Hipolet Moncevicz, Judy Anderson Moore, Bob Noble, Dave Perini, Erwin Prasse, Vince Promuto, Vic Rimkus, Mike Ryan, Bill Samko and Terry Wadsworth.

INDEX

Numbers in *bold italics* indicate pages with illustrations.

Index